PURITANISM AND
RICHARD BANCROFT

PURITANISM AND RICHARD BANCROFT

STUART BARTON BABBAGE

Sometime Dean of Melbourne and Principal of Ridley College

with a Foreword by the late

NORMAN SYKES

Sometime Dean of Winchester and
Dixie Professor of Ecclesiastical History
in the Univerity of Cambridge

Published for the Church Historical Society

LONDON

S·P·C·K

1962

First published in 1962
by S.P.C.K.
Holy Trinity Church
Marylebone Road
London N.W.1

Made and printed in Great Britain by
William Clowes and Sons, Limited, London and Beccles

CONTENTS

FOREWORD

"**M**ATTERS OF such weight and consequence are to be speeded with maturitie", wrote Miles Smith in his Preface to the Authorized Version of the Bible, itself a product of the Hampton Court Conference in which Richard Bancroft as one of the Anglican members met the leading Puritans face to face. The observation may perhaps be pardonably applied to the Dean of Melbourne's present study; for I remember its beginnings in the years preceding the second world war of 1939–45, when I had the pleasure of supervising the author's studies. The events of war carried him to very different occupations and to far-off lands; and when hostilities ended he thought it a duty to relinquish the research studentship into which he had been elected at Trinity College, Cambridge, in order to return to the service of the Church in Australia. This enforced deferment of the completion of his work was prolonged by those thieves of learned leisure, the pastoral cure of his Deanery of Melbourne and the office of Principal of Ridley College. It is an additional pleasure therefore to welcome now the completed study.

The importance to the student of English Church history of this careful, thorough, and detailed survey of Puritanism during the vital first septennium of the reign of James I, embracing the Hampton Court Conference, the passing of the canons of 1604, and their enforcement by the new primate, Bancroft, is indubitable. More particularly Dr Babbage by his investigation of the individual cases of deprivation of ministers for refusal to conform to the canons in the dioceses of London, Lincoln, Chichester, Norwich, and Peterborough, has been able to produce convincing evidence for estimating the total number of such deprivations as between eighty and ninety; a figure far below the exaggerated claims of Puritan supporters but larger than that accepted by

vii

Dr R. G. Usher. Dr Babbage has also shown by the valuable use which he has made of the *detectiones* and *comperta* resulting from Bancroft's visitations, the injustice of Usher's dismissal of these sources as of little value. Furthermore, he has given a detailed account of the attempts of lay sympathizers with the Puritan ministers to secure a reversal of the ecclesiastical sentences by parliamentary action; and of the endeavours of the common law judges to hinder the process of ecclesiastical causes in the High Commission Court by the issue of Prohibitions. In addition, he has examined thoroughly Bancroft's valiant, if vain, endeavours to solve the problems of non-residence and pluralism by improving the value of benefices, either by the recovery of impropriations or by the restoration of payment of tithe in kind instead of by *modus decimandi*, a subject to which much attention has been given in Mr Christopher Hill's recent study of *Economic Problems of the Church from Whitgift to the Long Parliament*. In all these respects, Dr Babbage has made a valuable contribution to the history of Puritanism during Bancroft's primacy.

Bancroft himself likewise appears in a more favourable aspect than many historians, and particularly the historians of Puritanism, have allowed. Dr Albert Peel indeed saw in him only "an able careerist, one of those who, by dint of much pushing, get to the top"; though he admitted that Dr Babbage has "generally portrayed him in a favourable light". Bancroft indeed is regarded by the Dean of Melbourne as a prescient primate, who saw the fundamental character of the Puritan menace to the established order of the Church of England and who strove by his enforcement of conformity to stem the tide of its penetration of the clerical order. Yet, together with many of the bishops of his province, in his enforcement of the canons of 1604 he sought so to minister justice as to forget not mercy. I esteem it an equal privilege and pleasure to commend the Dean of Melbourne's study to all who are interested in the history of religion in England, both as a memento of our former association and with the confidence that it constitutes a valuable and authoritative interpretation of its subject.

NORMAN SYKES

ACKNOWLEDGEMENTS

NORMAN SYKES was, by general consent, the doyen of English ecclesiastical historians. His untimely death has bereft English historical scholarship of its most distinguished ornament. He was a meticulous scholar and a polished writer. His gifts were not only professional but also personal. He gave unstinted help and encouragement to his students, and I would be less than generous if I failed to pay posthumous tribute to his memory. In my younger days as a student he gave me invaluable guidance and advice together with the gift of friendship. One of his last acts was to write the foreword which appears in this book.

I would also thank my long-suffering wife and daughter for undertaking the tedious labour of compiling the index and seeing the book through the press.

S. B. B.

I must add my thanks to the Reverend Dr L. L. Morris for the use of the Tyndale House Library. His willing assistance and the hospitality of his wife made light of our "tedious labour".

J. E. B.

1

PURITANISM AND THE RISE OF
RICHARD BANCROFT

JOHN WHITE, Bishop of Winchester, in the course of his
panegyric at Queen Mary's funeral, made pointed reference
to the ominous signs of impending religious revolution: "I
warn you, the wolves be coming out of Geneva, and other places
of Germany, and have sent their books before them, full of
pestilent doctrines, blasphemy, and heresy, to infect the people."[1]
For his temerity he was summoned before the Council and placed
under house arrest.

With the accession of Queen Elizabeth, the protestant *émigrés*
came hastening back to the Kingdom. On the Continent they
had enjoyed fellowship with the best reformed churches, and they
were resolved that England should now enjoy the like blessing
of a "godly reformation". At Frankfurt Dr Richard Cox (soon
to become Bishop of Ely) had produced a simplified version of the
1552 Prayer Book in which certain ceremonies had already been
abandoned as "in their own nature indifferent".[2]

Within the House of Commons, which assembled on 25
January 1558/9, the advocates of reform were confident and
resolute. Sir Anthony Cooke, the ardent protestant and erstwhile
tutor to Edward VI, wrote exultantly to Peter Martyr: "We are
busy in Parliament about expelling the tyranny of the pope
and restoring the royal authority, and re-establishing true
religion."[3]

Elizabeth did not share the prevailing mood: she was no
iconoclast: she wanted a religious settlement that was both

---

[1] J. Strype, *Ecclesiastical Memorials, relating chiefly to Religion and the Reformation
of it, and the Emergencies of the Church of England, under King Henry VIII, King
Edward VI, and Queen Mary I*, Oxford, 1824, Vol. III, pt. 2, p. 542.

[2] Cox to Calvin. 5 April 1565. Quoted, *Troubles at Frankfort*, ed. E. Arber,
1908, p. 77.

[3] *Zurich Letters*, Vol. II, p. 13.

cautious and conservative.[1] It now appears, if the convincing reconstruction of J. E. Neale is to be accepted,[2] that she favoured the passage, in the first session of Parliament, of an Act abrogating the papal, and restoring the royal supremacy, with the further authorization of communion in both kinds, thereby postponing to a later date the vexed problem of the Prayer Book. This purpose, however, was defeated by the resolute determination of the radicals in the House of Commons, with the result that the Act of Uniformity was finally passed at the same time as the Act of Supremacy.

The Prayer Book, as authorized, was the Prayer Book of 1552, with several significant changes of a conservative nature: the petition in the Litany, praying for deliverance "from the tyranny of the Bishop of Rome and all his detestable enormities", was omitted; and, in connection with the administration of the Sacrament of Holy Communion, the commemorative words of the Prayer Book of 1552 were prefaced by the sacramental words of 1549. The "Black Rubric", which had been inserted in 1552 without parliamentary sanction, was omitted; and, crucially important, the Queen had a conservative proviso concerning the ornaments of the Church inserted in the Bill. The Bill passed the Commons without difficulty, but, according to the Spanish ambassador, only passed the Lords by a margin of three votes.[3]

The private beliefs of the Queen are a matter of speculation and conjecture. She was educated by Renaissance scholars of liberal views and she proved an apt student. More important, her experiences during the turbulent days of her brother's reign and the unhappy reign of her sister implanted in her a deep and abiding fear of fanaticism. She was determined to countenance no fierce counter-reformation. She wanted no extremism: she wanted a settlement at once broad and generous. She had no desire to open "windows into men's hearts and secret thoughts".[4]

---

[1] The Spanish ambassador reported the Queen as saying "that she differed very little from us, as she believed that God was in the Sacrament of the Eucharist, and only dissented from three or four things in the Mass". *Spanish Calendar Eliz.*, Vol. I, p. 61.

[2] *Elizabeth I and her Parliaments, 1559–1581*, London, 1933.

[3] *Spanish Calendar Eliz.*, Vol. I, p. 67.

[4] Sir Francis Bacon is our authority for this phrase: J. Spedding, *An Account of the Life and Times of Francis Bacon*, Boston, 1878, Vol. I, p. 97.

Years later she made her famous *apologia*: "We know not, nor have any meaning to allow that any of our subjects should be molested either by examination or inquisition . . . as long as they shall profess the Christian faith, not gainsaying the authority of the holy Scriptures and the articles of our faith contained in the Creeds Apostolic and Catholic; or for matters of ceremonies . . . as long as they shall show them selves quiet and conformable. . . ."[1] She would make no "examination or inquisition" of men's "secret opinions", no intrusion into men's "consciences for matters of faith". On the basis of a settlement both tolerant and comprehensive she hoped for a general conformity in practice. It was essentially the policy of a politique and a realist.

This accommodating ecclesiastical settlement was unacceptable to the Marian bishops, who, with the exception of Kitchin of Llandaff, refused the oath of supremacy and were deprived; and it was unacceptable to the returned *émigrés*, who objected to the embarrassing requirements concerning ceremonies and vestments. John Jewel, who was appointed Bishop of Salisbury in 1560, writing to Peter Martyr, complained indignantly:

> The scenic apparatus of divine worship is now under agitation; and those very things which you and I have so often laughed at, are now seriously and solemnly entertained by certain persons (for *we* are not consulted) as if the Christian religion could not exist without something tawdry. Our minds indeed are not sufficiently disengaged to make these fooleries of much importance. Others are seeking after a *golden*, or as it rather seems to me, a *leaden* mediocrity; and are crying out, that the half is better than the whole.[2]

Sandys, writing to Parker on 30 April 1559 concerning the Ornaments Rubric, said: "Our gloss upon this text is, that we shall not be forced to use them."[3] However, it would seem that he was mistaken, for when Thomas Sampson was offered a bishopric, he refused on the grounds that vestments were not things "indifferent". The Queen also seemed to be of a different mind, and it was thought that she might not have agreed to the Prayer Book without the ornaments rubric. Her retention of the crucifix and candles in the royal chapel was a further cause of offence, and Jewel, in a further letter to Peter Martyr, replied:

[1] S.P. Dom., Eliz. I, Vol. LXVI, no. 54. Published, *Queen Elizabeth's Defence of her Proceedings in Church and State*, London, 1958.
[2] *Zurich Letters*, Vol. I, p. 23.   [3] *Parker Correspondence*, p. 65.

"As to ceremonies . . . there is a little too much foolery. That little silver cross, of ill-omened origin, still maintains its place in the Queen's chapel . . . . The slow-paced horses retard the chariot."[1] In another letter he lamented that everything is being done with "deliberation, and prudence, and wariness, and circumspection". "This dilatoriness", he said, "has grievously damped the spirits of our brethren." "It is idly and scurrilously said, by way of joke, that as heretofore Christ was *cast out* by his enemies, so he is now *kept out* by his friends."[2] Sir Francis Knollys, that ardent and indefatigable protestant, presented an address to the Queen "against the use of images",[3] and wrote to Parker (consecrated Archbishop of Canterbury on 17 December 1559) of "the enormities yet in the Queen's closet retained".[4]

Elizabeth summoned her second Parliament in 1563, and Convocation met contemporaneously. The supporters of the papal supremacy had been removed by the application of the oath of supremacy, and the representatives of reform were now firmly entrenched. In the Lower House of Convocation a series of six articles was debated: they provided for the abolition of saints' days, the omission of the sign of the cross in baptism, and the removal of organs. Kneeling at the reception of the sacrament was to be optional at the discretion of the ordinary, and the surplice was prescribed as a sufficient garment for ministerial functions.[5] After heated debates, these articles were defeated by one vote—after proxies had been invoked. It was a bitter disappointment to the radicals: henceforth they would seek to work through Parliament rather than Convocation.[6]

Many of the newly consecrated bishops were drawn from the

[1] *Zurich Letters*, Vol. I, p. 55.
[2] Ibid., Vol. I, p. 17. 14 April 1559.
[3] Quoted, J. Strype, *Annals of the Reformation and Establishment of Religion, and other various occurrences in the Church of England, during Queen Elizabeth's Happy Reign*, Oxford, 1824, Vol. I, pt. 1, p. 331.
[4] *Parker Correspondence*, p. 97.
[5] Printed, G. W. Prothero, *Select Statutes and Other Constitutional Documen s*, Oxford, 1949, p. 191.
[6] J. E. Neale comments: "Having failed to mould their own assembly to their wishes and thus exploit the proper constitutional machinery, the left-wing of the clergy was driven back, for future occasions, on the irregular expedient of 1559—on organizing its agitation through the House of Commons. In consequence, not only the quality of Elizabethan parliamentary history but the whole future of English constitutional development was profoundly affected." Op. cit., pp. 89–90.

ranks of the returned *émigrés*, and were exceedingly reluctant to enforce the ceremonial requirements of the ecclesiastical settlement. Cecil indignantly protested to Parker: "The Bishop of Norwich winketh at schismatics and anabaptists. . . . A surplice may not be borne here."[1]

The Queen was implacably opposed to any further concessions to the left. She had already been driven by Puritan pressure to concede more than she approved. She upbraided the Archbishop for his laxity in enforcing conformity, and, in a letter dated 25 January 1564/5, complained that "in sundry places of our realm of late . . . not only in opinions, but in external ceremonies and rites, there is crept and brought into the Church by some few persons . . . an open and manifest disorder and offence. . . . We intend to have no dissension or variety grow by suffering of persons which maintain dissension to remain in authority."[2] Parker, in a letter to Grindal, Bishop of London, spoke of the Queen's indignation concerning those who maintained "disordered dissension", and her determination that "none hereafter be admitted to any office . . . but such as shall be disposed to follow common order, and shall also before their admittance orderly and formally promise to use themselves in truth, concord, and unity, and to keep . . . order and uniformity in . . . external rites and ceremonies".[3] Grindal communicated these instructions to the bishops of the provinces, and demanded returns concerning existing diversities. It appeared that there was widespread lawlessness.

> Some say the service and prayers in the chancel, others in the body of the church . . . some say in a surplice, others without a surplice; the table standeth in the body of the church in some places, in others it standeth in the chancel . . . administration of the Communion is done by some with surplice and cope, some with surplice alone, others with none; some with unleavened bread, others with leavened; some receive kneeling, others standing, others sitting; some baptise in a font, others in a basin; some sign with the sign of the cross, others sign not. . . .[4]

Notorious offenders were summoned to London for examination, including Sampson, Dean of Christ Church, Oxford, and

[1] *Parker Correspondence*, p. 149.
[3] Ibid., p. 229.
[2] Ibid., pp. 224, 227.
[4] *Lansdowne MSS.*, VIII.

His early life is shrouded in obscurity. His father was apparently a man of little note, and Richard was sent to the local Grammar School at Farnworth. The county of Lancashire was deeply divided religiously: the Roman Catholics were firmly entrenched in the conservative north and west, and the protestants in the south-east. We do not know what influences were brought to bear upon him. He was probably ignorant of the conflicts and tensions which were present in Elizabeth's first Parliament. In due course he would learn of the growing catalogue of Puritan complaints against the vestments and ceremonies of the Church.

It was through the generosity of his maternal great-uncle, Hugh Curwyn, that Bancroft proceeded to Christ's College, Cambridge. Cambridge was a centre of turbulent religious controversy.[1] Among Bancroft's contemporaries were such convinced Puritans as Edmund Chapman, Humphrey Fenn, John Knewstubs, and Laurence Chaderton. According to tradition, Bancroft was noted for sport rather than for learning; for boxing, wrestling, and the quarter-staff rather than for diligence: he is said to have owed his life during a town-and-gown fight to Chaderton's intervention.[2] It was because of Puritanism at Christ's College that Bancroft joined Jesus as a tutor, after graduating Bachelor of Arts in 1566/7. He graduated Master of Arts in 1572, and two years later he was ordained priest at Ely.[3] He was presented by his uncle to a prebend in St Patrick's, Dublin, and a little later to a prebend at Ely,[4] thereby joining the ranks of the pluralists. He was appointed chaplain to the Bishop of Ely, Richard Cox; and on 24 March 1576, he was collated by the Bishop to the rectory of Teversham, near Cambridge.[5] Before the end of the year he was appointed one of the twelve preachers licensed by the University.

While Bancroft was industriously ascending the ecclesiastical ladder, Puritanism was growing in militancy and strength.

[1] For details, see H. C. Porter, *Reformation and Reaction in Tudor Cambridge*, Cambridge, 1958.

[2] R. G. Usher, *Reconstruction of the English Church*, 1910, Vol. I, p. 26.

[3] There is no record of his ordination as a deacon in the Ely Registers.

[4] *Carta Miscellanea*, Vol. XII, f. 23, Lambeth Palace Library, 21 December 1575.

[5] *Institution Book*, Diocesan Registry, Ely. 24 March 1575/6. Bancroft, like his predecessor in the primacy, Whitgift, was both Rector of Teversham, and chaplain to Richard Cox, Bishop of Ely.

Thomas Cooper, reviewing Puritanism in 1589, noted different phases:

> At the beginning some learned and godly preachers, for private respects in themselves, made strange to wear the surplice, cap, or tippet: but yet so that they declared themselves to think the thing indifferent, and not to judge evil of such as did use them. Shortly after rose up another defending that they were not things indifferent but disdained with antichristian idolatry, and therefore not to be suffered in the Church. Not long after came another sort affirming that those matters touching apparel were but trifles, and not worthy contention in the Church, but that there were greater things of far more weight and importance, and indeed touching faith and religion, and therefore meet to be altered in a church rightly. As the Book of Common Prayer, the administration of the Sacraments, the government of the Church, the election of ministers, and a number of other like. Fourthly, now break out another sort earnestly affirming and teaching, that we have no Church, no bishops, no ministers, no sacraments; and therefore that all that love Jesus Christ ought with all speed to separate themselves from our congregation, because our assemblies are profane, wicked and antichristian.[1]

It is not difficult to understand some of the reasons for this development. The radicals had been frustrated in their endeavours to secure a more thorough reformation either through Convocation or Parliament. They now found themselves increasingly harried by the bishops. It is not surprising, in these circumstances, that they turned against the bishops. They began to question the institution of episcopacy, its validity and genuine apostolicity. Controversy concerning ceremonies merged into a more fundamental controversy concerning the government of the Church, its polity and form.

Thomas Cartwright was the chief agent and architect of this change. He was an effective and able preacher. He was appointed Lady Margaret Professor of Divinity in the University of Cambridge in 1569,[2] and, in his lectures on the Acts of the Apostles, claimed that presbyterianism was the primitive and apostolic form of Church government. He advanced six propositions: the names and offices of archbishops and bishops ought to be abolished;

---

[1] *An Admonition to the People of England*, 1589, ed. E. Arber, p. 119.
[2] A. F. S. Pearson, *Thomas Cartwright and Elizabethan Puritanism, 1535–1603*, Cambridge, 1925, pp. 28–9.

the offices of bishops and deacons ought to be established as in the New Testament; the bishops ought to have purely spiritual functions, and the deacons ought to care for the poor; the government of the Church ought to be entrusted to the ministers and presbytery of the Church; each minister ought to be attached to a definite congregation; and a minister ought to be elected by the congregation of a Church.[1]

The immediate effect of the lectures was vigorous debate and dissension. William Chaderton of Queens' wrote to Cecil that Cambridge was "all in a hurly-burly and shameful broil". Cartwright was determined, he said, "to overthrow all ecclesiastical and civil governance that now is, and to ordain and institute a new found policy".[2] Grindal protested that Cartwright's "busy head" was "stuffed full of singularities".[3] Cartwright was summarily suspended from his lectures by the University authorities, and later deprived of his Chair.

As a means of defence against the seductions of Rome, some of the bishops encouraged the use of "prophesyings" or "exercises". The ostensible purpose of these gatherings was mutual exhortation and edification with the exposition of Scripture. But there were others who suspected that these gatherings might become revolutionary party-cells for the practice of the Geneva-discipline. Bishop Aylmer related that "there is of late a rank of rangers and posting apostles that go from shire to shire, from Exercise to Exercise, namely Patchet, Standon, etc. accompanied, countenanced and backed with Sir R. Knightley, Mr Carlett, and others out of Warwickshire, Northamptonshire, and other shires, to Ashby where Gilby is bishop, to Leicestershire, where Johnson is superintendent, to another place where the monk Anderson reigneth to Coventry, etc."[4]

Bishop Scambler of Peterborough addressed an urgent plea to Burghley:[5]

Vouchsafe ... to looke upon theis sheires of Northampton and Rutland ... and ayde me with your counsaile. ... Those whom men

---

[1] *S.P. Dom.*, *Eliz. I*, Vol. LXXIII, p. 26.
[2] Ibid., Vol. LXXI, p. 11.
[3] Ibid., Vol. LXXI, pp. 23, 58.
[4] *Additional MSS.*, 29,546, f. 56.
[5] William Cecil was created Baron of Burghley in 1571.

doe call puritans and their fautours . . . are growen apparentlie to neglecte, if theie doe not abhorre, the devine service sett owte by publique aucthoritie. So that in the towne of Overton where Mr Carleton dwelleth there is no devyne service upon most Sondayes and hollidaies according to the booke of commen prayer, but in steede thereof ij sermons be preached most commenlie by one Mr Standen and one Mr Kinge, men for their opinions not licensed by me to preach at this daie. When they are determined to receyve the communion theie repaire to Whiston, where it is theire joye to haue manie owte of diuers parishes, principallie owt of Northampton towne and Overton aforesaid with other townes thereabowte, theare to receive the sacramentes with preachers and ministers to their owne likinge, and contrarie to forme prescribed by the publique order of the realme. . . . To their purposes they have drawen diuers yonge ministers, to whome it is plausible to have absolute authoritie in their parishes. In their waies theie be verie bolde and stowte, like men that seme not to be without great frendes.[1]

The organizing secretary behind this radical movement was John Field. He was a brilliant tactician. Bancroft later described him as "a great and chiefe man amongst the brethren of London: and one to whome the managing of the discipline (for the outward practice of it) was especially (by the rest) committed. So as all the letters, that were directed from the brethren of other places; to haue this or that referred to the London assemblies, were for the most part directed vnto him."[2]

The Bishop of London reported that "there is a conuenticle or rather conspiracie breedinge in London. . . . The citie will neuer be quiet untill theese authors of sedicion who are now esteemed as godds, as Fielde, Wilcocks, Cartwright, and others, be farre removed. . . . The people resorte unto them as in poperie they were wonte to runne on pilgrimage."[3] According to Bancroft, it was this cell which decided to address *An Admonition to Parliament*.[4]

The time was propitious. The Ridolfi plot had just been discovered. This sinister plan envisaged the rescue of Mary, Queen of Scots, the deposition or death of Elizabeth, and the re-establishment of Roman Catholicism. The discovery resulted in

[1] *Lansdowne MSS.*, XVII, f. 27. 13 April 1573.
[2] *Suruay of the Pretended Holy Discipline*, p. 369.
[3] *Landsdowne MSS.*, XVII, f. 43.
[4] Printed, *Puritan Manifestoes*, ed. W. H. Frere and C. E. Douglas, London, 1954.

an intense outburst of protestant patriotism. The radicals were not slow to take advantage of this situation. The campaign opened with the publication of the *Admonition*. Its significance cannot be overestimated. This masterly document marked the explicit adoption of the presbyterian platform by the Puritan reformers. It professed to offer "a true platform of a church reformed", affirming that "the offices of a Church are chiefly three, ministers or pastors, elders and deacons". Furthermore, "the outwarde markes whereby a true christian church is knowne, are preaching of the word purely, ministring of the Sacraments sincerely, and ecclesiastical discipline which consisteth in admonition and correction of faults severelie".[1] An additional tract, *A View of Popishe abuses yet remaining in the Englishe Church, for the which Godly Ministers have refused to subscribe*, was attached to the *Admonition*. The Prayer Book was bluntly described as "an unperfecte booke, culled and picked out of that popishe dunghill, the Masse boke full of all abhominations".[2] Vestments were dregs of popery: "Copes, caps, and surplesses, tippets, and such lyke baggage, the preachyng signes of popysh priesthode . . . are as the garments of the Idole, to which we . . . say, avaunt and get thee hence. They are as the garments of the Balamites, of popish priestes, enemies to God and all Christians. They serve not to edification, they have the shewe of evyll . . . they worke discorde . . . they bryng the ministerie into contempte, they offend the weake, they encourage the obstinate."[3] There were, however, more fundamental questions at issue. An additional note in the second edition was concerned to underline and stress this fact: "Neither is the controversie betwixt them and us as they would beare the world in hand, as for a cap, a tippet, or a suplesse, but for great matters concerning a true ministerie and regiment of the churche, according to the word. Which things once established the other melt away of them selves."[4]

The *Admonition* was an astute and able piece of propaganda. Written in a robust and vigorous style, it proved a best seller. A third edition appeared in August and the authorities found themselves unable to suppress it. Bishop Cox, writing to Bullinger, expressed a fear lest these "factious and heady men" pull "in pieces the whole economy of our Church". "Their object", he said, "is

---

[1] Quoted, ibid., p. 9.
[2] Ibid., p. 21.   [3] Ibid., p. 35.   [4] Ibid., p. 36n.

to revive the ancient presbytery of the primitive church, and to establish an equality of ministers."[1] The bishops determined that the challenge must be met, and the episcopal government of the Church defended. Whitgift was commissioned for the task.

An Answere to a certen Libel intituled An Admonition to the Parliament . . . appeared in February 1572/3. The text of the *Admonition* was reproduced page by page, and was refuted paragraph by paragraph. Cartwright responded with, *A Replye to An Answere made by M Doctor Whitgifte Agaynste the Admonition to the Parliament* (1573). *A Defense of the Answere* came from Whitgift's pen in 1574, and *The Second Replie* from Cartwright in 1575, and *The Rest of the Second Replie* in 1577. Whitgift resisted the claim that ecclesiastical polity must find its justification and support in Holy Scripture:

> I find no one certain and perfect kind of government prescribed or commanded in the scriptures to the church of Christ; which no doubt should have been done, if it had been necessary unto the salvation of the church. . . . Some kind of government may be a part of the church, touching the outward form and perfection of it, yet it is not such a part of the essence and being, but that it may be the church of Christ without this or that kind of government: and therefore the kind of government of the church is not "necessary unto salvation . . .".[2]

Cartwright, however, argued strongly that "the discipline oi Christ's Church, that is necessary for all times, was delivered by Christ and set down in the Holy Scriptures".

The Queen intervened by issuing a royal proclamation, dated 11 June 1573, which denounced religious dissent in general and the publications of the Puritan press in particular. All copies of the *Admonition* and of Cartwright's *Reply* were to be surrendered. Sandys, Bishop of London, complained that not a single copy of the specified books had been surrendered to him.[3] A warrant was issued for Cartwright's arrest but he succeeded in escaping to Germany.

[1] *Zurich Letters*, Vol. I, pp. 284–5.
[2] J. Whitgift, *Works*, Vol. I, pp. 184–5.
[3] J. Strype, *The Life and Acts of John Whitgift, D.D., the third and last Lord Archbishop of Canterbury in the reign of Queen Elizabeth*, Oxford, 1822, Vol. I, p. 107.

The following year there was published anonymously at La Rochelle *Ecclesiasticae Disciplinae et Anglicanae Ecclesiae ab illa aberrationis plena e verbo Dei et dilucida explicatio*. The authorship is generally ascribed to Walter Travers, although Cartwright was responsible for the preface. Cartwright made an English translation: *A full and plaine declaration of Ecclesiasticall Discipline owt off the word of God, and off the declining off the churche off England from the same*. It was an effective and persuasive exposition of the presbyterian form of Church government.

This literary warfare had been accompanied by intensive parliamentary activity.[1] On 17 May 1572, the Commons had given a first reading to a Bill concerning rites and ceremonies. The preamble stated that the Prayer Book, though sound enough in substantial doctrine, contained "divers orders of rites, Ceremonies and observacions" which were permitted in "respecte of the greate weakness of the people" when "blynded with supersticion". The time was now ripe for further reformation: already "many Congregationes" had "grown to desire of attenying to some further forme than in that book is prescribed". God had "raysed up a grate nomber of lerned pastors and zealous minysters": these men, "in discharge of theire consciences", had adopted the practice of omitting "the precise rule and strayt observacion of the forme and order prescribed in that booke, with some parte of rites and ceremonyes therin apoynted", in an endeavour to conform "themselves more neerlie to the Imitacyon of thauncyent apostolicall churche and the best reformed churches in Europe, as well in the forme of comon prayer mynistracion of the sacraments, examinacion of the communycants, catechisying of the youth and instruction of the older with divers other profitable exercises to the great encrease of treu knowledge, furtherances of gods Glorye and extinguishynge of the supersticion and the advancyne of true religion". Because "a nomber of maliciouse adversaries of the trueth" had sought "by all mens to hinder and disturbe theise godlie proceedyngs" this Bill enacted

. . . that it shall and may be lawful to and for all and every persone vicar and mynister beyng a preacher allowed and havyng the charge of any congregacion with the consent of the most part of Bishopps of

1 For details, see J. E. Neale, op. cit., p. 298.

this Realm to omytt and leave any parte of the same prescribed forme appoynted by and in the same booke of comon prayer in suche sorte, and at tymes, as to such personne, vicar or minyster shalbe thoughte most necessarie and expedyent to preache the woord of God or to use any other godlie exercise, for the instruction of his congregation . . . and with like consent to use such forme of prayer and mynistracion of the woorde and sacraments, and other godlie exercises of religion as the righte godlie reformed Churches now do use in the ffrenche and Douche congregation, within the City of London or elsewhere in the Quenes maiesties dominions and is extant in printe, any acte or acts, Iniunction, advertisement or decree heretofore had or made to the contrarie notwithstandynge.[1]

A peremptory message arrived from the Queen "that from henceforth no Bill concerning Religion shall be preferred or received . . . unless the same should be first considered and liked by the Clergy".[2]

"Prophesyings" were being increasingly subverted into secret sessions for the practice of the "discipline", until finally the Queen, who had always regarded them with intense suspicion and hostility, insisted on their suppression. Grindal, who was made primate in 1575, obstinately refused. "I am forced, with all humility, and yet plainly, to profess that I cannot with safe conscience and without the offence of the majesty of God, give my assent to the suppression of the said exercises, much less can I send out any injunction for the utter and universal subversion of the same."[3] Grindal was sequestered for his temerity, and the Queen without further ado admonished the bishops herself, commanding them to put an end to these "disputations and new devised opinions upon matters of divinity . . . by which manner of assemblies great numbers of our people . . . are brought to idleness and seduced and in a manner schismatically divided among themselves".[4]

[1] S.P. Dom., Eliz. I, Vol. LXXXVI, p. 45. Printed, Frere and Douglas, op. cit., p. 149.
[2] Sir S. D'Ewes, The Journals of all the Parliaments during the reign of Queen Elizabeth, both of the House of Lords and House of Commons, London, 1682, p. 213.
[3] Grindal's Remains, p. 387.
[4] "Queen Elizabeth's letter to the bishops throughout England against conventicles, and for the suppressing the exercise called prophesying." 7 May 1577. Printed, E. Cardwell, Documentary Annals of the Reformed Church of England, Oxford, 1839, Vol. I, p. 373.

Parliament met again in 1576, having been kept in being by a series of prorogations. Once again, the Puritans seized the occasion to ventilate sundry grievances. It was astute tactics: it served to discredit the administrative organization of the Church, and it fed an incipient anticlericalism. On 29 February 1575/6, Thomas Cromwell, the diarist, reported: "Mr Pistor, with great zeal, declared to the House the great prejudice [that] grew to the realm by the unlearnedness of the ministry, abuses of excommunication, want of discipline, dispensations, and tolerations for non-residency, and such like."[1] He moved "that an humble petition may be made to the Queen's Majesty for reformation". This was a different and more constitutional method of procedure: previously the Puritans had attempted direct statutory action. A committee, containing some of the most stalwart Puritan laymen—Snagge, Lewkenor, Yelverton, and Audley among others—was appointed. The petition was duly presented. The preamble stressed the evils of ignorance and non-residence:

> Whereas by the lack of the true discipline of the Church a great number of men are admitted to occupy the place of ministers in the Church of England, who are not only altogether unfurnished of such gifts as are by the word of God necessarily and inseparably required to be incident to their calling, but also are infamous in their lives and conversations; and also many of the ministry whom God hath endowed with ability to teach are by means of non-residence, pluralities, and such-like dispensations so withdrawn from their flock that their gifts are almost altogether become unprofitable; whereby an infinite number of your Majesty's subjects, for want of the preaching of the word—the only ordinary means of salvation of souls and the only good means to teach your Majesty's subjects to know their true obedience to your Majesty . . . have already run headlong into destruction, and many thousand of the residue yet remain in great peril. . . .

The petitioners earnestly requested the Queen "that . . . provision may be made for supply and reformation of these great wants and grievous abuses . . .". The queen was gratified that the Commons had learnt the propriety of proceeding by petition, instead of demanding statutory action. She promised to confer with the bishops concerning measures of reformation.[2] It would

---

[1] *Trinity College, Dublin, MSS.*, N.2/12.
[2] *Additional MSS.*, 33,271, f. 13 b.

appear that the articles passed by Convocation at this session, concerning the admission of fit persons to the ministry, were an outcome of this petition and the Queen's subsequent conference with the bishops.

In the year 1583 Edmund Grindal, blind and sequestered, died, and John Whitgift, known anti-Puritan and stern disciplinarian, was appointed Archbishop of Canterbury in his stead. He was the Queen's own personal choice, whom she greeted affectionately as her "little black husband".[1] He was sworn to reduce the Puritans to order and conformity: "Her Majesty moveth and earnestly exhorteth me therunto with straight charge as I will answer the contrary."[2] His mettle was soon seen in a letter which was forwarded to the clergy on 19 October 1583, four days before his enthronement. Certain articles, which had received the Queen's approval, were enclosed: all private preaching, reading, or catechizing was to be abolished, and none was to preach, read, or catechize, unless he ministered the sacraments publicly four times a year according to the Book of Common Prayer; all must "wear and use such kind of apparel as is prescribed ... by the book of Advertisements"; and none must preach, read, or catechize unless subscription had first been given to the *Three Articles*:

I. That her Majesty, under God, hath, and ought to have, the sovereignty and rule over all manner of persons born within her realms and dominions, and countries, of which estate ecclesiastical or temporal whatsoever they be. And that none other foreign power, prelate, state, or potentate hath, or ought to have any jurisdiction, power, superiority, preeminence, or authority ecclesiastical or temporal within her Majesty's said realms, dominions, and countries.

II. That the Book of Common Prayer, and of ordering Bishops, Priests, and Deacons, containeth nothing in it contrary to the Word of God. And that the same may be lawfully used; and that he himself will use the form of the said book prescribed, in public prayer, and administration of the sacraments, and none other.

III. That he alloweth the book of Articles of Religion, agreed upon by the Archbishop and Bishops in both provinces, and the whole clergy in the Convocation holden at London in the year of our Lord

---

[1] Cf. H. Peachman, *The Compleat Gentleman*, London, 1661, p. 165.
[2] H.M.C., *Marquis of Bath MSS.*, Vol. II, p. 26.

1562, and set forth by her Majesty's authority. And that he believeth all the articles therein contained to be agreeable to the word of God.[1]

Whitgift was fully alive to the dangers of Puritan infiltration, and he was determined to resist, by all means in his power, the alteration or subversion of the Church as by law established.

In 1582 an attempt had been made to set up a "presbytery in episcopacy". Delegates from the counties of Essex, Cambridge, and Norfolk had met in Suffolk to determine what might be tolerated and what ought to be refused in the Prayer Book. They agreed that the Articles of Subscription might be consented to only in accordance with the statute of 1571, which limited subscription to such Articles as contained the sum of the Christian faith and the doctrine of the Sacraments. Subscription to the Prayer Book and to the rest of the Articles should be resisted, even though a man should be deprived of his ministry for so refusing.

In this connection Puritan "classes" had been organized for prayer and fellowship to enable ministers to meet and confer over matters of common concern.[2] John Field had hoped that these "classes" might form the basis of a wider organization and make possible the holding of general conferences. Now, threatened by Whitgift's coercive tactics, they anxiously discussed ways and means of resistance. They resolved to compile a statistical and descriptive survey of the state of the ministry, with the names of ministers, whether resident or non-resident, preacher or non-preacher, etc. They hoped that this information, with its damaging revelations, would discomfort and discredit their adversaries.

In the meantime, Whitgift secured a new authorization of the Ecclesiastical Commission, for the purpose of enforcing ecclesiastical discipline. Richard Bancroft, whose anti-Puritan fervour was well known, was entrusted with its administration. It revived the use of the oath *ex officio* and provided two dozen Articles for the examination of suspects. (The oath *ex officio* was one which ecclesiastical authorities, by virtue of their office, might administer to an accused person, thereby forcing him, if guilty, to incriminate himself.) The revival of these procedures produced an

---

[1] J. Strype, *Whitgift*, Vol. I, p. 229.
[2] Cf. R. G. Usher, *The Presbyterian Movement in the Reign of Queen Elizabeth as illustrated by the Minute Book of the Dedham Classis, 1582–9*, London, 1905.

immediate outcry. Burghley wrote to the Archbishop: "I think the Inquisitors of Spain use not so many questions to comprehend and to trap their preyes. . . . According to my simple judgment, this kind of proceeding is too much savouring of the Romish Inquisition; and is rather a device to seek for offenders, than to reform any."[1] Whitgift assured Burghley that ministers were deprived, not simply for refusing subscription, but for stubborn nonconformity.

> I would not towch anie for not subscribing onelie, but for breach of order in celebrating divine service . . . not according to the forme by law prescribed.
> Towching the twenty-four articles, which your Lordship semith so much to mislike . . . I cannot but greatlie mervale at your Lordships vehement speaches against them, (I hope without cause.) Seeing yt ys the ordinarie cowrse in other courts likewise: as, in the Starchamber . . . I think these articles to be more tollerable, and better agreeing with the rule of justice and charitie, and less captious, then those in other courts. . . .
> I know your Lordship desireth the peace of the Church; but how ys yt possible to be procured, (after so long libertie and lack of discipline) vf a few persons so meanelie qualified as most of them are, shold be countenanced against the whole state of the Clergie of greatest account. . . .[2]

Members of the Privy Council were not convinced. They contrasted the immunity of "lewd, evil, unprofitable and corrupt" clergy with the treatment meted out to "diligent, learned and zealous" Puritans—"though in some points of ceremonial they might seem doubtful, only in conscience and not of wilfulness".[3] Whitgift, obstinate and unbending, refused to give way.

The struggle was continued by sympathetic supporters of the Puritan cause in Parliament (1584). Petitions were presented concerning the deplorable state of the ministry and the restraint of "so many good preachers". It was resolved to trust that the Queen would take speedy order. Dr Peter Turner introduced "a bill and a book": the "book" was the Genevan Prayer Book, the "bill" was to authorize this in the stead of the 1559 Prayer

---

[1] J. Strype, op. cit., Vol. III, pp. 104–7.
[2] Ibid., Vol. III, pp. 107–12.
[3] Ibid., Vol. I, pp. 328–30.

Book. The motion "stayed". In 1586 Cope introduced another Bill and a Book, declaring "utterly void" all existing ecclesiastical laws and statutes and substituting a presbyterian form of Church government. Elizabeth peremptorily sent for both Turner's Bill and Book and Cope's Bill and Book, and imprisoned their sponsors.

The Puritan movement began to show that fissiparous tendency which became its besetting weakness. The moderates still hoped for reformation from within the established Church either through the instrumentality of Parliament or the intervention of the Church; a new school of radicals, despairing of reform, insisted on the duty of immediate separation from the established Church "without tarrying for anie".[1] Cartwright contended that the apparel of the clergy and the ceremonies of the Church of England were not sufficiently evil in themselves to warrant secession. They were things "indifferent", and a minister's primary duty was to preach the gospel. Cartwright, though eager for reform, counselled patience. He hoped that a government of pastors and ruling elders would replace a government of archbishops and bishops, chancellors and archdeacons, and that it would be possible to organize the parishes of England into a connected system of presbyteries and synods, with assemblies, provincial and general. But the achievement of these things was dependent upon the goodwill of the Supreme Governor of the Church.

The separatists, however, adopted a different point of view. They denied that vestments and apparel were things "indifferent", and they did not believe that it was possible to reform the Church from within. The apostolic injunction was unambiguous: "Come out from among them, and be ye separate, saith the Lord, and touch not the unclean thing, and I will receive you, and will be a Father unto you, and ye shall be my sons and daughters, saith the Lord Almighty."[2] They enumerated fifteen "causes and reasons out of the mighty word of God that do move us . . . not to consent or be present in prayer and hearing the word of God, neither to communicate with those that do either receive or mainteine the remnants, reliques, and levings of the pope and papistry". "The filthy rags", they affirmed, bring the "heavenly

[1] Cf. R. Browne, *A Treatise of Reformation without Tarrying for Anie*, 1582.
[2] 2 Cor. 6.17–18.

word of our eternall Lord God into bondage, subjection, and slavery."[1]

Robert Browne,[2] a kinsman of Lord Burghley, was the first to teach the concept of the "gathered church" composed of "the worthiest, be they never so few".[3] He declared that the Church ought to be reformed without tarrying for the magistrate to do it, or for any other.[4] He acted on the principle that no bishop's licence to preach was necessary when a man felt called of God to do so. Confronted by "Bancroft, the Bishop's officer", who read him the Privy Council injunction forbidding unauthorized preachers, Browne replied that he was no longer preaching in Cambridge, but that, if he desired to do so, he would ignore the Council's commands.[5] Browne was thereupon imprisoned. After his release the Bishop of Norwich complained that he was now in Bury St Edmunds stirring up trouble. In 1583 the Sheriff asked the University of Cambridge to arrange for the visit of a University Preacher to silence objectors and defend the Church. Bancroft was chosen. During the course of his visit, Bancroft discovered, attached to the Queen's Arms, a libellous inscription, which compared the Queen to "that woman Jezebell".[6] Two laymen, Copping and Thacker, who had distributed books written by Browne and Harrison, were arrested and put to death. Bancroft was warmly congratulated by the authorities for his efficient detective work.

[1] *Morrice MSS., Seconde Parte of a Register*, Part 1, ff. 619–22. Quoted, A. Peel, *The Second Parte of a Register, Being a Calendar of Manuscripts under that title intended for publication by the Puritans about 1593, and now in Dr Williams' Library, London*, Cambridge, 1915, Vol. I, p. 55.

[2] There were several earlier separatist gatherings: see C. Burrage, *The Early English Dissenters in the Light of Recent Research (1550–1641)*, Cambridge, 1912, Vol. I, pp. 68 ff.

[3] For the fundamental points of difference between Cartwright and Browne: see *Lambeth MSS.*, 113, f. 187: "Cartwright's Reproof of Certain schismaticall persons and their doctrine concerning the hearing and preaching of God's Word." Ibid., 113, f. 203: "Browne's Answer to Cartwright's letter for joining with the Church of England."

[4] *A Treatise of Reformation without Tarrying for Anie.* Cf. *The Articles of Brownissian.* H.M.C., *Various*, Vol. IV, p. 166.

[5] R. Browne, *A True and Short Declaration*, 1584.

[6] *Camb. Univ. Lib. MSS.*, Mm. 1, 47, f. 332. A copy of Harrison's *Three formes of catechismes* (1583) in the Lambeth Palace Library, with Bancroft's initials on the cover, has an inscription on the title-page in Bancroft's hand: "The booke was geven me by the Lord cheefe Justice of the Common place; at Burie Assises 1583 the sixt of Julye."

Between 1583 and 1585 Bancroft prepared a circumstantial and documented account of the principles, platform, and practice of the Puritans.[1] He devoted the first section to a discussion of the "Heresies in R. Brownes Booke"; the second, to an account of the "Opinions and Dealings of the Precisians". "Item they generallye condemne all Bishops, Deanes, and Archdeacons, and desire to haue certen Elders, or Superintendents (as they call them) to be placed in theire roomes, and therefore they refuse to pray for them. Some also refuse to pray for the Queene, as supreme Governor in all causes ecclesiasticall."[2] Field was the active organizer, both secretary and treasurer: "Item they vse to make collection of money for their brethren that travelle for them beyond the Seas, and the monye gathered is comonlye delivered to one Field a Preacher in the Citie, and one Culverwell in Tamyse street. . . ."[3] Bancroft dwelt upon the divergent views of Cartwright and Browne, united only in their common opposition to the Church as by law established.

Some doe follow T.C. or rather in deede runne before hym, and yet they are more tollerable. Other some doe followe Browne, who are most detestable and licentious Libertynes. . . . Howbeit in the matter questioned for the present estate and governement of the Churche, both the sortes doe ioyne against vs almost in one manner.

For, the same faultes that the one fyndeth therein, the other dooth also charge vs withall. The same order and governement for a perfect Reformacion is of both partes equallye vrged.

The difference that is herein betwixt them, may well be resembled to one and the same lute string sett vp a note or two higher.

For the Brownists vppon the same propositions doe but conclude more furiouslye: as for example. If the Prynce doe hinder this Government, she is no Christian. If the Prynce will not hasten the same, the Ministers must not tarye her leysure.

The estate of the Churche is thus and thus, therefore to be reformed saith the one sorte, or else there can be no right Religion. Nay saith the other to be eschued as a nest of devilles, and vtterlie forsaken of all true Christians.[4]

In the fourth and final section Bancroft recounted "Certen

---

[1] St John's College Library, Cambridge, M.9. Printed, A. Peel, *Tracts ascribed to Richard Bancroft*, Cambridge, 1953.

[2] A. Peel, op. cit., p. 12.

[3] Ibid., p. 12.   [4] Ibid., pp. 18–19.

slaunderous speeches against the present Estate of the Church of Englande published to the people by the Precisians". As a result

> they haue brought the people in manye places to forsake theire parrishe Churches, and to frequent private Conventicles, sometyme in howses, sometymes in feeldes and woodes (as though the word of God might not be preached syncerelie and publiquelye in theise dayes) to forsake theire owne Pastors, and to followe them vp and downe the Contrye, and to leave theire trades and occupations, almost every daye in the weeke (to theire great impoverishing), for the attendance of theire novelties.[1]

They reject the authorized services of the Church, meeting as a coterie of the elect:

> Touchinge the Communion, they brought their disciples to this order, that most of them will not communicate with anye, but suche as be of theire owne crew, and therefore they forsake theire owne Churches to assemble them selves for that purpose. And in this meetinge the whole order sett out by lawes and authorities is wilfullie contemned: This is, or at the leaste hath bene their manner, (as a Preacher enformed me) who said he was present. After the Minister hath saluted everie one both man and woman, at theire comynge into the Chamber with a kysse, a longe Table beinge prepared for the purpose, (which holdeth fortie or fiftie persons) he taking the chayre at the end thereof, the rest sitt downe everie one in order: And then after the Wordes of Christes institution, the Minister hym self having receaved in both kyndes: the breade and the wyne which is left, passeth downe, and everye man without more a doe is his owne Carver.[2]

Bancroft made useful capital out of the recurrent dissensions and personal rivalries that rent the separatist congregations, particularly the emigrant settlements at Middleburg in Zeeland.

> Certeyne Schismaticall Reformers, as Robert Browne, Robert Harrison, Tobye Henson, John Chamler, Charles Moneman, Will'm Harrison, and a greate companye of other seditious persons both men and women, some havinge forsaken theire wyves, and other some theire husbands aboute two years synce, the estate of the Churche of England beinge first condemned as vnlawfull for them to tarrye in: and having layed downe the whole order of theire new governement, theire orders lawes and fasshions, appoynted Browne the Pastor, Robert Harrison the Doctor, and the rest to be Seniors

---

[1] Ibid., p. 70.   [2] Ibid., p. 70.

&c, lyke rebellious people departinge the Realme, did sayle into Flaunders. Where they had not bene (I thinke) a moneth in theire new Kindome of Christe, and most gloryious Syon, but (as Browne hym selfe dothe witnes) theire holye decrees were broken, there fell out questions, offences, partes takinge, and greate presumption encreased.

The myndes of the people were estraunged from theire Pastor, accusations, slaunders, and quarrells being caste abroade by the cheife of them, they grew to open defiance and raylinges. Browne the Pastor was accused for a Schismatike and a slaunderer, by Harrison the Doctor: At the first Harrison faylinge of the successe he looked for, did in a rage caste of his charge, and would no longer entermeddle therewith: except that Browne might be punished. Wherevpon the Seniors and people agreinge to his desire, Browne was twise condemned for an vnlawfull Pastor. This geare netled Pastor Browne: He forbiddeth the Congregacion anye more to resorte to his Chamber, (which was belike the place of theire meetings) and renouncinge in a rage his pastorall charge, Harrison agayne vndertaken his burden.

It were too longe to recount their quarrelles. Some grew wearie of Flaunders, and wisshed themselves agayne in England: others misliked that counsell. Harrisons sister was condemned by Browne for a reprobate, and he hym self also accused (by hym also) aboute the gaginge[1] of a sylver spoone: Muche a doe there was amongest them. Browne was condemned for a Schimatike and lewde Pastor three severall tymes, and always some kynde of agreement was made from the teeth outward, which lasted so longe as it was in makinge. So that in the end theire contentions and spight still encreasinge, Pastor Browne being the fourth tyme condemned and judged for an hereticke, and for a more wretched caytiffe then either the Pope or Antichriste, A generall breache was made of the Presbiterye. And thus the new government being dissolved, and everye man repayringe to his owne Contrye, the glorye of their Sion was vtterly defaced.

This Storye is written in a little Pamphlett, whiche is supposed to haue bene published by Browne, the tytle thereof is. *A true and short declaracon both of the gatheringe and ioyinge together of certyne persons; and also of the lamentable breache and division which fell amonge them.*[2]

It is difficult to exaggerate the polemical power of Bancroft's historical account. He used to advantage every discreditable incident, every squabble, and every scandal. The final picture of Puritanism was repellent and unattractive: and the mud has stuck.

---

[1] Pledging.   [2] Peel, op. cit., pp. 88–90.

Bancroft was also concerned to justify the episcopal form of government and, in the course of doing so, he asserted its apostolic authority:

It appeareth *Actes 18.* that St Paule havinge taken paynes by the space of A yere and sixe monthes to plant the Churche of God in Corinth, was no sooner departed thence into Syria, but certen light heades began to raise vp factions, and schismes, leadinge and driving after them their severall companyes of disciple [*sic*] & scollers.

For it was the order generallye amongest them that everie minister accompted suche as he had baptised to be his Sectaries and followers; And the people also beinge tumultuous, acknowledged them for their capteynes, directors and leaders: so that some holdinge of Paule, some of Apollo, some of Cephas, some of this man, some of that man, there grew in short tyme at Corinth as manye sectes and schismes in a manne as there were Preachers and teachers.

Wherevpon saith St Jerome, there was order taken and a decree made that (for the repressing of theise mischiefes, least everie man still should deale as he list) there should be certeyne choise Ministers appoynted for Bisshops in everye Coaste, and cheife Citie, who having the Rule and governement of the Clergye there committed vnto them, might by their authoritie prevent or redresse suche outragious enormyties. . . .

After the Apostles tymes therefore all the first Councells both pro-vinciall and generall as hath bene alledged did so diligentlye provide that Preists should attempt no matter without the conference of theire Bisshops, nor Bisshops but by likinge of their Metropolitanes: It was for no other cause, but for avoydinge contentions, sects schismes and heresyes.[1]

Bancroft had a gift for painstaking research and exhaustive inquiry. He demonstrated his ability as an ecclesiastical sleuth by publishing a *Discourse upon the Bill and Book exhibited in Parliament by the Puritans for a further Reformation of the Church Principles.*[2] He asserted that sinister and subversive plans lay behind the innocent demand for "a learned Ministry and the amendment of things amiss in the Ecclesiastical Estate".[3]

On 23 June 1586, a further stringent ordinance was issued by the Star Chamber to restrain the products of the Puritan press. No manuscript was to be set up in type until it had first been

[1] Ibid., pp. 132–4.
[2] *S.P. Dom.*, *Eliz. I*, Vol. CXCIX, no. 1.
[3] Sir S. D'Ewes, *Journals*, p. 410.

licensed by the Archbishop, or the Bishop of London, and any printer who disobeyed was to be liable to six months' imprisonment.[1] On 16 April 1588, Whitgift, on the strength of this ordinance, ordered the printing press of Robert Waldegrave in St Paul's Churchyard to be seized, and, among other works, copies of *The State of the Church of England laid open in a Conference*, by the learned extremist, John Udall, Vicar of Kingston-on-Thames, were discovered.

Six months later *An Epistle to the terrible Priests* written "by the reverend and worthy Martin Marprelate, Gentleman", appeared.[2] It was the first of a notorious series of tracts. They were ribald and abusive. The "Canterbury Caiaphas", the "froth and filth" of ecclesiastical laws, "the squeaking and chanting choristers", the "idle loitering lubbards", the "cursed uncircumcised murdering generation" of clergy, the "horned monsters of the Conspiration House", the "pageant and stage play" of the service of Holy Communion, all were "run down with a saucy pertness". The bishops were lampooned with alliterative ingenuity as "proud, popish, presumptive, profane, paltry, pestilent and pernicious prelates". Thomas Cooper, Bishop of Winchester, who endeavoured an episcopal reply,[3] was ridiculed and abused: *Hay any Worke for the Cooper*.

The pert author of these scurrilities was a past master at mockery and abuse. But he had a more serious purpose: the form of a Church both godly and reformed. Was the external government of the Church a matter "so prescribed by the Lord in the New Testament" as to be unalterable without sin by any man? The answer was emphatically: Yes. The one who denied this was "so mad and wicked as to say that our Saviour Christ left behind Him, here on earth, an unperfect and maimed body".

Bancroft, whose proved ability for inquisitorial work was more and more appreciated, was charged by Whitgift with the task of tracking down the press and of discovering the identity of the author. After intensive investigation the press was finally dis-

---

[1] Printed, G. W. Prothero, op. cit., p. 169.

[2] The writer promised to make public the iniquities of the clergy, and to put "a young Martin in everie parish . . . everie one of them able to mar a prelate". Hence the pseudonym.

[3] *An Admonition to the People of England.* January 1588/9.

covered at Newtown, near Manchester, and both press and printers were sent back to London under escort.[1] The identity of the author was never discovered.[2]

Bancroft was invited to preach at St Paul's Cross on 9 February 1588/9,[3] on the first Sunday of the new session of Parliament. Taking as his text the topical words: "Dearly beloved, believe not every spirit, but try the spirits whether they be of God. For many false prophets have gone out into the world", he used the occasion to launch a comprehensive attack on all separatists and schismatics: on all "Arians, Donatists, Papists, Libertines, Anabaptists, the Familie of Love, and sundrie other";[4] and to defend and vindicate the episcopal order of government, which had existed "ever since St Mark's time". "The Church of God ever since the apostles time hath distributed the ecclesiastical ministry principally into these other parts, bishops, priests and deacons."[5] Concerning presbyterianism:

There are verie manie now adaies who do affirme that when Christ used these words, *Dic ecclesiae*, he ment thereby to establish in the church for ever the same plat and forme of ecclesiasticall government, to be erected in everie parish, which Moses by Iethroes counsell appointed in mount Sinaie. . . .

They had (saie these men) in their synagogs their priests, we must have in every parish our pastors: they their rulers of their synagogs, we our elders: they their leviticall treasurers, we our deacons.[6]

But this interpretation, he held, lacked historical support:

There was never particular church, councell or synode, or any man of judgment that ever lived till these latter times (as I thinke, and I

---

[1] *Baker MSS.*, M.m. 1, 47, p. 333.

[2] Perhaps it was Job Throckmorton aided by John Penry. Professor A. L. Rowse has an ingenious and attractive suggestion: "Far too secular and amusing to have been written by the earnest Penrys of this world, were they, I wonder, written by such a person as Michael Hicks? They were clearly written by someone in a position to know everybody who was anybody, and the absolute certainty of Martin that he would never be brought to book points to someone safely ensconced high up at Court. Michael Hicks, Burghley's secretary, was a supporter of the Puritans, and he had a merry facetious pen. But who could Martin have been? The secret seems lost forever." A. L. Rowse, *The England of Elizabeth*, London, 1950, p. 531.

[3] *A Sermon Preached at Paules Crosse the 9. of Februarie, being the first Sunday in the Parleament, Anno. 1588.*

[4] Ibid., p. 3.   [5] Ibid., p. 99.   [6] Ibid., pp. 8–9.

have taken paines for the search thereof) that did ever so expound
and interpret that place. . . . A verie strange matter if it were true,
that Christ should erect a forme of government for the ruling of his
church to continue from his departure out of this world untill his
comming againe: and that the same should never be once thought of
or put in practise for the space of 1500 years.[1]

Basic to Puritanism was its contempt for episcopacy: "there are
many causes set downe by the said ancient fathers why so many
false prophets do go out into the world . . . whereof I finde the
contempt of Bishops especiallie to be one."[2] There was also the
alluring prospect of economic gain and material advantage:

I am fully of this opinion, that the hope which manie men have
conceived of the spoile of Bishops livings, of the subversion of
cathedrall churches, and of a hovocke to be made of all the churches
revenues, is the cheefest and most principall cause of the greatest
schismes that we have at this day in our church.[3]

Satirically and scornfully, Bancroft pressed his attack:

They will furthermore (the better to creep into your harts) pretend
great humilitie and bitterly exclaime against the pride of Bb. as
though they affected nothing else by their desired equalitie, but some
great lowlines, and to prostrate themselves at your feet for your
service; whereas in deed they shoote at greater superioritie and
preeminence, then ever your Bishops did use or challenge unto
them: and would no doubt tyrannise by their censures over both
prince and people at their pleasure, in most untollerable and
popelike maner. . . .[4]

It was a bitter, polemical sermon. The Puritans were incensed
at the base motives attributed to them, and the description of their
activities as subversive and revolutionary. Nevertheless, Bancroft
had raised certain fundamental questions of fact: was it possible
to claim apostolic and scriptural support for the institution of
episcopacy? Lord Burghley sought the opinion of Dr Hammond,
Chancellor of the diocese of London. The Chancellor replied,
4 November 1588, that the name of bishop, as an office having
superiority over many churches, was not to be found in the
Scriptures, and that

[1] Ibid., pp. 10–11.   [2] Ibid., p. 14.
[3] Ibid., pp. 23–4.   [4] Ibid., p. 93.

the Bysshops of our realm do not . . . nor may not, clayme to themselves any other authoritie than is geeven them by the statute of the
25 of Kynge Henry the 8, recited in the fyrst yaere of her Majesty's
raygne, neither is it reasonable they should make other clayme, for
had it pleased her Majesty, with the wysdome of the realme to have
used no bysshopps at all, we could not have complayned justly of
any defect in our Churche.[1]

Sir Francis Knollys, that doughty Puritan, desired the judgement
of Dr John Reynolds, subsequently to be President of Corpus
Christi College, Oxford. Reynolds replied:

he seemeth to avouch the Superioritie which Bishops haue amonge vs
ouer the Clergie to be of gods owne ordinaunce, though not by
expresse words yet by necessarye consequence, in that he affirmeth
their opinion who impugne that superioritie to be heresie. Wherein
I must confesse he hath committed an ouersight in my judgment.

Again:

he affirmeth that St Jerom saith, and Mr Calvin seemeth on his
report to confesse that Bishops haue had the said superioritie euer
since the tyme of St Marke the Evangelist, of the which pointe I
thinke as of the former, sith neither Jerom saith it, neither doth
Calvin seeme to confesse it on this report . . . it is certaine that
neither of them doth affirme that Bishops haue so long tyme had
such superioritie as Dr Bancrofte seemeth to father vpon them.[2]

Four days after the delivery of Bancroft's sermon a Royal
Proclamation (13 February 1588/9) expressed in unmistakable
terms the Queen's dislike of the Martinist writings "in railing sort
and beyond the bounds of all good humanity". With remarkable
prescience she saw that they threatened not only the government
of the Church, but her own prerogative. Any who possessed
copies were to surrender them.

The Scottish Presbyterians were greatly incensed by Bancroft's
description of John Knox as "a man of nature too contentious"
and of "perverse behaviour", and furthermore, his assertion
that the Scottish ministers had usurped the whole ecclesiastical
jurisdiction during the minority of the King. On 29 April 1589,
a meeting of the Edinburgh presbytery resolved to depute three
ministers—Robert Pont, Robert Bruce, John Davidson—to draft

[1] Quoted, J. Brown, *The English Puritans*, Cambridge, 1912, p. 80.
[2] *Sloane MSS.*, 271, f. 41 b.

a reply to Bancroft. On 10 June the Edinburgh presbytery resolved
that they should present their report to the next General Assembly.[1]

Some months later, Sir Robert Naunton, writing from the
embassy in Scotland, reported to Dr John Copcot,[2] Master of
Corpus Christi College, Cambridge, that

> At ye first publishing of Mr Bancrofts sermon, there was nothing
> but breathing out threatenings of I know not what Canonicall
> confutacion to be set forth by ye generall consent of their provinciall
> Syndode, anathematizing as well ye readers as ye author of that
> schismaticall libell for so it pleased some of their brotherhoods to
> intitulate that booke.[3]

The Edinburgh presbytery finally resolved upon a direct "Sup-
plicatioun" to the Queen desiring her to "take order" with Dr
Bancroft for "that Infamous Sermon". Bancroft, in a letter to
Naunton, pointed out that he had not intended directly to attack
the presbyterian ministers of Scotland, but he emphatically
declined to retract from his main position:

> yow know we are pressed with examples of other Churches to the
> imbracinge of that most counterfeyt and falsly patched vp govern-
> ment which is tearmed the presbitery, a meere humane device
> devised by shiftinge and sleight, attayned by tiranny and bloud,
> and mainteyned with vntollerable pride and with most straunge
> boldness in expoundinge the scriptures and falsifyinge of all anti-
> quitye.[4]

Bancroft was not content with a policy of defence. Cartwright
insisted that presbyterianism was the scriptural form of Church
government; Bancroft countered by arguing that episcopacy was
the apostolic form of Church government. Bancroft carried the
war into the enemy's camp, and it is the measure of his achievement that he altered decisively the basis of the controversy. He was
bitterly attacked: John Penry, whose implication in the *Mar-prelate
Tracts* was widely suspected, replied with an anonymous work:
*A Briefe Discovery of the Untruthes and Slanders (Against the true
Government of the Church of Christ) contained in a Sermon preached the
8. of Februarie 1588 by D. Bancroft.* It was printed in Edinburgh

---

[1] *Minutes of the Presbytery.* Miscellany of the Woodrow Society, Vol. I, p. 470.
[2] Or Copcoat.
[3] *Additional MSS.*, 32,092, f. 106. Printed C. Burrage, op. cit., Vol. II, p. 127.
[4] *Egerton MSS.*, 2,598, f. 242. Printed C. Burrage, op. cit., Vol. II, p. 130.

without any indication of either author or printer.[1] Concerning the bishops, he wrote:

> Those that will needs be our pastors and spiritual fathers are become beasts, as the Prophet Jeremy saith, and have not sought the Lord. . . . They every way labour to keep us in bondage: they hide the truth, and will not suffer others to see the same. If the Lord in mercy do open the eyes of any man, he must not for his life make it known that he hath seen the light, much less walk in the same. . . .

In September 1590, another pamphlet appeared: *D. Bancrofts Rashness in Rayling*. It carried the initials of the author, John Davidson, and the familiar name of the printer, Robert Waldegrave. The author attacked Bancroft's "cartload of calumnies", and assailed "that heavy bondage of Antichristian government by loftie lords, wrongfully called Bishops (an hurtfull relicke of Romish confusion)". Davidson explained that the long delay in publication was due to the fact that the Scottish ministers had hoped for due redress from the Queen and Council of England.[2]

There were also repercussions in Scotland following Bancroft's sermon. Bancroft relied on a royal declaration issued in 1585, which he assumed to reflect the views of the King. It was, in fact, written by Patrick Adamson, Archbishop of St Andrews. Bowes, the English ambassador, wrote to Burghley: "It is stomaked here, that Mr Bancroft should in his booke charge the King bothe with manyfest dissimulacion, and also to have given out the declaration which was not authorised by the King, but sett fourth by the archbisshop of St Androes." The King and Chancellor were anxious that Burghley should do something in this matter for the satisfaction of the King's honour.

Bancroft was duly summoned before Lord Burghley. He had prepared a defence, but was not permitted to speak, and was peremptorily ordered back to his lodging at the Bishop of Ely's palace in Holborn to prepare a Submission for transmission to the King.

Bancroft humbly confessed his error, both in attributing the declaration to the King and in imputing to the King inconstancy of mind. Nevertheless Bancroft made it clear that he did not

[1] W. Pierce, *John Penry: His Life, Times, and Writings*, London, 1923, p. 263.
[2] See O. Chadwick, "Richard Bancroft's Submission", *Journal of Ecclesiastical History*, Vol. III, no. 1, p. 58.

repent of anything which he had written concerning the presbyterian ministers of Scotland. On the principle that offence is the
best form of defence, he renewed his attack:

> Your Lordship seeth how hott and angrye the ministers are in this
> last treatise . . . bicause I used the wordes and speaches before
> mentioned: and yet even with the same breathe, that they complayne
> of me (such is theyr pride) they write in this sorte of the Church of
> England. That the same is still under the bondage of an Anti-
> christian government:[1] that our Bishops are a hurtfull relique of
> Romishe confusion; that they thrust with side and shoulder to push
> all the weake with theyr hornes, till they have scattered them abroad,
> and to make havocke of the Church by a disguised persecution; and
> that they doe tirannise above theyr brethren with violence and
> crueltye. They doe iustifye the proceedings of the disturbers of our
> quiet and animate them to goe forwarde as they have begonne: they
> say they must not cease to commende theyr troubled state unto god
> in theyr private and publick prayers: they compare our hinderance
> of theyr discipline unto the hinderance which gods enemies made to
> the buildings of Jerusalem: they call the favorers of our church
> government a generation of Bishopists: and doe insinuate that there
> are in courte some craftye miscreats which doe abuse her majestie.
> Doth not your Lordship wonder at this theyr great presumption
> and libertye of speache?[2]

The Submission was forwarded by Burghley to Bowes for transmission to the King. On 7 December Burghley received a message:

> His hignes hes seine the apologetik submission of Dr Bancroft . . .
> His majesties desyre is that he shoulde tak occasioun ather in the
> same or lyke publick place to interprete suche his speaches as have
> bene mistaken, and to utter what was his good and verye meaning;
> which wilbe a full satisfactioun to his highnes heir, and no palinodye
> to him.[3]

On 22 December Burghley replied that he thought no good could
come from reopening the sore place by forcing Bancroft to explain
himself in public; and, on 13 January, Bowes wrote to tell
Burghley that the King and the Chancellor were content to let
the matter rest.[4]

[1] From *D. Bancrofts Rashness in Rayling.*
[2] National Library of Scotland, Adv. Ms. 6.1:.3, f. 51ᵛ. Quoted, O. Chadwick, op. cit., p. 67.
[3] *S.P. Scot.*, Vol. X, no. 505.
[4] Ibid., Vol. X, no. 517.

A new and significant line of Puritan attack against episcopal regimentation was adopted by Humphrey Davenport in the Parliament of 1589. The method of direct attack had failed: those who had submitted a Bill and a Book in 1587 had been decisively defeated and discredited, and it was now time to attempt a different kind of strategy. The method of attack was no longer legislative but constitutional and legal. In the Journal of the House the Clerk noted: "Mr Davenport moved neither for making any new laws, nor for abrogating of any old laws, but for a due course of proceeding in laws already established, but executed (he thinketh) by some ecclesiastical governor[s] contrary both to the purport of the same laws and also to the minds and meanings of the law-makers, to the great hurts and grievances of sundry of her Majesty's good subjects."[1] It was an astute move, challenging and threatening the administrative machinery of the Church. The innocent question was raised: "Whether the desire of a further and better reformation in the Church of England, in dutiful manner, be not warranted by the word of God and the law of England?"

In 1593 Bancroft produced another substantial study: *A Suruay of the Pretended Holy Discipline, Containing the beginninges, successe, parts, proceedings, authority, and doctrine of it: with some of the manifold and materiall repugnances, varieties, and uncertaineties, in that behalf. Faithfully gathered, by way of historicall narration, out of the bookes and writings of principall fauorers of that platforme.* In this expanded work (a greatly enlarged version of the sermon) Bancroft described the early genesis of Puritanism: its origin in Geneva under Calvin, and its subsequent propagation in England by means of the *Admonition.* "It was agreed upon ... that an admonition ... should be compiled and offered unto the Parliament approaching, Anno 1572. Against which time it was also provided, that Beza should write his letter to a great man in this land, for ... the admitting in England of the said Allobrogicall Discipline."[2]

Accordingly, Beza had written "to the Queens Majesty ... that her Majesty should conform the present Apostolicall and most ancient estate of the Church of England, unto that newly

---

[1] For detailed discussion and documentary analysis, see, J. E. Neale, *Elizabeth I and her Parliaments, 1584–1601,* London, 1959, pp. 222 ff.

[2] Op. cit., p. 42.

devised and unbridled new platform of that demy-Parish of Geneva".[1] Beza's letter was mistimed, for it arrived after the end of Parliament. Cartwright and Travers had prosecuted the matter, and had actually set up the discipline in secret: "They have had their Subscriptions, their Synods of divers sorts; Classicall, Provinciall, and Generall. In those Synodes they have practised Censures, made Laws of their own, and disallowed some of those which the State of this Realm hath made. Unto these and such like their private Conventicles they have appropriated the name of the Church."[2]

The crucial issue was the nature of the ministry. Bancroft emphatically asserted that there was neither scriptural authority nor historical support for the presbyterian form of Church government: "the institution of this pretended Government cannot be shewed out of the Old Testament: and then by their own confessions . . . it may not be urged out of the New . . . the first time that ever this feigned genevian device saw light (for ought that I can read or Judge) was at Geneva."[3] He was emphatic that episcopacy was both scriptural and historical:[4]

In the Old Testament, the high Priest, besides that he was a figure of Christ, had also under Moses, Joshua, the Judges and the Kings . . . authority and jurisdiction Ecclesiasticall within that Countrey of Canaan, under whom for the same purpose were other Priests, at least 24, that were called *Principes Sacerdotum*, Princes of the Priests, all of them inferior to the high Priest, but superior to the rest. In the New Testament, our Saviour Christ, whilst he lived on earth, had his Apostles, and in degree under them his 70. Disciples. After his ascension, the same inequality of the Ministry of the Word continued in the Church . . . For as much as God himself appointed an inequality amongst the Priests in the Old Testament; forasmuch as Christ, though he called himself a Minister to minister unto others, was yet the Master over his Apostles and Disciples; forasmuch as by Christs institution, and in his own time, the Apostles were superior unto the seventy Disciples; forasmuch as the Apostles,

---

[1] Ibid., p. 43.
[2] Ibid., p. 44.   [3] Ibid., p. 69.
[4] It is important to note the exact nature of Bancroft's claim: "Episcopacy was defended as being of apostolic, not of dominical, provenance; and the appeal to history and tradition constituted the ground of its justification, not the allegation of any exclusive prescription of scripture." N. Sykes, *Old Priest and New Presbyter*, Cambridge, 1956, p. 26.

when the Gospel began to spread it self, appointed sundry Timothies and Titus's, to govern the Churches in divers countries and Territories; forasmuch as all the Ecclesiasticall Histories doe record the Superiority of Bishops, and doe set down the Catalogues of many of them, and which of the Apostles and Apostolical Bishops, and in what Cities and Countries they succeeded ... forasmuch as Beza for his own part hath written so honorably to the now L. Archbishop of Canterbury, and so generally to all our Bishops now professing the Gospell, condemning those of great arrogancie that shall presume to speak against them ... I see no reason why this Anabaptistical dream of equality amongst Pastors whould not be sent back to the place from whence it issued.[1]

Within a decade men would hear the famous slogan: "No bishop; no King". It was a view to which Bancroft strongly subscribed: the Puritans, he said, were seeking to take from Christian Princes their authority in ecclesiastical affairs, with a view to substituting for it the supreme authority of the presbytery in causes ecclesiastical. Bancroft declared that "Calvin could not abide that King Henry the Eighth should be termed the Head or Supreme Governor in earth of the Churches of God within his Dominions".[2] His followers,

Cartwright and some others with him do affirm ... that all Kings (as well heathen as Christian) receiving but one Commission and equall authority immediately from God, have no more to doe with the Church the one sort then the other, as being in no respect deputed for Church-Officers under Christ, otherwise then, if they be good Kings, to maintain and defend it. And secondly, that as God hath appointed all Kings and Civill Magistrates his immediat Lieutenants for the government of the World in temporall Causes; so Christ, as he is Mediator and governor of his Church, hath his immediate officers to rule in the Church under him, and those they say are no other then Pastors, Doctors and Elders, to whom they ascribe as large authority in Causes Ecclesiasticall.[3]

Bancroft's fervent hope was that the Church of England might "be never troubled with such a discipline", but might continue to preserve the "old and present Apostolicall forme of Church-government under her excellent Majestie, by Archbishops or Arch-builders, and Bishops, practised in the Apostles times,

---

[1] Ibid., pp. 83, 112–13.　　[2] Ibid., p. 202.
[3] Ibid., p. 205.

approved by all the ancient Fathers and generall Councils, and continued in this Land since the time that it first professed Christianity".[1]

Bancroft renewed his charges in *Dangerous Positions and Proceedings, Published and Practiced within this Iland of Brytaine, under the Pretence of Reformation, and for the Presbiterial Discipline*, published the same year. Once again he accused the Scottish Presbyterians of meddlesome interference in the affairs of the English Church:

> They do justifie the Proceedings of our Disturbers here, and animating them to go forward as they have begun, do tell them that both their Causes (viz. their own in Scotland, and of our Factions in England) are most nearly linked together: And do promise that they will not cease to commend their troubled Estate unto God, in their private and publick Prayers.[2]

Reviewing the course of the controversy, Bancroft pointed out that the Puritan controversy was, in the first place, a question of vestments, so that

> for the first Ten or Eleven Years of her Majesty's Reign, through the peevish Frowardness, the Outcries and Exclamations of those that came home from Geneva, against the Garments prescribed to Ministers ... no man ... is ignorant what great Contention and Strife was raised; Insomuch as their Sectaries divided themselves from their ordinary Congregations, and meeting together in private Houses, in woods and Fields, had and kept there their disorderly and unlawful Conventicles.[3]

The publication of the *Admonition* and the erection of a presbytery at Wandsworth in Surrey had marked a further stage. Conferences were then held at London, where at first "little was debated, but against subscription, the Attire and Book of Common Prayer, [but] about the year 1583 the Form of Discipline ... was compiled: And ... certain Decrees were made concerning the Establishing and the Practice thereof."[4] Subsequently, the *Book of Discipline* had been revised, and sent abroad about 1587; later, it had been used at "classes" in Northamptonshire.

It was an extraordinarily circumstantial account, both detailed and precise. Bancroft made public the decrees and decisions of

---

[1] Ibid., p. 371.
[3] Ibid., p. 65.
[2] Op. cit., p. 31.
[4] Ibid., p. 69.

the "classes"; he enumerated the names of the chief members; and he described the manner in which they conducted their "classes".

> The manner of every particular Classis is this: At their Meeting (which is always in some private House, but yet in their Mother Cities) first a Moderator is chosen in this sort: One of them conceiveth a Prayer for God's Direction in that Choice. Then he that conceived the Prayer, sitteth alone in Scrutiny; and every one giveth his Voice secretly unto him. He that hath the most Voices is chosen.[1]

The secret practice of the "discipline" was simply a preparation for the public introduction of the full presbyterian system.

> About Four Years since, it should seem that some of the Brethren were of Opinion, that they had dealt long in the Practice of their Discipline, after such a secret manner: And that then they were bound in duty to proceed to the publick Exercise of it, notwithstanding any danger that might thereby ensue.[2]

This revolutionary and reckless policy, however, was only advocated by a few "desperate Reformers". Nevertheless, Cartwright was not without blame for he had not restrained them.

> And who knoweth not, that if Cartwright and the rest, had not secretly clapped such Fellows on the Backs for their Zeal, and laughed in their Sleeves to see them go so forward, but had disliked them: His earnest Reproof on the First (being their Apostle and Worthy) would have prevented all the others that followed, being his Disciples.[3]

Once again Bancroft dwelt upon the potential dangers to both Church and Commonwealth:

> I would not have urged Matters in this sort, were it not that I think (in my Conscience) it is more than high time, that her Majesty's faithful Subjects should learn to know these Practices, and withal to beware of such Sectaries, as (under their many, both godly and goodly Pretences) do thus seditiously Endeavour to disturb the Land.

He had done his duty:

> it will be apparent to our Posterity, that if any such Mischiefs (which God forbid) shall happen hereafter, they were sufficiently

[1] Ibid., p. 78.   [2] Ibid., p. 133.   [3] Ibid., p. 169.

warned that both should and might (in good time) have prevented them.[1]

These works were designed to vindicate the policy sponsored by Whitgift and implemented by Bancroft. They were published to justify the coercion and suppression of the Puritans. The bishops had outwardly triumphed. The bishops were consistently supported and encouraged by the Queen. The "classis" movement was destroyed. In the minute book of the Dedham "classis" this entry appears: "The 2nd June [1589] was our 80th meeting." Plans were made for the next meeting, but it was not held. The following entry tells the story of the progress and conclusion of the Dedham "classis": "Thus long continued through God's mercy this blessed meeting, and now it ended by the malice of Satan."

Cartwright was summoned before the Ecclesiastical Commissioners, and, on refusing the *ex officio* oath, was imprisoned; the more extreme radicals—Barrowe, Greenwood, and Penry— were executed under the Act of 1581, which forbade seditious writings. Bancroft had succeeded in intercepting in Scotland the private papers of Penry,[2] and these were used during his trial to secure his conviction and condemnation.

One last minute effort was made in Parliament to end the repressive and coercive policy of Whitgift and Bancroft. James Morice, Attorney of the Court of Wards, launched an attack on the legality of proceedings in the Court of High Commission. He described the oath *ex officio* as "an ungodly and intolerable inquisition", and Whitgift's articles as "a lawless subscription". He denounced both the oath and articles as contrary to law and common justice. Let the bishops "declare to the world by what authority they do these things". Morice, having spoken generally, announced that he had drawn up two bills, in the form of petitions: the one against unlawful oaths, inquisitions, and subscriptions; the other against unlawful imprisonment and restraint of liberty. The Queen promptly intervened to stifle further discussion, and the Lords of the Privy Council ordered Morice's confinement.

Morice failed in his immediate purpose. Nevertheless, he had

---

[1] Ibid., p. 182.
[2] *Cam. Univ. Lib. MSS.*, Mm. 1, 47, f. 334.

raised constitutional questions of the highest importance, and the debate was only adjourned and not concluded. It would be resumed at a later date in a more bitter and violent form.

In this Parliament (1593) an Act, directed against "seditious sectaries and disloyal persons",[1] threatened with imprisonment persistent abstainers from the authorized services of the Church, those who criticized those services or ecclesiastical authority, and those who associated with unlawful conventicles. The Barrowists, who were imprisoned, despairing of their liberty, petitioned for permission to emigrate. To all outward appearances Puritanism was crushed. Furthermore, those influential Puritan laymen, whose powerful mediation had meant so much, were now removed through the remorseless march of death. The Earl of Leicester had died in 1588, Sir Walter Mildmay[2] in 1589, the Earl of Warwick and Sir Francis Walsingham in 1590.

"In due season we shall reap, if we faint not." Bancroft's reward came with his elevation to the bishopric of London in 1597.[3] Whitgift earnestly pressed his suit and testified:

His Conversation hath been without blame in the world, having never been complained of, detecteth [sic], or for ought he knoweth suspected any extraordinary enormity.

He hath taken all the Degrees of Schools, as other men have done, & with equall credit.

He hath been a Preacher against Popery, about 24: years, & is certainly no Papist, Indeed he is not of the Presbyterial Faction.

Since he hath professed Divinity, he hath ever opposed himself, against all Sects & Innovations.

By the appointment of Archbishop Grindall, he did once visit the Diocese of Peterborough: About 12: years since, he was likewise a Visitor of the Diocese of Ely.

He was sent for from Cambridge, to preach at Bury, when the pretended Reformation was begun there, without staying for the Magistrate, as the term was then; & when the Sheriff, as he said,

---

[1] 35 Eliz. I, c. 1.

[2] Mildmay was the founder of Emmanuel College, Cambridge. "Sir Walter," said the Queen, "I hear you have erected a puritan foundation." To which Mildmay replied: "No, Madam: far be it from me to countenance anything contrary to your established laws, but I have set an acorn, which, when it becomes an oak, God alone knows what will be the fruit thereof."

[3] Bancroft had been appointed treasurer of St Paul's in February 1585/6; prebendary of Westminster in July 1587; prebendary of St Paul's in 1590; and chaplain to Archbishop Whitgift in 1592.

4

could hardly get any Preacher in that country, that either would or durst oppose themselves against it.

At his being at Bury, he detected to the Judges, the writings of a Poesie, about her Majesties Armes, taken out of the Apocalyps, but apply'd to her Highness most falsely & seditiously. It had been sett up a quarter of a year, in a most publick place, without controulment. I note these two last points, partly for the effects that followed of them, & because he was greatly maligned, by no mean persons, for doing his Duty in both.

He remained with the late Lord Chancellor 12: years at the least for the most part in her Majesties Court, & was in good Reputation with him, & often employed in sundry matters of great Importance, for her Highness service. Since his said Lordship's death, he hath remained with the like credit five years almost, with the L: Archbishop of Canterbury.

He hath been of her Majesties Commission general, for cause ecclesiasticall, throughout England, almost 12: years, in which time there have been few causes of any Importance dealt in, either at Lambeth or London, wherein he hath not been an Assistant.

He was by his diligent search the first Detector of Martin Mar-Prelats Press & Books, where & by whom they were printed.

He was an especial Man, that gave the Instructions, to her Majesties learned Council, when Martin's Agents were brought into the Star Chamber.

By his advice, that Course was taken, which did principally stop Martin & his Fellows' mouths viz: to have them answered after their own vein in writing.

By his diligence to find out certain Letters & writings, Mr Cartwright and his complices, their setting up their Discipline secretly in most shires of the Realm, their Classes, their Decrees, & Book of Discipline were first detected.

The chief Instructions were had from him whereby her Majesties Learned Counsell framed their Bill & Articles against Mr Cartwright, & the rest in the Star Chamber.

By his letter written, at the Commandment of the L: Chancellor to himself, her Majestie was throughly informed of the state of the Church, how it then stood, & how far the said factious persons had impeached her Highness authority & the government established.

By his own diligence, Penry's seditious writings were intercepted, as they came out of Scotland, & delivered to the now L: Keeper.

His earnest desire, to have the Slanderous Libels, against her Majestie answered, & some Pains of his taken therein, would not be omitted, because they show his true Affection, & dutiful heart unto her Highness.

His Sermon at Paul's Cross the first Sunday in the Parliament 1587 [*sic*, 1588/9]: being afterwards printed by direction, from the Lord Chancellor & L: Treasurer, was to special purpose, & did very much abate the edge of the Factious.

The Last Parliament, he did sett out two Books in defence of the State of the Church, & against the pretended Holy Discipline: which were liked and greatly commended, by the learnedst Men in the Realm.

He hath been an especiall Man of his calling, that the L: Archbishop of Canterbury hath used for the space of 9: or 10 years, in all the Stirs which have been made by the factious, against the good of the Church, which hath procured him great dislike amongst those, who are that way inclined.

Though he hath been carefull and zealous to suppress some sort of sectaries, yet hath he therein shewed, no tyrannous Disposition, but with Mildness and kind dealing, when it was expedient, hath reclaimed diverse.

Whilst he had been occupied for 15, or 16: years, as hath been expressed, 17: or 18: of his Juniors (few or none of them being of his experience) have been preferred, eleven to Deaneries, & the rest to Bishopricks. Of which number, some have been formerly inclin'd to Faction, & the most as neuters have expected the Issue, that so they might, as things should fall out, run with the time. They that list may enter into the consideration hereof particularly.

He hath been long in speech for the Bishoprick of London, his late good L. told him, the summer before he died, that her Majesty was purposed, to have removed Bishop Elmer to Worcester, & to have preferred him to London.

Bishop Elmer offred thrice, in two years, to have resigned his Bishoprick with him, upon certain conditions, which he refused. Bishop Elmer signify'd the day before his death, how sorry he was, that he had not written to her Majestie, & commended his last suit unto her Highness viz: To have made him his Successor.

Since the death of the last Bishop, no man hath been so commonly named, for that place as he, nor is generally thought to be more fit for it.[1]

The Archbishop's intervention was successful: on 21 April 1597, Bancroft was formally elected Bishop of London by the Dean and Chapter of St Paul's, the election being confirmed on 6 May in the church of St Mary le Bow, before Richard Cosin, the Archbishop's Vicar-General and principal official. Whitgift wrote to

---

[1] *Baker MSS.*, Mm. 1, 47, f. 333. Printed, J. Strype, *Whitgift*, Vol. II, p. 386; A. Peel, *Tracts*, p. xvii.

Cecil: "Good Mr Secretarie you have bownd me unto you in this action for ever. Neither by God's grace shall you at anie time haue cause to repent you of your most faithful and kinde dealing with me. And as for Dr Bancroft, I dare assuer you shal finde him a honest, true and faythfull man."[1] Two days later Bancroft was consecrated at Lambeth by the Archbishop, assisted by John Yong, Bishop of Rochester, Anthony Rudd, Bishop of St David's, Richard Vaughan, Bishop of Bangor, and Anthony Watson, Bishop of Chichester.[2]

Whitgift was failing rapidly, and increasingly Bancroft took the reins of ecclesiastical affairs. Thomas Fuller observes: "indeed he was in effect Archbishop whilst Bishop, to whom Doctor Whitgift in his decrepite age remitted the managing of matters, so that he was the Soul of the high Commission".[3] Whitgift died shortly after the accession of James, and Bancroft was the obvious candidate for the primacy. The election, however, was not made for several months. He was one of the episcopal representatives at the Hampton Court Conference, and, on Whitgift's death, was appointed President of Convocation. The Venetian ambassador, Girolamo Girardo, wrote to the Doge and Senate on 20 October 1604, "after some opposition the Bishop of London has been named Archbishop of Canterbury".[4] Bancroft was nominated to the primatial see of Canterbury on 9 October, elected by the Chapter on 17 November, and confirmed on 10 December.[5] But this is to anticipate the more immediate events associated with the accession of the new monarch to the throne.

---

[1] *Hatfield MSS.*, 49, f. 108.
[2] G. Hennessy, *Novum Repertorium Ecclesiasticum Parochiale Londinense*, p. ix.
[3] T. Fuller, *The History of the Worthies of England*, London, 1662, p. 112.
[4] *C.S.P.*, *Venetian*, Vol. X, no. 288.
[5] J. Le Neve, *Fasti Ecclesiae Anglicanae*, London, 1716, Vol. I, p. 26.

2

THE MILLENARY PETITION AND HAMPTON COURT CONFERENCE

THE ACCESSION of James VI of Scotland to the throne of England was the signal for renewed Puritan propaganda. The Puritans were convinced that the new King would be sympathetic to the godly work of further reformation. He was reputed as saying, at the General Assembly of the Church of Scotland in 1590, "As for our neighbour Kirk in England, it is an evil mass said in English, wanting nothing but the liftings".[1] It is not surprising that the Puritans awaited his arrival with eager expectancy.

The King, however, was far from sympathetic to the Puritan cause. He held an exalted conception of the royal prerogative and he adopted a high view of his rôle as "God's lieutenant". This conception was incompatible with the claim of the Presbyterian Church to spiritual independence and autonomy. On the occasion of a memorable interview, held at Falkland Palace in 1596, Andrew Melville had laboured, with painful bluntness, the supremacy of the Church in spiritual things. According to the chronicler:

Mr Andro brak af upon the King in sa zealus, powerfull, and unresistable a manner, that, whowbeit the King used his authoritie in maist crabbit and colerik maner, yit Mr Andro bure him down, and outtered the Commission as from the mightie God, calling the King, but "God's sillie vassall"; and, taking him by the sleive, says this in effect, throw mikle hot reasoning and manie interruptiones: "Sir, we will humblie reverence your Majestie alwayes, namlie in publick, but, sen we have this occasioun to be with your Majestie in privat, and the countrey and Kirk of Chryst is lyk to wrak for nocht telling yow the treuthe, and giffen of yow a faithfull counsall, we maun discharge our dewtie thairin, or else be trators bathe to Chryst and yow. And theirfore, Sir, as dyvers tymes befor, sa now

---

[1] *S.P. Scot., Eliz. I*, Vol. XLVI, nos. 48, 58.

again I mon tell yow, thair is twa Kings and twa kingdomes in
Scotland. Thair is Chryst Jesus the King, and His Kingdome the
Kirk, whase subject King James the Saxt is, and of whase kingdome
nocht a king nor a lord nor a heid, bot a member."[1]

This was shocking and unacceptable doctrine to a monarch who
held that kings were "the breathing Images of God upon earth".[2]
It is not surprising that James was hostile to presbyterianism
and that he viewed the demands of the English Puritans with
distrust.

The Millenary Petition was submitted to the King soon after his
arrival in London in the early part of 1603. The Puritans declared
that they were "Ministers of the Churche of England desiringe
reformation of certaine ceremonies and abuses in the Churche".[3]
It is true that in times past they had subscribed:

> Diuerse of vs that sue for reformation, haue formerly, in respect of
> ye tymes, subscribed to the booke, some vppon protestation, some
> vppon expositions giuen them, some with Condition, rather then
> the Churche should haue been depriued of our Labours and minis-
> terie: yet nowe wee to the number of more than a thowsand of
> your Maiesties subiects and ministers, all groning as vnder one
> Common burthen of humane rites and ceremonies, Doe, with one
> ioynt Consent, humble ourselves at your Maiesties ffeete, to bee
> eased and releyued in this behalffe. . . .

Their present objections concerned the Church service, ministers,
livings and maintenances, and Church discipline. They particularly desired

> that ye crosse in Baptisme: interrogatories ministred to infantes:
> Confirmation as superflous maye bee taken awaye: Baptisme not to
> bee ministred by weomen, and so explained: the Capp and suplesse
> not vrged: that examination maie goe beefore ye Communion: that
> it bee ministered with a Sermon: That diuerse termes of Priests and
> absolution, and some other vsed, with the ring in marriage, and
> other such like in the booke, maye bee corrected: the Longsomnes of
> Service abridged: Church songes and musick, moderated to better
> edifieng: that the Lordes daie bee not prophaned: the rest vppon
> holye daies not so strictlie vrged: that there maye bee an vniformitie

---

[1] Quoted N. Micklem, *The Theology of Politics*, London, 1941, pp. 87–8.
[2] James I, *Political Works*, Cambridge (ed. C. H. McIlwain, 1918), p. 464.
[3] *Additional MSS.*, 8,978, f. 107; 28,571, f. 175; *Egerton MSS.*, 2,877, f. 174 b;
Stowe MSS., 180, f. 7; quoted, inaccurately, E. Cardwell, *A History of the
Conferences . . .*, Oxford, 1841, p. 130.

of doctrine prescribed: No popish opinion to bee any more taught or Defended: nor ministers charged to teache their people to bowe at the name of Jesus: That the canonicall scriptures onelye bee read in the Church.

They were concerned about the grievous lack of a preaching ministry, and wished

> that none hereafter bee admitted into ye ministerie, but able and Sufficient men, and those to preache Diligentlie, and especiallie vppon the Lordes day, And such as bee allreadie entered, and cannot preach, maye either bee removed, and some charitable Course taken with them for their relieffe, or ellse bee forced according to the vallue of their Livings to meynteyne preachers. That Non-residence bee not permitted: That King Edwardes Statute for the Lawfulness of ministers marriage bee revived. That ministers bee not vrged to subscribe, but according to the Lawe, to the Articles of Religion, and the Kinges supremacie onelie.

They were also concerned about the evils associated with pluralities, urging "that Bisshopps Leave their Commendams, some holding Prebends, some Parsonages, some vicaridgs, with their Bisshoppricks"; and "that double beneficed men bee not suffred to hold some two, some three benefices, with Cure, and some two three or fower dignities beesides". Finally, they earnestly desired the exercise of the "discipline of Christ":

> That the discipline and excommunication maye bee administred according to Christ his owne institution, or att Leaste, that theise enormities may bee redressed. As namelye that excommunication come not forth vnder the name of Lay persons, Chaunccellors, officialls: that men bee not excommunicated for triffles, and twelv-pennie matters: that none bee excommunicate without Consent of his pastor, that the officers bee not suffered to extorte vnreasonable ffees: that none having iurisdiction or Registers place put out the same ffarme: that diuerse popish Canons (as for the restraint of marriage at certaine tymes) bee reversed, that the Longsomnesse of suits in ecclesiasticall Cowrts which hange sometyme. 2.3.4.5.6.7. yeares maie be restrayned, that the oath ex officio, whereby men are forced to accuse themselues, bee more sparinglie vsed, that Lycences for marriage without banes askinge, be more cautiously graunted.

This list of abuses was not exhaustive but typical:

> theise, with other suche abuses yet remayning and practised in the Church of England, wee are able to shewe not to bee agreeable to

the scriptures, if it shall please your highnesse further to heare vs, or
more at large by wryting to bee informed, or by Conference among
the Learned to bee resolued.

The petitioners concluded with a confident appeal to the Christian
judgement and godly zeal of the King:

Wee doubt not, but that, without any further processe, your majestie
(of whose Christian judgment wee haue receaued so good a taste
allreadie) is hable of yourself to iudge of the equitie of this Cause.
God, wee truste, hathe appointed your highness our phisitian to
heale those diseases, and wee saye with Mordecai to Esther, Who
knoweth whether you are come to the Kingdome for such a
tyme.

The beneficial consequences of such a godly reformation were set
forth:

Thus your Maiestie shall doe that which wee are persuaded shalbee
acceptable to god, honorable to your Maiestie in all succeeding
ages; profitable to his Churche, which shalbee thereby increased,
Comfortable to your ministers, which shalbee no more suspended,
silenced, disgraced, imprisoned for mens traditions, and preiudiciall to none, but to those that seeke their owne quiett creditt and
profitt in the world. Thus, with all dutifull submission, referring
our selues to your Maiesties pleasure for your gracious aunswere, as
God shall direct you, wee most humblie recommend your Highness
to the Devine Maiestie, whom we beeseech for Christ, his sake to
dispose your royall harte to doe herein what shalbee to his glorie,
the good of his Churche, and your endles Comforte.

The petitioners subscribed themselves: "Ministers of the Gospell,
that desier not a disorderly innovation, But a due and godlie
reformation."

Fuller said that the petition was signed by seven hundred and
fifty preachers,[1] but apparently he was confusing the *Millenary
Petition* with the petition from the Lincolnshire ministers in 1604,
which has this number of signatures.[2] The Puritans themselves,
when replying to the *Confutation* published by the University of

[1] T. Fuller, *The Church History of Britain from the Birth of Jesus Christ., until
the Year MDCXLVIII* (ed. J. S. Brewer), Oxford, 1845, Vol. V, p. 265.

[2] *An abridgment of that Booke which the Ministers of Lincoln Diocess deliuered to
his Maiestie upon the first of December last 1605.*

Oxford, denied that signatures were solicited: "neither before were any hands required of it, but only consent."[1]

The King was eager to win the approval of his new subjects. His progress south was slow and leisurely. The King was determined to indulge his passion for hunting. The stream of place-hunters continued to grow: suitors for places soon found themselves joined by petitioners with grievances. In due course the Millenary Petition was presented. It struck a responsive chord. The King was not averse to the idea of a Conference, nor did he object to playing the rôle of arbiter in the affairs of the Church. His mind was acute and argumentative. He enjoyed the thrust and parry of vigorous theological controversy. He readily agreed.

The aged Archbishop was disconcerted and dismayed. His enemies had become his accusers, and the Church was now in the dock. The King agreed that the ministers should meet the bishops in Conference as equals. The King, by his foolish and precipitate action, had committed a tactical blunder of the first order. Gravely concerned, Whitgift wrote letters to the bishops requiring them to furnish him immediately with statistics and particulars of beneficed clergy and preachers:

> Theise are to require your lordship for certeine causes me especially moving, that with all convenient speed, after the receipt hereof, you certifie me, under your hand, the names and surnames of all the preachers within your dioces, what degree of schole they and every of them be of, by whom they are allowed preachers, and whether they be beneficed curates, or stipendary preachers, together with the parishes name where they lyve and preache. And thus praying your lordship to be very carefull in the premises, I commit your lordship to the protection of Almighty God.[2]

A month later the Archbishop sent another anxious letter urging expedition.[3]

---

[1] *A true modest and iust defence of the petition for Reformation exhibited to the Kings most excellent Maiestie, Containing an Aunswere to the Confutation published vnder the names of some of the Vniuersitie of Oxford. Additional MSS.,* 8,978.

[2] 12 May 1603. Quoted, D. Wilkins, *Concilia,* London, 1737, Vol. IV, p. 368.

[3] The Archbishop and the bishops found it difficult to secure the particulars required. On 6 September 1603, the Bishop of Lincoln wrote:

> By the copie of the right Reuerend father in god my very good Lo: and brother the archbushop of Cant. his G: lettres lately written vnto mee you shall vnderstand how long and earnestly the Certificates haue been looked for and how slowly sente, and that without copies, and some not at all.

In the meantime the Puritans were not negligent: they gathered their own statistics. A circular was distributed with detailed directions:

> Whereas the Archbishop said of 8000 benefices, there are but 500 competent, and therefore Learned men must either Lacke competent Living, or else haue mo benefices then one. And whereas also Bishops make their enquirie of the number of graduats in the ministerie, of licenced preachers, and how often they preache: And sithe it is knowne that many be graduats that cannot preache, And many be licenced that deserve for their insufficiencie to be hissed out of the pulpitt, And that yf one be licenced in many Dioceses, he is accounted for so many preachers, and some sett downe themselves to preache once everie Sabaoth, which scarce preache once a quarter: There would therefor (to discover the skirt of the highe Preist) *be a diligent and faithfull* enquirie made. 1. of the nomber of benefices that be in everie diocese. 2. The valewe of them by a common estimation. 3. the number of soules to be taught of the ministers, vnlearned, vnpreaching, scandalous, hauing no benefices then one, hauing but one, yet Non-resident, their preaching but seldome and vnprofitable. What be their names, livings, and causes of Non-residencie, how often, and what manner they preache. In this inquirie notice would also be taken of populous townes. And lastlie of bishops, and Commissaries their conversation, wherein scandalous. The Bishops preaching where, and how often, their visitations, whether yeerelie, and to what purposes.[1]

A document, *Advice tending to Reformation*, indicated the strategy:

> it is thought fitt by some of creditt, and neere to his Maiestie, that both noblemen, gentlemen, and ministers (everie sort of themselves) complaine of corruptions, and desire reformation in severall petitions, signed with as many hands of everie sorte, as may be procured, and the same presented to his Maiestie by some in name of the rest.

Those referred to as "some of creditt, and neere to his Maiestie", were probably Galloway, a presbyterian minister, and Pickering,

---

By reason whereof I haue beene blamed without cause, wherefore I pray you to take this for a finall warninge, that if you shall not presently send vnto mee those certificates which are behinde And those which hereafter eyther by the Canons or by other lawfull authoritie you are to make, I will not beare with your negligence any more, but returne the same (though sore against my will) to your further charge and danger.

Quoted, C. W. Foster, *The State of the Church*, Lincoln, 1926, p. liii.

[1] *Additional MSS.*, 28,571, f. 199; 38,492, f. 62. Printed, R. G. Usher, *Reconstruction of the English Church*, Vol. II, p. 358.

a Northamptonshire gentleman, who were both described in another Puritan petition of the same year, as "friends of the petition in Court".[1] The tactics were to bring pressure to bear by means of petitions and steady propaganda:

> There must be sundrie petitions of Ministers of sundrie parts, and yet but a fewe in a petition to *avoyde the suspition of conspiracie*, and the petitions to varie in woords, but agree in the *desire* of reformation to be according to the woord, and all reformed Churches about vs: provided they do not expresslie desire the removing of Bishops. And *in complayning of speciall grievances as the oathe ex officio, Subscription, ceremonies.* . . .

In this agitation it was necessary to mobilize all available resources: ministers in parishes, gentry in Parliament, friends at Court.

> *The Ministers* are also to stirre vp the people to a desire, or a *Liking* of reformation, both in preaching as in praying against the supersitious ceremonies, and tirannie of Prelates, provyded that it be performed in judgement, and discretion. Some of the Ministers are also to be provyded to dispute vpon some propositions to sett out the corruptions that be in the present Hierarchy *and Liturgie*.
> Also Lawyers, against the tyme of the Parlement, are to provide and make readie penned Statutes tending to this purpose. And others are to write some learned treatises against that tyme.

The campaign was brilliantly conceived and efficiently executed. In Northamptonshire the Puritans met together on 16 May to formulate their plans and implement their programme.[2] It was decided, first of all, "that Judge Yelverton be solicited by some Lettre or personally to sett downe a petition to the which he, the justices and gentlemen of the countery may subscribe". The scandalous state of the ministry was to be the subject matter of the petition:

> dumb ministerie and who made them. . . . Under who they serve and what they have for their paines. . . . The non-residentes, and where they live, and who supply their places. . . . Pluralities and how many Livinges they have, and howe farre distante, and the valuations . . . Howe offensive in life, and howe longe they have continued soe notwithstanding all courtes of reformation, although they have bene presented.

---

[1] *Sussex Petitions*, 1603; *Cecil MSS.*, 101, ff. 160–1, H.M.C., Part XV, pp. 262–3.
[2] *Sloane MSS.*, 271, f. 20 b; quoted, R. G. Usher, op. cit., Vol. II, p. 361.

It was decided that matters of reform should be pursued in both Convocation and Parliament, and that two ministers should be made available, behind the scenes, to guide and advise. It was thorough and imaginative organization of a high order. Consequently, it was agreed that two ministers be "chosen for Northamptonshire to prosecute these causes at the Parliament, by common advice and consent, their places supplyed, their charges borne". Not only was a petition to be offered in the House of Commons, a supplication was to be offered in Convocation. It was agreed

> that according to the patterne of a supplication of Mr Dudley Fenners,[1] the ministers of the same shire make a supplication, and offer it at the convocation dore, or proffere it by some of the house, witnesse beinge taken. That everye minister not only by publique preaching doe urge Reformation, but also by worde and lettres doe labour the same. and also that the Bishops and Deanes be solicited by them that have acquaintance with them keepinge true copies of their lettres.[2]

On 12 November 1603, Thomas Cartwright wrote to Judge Yelverton, in accordance with the resolutions of the party cell, soliciting his assistance in the Puritan cause:

> I haue been (right worshipfull) intreated by those (I confesse) I owe much duetie vnto. I would become petitioner vnto you, for your good and helpful hand in the common cause of the Church . . . I humblye praye you . . . that in the loue you haue these many yeeres borne to the trueth, you would take the paynes to drawe a supplication to his Majestie in the behalfe of the Nobilitie and Gentrye of that shire, as for a reformation generally of things amisse, so more particularly, for the remoueall of th'ignorant, idle and vnresident ministerye, and consequently the pluralities, the subscription other then the statute requires, the burthen of Ceremonies, the abuse of the spiritual courts. . . .

Thomas Cartwright[3]

What happened in Northamptonshire is typical of what was happening throughout the country. In the county of Suffolk

---

[1] Dudley Fenner, expelled from Cambridge for Puritanism in 1575, was a friend and follower of Cartwright. He was in charge of the reformed church at Middleburg at the time of his death.

[2] There are sixteen signatories to this memorandum.

[3] *Sloane MSS.*, 271, f. 21 b. 12 November 1603.

certain knights and gentry addressed a petition to the King, concerning "sondry offensyve things remeyninge as yet in theise dominions in the service appoynted to god and the Ministerie and government of this Churche".[1] The "offensyve things" were particularized: "ye Ignorant and vnlearned Ministerie, the half Ministers called deacons,[2] the non Resident Ministery, the pluralitie of Lyvinge conferred to one, The many offensyve Ceremonies, As the Cornered Cappe, typpet, Cloake, and surplice".[3] In Oxfordshire the petitioners prayed that their "owne yooke may be made lighter in these things, viz. those ceremonies that seeme superstitious, as the crosse in Baptisme, and what els in the Lyturgie may require redresse, subscription not required by Lawe, othe ex officio: and the vnbounded power of the Ecclesiasticall gouernments and courts".[4] In Sussex, the ministers desired ease "of the burden of the subscription heretofore imposed otherwise than the laws of the land require, and of those ceremonies which press the conscience of many of God's servants, and hinder the execution of their ministry". They wanted the King "to set up among them that ancient form of the church's censure, as agreeable to his word". They had "faithfully taken" certain facts concerning the ministry in Sussex:

> The number of churches in their country is about 300, of which the impropriations are 108. The insufficient maintenances are many, and of the 23 not above 16*l.* by the year, and some of 4*l.* or 5*l.* Double beneficed men about 50. Single and yet non-resident 6. Non-preaching about 100; negligent in preaching about 60. Of all these many are scandalous for corrupt life or doctrine.[5]

The authors of the *Advice tending to Reformation* were past masters in the art of skilful and effective agitation. "Let this advice", they urged, "passe from one faythfull brother to another with all speede and heede." Prominent Puritans were given special responsibilities as organizers and promoters. Hildersham, Vicar of Ashby-de-la-Zouch in the Lincoln diocese,[6] Egerton,

[1] *Additional MSS.*, 38,492, f. 71.
[2] This clause has been erased in the original MS.
[3] Cf. *Tanner MSS.*, 280, f. 135: "Certaine grosse corruptions which all of any note for religion, and not som way tyed to the Bishops, wish to be amended."
[4] *Sloane MSS.*, 271, f. 20. 16 May 1603.
[5] *Cecil MSS.*, 103, f. 64. H.M.C., Part XV, p. 390.
[6] Hildersham was deprived of his rectory of Ashby-de-la-Zouch on 24 April 1605. For details, see, Ch. 6, "Deprivation".

preacher at Blackfriars in London,[1] and Jacobs, a separatist,[2] were those chiefly responsible for securing the presentation of petitions. "Mr Hildersham and some few others of his brethren were chosen, and chiefly intrusted to manage this important business to prosecute the Petitions, Sollicit that cause, and if required to dispute it."[3] Henry Jacobs, writing from Woodstreet, London, sought to enlist the support of Proctor Dale:[4]

> Moreover I ame to let you vnderstand, that many learned and godly Ministers are about to exhibite to the Kings Majestie a petition, for the reformation of things amisse in our Church. Wherevnto a consent of as many, as conveniently we can gett, is very behovefull. My opinion and truste is concerninge you, that you wilbe, not only a partaker, but also a furtherer of this Christian dewty. I haue sent you heere inclosed, the forme to be subscribed by all such as haue good will to this purpose. I praye you, let me haue an aunswere heerof from you asone as you may; with so many of your well affected frends hands therevnto as shalbe thought good. It is not intended, that your names shalbe rashly shewed to any mans preiudice, but reserved to a fitt opportunity, if we shall perceaue that they altogether beinge brought forth, will further our desires and sute, of the good succese whereof, we conceaue good hope, thancks be to god. Thus beseechinge god to keep and sainctify vs for his service and to geue vs wisedome in all things. I bid you hartely farewell.
>
> Woodstreet in London.   30. of Iune 1603.
>   Yours to his powre
>   Henry Jacob
>
> The copie of the Subscription.
>
> We whose names are vnder written, doe agree to make our humble petition to the Kings Majestie that the present state of our church be further reformed in all things needfull accordinge to the rule of gods holy woord, and agreeable to [the] example of other reformed

---

[1] Egerton was a prominent Puritan, but he was permitted to remain in his cure at St Anne's, Blackfriars, until his death in 1621. See, Ch. 7, "Conformity and Subscription".

[2] Jacobs was formerly a Brownist. See, Ch. 5, "Puritan Resistance".

[3] *Morrice MSS.*, G, f. 543.

[4] *Harleian MSS.*, 6,849, f. 271. 30 June 1603. R. G. Usher was apparently unaware of the name of the recipient, and quoted it from the copy printed in the preface of the *Answer of the Vice-Chancellor ... of the University of Oxford* to the *Millenary Petition*. Op. cit., Vol. I, p. 296. Printed, C. Burrage, *The Early English Dissenters in the Light of Recent Research (1550–1641)*, Vol. II, p. 146.

churches, which haue restored both the doctryne and disciplyne, as it was deliuered by our Sauior Christ, and his holy Apostells.[1]

Henry Jacobs, tireless and indefatigable, directed operations from Woodstreet:

> Reverend and well beloved, notwithstanding I suppose you have ben already written vnto or at at [sic] the least have ben communicated with by those who have ben written vnto by som from hence to procure a consent of the faithfull Ministers of your Country according to ye tenure of ye inclosed, yet I thought good againe and that by advice of others heere with vs by a word or two to stirre vp your godly minds to this necessary duty, and the rather because they to whom the blemishes of our Church are profitable and in their conceipt honorable leve no stone vnremoved to hinder a further reformation. Besides the tyme draweth neere wherein the declaration of your consent in this busyness will be of great vse, and therefore ye matter requireth the more expedition. It is not intended that your names, which we desyre to be sent vp hither, shall be rashly shewed to your prejudice, but reserved to a fit opportunity if vpon the exhibiting of our peticion the same shall be found expedient for ye furtherance of our cause, of ye good successe whereof we conceaue good hope thanks be to God.

The draft of the subscription was the same, but an additional section was provided, specifying precisely "the offensyve things":

> In particular we desyre the removing of the Ecclesiastical Courts, ye dumb and idle Ministers, Nonresidencyes, Offensive and superstitious Ceremonies, Subscription beyond Law, the Oth Ex Officio, Excommunication for trifles, by lay men etc.

A postscript added:

> If any think not good to go so far as the example of other Churches, etc. let them stay at the first line. If any thinke good to descend into particulars let them go beyond ye 2 line, and reckon vp as many and as few as they please.[2]

The Universities sprang to the defence of the ecclesiastical establishment. Cambridge indicated its attitude by a Latin grace, approved 9 June:

---

[1] The same form of subscription was used in Northamptonshire and Oxfordshire. Cf. *Sloane MSS.*, 271, f. 20.

[2] *Lambeth MSS.*, 113, f. 242. Quoted, C. Burrage, op. cit., Vol. II, pp. 147-8.

Placet vobis, ut quicunque doctrinam vel disciplinam Ecclesiae Anglicanae, vel ejus partem aliquam, dictis aut scriptis, aut quocunque alio modo in Academia Cantabrigiensi publice opugnaverint; ab omni suscepto gradu suspendatur, et a suscipiendo excludatur ipso facto.[1]

Oxford replied to the Millenary Petition with a vigorous denunciation of the Puritan agitators:[2]

For our parts we vtterly condemne the course, that these Schismatikes have therein taken. Who to bolster out their stale obiections and false calumniations, have trudged up and downe diverse Shires, to get the consent, of they care not whom; so they make vp the tale, and pretend a number.[3]

Their goal was the erection and establishment of the presbyterian order and discipline: "They will never have an end, till either they have set vp the Presbitery, Or else be cut of [sic] by Authority." The Puritans were not without guile: they had carefully disguised their real objective:

the experience that his most excellent Maiestie hath had, of the manifolde mischiefs and miseries, that attended their pretended Discipline, doth make them not dare to speake plainly for it. They therefore faulter in seeking to obtaine that, which yet in hart they do affect, and specially desire.[4]

The Puritans repudiated these base calumniations and replied with *A true, modest, and iust defence of the petition for Reformation exhibited to the Kings most excellent Majestie; Conteining an Aunswere to the Confutation published vnder the names of some of the Vniuersitie of Oxford.*[5] It was dedicated to the King. They frankly agreed that "the gouernment of the Churche" was one of the matters under consideration: "it hath pleased your Majestie in your princely wisdome to permit and will a Conference of the Learned concerning such matters."[6] They welcomed the forthcoming Conference and the prospect of reform and amendment.

---

[1] J. Strype, *Whitgift*, Vol. II, p. 483.

[2] *The Answere of the Vice Chancelovr, the Doctors, both the Proctors, and other Heads of Houses in the Vniversitye of Oxford: (Agreeable, undoubtedly, to the ioint and Vniform Opinion, of all the Deanes and Chapters, and all other the learned and obedient Cleargy, in the Church of England.) to the Humble Petition of the Ministers of the Church of England, desiring Reformation of certaine Ceremonies and Abuses of the Church,* 1603.

[3] Quoted from the *Epistle Dedicatorie.*

[4] *Ibid.,* p. 20.

[5] *Additional MSS.,* 8,978.

[6] *Epistle Dedicatorie,* p. 6.

Wee trust that God hath raised your Majestie vp as another Dauid to settle the pillars of the Earthe, that were shaken. And as the prophet saith *to take of the heauie burthen*; burthenous Ceremonies, burthenous Censurers, burthenous abuses, which many haue a long tyme groned vnder. . . .

The petitioners subscribed themselves: "Your Majesties most faithfull Subiects, The humble petitioners, the Ministers and Preachers, that desire Reformation According to the Worde of God."

The King recognized the justice of many of the Puritan complaints, particularly those concerning stipends. He was genuinely solicitous that something should be done. Without further delay he addressed a letter to the Vice-Chancellors of the Universities, dated 10 July 1603, informing them that he had resolved to devote all royal impropriations to the betterment of ecclesiastical livings.

The zeal, that religion might be well planted in this realm, and all other our dominions, hath caused us to enter into consideration of all means, that might best serve to the furtherance hereof. Wherein finding that no one thing is a greater impediment, than want of competent living to maintain learned men in such places of our Kingdom, where the ordinary benefit of the vicarages doth not suffice, and the parsonages are impropriate, and in laymens hands, we have found, that there could not be a readier way to supply that defect, than if those impropriations of tithes might be converted again to the right use, for which they were at present instituted; wherein by God's grace we have a purpose to do in such of them as now are, or shall be in our hands, whatsoever our state may well bear.[1]

He hoped that the Universities would gladly follow his good example:

In the meantime we haue considered that to giue beginning to so good a worke, none were more fitt then the Colledges of our Vniuersities, who being so eminent members of our State, and hauing diuers of them Impropriations, and some of them also a desire, as we are informed, to provide for such persons out of such liuings, as shall fall within their power to dispose, which example

---

[1] *S.P. Dom., Jas. I*, 11, Vol. XXXVIII, dated 8 July 1603; *Additional MSS.*, 1,856, f. 11, dated 10 July 1603. Printed, D. Wilkins, op. cit., Vol. IV, p. 369.

shall haue greater efficacy with all good men to aduance the glory
of Christs Gospell.

Whitgift, aged and failing, was greatly perturbed. He at once
communicated with the King and sought the powerful intervention of Cecil. He said that the King had been misguided "by Mr
Galloway and some others", who were "altogether ignorant of
this our State". He pleaded with the King to stay the order
"untill opportunitie may serue mee to attend uppon you and to
make knowen the Inconveniences that may ensue . . . for sure I
am, that it wil bee in tyme the ouer-throwe of the Universities
and of Learning". Impropriations, he explained, were used "to
provide for the generall necessities of the whole church".[1] The
same day[2] Whitgift wrote to Cecil:

> It is here reported that his Majesty, by the instigation of some of his
> ministers, not knowing the state of this Church, nor of the Uni-
> versities, hath written letters to the Universities that they shall
> hereafter grant no leases of their impropriations but to the curates
> or vicars thereof, which will breed so many and great inconveniences,
> that in time it will not only overthrow them, or at least greatly decay
> them, but also learning itself and a learned ministry. I have written
> to his Majesty as much in effect, and have entreated him to make
> stay of any such proceeding, till he may be better informed. You are
> Chancellor of one of the said Universities, and are in that respect
> bound to protect them. I heartily pray you to be a means to his
> Majesty to the same effect, and to join with me in this suit.
>
> From Croydon,
> 9 July 1603.[3]

The Puritan leaders assembled in London to report progress.
They had good grounds for sober encouragement. The campaign
was bearing fruit. It was resolved that the campaign be continued
along the same lines:

> That therefore you would labour, so many Ministers, Gentlemen,
> and so vpwarde, and commons, as you can, to complaine them-
> selues of the violences, greiuous burdens, and matters of iust dis-

---

[1] *S.P. Dom., Jas. I*, 11, Vol. XXXIX, dated 9 July 1603.
[2] The dates are confusing. The King's letter is dated 10 July (*Additional
MSS.*, 1,856, f. 11), but the Archbishop's letters to the King (*S.P. Dom.,
Jas. I*, 11, Vol. XXXIX) and to Cecil (*Cecil MSS.*, 101, f. 20) are dated 9 July.
[3] *Cecil MSS.*, 101, f. 20. H.M.C., Part XV, p. 177.

contentment, laid heretofore or still vpon all in generall or any one in particular by themselues or any of the Chauncelers, Commissaries, or any other of the Officers whatsoeuer.

Their advice was not to join "many Ministers or gentlemen together in one petition", but to "drawe seuerall ones as you dwell or haue vsed together seuerally for the avoydinge of the suspition of conspiracy".[1]

Having formulated their plans, the leaders dispersed. Henry Jacobs proceeded to Sussex. He was actively supported by prominent local Puritans, particularly by Norden, Frewen, Healie, Goldsmith, Goffe, and Erbury.[2] Norden drafted the petition, which was then forwarded to London for Galloway's approval. It was returned to Sussex so that signatures might be secured. Norden, examined before the Bishop of Chichester by order of the Privy Council, revealed how subscriptions were obtained: "sometimes at meetings at sermons, sometimes after evening prayers in church, where the petition was read unto the people, much by private solicitation, sometimes by a constable, and at one time by an officer or sergeant."[3]

Members of the Council were increasingly disturbed about the revolutionary implications of these proceedings. Lord Buckhurst, in a letter to the Archbishop, wrote: "May it please your grace, I must ask parden of you for that I have taken vpon myself your place and offis in complaining to his Majestie against the seditious and daungerous proceedings of these puritans." He reported that Jacobs had been described by the Bishop of Chichester as "a schismatical minister deprived", and confirmed that he "went about in Sussex to gather handes to a supplication to the King against the present government of the Church; Complaining therein of 2 things: first, of an vnlerned ministery, and secondly, against all the courts spirituall".[4]

The ecclesiastical authorities awaited the forthcoming Conference with considerable trepidation. They were exceedingly unhappy about its genesis and they were apprehensive about its outcome. The Archbishop of York, Matthew Hutton, in a long

---

[1] *Sloane MSS.*, 271, f. 20. 14 July 1603.
[2] See, Ch. 6, "Deprivation", Chichester Diocese.
[3] *Cecil MSS.*, 101, ff. 160-1. H.M.C., Part XV, pp. 262-3.
[4] *Additional MSS.*, 28,571, f. 179. September 1603.

letter to the Archbishop of Canterbury, dated 9 October 1603, discussed the implications of the proposed Conference. He pointed out that the principles of presbyterianism were incompatible with the claims of an absolute monarchy:

> They that so much do magnify the government of the presbyteries, like better of a popular state than of a monarchy. Yea, Calvin himself, the chief patron of presbyteries, as he misliketh that a king should be supream head, so he commendeth, beyond all other, a mixt state of aristocratia and timocratia. Such was and is at Geneva. And so a popular government by presbyteries is more fit for a popular government than it is for a basilia. Therefore the King's majesty, as he is a passing wise King, and the best learned prince in Europe, had need to take heed, how he receiveth into his kingdom such a popular government ecclesiastical as is that of the presbyterie.

Hutton was convinced that the intention of the Puritans was "to disgrace and deface the Book of Common Prayer and the ministration of the sacraments; either to overthrow it, or (at least) to alter it". Admittedly some of the points at issue were trivial ("things indifferent") yet, having been "set down in this church by publick authority", they ought "not be spurned at by private men". He piously opined: "Humility and obedience to the prince and his laws, in all things not contrary to God's laws, beseem best for all subjects and private men." He devoutly prayed that the "gyddie headed puritanes" would not achieve "their fantasticall platforme of their reformation".[1]

Episcopal apprehension was not allayed by some ill-advised remarks of the King, which were eagerly seized upon by the Puritans and disseminated abroad. Galloway, preaching before the King, strongly urged "the necessitie of a learned and resident ministerye". The King assured the Scottish preacher that it was his "full Resolution and purpose . . . to establish such a ministerye through out all his Dominions as fast as God might give him means unto it".[2] This assurance fortified the hopes and strengthened the resolution of the Puritan reformers. In a letter, Galloway reiterated that the King had promised "that all

---

[1] *Tanner MSS.*, 280, f. 168; printed, J. Strype, *Whitgift*, Vol. III, pp. 392–402; E. Cardwell, op. cit., p. 511.
[2] *Sloane MSS.*, 271, ff. 23–4.

corruptions dissonant from the Word, or contrary thereto, should be amended"[1] at the forthcoming Conference.

The monarch's reckless indiscretions lent wings to rumour. It was apparent that the forces of revolution were gaining in confidence and gathering strength. The defenders of the establishment urged the King to make an unambiguous declaration of policy. The result was a royal proclamation, dated 24 October 1603, "concerning such as seditiously seek reformation in church matters".[2] There was emphatic support for the episcopal form of government: "since we understood the form and frame, we are persuaded that both the constitution and doctrine thereof is agreeable to God's word, and near to the condition of the primitive church." Nevertheless, this approval did not exclude a recognition that reforms might be needed in certain particulars:

> forasmuch as experience doth shew daily, that the church militant is never so well constituted in any form of policy, but that the imperfections of men, who have the exercise thereof, do with time, though insensibly, bring in some corruptions; as also for that informations were daily brought unto us by divers, that some things used in this church were both scandalous to many seeming zealous, and gave advantage to the adversaries.

The King had nominated 1 November 1603 for a Conference with "the bishops and other learned men" relative to the affairs of the Church. The Conference had been postponed: "By reason of the sickness reigning in many places of our kingdom, the unseasonable time of the year for travel, and the incommodity of the place of our abode for such an assembly, we were constrained to defer it until after Christmas." No erroneous conclusions were to be drawn from the fact of postponement:

> But this our godly purpose we find hath been misconstrued by some men's spirits, whose heat tendeth rather to combustion than to reformation, as appeareth by the courses that they have taken; some using public invectives against the state ecclesiastical here established, some contemning their authority and the processes of their courts, some gathering subscriptions of multitudes of vulgar

[1] Quoted, D. Calderwood, *History of the Kirk of Scotland*, Edinburgh, 1845, Vol. VI, p. 243.

[2] *Patent Roll*, Jas. I, 1, Part 3; printed, D. Wilkins, op. cit., Vol. IV, p. 371; E. Cardwell, *Documentary Annals*, Oxford, 1844, Vol. II, p. 43.

persons to supplications to be exhibited to us, to crave that reformation, which if there be cause to make, is more in our hearts than
theirs. All which courses, it is apparent to all men, are unlawful,
and do savour of tumult, sedition, and violence, and not of such a
Christian modesty, as beseemeth those who for piety's sake only
desire redress of things they think to be amiss, and cannot but be
the occasions of disentious partialities.

It was not proposed to alter the polity of the Church: "we have
reason to think the estate of the church here established, and the
degrees and orders of ministers governing the same, to be agreeable to the word of God, and the form of the primitive church."
The purpose of the Conference was simply to consider "corruptions which may deserve a review and amendment". In the
meantime propaganda was to cease:

Our pleasure is, that all our subjects do repose themselves, and leave
to our conscience, that which to us only appertaineth, avoiding all
unlawful and factious manner of proceeding; for that hereafter if
any shall either by gathering the subscriptions of multitudes to
supplications, by contemptuous behaviour of any authority by the
laws resting in ecclesiastical persons, by open invectives and in-
decent speeches either in the pulpit or otherwise, or by disobedience
to the processes proceeding from their jurisdiction, give us cause to
think, that he hath a more unquiet spirit, than becometh any private
person to have toward public authority, we will make it appear by
their chastisement, how far such a manner of proceeding is displeasing to us . . . Wherefore we admonish all men hereby to take
warning, as they will answer the contrary at their peril.

The Archbishop was immensely relieved. Writing to Gilbert,
Earl of Shrewsbury, 12 December 1603, he expressed the measure
of his relief:

Although our humourous and contentious brethren have made many
petitions and motions correspondent to their natures, yet your lordship may perceive by the proclamation published, and to my
comfort I am assured by his Majesty's letter writ to me, that they
have not much prevailed. Your lordship, I am sure, doth imagine
that I have not all this time been idle, nor greatly quiet in mind.
For who can promise himself rest among so many vipers?[1]

The King's public rebuke of reforming agitation did not
preclude the prosecution of private inquiry or investigation.

[1] J. Strype, op. cit., Vol. III, pp. 391–2.

Writing to the Archbishops of Canterbury and York,[1] he described the number of petitions that had been presented to him. He desired a thorough investigation to be made: "Wee haue thought it convenient to lett you vnderstand yt informations from many places of our kingdome, and from persons of good sort, are so continually and so credibly deliuered vnto us, as we can not but giue some credytt vnto them." The information might well be false: "which information notwithstanding we are not so transported withall, but we would first heare from you how farr they are true or false." He desired a census of the clergy:

> We require you for our satisfaction to cause ye seuerall Bishopps of your province within some convenient time to make certificate to you in writing what nomber of churches with cures of soules be vnder each of them, what ye Incumbents are, of what degree in schoole and how qualifyed to preache, and what ye seuerall liuings of each church is worth, which certificates you shall send vnto us, or bringe them your selfe.

He was ready and willing to assist in the augmentation of ecclesiastical incomes: "yet shall we be content in all such vicarages, whereof ye tythes be impropriate and are in our hand, if they be not able to mainteyne a sufficient minister, to add some reliefe to them by some convenient meanes, as we may and as vpon deliberation of our Councell shalbe thought fitt." This concern was not to be misconstrued. He did not intend to tolerate nonconformity:

> We heaure that some ministers in ye celebration of diuine seruice and sermons, do vse new formes not prescribed by aucthority, which we take to procede of humor, affectation, or of novelty, and hauing by our proclamation made knowne our meaning in these thinges, we require you to cause those novelties to be seuerally reformed, and all men to conforme themselues.

Whitgift accordingly wrote to each of the bishops:

> I heartely pray your Lo: with all the speede you can, to sende vnto mee the Certificate promised in your last lettres. For I receaued Commandement from his highnes by lettres from him dated 29.

---

[1] The King to the Archbishop of York. *Egerton MSS.*, 2,877, f. 172 b. 29 October 1603. The King to the Archbishop of Canterbury. *Harleian MSS.*, 677, f. 107; *Additional MSS.*, 38,139, f. 183. 29 October 1603.

October wherein hee requireth the same. In which lettres also his majestie signifieth that hee is enformed that some ministers in the celebracion of divine service and Sacramentes do vse new formes not prescribed by authoritie, which hee taketh to proceede of an humour and affection of noveltie. And therefore requireth mee to cause the same to bee severely repressed and all men to conforme themselues to the due observation of the book of common praier, with signification, that herafter if there bee any omission in this kinde hee will aske accompt of yt onely at my hands. And therfore I do pray and require your L: to haue a due care herof and to suffer none within your dioces to alter anie thinge, but duely to observe the booke of common praier, as you will answere to the contrarie. For I meane not to beare eyther your burthen or anie others But to do that which my place and authoritie vnder his majestie requireth, without respecte of person.[1]

The returns were duly forwarded to the Archbishop and communicated to the King, for use at the forthcoming Conference.[2]

There was some speculation concerning the identity of the Puritan representatives. On 23 August 1603 it was anticipated that the disputers would be Reynolds, President of Corpus Christi College, Oxford; Chaderton, Master of Emmanuel College, Cambridge; Travers, who had been Hooker's great adversary at the Temple; Knewstubs, Rector of Cockfield in Suffolk; Jerton; and Hildersham, Rector of Ashby-de-la-Zouch.[3] Another list, probably compiled by Galloway, suggested Reynolds; Sparke, who was at one time Archdeacon of Stow in Lincoln; Field, subsequently to become Dean of Gloucester, or Hildersham; Chaderton; Fenn, who had been suspended several times from his ministry at Holy Trinity, Coventry; and Knewstubs. Cartwright's name was placed on the list, but was later crossed out, for he died in December 1603.[4] These drafts[5] included Puritans of various schools of thought, but the final list restricted representation to the moderates: Reynolds, Sparke, Chaderton, and

[1] *Brown Book*, Lincoln Record Office, f. 195 d; quoted C. W. Foster, op. cit., p. liii.
[2] *Harleian MSS.*, 280, ff. 157 ff.
[3] *Sloane MSS.*, 271, f. 21 b.
[4] *S.P. Dom., Jas. I*, 14, Vol. VI, no. 15.
[5] Cf. also *Beaulieu MSS.*, ff. 33–44. H.M.C. "Preliminary Puritan Draft for the Hampton Court Conference . . . Ministers of the Conference: Dr Reinolds, Dr Sparkes, Dr Fielde, Mr Chaderton, Mr Knewstubs. At their Conference and in place: Monsieur Gourden, Mr Galowaye."

Knewstubs. It is possible that others were also present, either officially or unofficially.[1]

The radicals, undeterred by their exclusion from the Conference, prepared a series of "instructions":

> Mr Arthur Hildersham, Mr Stephen Egerton, Mr Edward ffleete-wood of Lancashire and some other Ministers delivered to these Conferences Ten Demands, made by Thirty Reverend Divines, in the name of themselves and others, which they humbly desired them to sollicit his Majestie to grant.[2]

There was a familiar ring about the "demands" of these earnest and zealous reformers:

> Our earnest suit to our reverend brethren, chosen to deal for the cause in the conference, is that according to the calling and opportunity that God hath given they would solicit his Majesty in the behalf of the Church in these points.

> That there may be order taken for establishing of such ministers in any congregation as are well approved to be sound in religion, able to teach, diligent in teaching, and of unblameable life, and for the avoiding of all dispensations for pluralities, non-residents, and commendams.

> That order may be taken for raising a competent maintenance for the ministry by uniting of small parishes. . . .

> That the articles of religion may be reviewed, and more particularly and plainly and fully set down, that so all erroneous doctrines may be prevented, and the doctrine of the church touching all the points controverted at this day may be clearly known, and that subscription may be required only to those articles as to the confession of the faith of our churches;

> That all ceremonies that have been known to be offensive, and which very many profitable ministers in the land cannot be persuaded to use, may be abolished, or at least left free to use or refuse according to the conscience and discretion of the faithful minister; That the liturgy may be corrected according to the Word, and that for the better fitting and enabling men for the ministry the exercise

---

[1] *Harleian MSS.*, 3,795, f. 7 b. Galloway is described as one of the "Puritan actors in these pointes". "Dr Feythe [Field?] went in with the Puritans, he neuer spake but once, and that altogether against them."

Dr Montague, Dean of the Chapel Royal, says that the Puritan representatives were, "Dr Reynolds, Dr Sparkes, Dr Field, Dr King, Mr Chaderton, and Mr Knewstubbs".

[2] *Morrice MSS.*, G, f. 541.

of prophecying may be established, both in the universities and in every parish in the land.

That his Majesty may be satisfied concerning the imputation of puritanism, disloyalty, innovation and faction that have been laid upon the faithful ministers and people of the land, and that humble suit be made to his Highness that either by proclamation or otherwise, they may be freed from those reproaches, and that the ministers within any diocese [*who*] are now troubled by the bishops for ceremonies, subscription, and such like, may be thereby set free, at the least till such time as these matters shall be by his Majesty and the parliament fully determined, and that the bishops and their officers may not till then be permitted to molest them for the matter above named.[1]

The representatives of the established Church were bidden to assemble before the King on 12 January 1603/4. They consisted of John Whitgift, Archbishop of Canterbury; Richard Bancroft, Bishop of London; Toby Matthew, Bishop of Durham; Thomas Bilson, Bishop of Winchester; Gervas Babington, Bishop of Worcester; Anthony Rudd, Bishop of St David's; Anthony Watson, Bishop of Chichester; Henry Robinson, Bishop of Carlisle, and Thomas Dove, Bishop of Peterborough, and several lesser dignitaries.[2] They were received privately by the King, who informed them that the Conference was postponed until the following Saturday. On Saturday "his Highness about xj of ye clock in his privy chamber, in ye presence of ye privy council only sitting on his right hand and all ye Bishops on his left made an excellent oration of an houre long, declaring yt religion was ye soule of a Kingdome and vnity ye life of Religion".[3] The King traced the successive stages of the Reformation, praising Queen

---

[1] *Beaulieu MSS.*, Hampton Court Conference, January 1603/4. H.M.C., *Report on the MSS. of Lord Montagu of Beaulieu*, pp. 32–3; cf. *Egerton MSS.*, 2,884, f. 8.

[2] W. Barlow, *The Svmme and Svbstance of the Conference, which it pleased his Excellent Majestie to haue with the Lords Bishops, and other of his Clergie, (at which the most of the Lordes of the Councell were present) in his Maiesties Priuy-Chamber, at Hampton Court, Ianuary 14, 1603*. Cf. *Harleian MSS.*, 3,795, f. 7 a; *Additional MSS.*, 38,492, f. 81; *Baker MSS.*, M.m. 1, 45, ff. 155–7 (printed R. G. Usher, op. cit., Vol. II, p. 335); *Egerton MSS.*, 2,877, f. 173 b. See, letters from King James to some person in Scotland; from Toby Matthew to Matthew Hutton, Archbishop of York; and from Patrick Galloway to the presbytery in Edinburgh, Scotland; printed, E. Cardwell, *A History of the Conferences . . .*, Oxford, 1841, pp. 146 ff.

[3] *Egerton MSS.*, f. 173 b.

Elizabeth, who had "reformed her sisters superstitions and established ye churche of god here in ye doctrine of Christ and discipline agreeable to ye same". He had not summoned "them as persons accused, but as men of choice by whom he sought to receaue instruction".[1] He desired to be enlightened on several points:

1. ye fourme of absolution after ye publique confession of sinnes.
2. ye manner of confirmation of children.
3. ye tolleration of priuate Baptisme to be done by lay men, or women.
4. Many great errors and abuses crept in vnder ye tytle of excommunication and by ye corrupt dealing of Chancellors, officialls, etc.[2]

According to Dudley Carleton, who wrote next day to his friend, John Chamberlain, "the Arch. bishop of Canterbury, with the Bishop of Winchester and Durrham made milde and goode answeare, And the Bishop of London spake well to the purpose but with too ruf boldness".[3] Dean Montagu testifies that the King spoke "so wisely, wittily, and learnedly, with that pretty patience, as . . . never man living heard the like".[4] James closed the day's discussion by decreeing that "for ye better clearing of some doubts and misconstructions here and there some few words not in ye body of ye text, but in ye rubricks or tytles of some of th' aforesaid particulars, should in ye next edition of ye common prayer booke be inserted by waie rather of some explanation then of any alteration at all".

On 16 January 1603/4 the Puritan representatives appeared before the King, robed (according to the derisive comment of one observer) "in clokes and Nitecaps".[5] The king invited two

[1] *S.P. Dom., Jas. I*, 14, Vol. VI, no. 21. Patrick Galloway's account to the Edinburgh presbytery, written a month later (10 February 1603/4), gives a very different picture. The bishops "returned to his Majesty, and . . . answered all was well. And when his Majesty in great fervency brought instances to the contrary, they upon their knees with great earnestness craved that nothing should be altered . . . after five hours dispute had by his Majesty against them, and his Majesty's resolution for reformation intimated to them, they were dismissed for that day." (Quoted, D. Calderwood, op. cit., Vol. IV, pp. 243 f.)

[2] *Egerton MSS.*, 2,877, f. 173 b.

[3] *S.P. Dom., Jas. I*, 14, Vol. VI, No. 21.

[4] Quoted, R. Winwood, *Memorials*, London, 1725, Vol. II, p. 13.

[5] *S.P. Dom., Jas. I.* 14, Vol. IV, no. 21.

bishops to be present. Bancroft and Bilson were nominated by the Archbishop. Dr Reynolds, as spokesman, "named diuers abuses, but insisted cheifly vpon the confirmation: ye crosse in Baptisme, ye surplice, priests baptisme, kneeling at ye communion, reading of ye Apocrypha, subscription to ye booke of common prayer and articles, one only translation of ye byble to be authenticall and read in ye churche . . .". After the bishops had replied,

> the King pleaded hard to have a good proof against the ceremonies, and if they had the Word of God against them or good authority, he would remove them: but if they had no Word of God against them, but all authority for them, being already in the church, he would never take them away: for he came not to disturb the state nor to make innovations, but to confirm whatever he found lawfully established, and to amend and correct what was corrupted by time.[1]

According to the fulsome testimony of an eyewitness "his Majestie in most excellent and extraordinary manner disputed and debated with them and confuted their obiections, being therin assisted now and then for variety sake, rather then for necessity, by ye two Bishops before named from xj of ye clock vntill after iiijer". These matters having been dismissed, Reynolds raised the question of the form of Church government. He argued that bishops should not exercise jurisdiction alone,

> but ioyntly with a Presbiterie of their brethren the pastors and Ministers of the Churche. Whervnto the Kinge replied merily sayeinge, he would haue the Presbitery buried in silence for these 7 yeares, and yf then he grewe idle, lasie, fatt, and pursie, I will set vp a Presbitery (saith he) to exercise my body and my patience. . . .[2]

The Puritans were utterly disconcerted. They had been invited to make serious submissions: their submissions were treated with ridicule and disdain. Galloway bitterly complained that their grievances were "very loosely and coldly answered".[3]

A final meeting took place on Wednesday 18 January when a document was read summarizing the changes agreed upon by the King, the bishops, and the Council. The King, "in an excellent

---

[1] Quoted, R. Winwood, op. cit., Vol. II, p. 13.
[2] *Harleian MSS.*, 3,795, f. 7 a; *Additional MSS.*, 38,492, f. 81.
[3] *S.P. Dom., Jas. I*, 14, Vol. VI, no. 25, 18 January 1604. Cf. *Egerton MSS.*, 2,844, f. 8; *Lansdowne MSS.*, 89, no. 17; *Additional MSS.*, 38,139, f. 24.

oration", expounded the things requiring alteration. The first main head

> whereof was concerning the Booke of Common Prayer, wherein former things were concluded to be amended.
>
> First the Absolution, which containeth nothing amiss in the matter, and only quarreled for the name, therefore hereafter it shalbe called the absolution or generall remission of sinnes.
>
> Secondly, the Confirmation: which being shewed to be no Sacrament with us, but of very good use for preparing children to the Communion, it was concluded it should remain only with the alteration of the name, that it should be called the Confirmation, or rather the examination of the said children.
>
> Thirdly, the Priuat Baptisme nowe by Laymen or Women shalbe called the Private Baptisme by the Ministerie or Curacie only, and all the questions in that Baptisme that insinuate it to be done by women taken away.[1]

The second main head concerned the Court of High Commission. The King desired that the power of the court in relation to ecclesiastical affairs should be "somewhat attenuated". Thirdly, concerning preaching, the King desired

> a more learned Ministerie and maintenance for them, to be provided in such places in England where there is want.
>
> Then, as few double beneficed men and pluralities as may be, where they have double benefices to maintaine preaching, and to have their livings neare one to the other. . . .
>
> For Doctrine, that there be one uniforme translation of the Bible to be made, and that only to be used in all the Church of England.
>
> And that the Articles of Religion made in primo Elizabeth be explained and enlarged, and that no man doe reade or preach against anie of them.[2]

Earlier in the Conference Knewstubs and Chaderton had

> moved his highnes with all submission to haue ye crosse in Baptisme vtterly foreborne, and kneeling at ye communion, which being for diuers causes denyed them, yet by their importunity on ye behalfe of certaine preachers in Lancashire, who had taken great paines against ye papistes and done much good among ye people, his Highnes was contented out of his princely clemency so farr to con-

---

[1] Quoted, E. Cardwell, op. cit., p. 212.
[2] Ibid. Cf. *S.P. Dom.*, *Jas. I*, 14, Vol. VI, no. 18; *Cotton MSS.*, *Cleopatra*, F.11, f. 120.

descend vnto them that a letter should be written to ye Bishop of Chester to beare with their weaknes for sometime and not to proceede ouer hastily or roughly against any of them, vntill by conference betwene ye Bishop and them they might be perswaded to conforme themselues to vs and ye rest of their brethren . . .[1]

In accordance with this resolution, it was urged that in "matters of Ceremonies and Order, being things indifferent, that the rule of the Apostle be kept, that all things be donne to edification, that so neither graue, sober, and peaceable persons be not to farre urged at first, nor turbulent or unquiet persons and busie spirits to doe what they list".[2]

A few verbal alterations to the rubrics, by way of explication: this was the fruit of the prodigious labours and the fervent hopes of the reformers. It was a meagre and miserable harvest. In the retrospect of time, however, one event redeems the barrenness of the debate. Despite Bancroft's opposition the King agreed to Reynolds' demand for "one only translation of ye byble to be authenticall and read in ye churche". The enterprise was begun which resulted in the publication in 1611 of that immortal classic: the Authorized Version of the Bible.

The Puritans had good reason to be discouraged and dismayed. In a letter to a Scottish friend, the King wrote exultantly:

We have kept such a revell with the puritans here this two days, as was never heard the like: quhaire I have peppered thaime as soundlie as yee have done the papists thaire. It were no reason, that those that will refuse the airy sign of the cross after Baptism should have their purses stuffed with any more solid and substantial crosses. They fled me so from argument to argument, without ever answering me directly, *ut est eorum moris*, as I was forced at last to say unto thaime; that if any of thaime had been in a college disputing with their scholars, if any of their disciples had answered them in that sort, they would have fetched him up in a place of a reply; and so should the rod have plyed upon the poor boyes buttocks. I have such a book of thaires as may well convert infidels, but it shall never convert me, except by turning me more earnestly against thayme.[3]

It was the typical utterance of a vain and frivolous man.

---

[1] *Egerton MSS.*, 2,877, ff. 172 b; 173 b.

[2] *S.P. Dom., Jas. I*, 14, Vol. VI, no. 25. Cf. *S.P. Dom., Jas. I*, 14, Vol. VI, nos. 16, 17, 18, and 26.

[3] *Cotton MSS., Vespasian*, f. 3. Quoted, E. Cardwell, op. cit., p. 160; J. Strype, op. cit., Vol. III, pp. 407–8.

According to one commentator, Dr Reynolds was "the principall mouthe and speaker". Dr Sparke "spake verie sparingly", and Mr Chaderton was "mute as any fishe", but Knewstubs was "feirce against the Crosse". It was reliably reported that

> Chaderton must conforme his irregular Colledge to weare the surplice, and receive the Communion knelinge, or els to be putt out of yt. The King imposed this by Reason of informacon gyven him from the Lord Henry. The Chancellors of both the Vniuersities must send their letters downe, that none shalbe admitted without subscription. This is the Triumphe they so longe expected. Dr Reynolds and his brethren are vtterly condempned for silly men.[1]

There is evidence that Chaderton, Master of Emmanuel College, Cambridge, did conform his College. On 21 November 1604 Sir Thomas Lake complained "that Dr Chatterton, who was one of the disputers at the Conference, does not only not conform himself as he seemed to promise at the Conference, but rather gives ill example in the University", and desired Cranborne, as Chancellor of the University, to take disciplinary action: "His Highness thinks it fit you should consider what is meet to be done with him if he persist, and what you as Chancellor may do to remove him if he continue obstinate."[2] But the following month Chaderton sent a certificate regarding the conformity of Emmanuel College.[3]

> I know neither Popish nor Puritan Recusant in Emmanuel College.
> The booke of Common Prayer and Ceremonies therin prescribed are observed in the said Colleg, according to the order of our English church.
> The surplis, with the other scholasticall habit, is used in the College according to the Universitie statute.
> All such as are professed Ministers in the said College have exhibited their lettres of orders, whereby I find them lawfully authorized, and canonically ordeyned to that function.[4]

---

[1] *Harleian MSS.*, 3,795, f. 7 b.

[2] *Cecil MSS.*, 107, f. 148. H.M.C., Part XVI, p. 367.

[3] Emmanuel long continued as a stronghold of Puritanism. The King, writing to Cranbourne, said: "I doubt not also but ere this time ye have received the puritans' catholic petition, for it neither names county, parish nor pastor ... that knave that was the framer of the petition ... is so near kin to Emmanuel as I shall distrust that race the more while I live. ..." *Cecil MSS.*, 134, f. 53. H.M.C., Part XVI, p. 363.

[4] *S.P. Dom., Jas. I*, 14, Vol. X.A, no. 73.

An official report of the Conference by William Barlow, Dean of
Chester, was published: *The Svmme and Svbstance of the Conference
which it pleased his Excellent Maiestie to haue with the Lords Bishops,
and other of his Clergie, (at which the most of the Lordes of the Councell
were present) in his Maiesties Priuy-Chamber, at Hampton Court,
Ianuary 14, 1603.* Written at Bancroft's request,[1] it was perused by
the King before publication.[2] Henry Jacobs scorned the ten-
dentious travesty:

> That which is set forth as the true report of it, being published
> onely by the Prelates (who are partiall) without the knowledge,
> aduise, or consent of the other side, deserues no credit . . . sith the
> Kings owne speeches be, as it seemeth grossly abused by the author,
> it is much more likely that speeches of other men are abused. Besides,
> none but Prelats, and such as were partiall, being present at the
> first dayes Conference, there can be no credit at all given to the
> report thereof: for it is more than apparent, that they haue fraudu-
> lently cut of, and concealed all the speeches (which were many)
> that his Maiestie vttered against the corruptions of our Church,
> and Practise of the Prelats: as appeareth by that testimony of the
> Deane of the Chappell, which he gaue thereof, saying, "That his
> Maiestie did that day wonderfully play the Puritan". But if he
> playd that part no otherwise then is specified in the Prelats report,
> he acted it very poorely, or rather never a whit. . . .[3]

It was a question whether the Conference was ever intended to
serve any honest purpose: "Such a Conference as that was never
desired by the Ministers, and it seemeth by the whole managing
of it that it was undertaken plotted and procured by the Prelatists
themselves, abusing therein his Majestie by useing Mr Galloway
as an instrument in the matter."[4]

Jacobs urged the convening of another Conference. In a
further pamphlet he enlarged on this necessity:

> Your Maiesties loyall and devoted Subjects, who for the safetie of
> our soules desire the Reformation of our Churches according to

[1] *Cecil MSS.*, 188, f. 109. H.M.C., Part XVI, p. 95. Dr W. Barlow to Lord
Cecil, 12 May 1604.
[2] Ibid.
[3] *A Christian and Modest Offer of a most Indifferent Conference or Dispvtation,
abovt the maine and principall Controversies betwixt the Prelats, and the late silenced
and deprived Ministers in England: Tendered by some of the said Ministers to the
Archbishop and Bishops, and all their adherents. 1606. Morrice MSS.*, G, f. 541.
"Colloquium Hamptoniense."
[4] Ibid.

Gods word, do cast downe our selves in the true affection of our heartes before your Royall presence, who we acknowledge to be the noblest pillar of the Gospell and the greatest hope for the propagation and establishing thereof that is in all Christendom Beseeching your Highnes to extend your kingly ayde and furtherance unto us in our foresaid most necessarie and iust desire, with protection also toward our innocencies against the Oppression of our Adversaries in this cause.[1]

The radicals disowned those who had represented the Puritan cause at the Hampton Court Conference: "most of the persons appointed to speake for the ministers were not of their Chusing or nomination, nor of their judgement in the matters then and now in question, but of a clean Contrary."[2] In their "instructions" they had insisted that ceremonies were "not indifferent, but simply unlawful". These "instructions" had been ignored:

Being intreated at that time by Ministers to dispute against those things *as simply evill and such as cannot be yielded unto without sin,* they professed to them that they were not so perswaded, and therefore could not so do. Being then requested to let his Majestie understand that some of their Brethren were further perswaded *touching the unlawfullness of these things* then themselves they refused that also. Lastly, Being intreated either to give them in Writing their reasons to prove ... those things indifferent, or give them an answer in Writing, to prove them simply evill, they would do neither the one nor the other.[3]

In the bitterness of defeat, it was tempting to attribute blame and to apportion responsibility.[4]

There were, however, other reactions. Thomas Sparke, one of the disputants, thought better of his nonconformity, and penned a pamphlet entitled, *A Brotherly Perswasion to Unitie, and Uniformitie in iudgement, and Practise touching the Received and present Ecclesiasticall gouernment, and the authorized rites and ceremonies of the Church of England. ...*[5] It all depended, he said, upon the cultivation of a spirit of charitable goodwill:

[1] *Reasons taken out of Gods word and the best humane Testimonies proving a Necessitie of Reforming Our Churches in England. Framed and Applied to 4. Assertions wherein the aforesaid purpose is contained,* 1604.
[2] *Morrice MSS.,* G, f. 541. "Colloquium Hamptoniense."
[3] Ibid.
[4] Cf. *Additional MSS.,* 38,492, f. 12. "The matters not reformed whereof pretence was made that they should be reformed."
[5] 1607.

6

if we could and would once learne to bend our wits as well to make the best constuction of euerie thing hereafter, as heretofore, to make the worst, both the practise of the book and the subscription thereunto and to the rest, would now be doubtlesse far easier then heretofore it hath, or yet is, vnto many. . . .

In the meantime, royal approval was given to the alterations and amendments agreed upon at the Conference. They were drafted by the bishops and submitted to the King, who replied:

wee . . . haue since receaued from you the said particular things in the said booke declared and enlarged by waie of explanation . . . Wee, hauing maturely considered of them, doe hold them to bee very agreeable to our owne severall directions vppon Conference with you and others, and that they are in no parte repugnant to the Worde of god.

The King declared: we do "fully, approue, allowe, and ratifie all and every one of the said declarations and enlargements by waye of Explanation". The King's Printer was ordered to print the new book, incorporating the alterations.[1]

On 5 March 1603/4 a proclamation was issued "for the authorizing and uniformity of the book of Common Prayer to be used throughout the realm".[2] The King, reviewing the circumstances which had led him to convene the Conference, mentioned how, at his first coming into the realm, he was "entertained and importuned with informations of sundry ministers, complaining of the errors and imperfections of the church here, as well in matter of doctrine, as of discipline". "Because the importunity of the complainers was great, their affirmations vehement, and the zeal wherewith the same did seem to be accompanied, very specious", he had agreed to a Conference being convened to settle the affairs of religion.

Before ourself and our privy council were assembled many of the gravest bishops and prelates of the realm, and many other learned men, as well as those that are comfortable to the state of the church established, as of those that dissented; among whom, what our pains were, what our patience in hearing and replying, and what the indifferency and uprightness of our judgement in determining, we

---

[1] S.P. Dom., Jas. I, 14, Vol. VI, no. 27. 18 January 1603/4. Patent Roll, Jas. I, Part 5. 9 February 1603/4.
[2] Proclamation Book, p. 64. Printed, E. Caldwell, Annals, Vol. II, p. 56.

leave to the report of those who heard the same, contenting ourself with the sincerity of our own heart within.

He had soon discovered that the objections of the Puritans were trivial and tiresome:

But we cannot conceal that the success of that conference was such as happeneth to many other things, which moving great expectation before they be entered into, in their issue produce small effect. For we found mighty and vehement informations supported with so weak and slender proofs, as it appeareth unto us and to our council, that there was no cause why any change should have been made at all in that, which was most impugned, the Book of Common Prayer, containing the form of the public service of God here established, neither in the doctrine, which appeared to be sincere, nor in the rites and form, which were justified out of the practice of the primitive church.

To satisfy the consciences of the over scrupulous, a few small things in the Prayer Book had been "explained, rather than changed". It was now the duty of all men, whether ecclesiastical or temporal, "to conform themselves unto it, and to the practice thereof, as the only public form of serving God, established and allowed to be in this realm". The bishops were charged to enforce conformity, and every parish was to obtain one of the new books "so explained". No further alterations were intended:

neither will we give way to any to presume, that our own judgement having determined in a matter of this weight, shall be swayed to alteration by the frivolous suggestions of any light spirit; neither are we ignorant of the inconveniences that do arise in government by admitting innovation in things once settled by mature deliberation, and how necessary it is to use constancy in the upholding of the public determinations of states.

3

THE ECCLESIASTICAL CONSTITUTIONS
AND CANONS

THE ABORTIVE Hampton Court Conference was the prelude to a series of measures, both legislative and administrative, designed to end the Puritan challenge. Despite the coercive and repressive measures of the latter years of Elizabeth's reign, Puritanism was still a living subterranean movement. The Millenary Petition was both a portent and a warning. With the Hampton Court Conference the first round had been won, and the authorities were now in a position to launch a determined counter-offensive. A necessary prerequisite, however, was the possession by the Church of an effective body of rules and regulations in the form of a consistent and coherent body of constitutions and canons.

The existing situation was far from clear. The question was to what extent pre-Reformation canon law was still binding in the reformed Church of England. The "Acte for the submission of the Clergie to the Kynges Majestie" declared that the ancient canons were still in force, except in so far as they were abrogated or annulled by subsequent legislation and the publication of more recent canons: "such canons . . . being already made which be not contrariant or repugnant to the laws, statutes and customs of this Realm, nor to the damage or hurt of the King's Prerogative Royal, shall still now be used and executed as they were afore the making of this act."[1]

Nevertheless, there was much uncertainty. The position is well summarized by the compilers of the *Report on the Canon Law of the Church of England*:

The effect of the Tudor legislation was to leave the Church in possession of its traditional jurisprudence and the legislation of the medieval popes as the basis of its law. But exactly what chapters

[1] 25 Henry VIII, c. 19.

either in the *Decretum* or in the papal codes had been abrogated by the Reformation statutes or were contrary to the Laws, statutes, and customs of the realm or damaging to the King's prerogative was never officially defined. Nobody attempted to disentangle what parts of the Canon Law were still in force from the parts which were no longer binding either on the principle laid down in the Act for the Submission of the Clergy or because they had never been observed as law in this country.[1]

The act for the Submission of the Clergy laid it down that canons could not be made unless the clergy were assembled by the King's writ, and licensed by the King to proceed to the formulation and execution of canons:

> Where the Kynges humble and obedyent subjects the clergy of this realme of England have not only knowledged accordyng to the truthe that the Convocacions of the same clergye is always hath byn and ought to be assembled only by the Kynges writt, but also sub-myttyng theym selfes to the Kynges Majestie hath promysed *in verbo sacerdocii* that they wyll never frome hensforthe presume to attempte allege clayme or putt in ure or enacte promulge or execute any newe canons constitucions ordynaunce provynciall or other, or by what soo ever other name they shall be called in the Convocation, onles the Kynges most royall assente and licence may to theyme be had to make promulge and execute the same, and that hys Majestie doo geve hys most royall assente and auctorytie in that behalf.

It further provided that the existing canons should be revised by thirty-two persons, sixteen being of the upper and nether house of the temporalty, and sixteen of the clergy, all being appointed by the King. The Act of 1534 further stipulated that no canons should be promulgated that had not previously received the royal assent:

> Be it therefore now enacted by auctoritie of this present Parliament accordyng to the seid submyssyon and peticion of the seid clergie, that they ne any of theym from hensforth shall presume to attempte allege clayme or put in ure any constitucions or ordynances pro-vynciall or synodalles or any other canons, nor shall enacte promulge or execute any suche canons constituciouns or ordynaunce pro-vynciall, by what soo ever name or names they may be called in theire Convocacions in tyme commyng, which alway shalbe assembled by auctoryte of the Kynges wrytte, onles the same clergie may have

[1] London, 1947, op. cit., p. 47.

the Kynges most royal assent and lycence to make promulge and execute suche canons constitucions and ordynaunces provynciall or synodall.[1]

The commission for the revision of the canons was in due course appointed. Its findings, however, were never ratified by the King. In the reign of Edward VI Parliament again authorized the setting up of a commission (3 & 4 Edward VI, c. 11), and eight persons were appointed with instructions to complete the work within three years. King Edward died before the canons could be promulgated. During the reign of Mary no action was taken. In the reign of Elizabeth I it was again suggested that the work of revision should be resumed and finished. In 1571 Archbishop Parker agreed to the publication by Foxe the martyrologist of the *Reformatio Legum Ecclesiasticarum*: the draft prepared by the Edwardian commissioners. The Queen, who disliked the meddling of Parliament in ecclesiastical affairs, stopped Parliament's discussion of the book, and it was published without official authority.

Nevertheless, several short series of canons and articles were proposed during Elizabeth's reign. In 1571 a series of canons under eleven titles, subdivided into paragraphs, was agreed to by the Upper Houses of the Convocations; but the canons never received the assent of the Lower Houses nor royal confirmation. In 1575 a series of *Thirteen Articles* "touching the admission of apt and fit persons to the ministry and the establishing of good order in the Church" was drawn up by the Convocation of Canterbury and authorized by the Queen. In 1585 *Six Articles*, as they were called, received the sanction of both Houses of the Convocation of Canterbury, but were not confirmed by the Queen. In 1597 these *Six Articles*, with additional matter, were formed into a collection of twelve canons which this time were passed by both Houses of the Convocations and were confirmed by the Queen's Letters Patent.

It was recognized that a thorough and comprehensive revision and review of the existing canon law was long overdue. The Puritans were anxious that the work of godly reformation, in this field, as in others, should be made more fully perfect, and, in the

---

[1] 25 Henry VIII, c. 19. Printed, *The Report of the Commissioners appointed to inquire into the Constitution and Working of the Ecclesiastical Courts* (1883), Historical Appendix (XII), p. 216.

"instructions" preparatory to the Hampton Court Conference, the radicals demanded "that according to the statute 25 Henry VIII, the canons and ecclesiastical laws may be reviewed, and that so all which are not sound and agreeable to the word may be abolished, and the rest publicly and plainly set forth, that we may know what laws we are bound to obey".[1]

In 31 January 1603/4 a royal writ was directed to John Whitgift, Archbishop of Canterbury, empowering him to summon the bishops, deans of the cathedral churches, archdeacons, chapters and colleges, and proctors of the clergy of every diocese within the province of Canterbury, to assemble in Convocation on 20 March. Before Convocation could assemble, however, John Whitgift died on 29 February, and a second writ was then directed to Richard Bancroft, Bishop of London, as dean of the province, on 9 March 1603/4, authorizing, appointing, and constituting him "President of the said Convocation, to execute those things, which, by virtue of our first writ, did appertain to him the said archbishop to have executed, if he had lived".[2] In the royal licence to Convocation, dated 12 April 1604, full authority was given to proceed to the preparation of ecclesiastical canons:

> Know ye that we, for divers urgent and weighty causes and considerations us thereunto specially moving . . . do give and grant full, free and lawful liberty, licence, power and authority unto the Reverend Father in God, Richard, Bishop of London, president of this present Convocation for the province of Canterbury at this present parliament now assembled, and to the rest of the bishops of the same province. . . . That they . . . shall and may from time to time confer . . . and agree of and upon such canons . . . as they . . . or the greatest number of them shall think necessary . . . for the honour and service of Almighty God, the good and quiet of the Church and the better government thereof. . . .[3]

Some of the Puritans were clear-sighted enough to see that the promulgation of revised canons would not be to their advantage but to their detriment. The Hampton Court Conference was sufficiently indicative of official policy. On the principle that offence is the best form of defence, one apologist raised the whole

---

[1] *Beaulieu MSS.*, H.M.C., p. 33.
[2] *Tanner MSS.*, 282, f. 20 b.
[3] *Patent Roll*, 2 Jas. I, Part 25.

question of ecclesiastical law and denied the right of the King
to authorize Convocation to proceed to the preparation of canons:
"The Canons and Constitutions of the Convocation house are
not the lawes of England, though that the Clergie of both provinces,
to witt of Canterbury and Yorke, meete there and conclude the
same, no though the Clergie be called thither, by the Kings Writt,
and the Canons and Constitutions themselues, be confirmed by
the greate seale of England."[1] He took his stand on the fact that
there are "but two sorts of Lawes in the Kingdome. The one
customary or Common Lawe as we call it: the other statute or
Parliament Lawe. But the Canons and Constitutions of the
Convocation house, are neither Common Lawe nor Statute
lawe, therefore, no Lawes of England or of the Kingdome." It
was not sufficient for canons to be confirmed by Parliament; they
must also be compiled by Parliament:

> vnlesse the parties concludinge and Constitutinge Cannons, haue
> power and right to ordayne, constitute, and enact, all callinge of
> them together, all constitutinge, ordayninge, and enactinge, yea all
> ratification and confirmation of them, by all outward meanes . . .
> are of no validitie and force at all, because the life and being of
> Lawes, consisteth in the lawfull power and authority of the lawe
> makers, and not in the outward ratification and confirmation of
> them. . . .

It was a good debating point, and it was to be raised again when
the binding character of the canons was to become a subject of
acrimonious controversy.

On 12 April 1604, the Bishop of London ordered the royal
warrant for the making of canons to be read before Convocation.[2]
Less than a month later, on 2 May, the canons were publicly
delivered to the prolocutor. *The Acts and Proceedings of Convocation*
tell the story:

> Haec dum agerentur, episcopus Londonensis, secundo die Maii
> prolocutor librum canonum perlegendum tradit, cujus examen
> utrique domui synodi in aliis sessionibus committit. Illo ipso die
> tres clerici, Egerton, Fleetwood, et Wotton, cum aliis sociis suis
> reformationem liturgiae Anglicanae per petitionem domui inferiori
> convocationis expetebant.[3]

[1] *Cotton MSS., Cleopatra*, F.11, f. 196.
[2] *Patent Roll*, 2 Jas. I, Part 25.   12 April 1604.
[3] E. Cardwell, *Synodalia*, Oxford, 1842, Vol. II, p. 584.

Egerton and Fleetwood again! It was Egerton and Fleetwood who, after their exclusion from the Hampton Court Conference, compiled the "instructions". It was Stephen Egerton who now took the initiative by delivering an *Address to Convocation, urging a revision of the newe booke of common prayer*.[1] There were still ambiguities in the Prayer Book, and there was urgent need for a further reformation in relation to the ministry, preaching, and ceremonies:

It seemeth theirfore a thinge right nessassarye and worthy to be considered of the Reuerend ffathers, with the rest of this learned and venerable assemblye of convocation, whether it would not tend to the high honner of god and the good of this our mother church:

1. First that ye purpose and intendment of his Majestie for a learned ministery and the reformation of Ecclesiasticall courts, be furthered and sett forward by vs, who are heare mett together for theise and the like considerations.

2. Secondlye that order be taken to compell such as are able to take paines in preachinge and Cathachisinge without the which the former wilbe in vayne.

3. Thirdlye that the newe booke of coman prayer be reuised and such additions and alterations as haue beene of late deuised be somewhat further considderd, that if upon good deliberation any defect shalbe fownd therein, it maye be by our godlye care amended, and the booke reformed. As namelie in theise points followinge. In the doctrine of the sacraments, newlie added to the Catechisme. Wheire first in the answer that is made touchinge the number of Sacraments it is said that theire are 2 only as generally nessassarye to saluation wheirbye in the vnderstandinge and iudgment of manye is implied a further number of sacraments then 2. for other particular ends and vses, though but too onlye for the generall end aforesaide, which seemeth to incline and drawe towards the popish doctrine, if not of 7 sacraments, yet of more then by our Church hath alwaiss bin acknowledged. ... All which matters of exception, howsoever at a blush they maye seeme to be vayne and friuilous, yet since they touch no longer the shadow and cerimonyes, but the very life and substance of religion, it is greatlie to be feared that if once they should be distasted, as they are of many already, it would breede a far greater inconuenience amongst vs, then ever before, since it is certaine that many of those who haue and can digest the former, will yett cast vp theise as lothsome puddle.

4. The fourth and last thinge to be considered is that since the

---

[1] *Additional MSS.*, 38,492, f. 1. 1604.

forcing of subscription, and vrginge of cerimonyes (accknowlledged by the Reuerend ffathers themselues to be things indifferent) hath been the cawses of so much broyle in the Church and hart burninge amonst those who professe one and the same religion, and which is greatlie to be feared, wilbe reuiued againe, vnlesse a godlye and a religious care be taken by a Christian and brotherlye moderation to preuent it. Theirefore if it be thought convinient to yeild no further vnto those our bretheren for the sattisfaction of theire conscience, yet at the least that they may be eased of subscription (further then to the articles of religion) the crosse in baptisme and the surplice, which more directlie then anie other doe seem to crosse the exercise of theire ministrie. . . .

Egerton was following the procedure established at the beginning of Elizabeth's reign. The reformers, having failed to secure a religious settlement after their own pattern, then pursued their aims in Convocation. They were only just defeated. The Puritans had failed once again at the beginning of a new reign to achieve their objectives: it was natural that another attempt should be made in Convocation.

Egerton found support in unexpected quarters. William Bedell, Fellow of Emmanuel, and later Bishop of Kilmore and Ardagh, distributed a tract[1] among members of Convocation pleading for tolerance and forbearance in the matter of ceremonies. It was true "that by the proclamation of March 5" the King had forbidden "any man to attempt any further alteration in the common and publick forme of ye service", but, in the absence of any explicit references to ceremonies, it was arguable that "his Majestie hath reserved this matter all entire". It was not a question of abandoning all solemn outward rites in the service of God, "for some suche rites . . . have a kinde of natural deriva-tion from the carriage of the mind in actions of gods service, as to uncover the head". Difficulty existed in connection with "a certaine kinde onely . . . which having no ground in nature, or necessity in reason, have by mans arbitrament a signification of some holiness, or opinion of some due sollemness put upon them, after the fancy of the founder: and which are urged as necessarily to be used by ministers of the gospel". He specified as offensive "the weareing of vestments which were used in popery, and the

[1] The ascription is a matter of internal evidence. See, Bedell's letters, *Tanner MSS.* (Bodl.), 75, f. 126 ff.

signe of the crosse in Baptisme". There were differences of interpretation and consequently differences of judgement:

> Some do take them to be remnants of Idolatry, and Superstitious traditions of men and therefor unlawful and wicked; others admitt them to be things indifferent, yet upon other, by reasons, as offence of the weake and the like, not expedient; and those that defend them, some commend them as ancient, as comely, and of ornament, others acknowledgeing no great excellency in them say no more but that they be not wicked, that they may be tolerated to heale inconveniences, that the magistrate and law requireing, they ought to be used for obedience. . . .[1]

Matters reached a critical juncture on 23 May in a discussion concerning the sign of the cross in baptism.[2] Bancroft vigorously defended the retention of the custom, but Anthony Rudd, Bishop of St David's, pleaded for the rights of conscience. He thought himself that men should submit rather than forgo their ministry. Nevertheless, he believed that the Church should deal tenderly with the convictions and scruples of men rather than pursue the paths of coercion and deprivation.

> For mine owne parte I acknowledg the antiquitie of the vse of [the] crosse as is mentioned in Tertullian, and after him Cyprian . . . likewise in Basil, Chrisostome, Augustine, and others. Allsoe I confesse the originall of the Paganes, who reproched the ancient christians for beleeuing in Christ crucifyed. I adde that in popery it hath beene superstitiously abused. And I affirme that it is in the Church of England now admitted and entertayned by vs as restored to the auncient integritie all supperstition abandoned.
>
> Likewise I wishe that if the Kinges highnes shall persist in the imposing of it, all would submit them selues vnto it (as we doe) rather then forgoe the ministerie in that behalf.
>
> But I greatly feare by report which I heare that very many learned preachers (whose consciences are not in our custodie, nor to be disposed of at our deuotion) will not be easily drawn therevnto. Of the which number if any shall come in my walke, I desire to be furnished beforehande, by these that be present, with sufficient reasons to satisfie them, if it be possible concerning such points which haue beene deliuered now: first of all, whereas there was euen nowe alleadged for the crosse, sundry places of scripture, as

---

[1] *Additional MSS.*, 38,492, f. 18.
[2] *Tanner MSS.* (Bodl.), 282, f. 22.

God forbid that I should reioyce, sauing in the crosse of Christ, and diuerse moe of the like sense: If any of the diuerse opinion fall into my company, and say that these scripture speaches be figuratiue implying the death and passion of our Saviour Christ with the fruits and effects thereof, and that to drawe an argument from them to iustifie the signall crosse is an insufficient kinde of reasoning and a fallacie, what answere shall I make vnto them to perswade them. . . .

Moreouer I protest that all my speaches now are vttered by way of proposition, not by way of opposition, by way of question, and not by way of contradiction. And that they all tende to worke pacification in the church (if it be possible) which I knowe to be very necessarie at this time. And that I put greate difference between *quod liceat* and *quod expediat*. And likewise betweene them that are Shismatticall or open disturbers of the state Ecclesiasticall established and them that are scrupulous only vpon the Ceremonies and other Circumstances, being otherwise learned, studious, graue, and honest men, whose labours haue beene both painfull in the Church and allsoe profitable to theyr seuerall congregations.

The deprivation of many godly and devoted men would bring the Church into grievous disrepute. There would also be the practical problem of providing suitable substitutes in the place of those deprived:

Concerning these preachers last mentioned, I suppose that if vpon the vrging of them to absolute subscription, and the vse of the ceremonies and the attire prescribed, they should stand out stifly and choose rather to forgoe theyr liuings, and the exercise [of their] ministery, though I doe not iustifie theyr doings herein, yet surely theyr seruice will be missed, at such time as neede shall require vs and them, to giue the right hands of fellowship one to another, and to goe arme in arme against the common aduersary. That soe there might be *vis unita fortior*. . . . Likewise consider who must be the executioners of the depriuation, euen we our selues the Bishops against whome there wilbe a greate clamour of them and theyr dependents and many other who are well affected toward them, whereby our persons should be in hazard to be brought into greate dislike, if not into extreame hatred; wherefore what inconveniences may issue I leaue to your wisdoms to be considered. . . . I thinke we should finde cause to bende our witts to the vttermost extent of our skill, to prouide some cures of soules for them wherein they might exercise theyr talents. Furthermore, if these men, being diuers hundred in number (as it is bruted abroad) should forsake theyr charges (as some doe presuppose they will) who, I pray you, shall succeede them? Verily I know not where to finde so many able preaching ministers within the realme unprovided for. But be it that soe many may be founde to supply these emptie roomes, yet they might more conueniently be setled in the seates of vnlearned, vnpreaching ministers, and soe the number of preachers should much be increased. But if they should be put into the places of these being dispossessed, therevpon would follow; first, that the number of preaching incumbents should not be multiplied by this supply. And secondly, the preachers could not in likly hoode be soe well and fittly furnished on a suddaine, for that though happily the supply should be of men as learned as the former, yet it is not probable, that they should be at theyr first comming from the vniuersities, or in a good while after, soe ready preachers, soe experienced in pastorall gouerment, soe well acquainted with the manners and vsage of the people, and soe discreete euery way in the carriage of them selues, as the others who haue spent allready many yeares abroad in theyr ministeriall charges.

All this was the more anomalous since papists at the most were exposed to recusancy fines, whereas Puritans were exposed to the total loss of their livelihood. The former differed from the Church in fundamental matters of doctrine, whereas the latter only differed in matters of ceremonies which were things indifferent. Rudd continued his plea:

Besides this, for as much as in the life time of the late Archbishop of Canterbury these thinges were not soe extreamly iudged but that many learned preachers enioyed theyr liberty herein conditionally that they did not by word or deede openly disgrace or disturbe the state established. I would know a reason why they should now be soe generally, and soe exceeding straitly called vpon, especially seeing that these mens labours are now the more necessary, by soe much as we see greater encrease of papists to be now of late, then was before. Againe, considering that the Romanists, who differe from vs in substance of Religion, are not for recusancy vtterlye disposed of all theyre liuely hood, but only haue a pecunial multe imposed vpon them, which many of them doe easily beare, as the matter vsed, I marueile why these men who dissent from vs only in Ceremony and circumstances, should there vpon be put to losse of theyr whole liuings and maintenances. To conclude, I wish that if by petition made to the Kings Majestie there cannot be obtained a quiet remoueall of the premisses which seems soe greious to diuerse (nor yet a tolleration for them, which be of the more stayed and temperate carriage) yet at the least there might be procured a mitigation of the penaltie, if they cannot be drawn by our reasons to conformitie with vs.[1]

Bancroft, Bishop of London, Bilson, Bishop of Winchester, Heton, Bishop of Ely, and Chaderton, Bishop of Lincoln, all spoke by way of reply, but unfortunately their speeches are not extant. Rudd would have spoken again, but Bancroft forbade further discussion:

> Ande he submitted himselfe obediently therevnto. Afferminge that because nothing was more deare vnto him then the peace of the Church, therefore he would still persue the course which he had allways held in vsinge the best meanes in perswasions that he could to drawe all others to vnitie and conformitie with himselfe and the rest of the reuerend companie.[2]

In the meantime Egerton and his followers were peremptorily ordered to conform. "Hos episcopus Londonensis et alii episcopi admonebant ab obedientiam at assensum praestandae liturgiae regia auctoritate stabilitae, illisque festum S. Johannis Baptistae assignabant ad consentiendum huic monitioni."[3]

The canons bear upon them clear evidence that they are a product of their historical time. There are numerous references to the controversies which convulsed the Church, and a recognition of the challenge from the right and from the left. There is an explicit allusion to the Hampton Court Conference: "We are sorry that his majesty's most princely care and pains taken in the conference at Hampton Court, amongst many other points, touching this one of the cross in baptism, hath taken no better effect with many, but that still the use of it in baptism is so greatly stuck at and impugned."[4] The form of the canon on the sign of the cross is unprecedented: it includes a lengthy historical excursion for the removing of all such scruples, "as might any ways trouble the consciences of them who are indeed rightly religious". By a remarkable transvaluation the cross—a symbol of shame—became, for the primitive Church, a symbol of triumphant

---

[1] *Harleian MSS.*, 677, f. 41.
[2] Ibid.
[3] *Acts and Proceedings of Convocation.* Printed, E. Cardwell, op. cit., Vol. II, p. 585. *Tanner MSS.*, 282, f. 22.
[4] Canon 30.

victory. The early Christians, "so far from being discouraged from their profession by the ignominy of the cross ... rather rejoiced and triumphed in it". They "signed therewith their children when they were christened, to dedicate them by that badge to his service, whose benefits bestowed upon them in baptism the name of the cross did represent". Although "the sign of the cross was greatly abused in the Church of Rome, especially after the corruption of popery had once possessed it", yet, "the abuse of a thing doth not take away the lawful use of it". It is lawful to preserve things which are edifying and spiritually helpful: "as the apology of the Church of England confesseth, it doth with reverence retain those ceremonies, which do neither endamage the Church of God, nor offend the minds of sober men." The use of the sign of the cross in baptism in the Church of England is "accompanied with ... sufficient cautions and exceptions against all popish superstition and error".

The canon concludes with three positive statements about the retention of this ceremony by the Church of England. First, the point is made that "the sign of the cross used in baptism is no part of the substance of that sacrament". After the minister has dipped the infant in water, or poured water upon it, with the use of the Trinitarian formula, "the infant is fully and perfectly baptized". This means that "the sign of the cross being afterwards used, doth neither add any thing to the virtue and perfection of baptism, nor being omitted doth detract any thing from the effect and substance of it". Secondly, attention is drawn to the fact that "the infant baptized is, by virtue of baptism, before it be signed with the sign of the cross, received into the congregation of Christ's flock, as a perfect member thereof, and not by any power ascribed unto the sign of the cross". In the third place, it is clearly stated that the use of the sign of the cross is in itself a thing indifferent. In the Church of England it has been reduced to its primary institution, and has been "purged from all popish superstition and error", so that it is now the duty of every man, "both minister and other, reverently to retain the true use of it prescribed by public authority".

Bancroft was impatient with those who took exception to this innocent ceremony. Writing to Salisbury in 1609 about a person who objected to the cross in baptism, he made the testy comment:

"I am sorie any christian man should shew so greate a detestation of the signe of the Crosse. Certaynely it argueth a neere affinitie to Atheisme. If any had so written in the dayes of the auncient fathers he wold have been accompted a most wicked wrecke."[1] This canon is unique among the 141 canons by virtue of its lengthy explanatory material and by virtue of its apologetic character.

The first twelve canons define explicitly what constitutes, and what does not constitute, membership of the Church of England. Positively, a member of the Church of England is one who confesses that the King's supremacy over the Church in causes ecclesiastical is legitimate;[2] that the Church of England is a true and apostolic Church;[3] that the Articles of Religion are scriptural and true;[4] that the rites and ceremonies are such as can be used with a good conscience;[5] and that the government of the Church by archbishops, bishops, and other clergy is agreeable to the Word of God.[6]

Direct and indirect references bear upon the rival pretensions of papists and Puritans. The papists who affirm "that the king's majesty hath not the same authority in causes ecclesiastical, that the godly kings had amongst the Jews and Christian emperors of the primitive church",[7] and who affirm "that the Church of England, by law established under the king's majesty, is not a true and apostolic church, teaching and maintaining the doctrine of the apostles",[8] are solemnly censured. Likewise those who impugn the validity of Anglican orders, teaching that "they who are made bishops, priests, or deacons, in that form, are not lawfully made, nor ought to be accounted, either by themselves or others, to be truly bishops, priests, or deacons, until they have some other calling to those divine offices", are excommunicated *ipso facto*.[9] Puritans who maintain "that the form of God's worship

---

[1] *S.P. Dom., Jas. I*, 14, Vol. XLVIII, no. 86. 5 October 1609.
[2] Canon 1. Cf. Article 37 in the Thirty-Nine Articles.
[3] Canon 3.   [4] Canon 5.   [5] Canon 6.
[6] Canon 7. Cf. Article 8 of Archdeacon King's *Visitation Articles for the Archdeaconry of Nottingham*, 1599. (Printed, W. P. M. Kennedy, *Elizabethan Episcopal Administration*, 1924, Vol. III, p. 319.)
[7] Canon 2.
[8] Canon 3. Cf. Article 10 of Archbishop Whitgift's *Visitation Articles for the Deanery of Shoreham*, 1597.
[9] Canon 8.

in the Church of England, established by law, and contained in the book of Common Prayer and Administration of Sacraments, is a corrupt, superstitious, or unlawful worship of God, or containeth any thing in it that is repugnant to the scriptures",[1] are also censured. Those Puritans who affirm that "the nine and thirty Articles" are in parts superstitious and erroneous, and such as they cannot "with a good conscience subscribe unto",[2] are also condemned.

> Whosoever shall hereafter affirm, That the rites and ceremonies of the Church of England by law established are wicked, antichristian, or superstitious, or such as, being commanded by lawful authority, men, who are zealously and godly affected, may not with any good conscience approve them, use them, or, as occasion requireth, subscribe unto them; let him be excommunicated *ipso facto*. . . .[3]

Those Puritans who

> separate themselves from the communion of saints, as it is approved by the apostles' rules, in the Church of England, and combine themselves together in a new brotherhood, accounting the Christians, who are conformable to the doctrine, government, rites and ceremonies of the Church of England, to be profane, and unmeet for them to join with in Christian profession

are to be excommunicated,[4] together with the authors of schism and the maintainers of schismatics:

> whosoever shall hereafter affirm, that such ministers as refuse to subscribe to the form and manner of God's worship in the Church of England, prescribed in the Communion Book, and their adherents, may truly take unto them the name of another church not established by law, and dare presume to publish it, That this their pretended church hath of long time groaned under the burden of certain grievances imposed upon it, and upon the members thereof before mentioned, by the Church of England, and the orders and constitutions therein by law established; let them be excommunicated. . . .[5]

[1] Canon 4. Cf. Article 7 of Whitgift's *Visitation Articles for Salisbury Diocese*, 1589. (Printed, W. P. M. Kennedy, op. cit., Vol. III, p. 238.)

[2] Canon 5.

[3] Canon 6. Cf. Article 20 of Bishop Bancroft's *Visitation Articles for the London Diocese*, 1601. (Printed, W. P. M. Kennedy, op. cit., Vol. III, p. 340.)

[4] Canon 9. Cf. Article 23 of Whitgift's *Visitation Articles for the Deanery of Shoreham in the Rochester Diocese*, 1597.

[5] Canon 10.

7

Two canons prohibit the establishment and secret practice of the Genevan discipline or the foundation of separatist conventicles:

> Whosoever shall hereafter affirm or maintain, That there are within this realm other meetings, assemblies, or congregations of the king's born subjects, than such as by the laws of this land are held and allowed, which may rightly challenge to themselves the name of true and lawful churches; let him be excommunicated. . . .

> Whoever shall hereafter affirm, That it is lawful for any sort of ministers and lay-parsons, or of either of them, to join together, and make rules, orders, or constitutions in causes ecclesiastical, without the king's authority, and shall submit themselves to be ruled and governed by them: let them be excommunicated. . . .[1]

Other canons lay emphasis upon the due and right administration of the sacraments and the services of the Church.[2] That subject of vexatious controversy, the surplice, is prescribed for "every minister saying the public prayers, or ministering the sacraments, or other rites of the church". "Every minister", so the canon reads, "shall wear a decent and comely surplice with sleeves, to be provided at the charge of the parish."[3] At the Hampton Court Conference the Puritan representatives "made a petition to be exempted from the superstitious surplice, in regard of the weakness of many Consciences, which thereby were dryven from their functions".[4] It was a perennial subject of querulous complaint: a few were even prepared to lose their livings rather than wear it.[5] Objections were sometimes raised on the ground of decency,[6] although the canon provides that "if any question arise touching the matter, decency, or comeliness thereof, the same shall be decided by the discretion of the ordinary". It is laid down that the Holy Communion in cathedral churches is to be administered upon principal feast days, "the principal minister using a decent cope, and being assisted with the gospeller and epistler agreeably, according to the advertisements

---

[1] Canons 11–12. Cf. Article 8 of Archdeacon King's *Visitation Articles for the Archdeaconry of Nottingham*, 1559.

[2] Canons 13–36.

[3] Canon 58. Cf. Whitgift's *Visitation Articles for the Deanery of Shoreham in the Diocese of Rochester*, 1597, no. 2: ". . . whether you have a decent and comely surplice and whether your minister useth ordinarily to wear the same in time of Divine Service or no . . . ?"

[4] *Additional MSS.*, 38,492, f. 81.

[5] E.g., Alexander Cooke, Vicar of Louth in the diocese of Lincoln.

[6] E.g., Christopher Dynys, Vicar of Calceby in the diocese of Lincoln.

published anno 7 Eliz.";[1] and, during other services, when there is no communion, all deans, masters, and heads of collegiate churches, canons and prebendaries, are to wear "daily . . . their surplices" and hoods.[2]

Some objection was taken to kneeling for the reception of the Sacrament in the service of Holy Communion on the ground that it encouraged idolatry. Under pressure from John Knox, the Black Rubric had been inserted at the last moment in the Prayer Book of 1552, by order of the Privy Council and without parliamentary sanction; the Rubric explaining that kneeling did not mean "that any adoration is done, or oughte to bee doone, eyther unto the Sacramentall bread or wyne there bodily receyued, or unto anye reall and essencial presence there beeying of Christ's naturall fleshe and bloude". This cautious qualification was omitted from the Prayer Book of 1559, on the ground that it had never received statutory authorization. It was restored at the request of the Presbyterian divines at the Savoy Conference in 1660, but then with an important modification, the words "corporal presence" being substituted for "reall and essencial presence". The absence of any rubrical statement in the Prayer Book of 1604 led some to argue that the act of kneeling implied idolatry and adoration;[3] and, as a result, some ministers adopted the practice of administering the Holy Communion to the congregation either sitting or standing.[4] An endeavour is made to curb liturgical innovations by stipulating that

> no minister, when he celebrateth the communion, shall wittingly administer the same to any but to such as kneel, under pain of suspension . . . nor to any that are common and notorious depravers of the book of Common Prayer and Administration of the Sacraments, and of the orders, rites, and ceremonies therein prescribed.[5]

[1] Canon 24.   [2] Canon 25.

[3] E.g., W. Bradshaw, *A Proposition on Concerning Kneeling in the very act of receiuing*, 1605; S. Hieron, *A Dispute upon the Question of Kneeling in the Acte of Receiving the Sacramentall bread and wine, proving it to be unlawfull. Or a Third Parte of the Defence of the Ministers Reasons for refusall of the Subscription and Conformitie requyred*, 1608.

[4] E.g., Thurlaston, Little Marlow, Fenny Drayton, in the diocese of Lincoln.

[5] Canon 27. Cf. Bancroft's *Visitation Articles for the Diocese of London*, 1601, no 16. "Whether doth your parson, vicar, or curate administer the Holy Communion unto any communicants which do not receive the same devoutly and humbly kneeling upon their knees; or whether doth he administer it confusedly to some kneeling, and to some either sitting, or standing, or walking?"

Again, the canons discourage the migration of people from one parish to another (the besetting sin of the evangelically minded), and churchwardens are to mark strangers who "come often and commonly from other parishes to their own church", and are "to remit such home to their own parish-churches and ministers, there to receive the communion with the rest of their own neighbours".[1]

Two canons regulate the administration of the Sacrament of Holy Baptism. Many Puritans objected to the institution of godparents as an unbiblical abdication of parental responsibility. Canon 29 deals with this point, ordaining that "no parent shall be . . . admitted to answer as godfather for his own child; nor any godfather or godmother shall be suffered to make any other such answer or speech, than by the Book of Common Prayer is prescribed in that behalf".[2]

Another subject of Puritan complaint was the ministry of "dumb dogs" who could not preach. Many Puritans had conscientious scruples about receiving the sacraments at the hands of such men and objected to the administration of the sacraments apart from the ministry of the Word.[3] The canon affirms that the efficacy of the sacraments is not dependent upon the minister's possession of preaching gifts, thereby ignoring the theological principle that the sign without the word is dumb:

> Whereas divers persons, seduced by false teachers, do refuse to have their children baptised by a minister that is no preacher, and to receive the holy communion at his hands in the same respect, as though the virtue of those sacraments did depend upon his ability to preach . . . we do require and charge every such person, seduced as is aforesaid, to reform that their wilfulness, and to submit himself to the order of the church in that behalf; both the said sacraments being equally effectual, whether they be ministered by a minister that is no preacher, or by one that is a preacher.[4]

---

[1] Canon 28. Cf. Ibid., nos. 15 and 49.

[2] Cf. Ibid., no. 4: "Whether doth your parson . . . baptise any without godfathers and godmothers . . . ?"

[3] Cf. Ibid., no. 49: "Whether any do refuse to receive the Holy Communion at their own minister's hands . . . because he is not a preacher . . . and who they be that do go from their own parish to receive at any other minister's hands?"

[4] Canon 57.

Canon 36 lays down the requirement of subscription, on the part of all occupying an ecclesiastical office, to the *Three Articles*.

> No person shall hereafter be received into the ministry, nor either by institution or collation to any ecclesiastical living, nor suffered to preach, to catechise, or to be a lecturer or reader of divinity in either university, or in any cathedral or collegiate church, city, or market-town, parish-church, chapel, or in any other place within this realm, except he be licensed either by the archbishop, or by the bishop of the diocese, where he is to be placed, under their hands and seals, or by one of the two universities under their seal likewise; and except he shall first subscribe to these three articles following, in such manner and sort as we have here appointed.

The *Three Articles* were based, with slight verbal alterations, on those issued by Whitgift in 1583. There was, however, one important modification: in the third Article subscription is now explicitly required to "all and every the Articles . . . being in number nine and thirty", instead of, as before, a general subscription to "all the articles". The concluding clause is carefully worded to exclude the possibility of casuistical equivocation or evasion:

> To these three articles whosoever will subscribe, he shall, for the avoiding of all ambiguities, subscribe in this order and form of words, setting down both his Christian and surname, viz. "I *N.N.* do willingly and *ex animo* subscribe to these three articles above mentioned, and to all things that are contained in them."

This canon, with its requirement of subscription "willingly and *ex animo*",[1] was bitterly resented.[2] Many, who had subscribed previously, refused to subscribe again, and others, who were prepared to conform and wear the surplice, were not prepared to subscribe in these terms.[3] The canon makes subscription a necessary requirement for the exercise of any ecclesiastical office: no one

---

[1] The same form of subscription was required to the *Three Articles* of 1583. In the archdeaconry of Buckingham in the diocese of Lincoln in 1584 most of the clergy subscribed: "Ego . . . ex animo subscribo", but David Powell wrote: "Ego David Powell rector de Foscot hiis articulis consentio et quaecunnque contra hos articulos noscci temporis scismatici scripserunt at docuerunt horreo et abominor"! C. W. Foster, op. cit., pp. 47 ff.

[2] *Rawlinson MSS.*, D.1, 352, f. 1.

[3] E.g., John Burgess in the diocese of Lincoln.

coming to reside in any diocese, shall be permitted there to preach, read, lecture, catechize, or minister the sacraments or to execute any other ecclesiastical function, by what authority soever he be thereunto admitted, unless he first consent and subscribe to the three articles before mentioned. . . .[1]

And

if any minister, after he hath once subscribed to the said three articles, shall omit to use the form of prayer, or any of the orders or ceremonies prescribed in the Communion Book, he shall be suspended and if obstinate, excommunicated.[2]

Ministers who, having been licensed, refuse to conform themselves to the laws, ordinances, and ecclesiastical rites of the Church of England, are to be admonished, and if after such admonition they do not conform themselves within the space of one month, their licenses are to be void and of none effect.[3]

In practice, it was not found possible to enforce these stringent requirements, and there are several cases of men who never conformed and yet who continued in the exercise of their ministry.[4] It would appear that in the eventuality no one was actually deprived solely for refusing to subscribe to the Articles mentioned in Canon 36. Making virtue of necessity the bishops were compelled to content themselves with only depriving those who refused both to conform and subscribe.[5]

The matter of pluralities was a subject calling for remedy and reform. The prevalence of pluralism was a cause of much scandal, and a frequent cause of just complaint. The official answer was that pluralism was part and parcel of the problem of ecclesiastical incomes, for (so the argument ran) the latter were so small that learned men could only be rewarded by the gift of several livings. The Puritans attributed to cupidity what the bishops attributed to embarrassing necessity. In an endeavour to limit the abuse the canons decree that

---

[1] Canon 37.
[2] Canon 38.
[3] Canon 54.
[4] E.g., Simon Bradstreet, Vicar of Horbling; John Jackson, Vicar of Bourne; Hugh Tuke, Rector of Silk Willoughby; Thomas Cotton, Rector of Laughton; John More, Rector of Knaptoft; etc., in the diocese of Lincoln. See, C. W. Foster, *The State of the Church*, pp. lxxiii–iv.
[5] See Bancroft's letter to the bishops, 22 December 1604.

no license or dispensation for the keeping of more benefices with cure than one, shall be granted to any but such only as shall be thought very well worthy for his learning, and very well able and sufficient to discharge his duty; that is, who shall have taken the degree of master of arts at the least in one of the universities of this realm, and be a public and sufficient preacher licensed.

The practice of pluralism is restricted to the learned. Other safeguards are included:

provided always, that he be by a good and sufficient caution bound to make his personal residence in each his said benefices for some reasonable time in every year; and that the said benefices be not more than thirty miles distant asunder; and lastly that he have under him in the benefice, where he doth not reside, a preacher lawfully allowed, that is able sufficiently to teach and instruct the people.[1]

Residence is enjoined upon deans[2] and prebendaries[3] in their churches, and both deans and prebendaries are to preach during their residence.[4] Unlicensed men are strictly forbidden to preach:

no person whatsoever not examined and approved by the bishop of the diocese, or not licensed . . . for a sufficient or convenient preacher, shall take upon him to expound in his own cure, or elsewhere, any scripture or matter of doctrine; but shall only study to read plainly and aptly (without glossing or adding) the homilies already set forth. . . .[5]

There are additional precautions. It is stipulated that "neither the minister, church-wardens, nor any other officers of the church, shall suffer any man to preach within their churches or chapels, but such as, by shewing their license to preach, shall appear unto them to be sufficiently authorized thereunto";[6] and furthermore, the names of strange preachers are to be noted in a book, "wherein every preacher shall subscribe his name, the day when he preached, and the name of the bishop of whom he had license to preach".[7] There is to be no public opposition between preachers,

[1] Canon 41. [2] Canon 42. [3] Canon 44.
[4] Canon 43. [5] Canon 49.
[6] Canon 50. Cf. Bishop Whitgift's (?) *Articles for the Worcester Diocese*, 1577 (?), no. 9: "Whether any minister take upon him not licensed to preach or expound the Scriptures. . . . ?"
[7] Canon 52.

"because upon such public dissenting and contradicting, there may grow much offence and disquietness unto the people".[1]

Certain directions concerning preaching, subsequent and supplementary to the canons, were issued under royal authority:

> Noe parson, vicar, curatt, lecturer, shall preach any sermon or collation hereafter, upon Sondayes and holydaies in the afternoone, in any cathedrall or parish church throughout the kingdome, but upon some part of catechisme, or some text taken out of the Creed, Ten Commandmentes, or the Lordes Prayer (funerall sermons onely excepted), and that those preachers be most incoraged and approved of whoe spend these afternoone exercises in the examining of children in their catechisme, and in expounding of the severall points and heads of the catechisme, which is the most ancient and laudable custome of teachinge in the Church of England.

The difficult doctrines of Calvinism are to be handled "tenderly":

> Noe preacher, of what tytle soever, under the degree of a bishop, or a deane, at the least, doe, from henceforth, presume to preach in any popular audience the deepe points of predestination, election, reprobation, or of the universality, efficacity [sic], resistability or irresistability of God's grace, but leave those thames to be handled by the learned men, and that moderatly and modestly by way of use and application, rather then by way of positive doctrine, as being [more] fitted for the schooles and universities then for simple auditors.

In view of the exalted conceptions which prevailed concerning the rôle of the godly prince, it is not surprising to find that preachers are forbidden "to declare, limitt, or bound out, any way of possitive doctrine, in any lecture or sermon, the power of prerogative jurisdiction, authority, or duty of soveraigne princes". Violent and immoderate attacks on sectaries are forbidden as needlessly provoking opposition and dissension:

> Noe preacher, of what title or denomination soever, shall causelessly and without invitation from the text, fall into bitter invectives and undesent raling speeches against the persons of either papists or puritanes, but modestly and gravely, when they are occasioned thereunto, by text of scripture, free both the doctrine and discipline of the Church of England from the aspersions of either adversarie,

[1] Canon 53.

especiallie where the auditorie is suspected to be tainted with the one or the other infection.[1]

Consequently, bishops are to be "more wary and choise in lycencing of preachers".

It was a well-known Puritan device to evade the practice of a compromising conformity by providing a curate to read the prescribed forms of service: this loophole was now closed:

> every minister, being possessed of a benefice that hath cure and charge of souls, although he chiefly attend to preaching, and hath a curate under him to execute the other duties which are to be performed for him in the church . . . shall twice at the least every year read himself the divine service upon two several Sundays publicly, and at the usual times, both in the forenoon and afternoon, in the church which he so possesseth, or where he readeth, catechizeth, or preacheth . . . and shall likewise as often in every year administer the sacraments of baptism, if there be any to be baptized, and of the Lord's Supper, in such manner and form and with the observation of all such rites and ceremonies as are prescribed by the Book of Common Prayer in that behalf.[2]

There is to be no secret and clandestine practice of Puritanism in the convenient obscurity of private houses: "no minister shall preach, or administer the holy communion, in any private house, except it be in times of necessity. . . . Provided, that houses are here reputed for private houses, wherein are no chapels dedicated and allowed by the ecclesiastical laws of this realm."[3] The canons rigorously proscribe every potential avenue for either the practice or propagation of Puritanism. Exercises are forbidden:

> No minister or ministers shall, without the license and direction of the bishop of the diocese first obtained and had under his hand and seal, appoint or keep any solemn fasts, either publicly or in any private houses, other than such as by law are, or by public authority shall be appointed . . . Neither shall any minister not licensed, as is aforesaid, presume to appoint or hold any meetings for sermons, commonly termed by some prophecies or exercises, in market-towns or other places. . . .[4]

[1] *MSS.* of *Lord Kenyon*, no. 13. H.M.C., Fourteenth Report, Appendix, Part IV, pp. 519.
[2] Canon 56.   [3] Canon 71.
[4] Canon 72. Cf. Archbishop Whitgift's *Articles for the Chichester Diocese* (*sede vacante*), 1585, no. 2: ". . . whether doth he or any other keep any exercise of expounding, or read any lecture in private houses whereunto other besides those of that family resort?"

Private conventicles and secret meetings are strictly forbidden:

> Forasmuch as all conventicles, and secret meetings of priests and ministers, have been ever justly accounted very hurtful to the state of the church wherein they live; we do now ordain and constitute, that no priests, or ministers of the word of God, or any other persons, shall meet together in any private house, or elsewhere, to consult upon any matter or course to be taken by them, or upon their motion or direction by any other, which may any way tend to the impeaching or depraving of the doctrine of the Church of England, or of the book of Common Prayer, or of any part of the government and discipline now established in the Church of England under pain of excommunication *ipso facto*.[1]

Other canons deal with such routine matters as "things appertaining to churches". Every church is to have the great Bible, and "the Book of Common Prayer, lately explained in some few points by his majesty's authority . . . and that with all convenient speed, but at the furthest within two months after the publishing of these Constitutions".[2] The substitution of basins for fonts is forbidden. A former constitution[3] about the provision of a font of stone in each church has been "too much neglected in many places": Canon 81 requires "that there shall be a font of stone in every church and chapel where baptism is to be ministered; the same to be set in the ancient usual places".[4] The position of the Holy Table is also defined. The *Injunctions* of 1559 required

---

[1] Canon 78. For an earlier reference to Puritan conventicles, see Bishop Aylmer's *Articles for the Diocese of London*, 1577, no. 55: "Whether any new presbytery or eldership be lately among you erected; and by them any ministers appointed with [*sic*] orders taking of the bishop, do baptise, minister the communion or deal in any function ecclesiastical, or gather any private conventicles whereby the people be drawn from the church?" For an earlier reference to papist conventicles, see Bishop Chaderton's *Articles for the Diocese of Chester*, 1580, no. 11: "Whether your parson, vicar, or curate, or any other within your parish be a favourer of the Roman Church or religion: . . . tending to the discredit and dispraise either of the Book of Common Prayer . . .: and whether they keep any secret conventicles, preachings, lectures or readings or private communions contrary to the law, and what be their names?"

[2] Canon 80.

[3] Probably a reference to Article 5, section 3, of the Canons of 1571.

[4] Cf. the many questions on this point in the *Visitation Articles*. E.g., Bishop Bancroft's *Articles for the Diocese of London*, 1601, no. 18: "Whether doth your parson, vicar, or curate, or any other minister or preacher baptize in your parish church or chapel any infants not in the font according to ancient custom, but in a basin . . . ?"

that the holy table in every church be decently made, and set in the place, where the altar stood, and there commonly covered, as thereto belongeth, and as shall be appointed by the visitors, and so to stand, saving when the communion of the sacrament is to be distributed; at which time the same shall be so placed in good sort within the chancel, as whereby the minister may be more conveniently heard of the communicants in his prayer and ministration, and the communicants also more conveniently, and in more number communicate with the said minister. And after the communion done, from time to time the same holy table to be placed where it stood before.[1]

The same requirement is laid down in Canon 82.

The final canons attempt to silence criticism by declaring, first of all, that a national synod is representative of the Church, and by threatening with the censure of excommunication any who affirm "that the sacred synod of this nation, in the name of Christ and by the king's authority assembled, is not the true Church of England by representation".[2] The Synod's decisions are declared to be binding on all clergy and laity, and not simply on those present:

> Whosoever shall affirm, that no manner of person, either of the clergy or laity, not being themselves particularly assembled in the said sacred synod, are to be subject to the decrees thereof in causes ecclesiastical, (made and ratified by the king's majesty's supreme authority) as not having given their voices unto them, let him be excommunicated, and not restored until he repent, and publicly revoke that his wicked error.[3]

Those who deprave the Synod by affirming that it is "a company of such persons as did conspire together against godly and religious professors of the gospel; and that therefore both they and their proceedings in making of canons and constitutions in causes ecclesiastical . . . ought to be despised and contemned",[4] are also solemnly threatened.

---

[1] E. Cardwell, *Documentary Annals*, Vol. I, p. 202. Cf. Bishop Middleton's *Injunctions for the Diocese of St David's*, 1583, no. 6: "When there is a communion to be ministered, that the Communion table be placed in the lower end of the chancel, as near unto the people as may be convenient, and when the ministration is done, remove it to the upper end of the said chancel."
[2] Canon 139.
[3] Canon 140.
[4] Canon 141.

On 6 September 1604, the royal confirmation was given to the book of canons,[1] the King declaring that he had "diligently with greate contentment and comfort read and considered of all theis theire saide Cannons", and that he found "the same such as wee are perswaded will be verie profitable not onlye to our Clergie but to the whole Churche of this our Kingdome, and to all the true members of it". He gladly gave them his royal assent: "Wee . . . have therefore, for us our heires and lawfull successors of our especiall grace certaine knowledge and mere motion given and by these presentes doe give our Royall assent according to the forme of the saide Statutes or Acte of Parliamente afore saide to all and euerye of the saide Cannons", and commanded that they be "diligentlye observed executed and equalie kepte by all our lovinge subiectes of this our Kingdome bothe within the province of Canterbury and Yorke." The clergy were to read the canons once a year on some Sunday or Holy Day in the afternoon before divine service, and every parish was to possess a copy of the book of canons "betwixte this and the feast of the Nativitie of our Lorde God nexte ensewinge". The archbishops, and others exercising ecclesiastical authority, were to enforce the strict observance of all canons, "not sparinge to execute the penalties in them seuerallie mentioned uppon anye that shall wittinglye or wilfullie breake or neglect to obserue the same".[2]

Little is known about the authorship of the canons themselves, although Usher surmises that three ecclesiastical lawyers, John Cowell, Sir Thomas Ridley, and Sir Edward Stanhope were Bancroft's assistants.[3] There is a rough list of twenty-one articles extant in the British Museum, endorsed, "Artickells agreed one by ye convocatione House, 1604",[4] clearly an early draft.[5]

This body of one hundred and forty-one canons enormously

[1] *Constitutiones sive Canones Ecclesiastici, per Episcopum Londinensum, Praesidem Synodi pro Cantuariensi Provincia, ac reliquos Episcopos, et Clerum ejusdem Provinciae, ex Regia Authoritate tractati, et conclusi. In ipsorum Synodo inchoata Londini, anno salutis millesimo, sexcentesimo tertio, regnique Serenissimi Principis, Clementissimi Domi nostri Jacobi, Dei gratia Angliae, Franciae, et Hiberniae Regis primo et Scotiae tricesimo septimo.* A copy of the original edition is extant in Lambeth Palace Library.

[2] *Patent Roll*, 2 Jas. I, Part V, 6 September 1604.

[3] R. G. Usher, *Reconstruction*, Vol. I, p. 345.

[4] *Additional MSS.*, 29,546, f. 77.

[5] Printed Appendix 1, below, p. 379.

strengthened the administrative machinery of the Church. At long last the unco-ordinated and diverse injunctions, interpretations, advertisements, orders, and articles, of the previous forty-five years,[1] were incorporated into a complete and coherent codification.[2] Furthermore, the bishops were now armed with a comprehensive and consistent code in relation to ecclesiastical discipline and the achievement of conformity.

In the House of Commons the canons were viewed with critical disapproval. A petition referred to

> sundrie great wronges, greevances, and oppressions, of late years committed by the Clergie, their Officers and Ministers, agaynst the Kings people and free men of the Realme, contraire to the good Lawes, statutes, and free Customes of the Realme: of all which the [people] of the Realme, assembled by the Kings writt in Parliament, in the name of all the Commons, most humblie praie remedie, of your Kings most excellent Majestie. . . .

The petitioners protested that the canons were illegal, being opposed to statute law:

> The Lords Bishopps and Prelates in the late convocation . . . in the late Synod begunne at London, 1603, did decree and publishe sundrie Canons and constitutions ecclesiasticall, in preiudice and impeachment . . . of the lawes, statuts, and free customes of the realme. And therfore the Commons most humblie praie the King, that the said canons, and constitutions, by the Lawes and statuts of the realm, being void canons, by the authoritie of this Parliament, maie be commanded, never hereafter, to be put in execution, vpon

---

[1] "The code of 1603, as it is usually called, consisted of one hundred and forty-one canons, of which ninety-seven were adaptations of previous canons, orders, and injunctions. Most of the canons which were actually new were those regulating and reforming the procedure in the ecclesiastical courts. Of the canons which were based on previous pieces of legislation, twelve were taken from the Injunctions of Edward VI, twenty-five from the Royal Injunctions of 1559, twenty-five from the Canons of 1571, and twelve from Archbishop Parker's *Advertisements*. The new code also incorporated the Canons of 1597. Although much of the material used in the compilation of the code was of sixteenth-century origin, the actual law contained in it is often only a re-enactment and adaptation of the provincial constitutions of the middle ages." *The Canon Law of the Church of England*, London, 1947, p. 73.

[2] Cf. "Observacions upon ye Ecclesiasticall Injunctions of 1 Elizabeth both how farr forth ye same are revived by the Canons made 1 Jacobi, as also which of ye said Injunctions may now be thought unfitt to be revived, though fitt for that time of ye Reformacion had 1 Elizabeth." *Rawlinson MSS.*, A.127, f. 69.

paine that the offenders incurre the penaltie appointed in the statute, 23 K. Ed. 3.[1]

The Act for the Submission of the Clergy (25 Henry VIII, c. 19), laid it down that no canon might be enacted contrary or repugnant to the laws, statutes, and customs of the realm. Consequently, "the Cannoniste cannot judge what is against the lawes, Statutes, and Customes of the Realme, but that Appertayneth to the Judges of the Law; therefore the Cannoniste ought not to interpret Statute".[2] It was for the common law judges to decide what was, and what was not, within the jurisdiction of the ecclesiastical judges: "It appeareth by the statute of 27 H. VIII, cap. 15, that though Cannons be made by the whole Convocation, and by the royall assent, yet if they be contrary or repugnant to the lawes or Customes of the Realme they be of noe force to bynde the subiecte."[3] The petitioners complained that Convocation had legislated in things affecting the laity, which should have been left to the temporal power: "The Commons complayne, that the said Synode, by force and virtue of thir speciall power, hath devised and decreed, certayne new and needlesse oathes, bonds and securities, to be made and taken by the laietie." These new oaths and securities should "onelie haue bin commaunded and enacted by the Kings temporall power, with the consent of his Lords and commons in parliament".[4] This argument was used again in a series of "Articles put up by the Commons A. 3 James 1, for the Reformation of certain abuses in the ecclesiastical State and Court". The claim was made that "the free men of the realme are not bound to obey any cannons, constitutions, or ordinances, made by the Clergie of the realme, in any of their convocations, vnlesse afterwards the said Canons be confirmed by authoritie of parliament".[5]

A draft Bill was also drawn up by the House of Commons entitled: "An Act for the due observation of the Great Charter of England". All the key canons of the late Convocation, including the canon requiring subscription to the *Three Articles*, were

---

[1] *Cotton MSS., Cleopatra*, F.11, f. 191.
[2] *Lansdowne MSS.*, 161, f. 254.
[3] Ibid.
[4] *Cotton MSS., Cleopatra*, F.11, f. 191.
[5] Ibid., f. 194.

declared invalid and void of effect.[1] The Bill declared that they
"conteyned many things which ar by experience since found to
be either hurtefull to your Majesties prerogatiue roiall, onrous to
your people, and contrariant and repugnant to the said great
charter": and enacted that

> everie matter, clause, and section conteyned in them, or any of them,
> shall from hence forth be vtterlie void, frustrate, and of no effect
> in lawe, to all intents, constructions, and purposes whatsoever ...
> and that all and singular processes, sentences, iudgements, and
> executions, of admonition, suspension, excommunication, inter-
> diction, deprivation, deposition, or degradation, had, made, giuen,
> or obtayned, agaynst any of the Kings people for violating, resisting,
> breaking, or not conforming, him or them selues, to all or any of the
> constitutions and canons aforesaid ... shalbe from henceforth
> vtterlie void.[2]

In the House of Lords "An Act restraining the executing of
canons ecclesiastical not confirmed by Parliament", was read
and engrossed. No canon, constitution, or ecclesiastical ordinance,
made within the previous ten years, or hereafter to be made, was
to have any force unless confirmed by Act of Parliament; and
any person executing any canon not so confirmed, was to incur
the dread penalties of *praemunire*. This Bill was actually read twice
in the House of Lords before being stopped.[3]

In pamphlets and tracts the legality of the canons was hotly
debated. The Puritans were under no illusions concerning their
sinister purpose:

> Sundry Canons seem to be made, quite on purpose to displace, and
> keep out such painful and godly Ministers, as make scruple of the
> Ceremonies, reviving, and pressing such Ceremonies, as by Disuse
> were almost buried; and for which her Majesty promised in the
> 14th of her Reign, that no Minister should be molested.[4]

Neither were they unmindful of their illegality: "We may safly
affirme, concernying many of the said late Canons, that they be

---

[1] The Canons were nos. 36, 37, 49, 53, 58, 62, 63, 67, 77, 80, 90, 97, 98,
101, 107, 115, 127, 130, 131, 135, 139, and 140.
[2] *Cotton MSS., Cleopatra*, F.11, f. 193.
[3] H. of L., Supplementary Calendar. *Lords' Journal*, Vol. II, pp. 425, 429,
6 May 1606. H.M.C., Appendix to the Fourth Report, p. 118.
[4] *Harleian MSS.*, 158, f. 183 b.

not to be put into execution within the Realme, unless they shall be confirmed by Act of Parliament."[1] In these circumstances

no loyall and honest subject [may] heereupon inferr, that his majestie intended by the generall wordes of his confirmation to authorize any particular matter, devised and decreed, by the Synod, contrary to the holy scriptures, hurtfull to the rights, prerogatives, and dignities of his Highnes Crown, repugnant to any lawes, statutes, or customes of the Realme, prejudiciall to his Lords and Commons in Parliament, or onerous to his people.

Since

sondry of the late Canons . . . tend to the blemishing of the liberty and franchise of the Kings will, grace, and power . . . it is a playne case, that every of the Kings liege and faithful subjects, ought to defend the Kings right, Honor, and dignity, against all such Canons.[2]

Despite the protests of parliamentarians and Puritan pamphleteers, however, the bishops proceeded forthwith to enforce the law of the Church as newly codified in the canons.

[1] This was the judgement of Lord Hardwicke, Chief Justice of the King's Bench, in *Middleton v. Crofts* (1736). Hardwicke's judgement was confirmed by the House of Lords in the case of the Bishop of *Exeter v. Marshall* (1868). Lord Hardwicke stated: "We are all of opinion that the Canons of 1603, not having been confirmed by Parliament, do not *proprio vigore* bind the laity; I say *proprio vigore*, by their own force and authority; for there are many provisions contained in these canons, which are declaratory of ancient usage and law of the Church of England, received and allowed here, which, in that respect, and by virtue of such ancient allowance, will bind the laity; but that is an obligation antecedent to, and not arising from this body of canons." Quoted, *The Canon Law of the Church of England*, pp. 76–7.

[2] *A Myld and Iust Defence of Certeyne Argvments, at the Last Session of Parliament directed to that most Honorable High Court, in behalfe of the Ministers suspended and deprived, etc.: for not Subscribing and Conforming themselues, etc. . . . .*, 1606, p. 118.

4

THE ENFORCEMENT OF THE CANONS

A ROYAL proclamation, dated 16 July 1604, stated that the Hampton Court Conference had shown no sufficient reason for any major alteration in the liturgy or government of the Church. Consequently, nothing was to be gained by further agitation. What was now required was conformity.

> We have thought good once again to give notice thereof to all our subjects by public declaration ... there appeareth no cause, why the form of the service of God, wherein they have been nourished so many years, should be changed; and consequently, to admonish them all in general to conform themselves thereunto, without listening to the troublesome spirits of some persons, who never receive contentment either in civil or in ecclesiastical matters, but in their own fantasies, especially of certain ministers, who under pretended zeal for reformation, are the chief authors of divisions and sects among our people. ... Our duty towards God requireth at our hands, that what untractable men do not perform upon admonition, they must be compelled unto by authority ... We have thought good to give time to all ministers disobedient to the orders of the church, and to ecclesiastical authority here by law established ... until the last day of November next ensuing, to bethink themselves of the course they will hold therein.[1]

There was much anxious consultation. A document entitled, "Directions to avoyde the proceedinges of the byshopps", was prepared. It was agreed that "if the Busshopps

proceed against any they must do it, ether

(quatūs)   they are Busshops.

or by vertue of the Commission."

There was much debate concerning the legal power of the bishops in relation to coercion. Admittedly "to send out processes to cite men and to sitt in Iudgment is a principall parte of the Judgment

[1] *S.P. Dom., Jas. I*, 14, Vol. LXXIII; *Proclamation Book*, p. 76; *Additional MSS.*, 38,139, f. 70 b. Printed, G. W. Prothero, *Select Statutes and Documents*, p. 420; D. Wilkins, *Concilia*, Vol. IV, p. 406; E. Cardwell, *Documentary Annals*, Vol. II, p. 60.

ecclesiastical", but "this being by statute 1 Elizabeth: annexed to the crowne, is an especiall prerogative Regall", and (so the argument ran) "doth leue the Busshop such priuiledges onely as are not preiudiciall, to the prerogative Royall or to the lawes and statutes of the realme". The urgent question was: "what Authoritie is then left to the Busshops?"

> If any be cited, they may appeare to avoyde occasion of sclander, but they are in open place to protest that sith all iurisdiction is in the Kinge, and that by their oathe to the supremacy they are bounde to acknowledge noe authoritie but that which is derived from his Majestie, that therefore they doe not appeare as of dutie, nether acknowledge the Busshopps authoritie or Iurisdiction in ecclesiastical causes, unlesse he haue sufficient warrant from his Majestie under the broade seale accordinge to the statute 1º Elizabeth Cap. 1.º

It was simply a question of legal fact:

> Towchinge the statute (1º Eliz: Cap. 1º) first it ratifieth neither the booke of comon prayer lately corrected, nether the former that was used in all the queenes tym, but only the booke of Ed. 6. with two alterations specified in the statute. Whereas that which hath byn hetherto used hath many alterations, and therefore they cannot proceed against any for the neglect of other of these bookes by vertue of the statute. Secondly, that statute dothe inflicte noe such penaltie for omission or refusall of the vestments or ornamentes of the ministers, and therefore none can be towched in his liuing for the surplesse by the statute, and there is not any other dothe commaund it.

Advice was given in anticipation of the ratification of the Canons.

> As for the Cannons, if they shalbe confirmed and soe the high Commission execute penaltie of them, it wilbe a verie doubtfull poynt whether they can stretche soe farr as to putt a subiect from his freehold, and if men putt it to the triall of the Comon lawe it will seeme a verie hard case, for admitt that the convocation howse may for breach of Church orders dispossesse a minister of his free hold, when not any other subiect, and soe by consequent the whole body of the Realme may (if they transgresse the Church Orders) be putt out of their landes and livinges, and be entralled to the clergy as in tymes past, which gapp will not easily be opened especially since it is graunted of all, that ecclesiasticall lawes doe properly tend only to the spirituall chastisements.

They drew comfort from the fact that

noe Busshopp except he haue a high Commission can with any couller of lawe proceede against a minister. The high Commission cannot inflict any warrantable penaltie for omission of the surplesse or the booke of comon prayer now extant and in use by vertue of the statute. If any be by Busshopp or Commission depriued he may notwithstanding keepe possession of his liuing untill by lawe it be tried whether the Busshopps act can dispossesse him of his freehold.

Detailed instructions followed on "the manner howe to keepe possession":

Lett him prouide that some one, ether wief, child, servaunt, or freind be alwayes in the Church, and in the howse night and day, soe noe other can be inducted. If any offer to thrust or pull him or his out of the Church, lett him not much contend, but being thrust out lett him goe to the Justices neer adjoyning, and deposing before them that he was thrust out of possession, they must of course lett him in possession agayne. If the Busshopp shall sequester his liuinge, the lawe hath a verie direct remidie to dissolve the sequestration.[1]

These directions, and others of a like character, were widely disseminated. When Melancthon Jewell[2] was arrested at the beginning of December 1604, he was carrying similar directions. Among his papers there was also a questionnaire which had been prepared by some of the Puritans in Exeter, addressed to their legal advisers in London. Their replies appear as marginal notes headed "certaine resolutions ... from certaine Lawyers at London". The questions, with their annotations, are indicative of a resolute determination to use all available legal means to frustrate the disciplinary activities of the bishops.

Not thoughte meete	To use meanes what may bee done by petition to his Majestie either for toleracion untill the bible be translated or to the ende of Parliament.
	What may bee done by appeale not withstanding the Canons.
May appeale	What may be done by prohibicion, either from the Kings Bench, or from the Chauncery or Common place [sic].
Noe.	Wheather the Bishop may proceede with Inhibicion to preache, or suspencion before the tyme that the Kings proclamacion bee ended.

[1] *Additional MSS.*, 28,571, p. 205. N.D.; *Cecil MSS.*, 109, f. 76; H.M.C., Part XVI, pp. 404–5. Printed, R. G. Usher, *Reconstruction*, Vol. II, pp. 362–5.
[2] Melancthon Jewell was in trouble with the High Commissioners for Puritan activity in 1591. J. Strype, *Whitgift*, Vol. III, p. 268.

Gotten.

To gett a Copie of the high Commission out of the Chauncerie.

voyde.

Wheather the Constitutions be not voyde by reason that many of them are against the lawe, customes, and usages, as by the statute 23 Hen. 8. title Roomes Abridgement.

Wheare as it was wont to be obiected that it was dangerous to alter any thinge though from worse to better, and for avoydinge of Innovacion, and yet this is not nowe regarded at all in bringinge in many straunge things, both in ministers and people as in the Canons.

Noe licence voyde before the tyme.

The Bishops maketh Licenses of all preachers, that appeared before and not conformed in apparrell, voyde by the 54th Canon, and inhibits them to preache contrarie to the Kings proclamacion which geives tyme till the laste of November to conforme themselves.

To assist Mr Carpenter for Travers his appeale.[1]

To shew Mr Nicholas Fuller what the Bishop proclaymeth of hime, and to requier his verie beste. ... Wheather the appeale may be beste before sentence or after, and to whome.

They be against lawe and voyde.

Wheather the 77 late Cannon requiringe Schoolmaisters to subscribe to 3 articles be not againste the law and soe voyde, and wheather or no by statute his Licence be not goode to teach, if he come orderly into church.

Wheather all former Licenses to preach be voyde by force of the Canon or wheather the Licence be not stronge which is given to the minister in his ordinacion in theise words viz. goe and preache the gospell. And soe the Canon voyde made againste this lawe.

This is in question.
It is extortion. In both if it may be till he bringe his action.

Wheather it bee extortion to Demaund money of Schoolmaisters for Licenses.

If deprivation be wheather possession may be kept in Church or personage.

---

[1] Another hand has interpolated: "This Carpenter dwellinge by the stockes is the generall agent for the Puritans and heretofore for Snape."

THE ENFORCEMENT OF THE CANONS

	Wheather the 36 Art: or any lawe requier anie ministers to subscribe to the 3 articles, wheather it
It is meete to supplicate.	be not meete to supplicate to the Kinge, that he would requier the Judges to enforme hime, wheather it be not against Lawe that the Bushop requier subscription to the 3 Articles.[1]

A limited period of grace was allowed in the royal proclamation during which period it was hoped that the wavering would conform. Bancroft was ordered to exercise patience. Sir Thomas Lake wrote to Viscount Cranborne 25 November 1604:

This morning his Majesty willed me to write to my Lord of North-ampton to deal with my Lord of Canterbury elect, touching the ministers not conformable: that where his Majesty conceives, so being informed, that many of them are disposed, though not to conform themselves precisely at the day, yet afterward within a month or two: his Majesty thinks fit that in that case where any shall be found of that disposition that will give hope of conformity, though not in the present, all proceeding against him may be for-borne for a month or two; and that if this disposition of theirs be but counterfeited and to win him, they may be the more roundly dealt with afterwards.[2]

In a letter to Bancroft, Cranborne said that the King wished certain ministers "suspended or imprisoned for refusinge sub-scription", to be reasoned with, and to have a time of probation assigned. The King had a shrewd suspicion that "such repugnancy agaynst the established order" was the product "of disobedience rather than of conscience", since they had confessed themselves that the things were indifferent. Cranborne continued:

[the King] hath demanded me to write vnto you privately that you do intymate to all the rest of my Lords the Bishops . . . that they do presently informe themselues of all such persons as stand in those terms within their dyocesses, and to cause them once agayne to appeare before them to see whether by dealinge with them more myldly and discreetly then peradventure some of them officially vsed to doe, they may be made more intelligible of their errour, and if not at the first Instant reformed, yet left some tyme of probation.

[1] *S.P. Dom., Jas. I*, 14, Vol. X.A, no. 81. Endorsed, "The seconde paper found aboute hime. Certaine resolutions brought downe this moneth by Melancthon Jewell from certaine Lawyers at London as he confesseth."
[2] *Cecil MSS.*, 107, f. 148. H.M.C., Part XVI, p. 366.

Severity was to be tempered with discretion:

> His Majestie meaneth you should make distinction of this favour
> betweene those whose lives of learninge and myld condition may
> promise hope of good to follow, and those in whome you observe
> lofty or turbulent humours, for whom punishment is more fitt then
> any other course.[1]

Chaderton, Bishop of Lincoln, at the beginning of the month
of December, wrote to Montagu, Dean of the Chapel Royal,
telling him that he had summoned the thirty nonconforming
ministers of his diocese before him at Huntingdon, but that he had
not proceeded to deprivation, because he had not received any
precise directions from the Archbishop.

> The unconformed ministers of my diocese ... stand all stiff in
> their former resolution ... I thought not good to deprive any of
> them, for I received letters this day from Mr Bullingham, my
> principal register, signifying that his Grace of Canterbury could not
> as yet send any certain direction for my proceedings against them;
> but as soon as they should be resolved upon he would send them,
> neither was there any other Bishop that had as yet censured any of
> the obstinate ministers with sentence of deprivation, neither yet
> with three admonitions, as I have done according to our agreement
> in Convocation, so far as he could learn.

He had therefore given them until

> the 30th day of the same month, *ad audiendam finalem sententiam*,
> hoping that before that time some sound course of proceeding
> against them will be resolved upon by my Lord of Canterbury, or
> the Lords of the Council, taking the opinion of the best lawyers in
> that behalf, and notified to all the Bishops of our Church, that we
> may all join in the execution thereof at one time, without prejudice
> one of another, for it would be a great grief and reproach to us all if
> we should attempt to do that which is not warrantable by law, or
> which being done should be reversed by law.[2]

The Bishop of Lincoln was not left long in a state of uncertainty.
The Council informed the Archbishop that

> the tyme is nowe expired, which by his Majesties late proclamation,
> daited the .16. th. daie of July last, was prescreibed and lymited to

---

[1] *S.P. Dom., Jas. I*, 14, Vol. VI, no. 89. March (?) 1605. (This letter is
wrongly dated in the *Calendar*.)

[2] *Cecil MSS.*, 108, f. 22, 12 December 1604. H.M.C., Part XVI, p. 379.

all those of the cleargie (for the conforming of themsealues unto the lawes and orders of the churche gouerment established within this Realme) that haue heretofore, under a pretended zeale of reformation, but in deed of a factious desire of innovation, refused to yield their obedience and conformitie thereunto; by means whereof, all such as persist in that wilful disobedience are subiecte to the penaltie of deprivation from their Benefices . . . and other Censures of the Churche, not only by any order and constitutions lately made, but by lawes of ancient tyme and by the Canons and Orders of the Church which were as well at all tymes heretofore as presently in vigour and force.[1]

The laws and constitutions were to be enforced for "the redressinge and reforminge of all offensive and scandalous divisions in the Church". This was the more necessary since some of the Puritans had "nourished and flattered their owne disobedience, presuming on a further enlargement of tyme and tolleration, than hath bein granted". A strict conformity was required:

Although yt bee much more agreable to his most gracious mynd and clemencie, to heale and cure suche distemperatures by lenity and gentleness, than by severitie; as hath well appeared by the conferences that his Majestie heretofore hath ordained to be had in his owne presence, by the course of advice and perswasion, as he hath prescreibed to be houlden by those, that are of chiefe place and authoritie in the Churche, and lastly by giuinge tyme and respite, (more than once), unto such persons either misled or unresolved, to conforme themsealues upon better advisement; nevertheless his Majestie is well pleased to have yt knowne that he is farre from alteration of his purpose to work an uniformitie, as they are importunate in their unjust desire of inovation, and expecteth that from henceforth, without delay, where advice prevaileth not, authoritie shall compell, and that the lawes shalbe put in execution, where admonition taketh not effect; the penaltie whereof they that will incurre muste impute it unto their owne obstinacie, being guiltie disobedience to his majestie, of uncharitablenesse unto any cure or of charge that they haue, and in dutifulnesse might holde, and themselues for any greivance or losse that they shall susteyne.[2]

Those instituted in the place of the deprived, were to be learned and capable, for "diuers turbulente persons haue mixed their

---

[1] *Additional MSS.*, 38,139, ff. 103 b. 10 December 1604. *Bancroft's Register*, f. 127 a. *S.P. Dom., Jas. I*, 14, Vol. X.A, no. 61. Quoted, E. Cardwell, *Documentary Annals*, Vol. II, p. 69.
[2] Ibid.

complaints with this affirmation: that the names of good and understandinge ministers shall nowe be supplyed with idle droanes and dumb images".

On 22 December the Archbishop wrote to each bishop enclosing a copy of the Council's letter:

> I doubt not but you will with all care, fayth, and diligence, accomplishe the effects thereof . . . I have furthermore sent you herewith, not without some direction, the manner of such proceedings with the obstinate of the ministery, as I thinke fitt to be generally obserued by your Lordship, and the reste of our bretheren. For it will much further the service committed unto us if we concurre together in that course.

On the same day a further letter was forwarded to each bishop with details of the methods to be adopted: "I haue thought it good to aduertise you of such a course and uniforme kynde of proceedinge with the disobedient and obstinate Ministers, as I thinke fitt to be obserued by my selfe, by your Lordship, and by the rest of my bretheren, the Bishops of this Province." Care was to be taken in future not to license those who refused to subscribe: "your Lordship will strictly obserue the XXXVIIth Canons made the last Convocation, so as none of them be admitted hereafter to execute any ecclesiasticall function without subscription, accordinge to the tenor of the saide Canons." A distinction needed to be made between those who, while willing to conform, hesitated to subscribe, and those who declined either to conform or to subscribe:

> they are of two kynds, and might both of them, hauinge heretofore subscribed be (as Revolters from the same) by an ordinarie course of iustice deposed from the ministerie; the one offereth and promiseth conformitie, but is as yet unwillinge to subscribe. The other in his obstinacie will be induced to yield to neither. Touchinge such as will be contented to obserue the orders and ceremonies prescribed in the Communion booke, and fully to conforme them selues accordinglie in the use of their ministerie: forasmuch as the neere affinitie betweene conformitie and subscription doth giue apparant hope that beinge men of sinceritie, they will in a short tyme frame them selues to a more constant course, and subscribe to that againe, which they by their practise, testify not to be repugnant to the worde of God; your Lordship may (an acte beinge made to remaine uppon recorde of such their offer and promise) respite their subscription

for some tyme: aduertisinge me of the names of euery such person with all conuenient speede, that thereuppon such further order may be taken as shalbe thought expedient in that behalfe.

In the case of the stubborn and the refractory, the bishops were to proceed at once to full deprivation.

Concerninge those that utterly refuse both conformitie and sub-scription: they are either Curates, or stipendiarie Preachers, com-monlie called Lecturers or men beneficed: For the two first, the interest they haue in their places is only by licence from their Ordinarie, and they are no longer to enioie them nisi quamdiu se gene gesserint. So as uppon such their refusall, your Lordship is to suspend them ab officio; which is in effect a deprivation to them, and consequently by the Lawe they are not to bee restored, untill they shall both conforme them selues and subscribe.

The intractable problem was the case of the beneficed clergy who refused to conform:

It would not much trouble them, nor worke the conformitie that is desired to put them to silence, if they might enioy their benefices, because I suppose they haue been heretofore particulerly admonished by your Lordship, but especially by his Maiesties Proclamation dated the 16th of Julie, MDCIV either to conforme them selues to the Church and obey the same, or else to dispose of them selues and their families some other waies as beinge men unfitt for their obstinacie and contempt to occupie such places: they are in an other sorte to be proceeded with: for in refusinge to conforme them selues to the use of the Communion booke, or in derogatinge or deprauinge any thing therein conteined, or anie part thereof, they fall within the compasse of diuers lawes, and particularly of the Statute Primo Elizabethae entituled An Act for Uniformity &c and so are subiect to deprivation.

The bishops had the undoubted legal power to proceed to deprivation: "the Lord Chief Justice, and Mr Attorney generall beinge conferred with, are verie resolute, that you may lawfully, by virtue thereof so proceede ageinst such obstinate persons". The canons must be enforced: "if anie of the saide disordered persons, shall willingly transgresse anye of the first twelue Canons, or of the three last: let the penalty therein mentioned be dulie and respectiuely inflicted uppon them." Bancroft was not acting out of malice or vindictiveness:

I haue not hitherto greatly liked of anie severe course : but perceiuinge by certaine instructions lately caste abroad, that the present opposition so latelie prosecuted, doth rather proceed from a Combination of sundrie factions, who in the pride of their mynde are loth to be foyled (as they terme it) then of anie religious care or true conscience; I haue thought it verie necessarie, for the repressinge of such irregular designements, earnestly to commend to your Lordship the careful execution of theise directions.[1]

The Council, according to the report of the Archbishop, were insistent that the nonconforming clergy were either to "be brought to good conformity or to be orderly removed". They complained

that sundry bishops . . . have stood as men at a gaze, and have done nothing . . . that the duties of their places do require . . . but still permit the froward and undutiful ministers of their dioceses to continue in their obstinate courses, as though they themselves were so obnoxious unto some exceptions that they durst not proceed against them. . . .

The bishops were to see that vacancies resulting from the deprivation of nonconforming ministers were filled by fit and worthy men :

we desire you to acquaint them all with another point of his Majesty's pleasure, which is that when they are deprived from their benefices, their lordships presently take such order with the neighbour preachers that their places may be conveniently by their charitable pains supplied; and that they signify to the patron of every such benefice as shall become void, that his Majesty very earnestly requires him forthwith to present an able and fit man to be admitted unto it, that so the parishioners (of whom his Majesty has a most tender respect) may not long be destitute of a pastor of their own amongst them to instruct them.[2]

The King was sensitive to the charge of vacillation. In a letter written to the Council he denied any real change of policy: although he admitted that he had once thought that verbal subscription was not so important as practical conformity :

I never before conceived the difference between real obedience and promise by subscription to obey, and if I erred anything herein, it

---

[1] *Bancroft's Register*, f. 127 b. Carelessly quoted by D. Neal, *History of the Puritans*, London, 1837, Vol. II, p. 38.
[2] *Cecil MSS.*, 108, f. 43. H.M.C., Part XVI, pp. 416–17.

was upon this respect, that I thought if there was any degree of difference between real obedience (I mean in absolute obedience to all the Church government) and promise by subscription to obey, I then thought that to wear the surplice indeed, to use cross after baptism and to do all the like, in effect was a greater obedience than to subscribe that they shall do it, and when the storm is past never perform a word, and protest that their subscription was only *ex justo metu*; and therefore I thought that if they presently conformed themselves, and after that would refuse to subscribe to that which in deed they had already performed, it would be a means to make their vanity appear, and every man to pity them the less.

He vehemently denied the charge of wavering indecision:

I am so far from yielding anything for fear of their popularity, as I am heartily glad of your stoutness in this case that are councillors, for if I be grown so easy now to be threatened, I am sure that it is in my last days, and therefore since I am interpreted to have inclined this way for fear of their mutiny, my resolution is that the bishops go on now with their own course according to the proclamation, and if my eye either spare or pity any of the disobedient, then let me incur both the shame and the harm in God's name.[1]

Matthew Hutton, Archbishop of York, in a letter to Viscount Cranborne, acknowledged the Council's communications:

I haue receiued lettres from your L: and others of his Majesties most honourable Priuie Counsell, conteyning two points. First, That the Puritanes be proceaded against according to Lawe, except they conforme themselues. Secondlie, That good care be had unto greedie Patrons, that none be admitted in their places, but such as are conformable, and otherwise worthie for their vertue and learning. I haue written to the three bishops of this Province, and in their absence to their Chancellors, to haue a special care of this service, and therein haue sent copies of your Lettres, and will take present order within myne owne Dioces.

He could wish that a like resolution was shown in relation to Roman Catholic recusants:

I wish with all my hart that the like order were geuen, not onely to all Bishops, but to all Magistrates and Justices of peace, etc., to procead against Papists and Recusants; who of late, partly by this round dealing against the Puritanes, and partly by some extra-

[1] Ibid., 134, f. 52. H.M.C., Part XVI, p. 399. King James to the Council (1604).

ordinary fauour, haue grown mightely in number, corage and insolencie. The Puritanes, (whose phantasticall Zeal I dislike), though they differ in ceremonies and accidents, yet they agree with vs in substance of religion; and, I thinke all, or the moste of them love his Majestie and the present Estate, and I hope will yealde to Conformitie. But, the Papists are opposite and contrary in verie manie substantiall points of religion, and can not but wish the Popes authority, and popish religion to be established. I assure your Lordship it is high time to looke vnto them; very many are gone from all places to London, and some are come downe into this Contrie in great iollitie, almoste triumphantly. But his Majestie, as he hath been brought up in the Gospell, and understandeth religion excellently well: so he will protect, maintaine and aduance it, euen vnto the end.[1]

Cranborne denied any suggestion of favour or partiality:

I would be loath, that your Lordship, who haue euer loued the truth, should liue in such a darknesse (through want of better information), as might obscure to you either his Majesties owne cleare, zealous, and constant resolution, for the preseruation of true religion, of the serious cares of my Lords of his priuy Councell to haue his godly and iust lawes duly executed.

The vital issue was not "ceremonies and accidents", as the Archbishop implied, but Church government. The presbyterian form of government was incompatible with the claims of absolute monarchy.

Although many religious men of moderate spiritts might be borne with, yett such are the turbulent humours of some that dreame of nothing but of a new Hierarchy (directly opposite to the State of a Monarchy) as the dispensacion with such men were the highe way to breake all bonds of vnity, to nourishe Scisme in the Church, and finally to destroye both Church and Commonwealth.

The Council did not intend to relax the laws against papists:

it is well said of a learned man, that there are Scismes in habite as well as in opinion, Et non seruator vnitas in credendo, nisi adsit in colendo, and therefore where your Lordship seemeth to speake

---

[1] *S.P. Dom.*, *Jas. I*, 14, Vol. X.A, no. 64. 18 December 1604. *Additional MSS.*, 30,662, f. 63 b (in French); 38, 139, f. 181; 12,497; 38,492, f. 93; *Egerton MSS.*, 2,877, f. 167 b; *Lansdowne MSS.*, 89, no. 28; *Harleian MSS.*, 677, f. 45; *Laing MSS.*, H.M.C., Report on Laing MSS., p. 99, 156; *Stowe MSS.*, 156, f. 50. Printed, R. Winwood, *Memorials*, Vol. II, p. 40; J. Strype, *Whitgift*, Vol. III, p. 420.

fearfully, as if in labouring to reforme the one, there were some purpose to tolerate the other, I must crave pardon of your Lordship, to replie this much, tyll I heare you touch particulars: That it is not a sure foundation to build vpon bruits.

The Archbishop was unduly apprehensive:

neither can I be perswaded otherwise (forasmuch as I haue obserued) in the place I haue held (within the compasse whereof some more then vulgar bruits do fall), but that whosoever shall behold the Papists with Puritane spectacles, or the Puritane with Papisticall, shall see no other certaintie then the multiplication of false images. Besides (my Lord) if that were true, which your Lordship reports (which God forbid) that Poperie and Papists should increase in those quarters: giue me leaue to tell your Lordship that you must either prouide to defend your owne challenge against your self, and blame your owne subordinates, if they haue dispensed, or else make knowne who gives impediment to that tymely woorke of reformation, for which you are so well authorised by our religious souueraigne.[1]

The Archbishop abandoned further procrastination, and, a month later, on 26 January 1604/5, writing to Henry Howard, Earl of Northampton, reported that he was enforcing conformity: "I am nowe dealinge againste the Puritanes of my dioces, which I thanke god are very few: and I hope I shall not be forced to proceede to depriuation of any, except some two or three." "The lesse learninge", he commented, "the more willfull and obstinate" such men are.[2]

The King prepared a "Memoriall" for the enforcement of conformity within the Universities "that a solid course be taken for the conformity of Cambridge to the Church's canons and for deposing all recusant puritans and to make it sure that the like course be kept with Oxford".[3] The Chancellors were informed that for the peace of the Church, the Universities were to "be kept in order and remaine freed from all Facions, novelties, and Schismes, the Cankers and banes of all Christian Vnity", so that students might be "knitt and joyned together in one profession of Christian Religion and true worship of God". No person was to be admitted to any degree of the schools whatsoever, unless he

[1] *S.P. Dom., Jas. I*, 14, Vol. X.A., no. 66. December 1604. *Harleian MSS.*, 677, f. 46; *Additional MSS.*, 38,139, f. 194.
[2] *Harleian MSS.*, 677, f. 53. 26 January 1604/5. *Egerton MSS.*, 2,877, f. 167 b.
[3] *Cecil MSS.*, 134, f. 51. H.M.C., Part XVI, p. 398.

had taken the oath of supremacy, and an oath approving the episcopal form of the government and the liturgy of the Church, and repudiating the presbyterian system of ecclesiastical government, in the following form:

> Ego, N.N. promitto et spondeo primum me vera Christi Religionem in Ecclesia Anglicana legibus hujus Regni jam stabilitam omni animo complexurum Scripturae authoritatem Hominum indicijs praepositurum. Regulam vitae ac summam fidei ex verbo Dei petiturum: caeterae, quae ex verbo Dei non probantur, pro humanis, et non necessarijs habiturum; Contrarias verbo Dei opiniones omni voluntate, ac mente refutaturum; vera consuetis, scripta non scriptis in Religionis causa antehabiturum; deinde me credere ac tenere formam Ecclesiastici Regiminis, quae apud nos est, per archiepiscopos et Episcopos legitimam esse, et sacris Scripturis consentaneam, novamque illam ac popularem, quae praesbyterij nomine usurpatur (utcumque alicubi approbatam) Monarchiae tamen certae institutae minime convenientem. Insuper iudicare me, ac pro virili mea astructurum, librum seu libros publicae Liturgiae, ac Episcopos, Presbyteros, et Diacones ordinandi et consecrandi nihil in se continere, quod verbi Dei sit contrarium, formamque precum publicarum, et administrationis Sacramentorum in eodem prescriptam, pie ac licite posse et debere observari, meque eandem vocatione mea id postulante, et non aliam, (quoties ita res feret) observaturum: Postremo me articulos Religionis (quo triginta novem, citra ratificationem, numerantur) in quos consensum est ab Archiepiscopis, et Episcopis utriusque Provinciae, ac reliquo omni Clero in Synodo Londinensi, anno domini 1562 ad tollendam omnen dissensionem, et consensum verae Religionis firmandum, pro veris et certis habiturum, et in omni loco tanquam consentientes cum verbo Dei, defensurum et Contrarios articulos in Scholis et Pulpitis vel alibi (pro vitae meae instituto) oppugnaturum. Haec omnia in me recipio, meque sedulo facturum promitto ac spondeo, ita me Deus Adjuvet per Christum Jesum.[1]

In pursuance of the King's directions,[2] Cranborne, as Chancellor

---

[1] *S.P. Dom., Jas. I*, 14, Vol. X.A, no. 68. December 1604. Ibid., Vol. XIII, no. 63. April 1605.

[2] James sent similar directions to the Chancellors of the Universities in 1616. *Lambeth MSS.*, 663, f. 97. "His Maiesties direction to the Vice-Chancellor: and Heads of Houses in the University of Cambridge . . . on the 3. of December. 1616." *Lansdowne MSS.*, 157, ff. 82, 123. James' directions to the Vice-Chancellor of Oxford University. 18 January 1616/7. These directions insist on the necessity for conformity and subscription to the *Three Articles*. No one is to be suffered "to mayntaine dogmatically any point of doctrine that is not allowed by the Church of England".

of the University of Cambridge, demanded that a "good conformity be observed in all members". The King had sought to yield satisfaction regarding "the lawful use, conveniency, nature, antiquity and good construction of such things in the Book of Common Prayer as by some unquiet spirits [had] been peevishly carped at, to the great scandal of the religion professed"; and was now resolved "to maintain the former constitutions . . . not permitting innovation, but requiring all men's conformity to things established". These good endeavours for the welfare of the Church, however, would be of little avail if "either the dregs of popery or intemperate humours of men that cannot submit to any order (with which their own inventions concur not) shall still remain to corrupt that famous nursery of learning".

> I have resolved . . . most earnestly to require you upon receipt of my letters presently to assemble your selves and take a diligent survey or ordering of every the colleges and halls in the University in Divinis Officiis according to the Statutes of the University, the constitutions of the Church and the orders prescribed in the Book of Common Prayer; and withal to take present order for the repressing of all liberty heretofore permitted in publishing or doing anything to the contrary, certifying me of the delinquents except they assure you of present reformation.

He wanted information concerning his powers as Chancellor in matters ecclesiastical:

> I do desire you advisedly (and yet with expedition) to inform me how the state of the University standeth for ecclesiastical jurisdiction, how far forth the same resteth in me, and by what charters or other good proofs the same may be avowed, that I may both know what power is in ourselves to reform the abuses or to remove the unconformable, especially in case (which I hope I shall not) there should any of your rank be found refractory; and also may be furnished with good reason to maintain the power in ourselves to perform this good work, if any go about to interpose any jurisdiction derogatory from the ancient charters we have.

He warned against the countenancing of any Puritanical practices:

> I may not also omit to remember you to be very diligent against private conventicles upon any pretence had in the University, neither that any sermons be suffered to be preached by unconformable men or at unseasonable times, contrary to the ancient orders of the university.

All ministers in the University were to exhibit their letters of orders, and all who preached at St Mary's church were first to subscribe to the *Three Articles* in the presence of some public officer of the University.[1]

The Chancellor's directions were duly heeded. On 10 December 1604, the Vice-Chancellor wrote that the Fellows of Emmanuel College had agreed on conformity:

> There came to me this present day three of the Fellows of Emmanuel College in Cambridge, Mr Gough, Mr Cudworth, Mr Warde, who testified to me upon their credits that the more use of the ceremonies touching divine service is all ready begun in that College, and that there is a full purpose and agreement among them that the Holy Communion shall from henceforth be administered, according to the course of the Church of England.[2]

Two days later, 12 December, the Master of the College, Laurence Chaderton, wrote to Dr Neyle to the same effect:

> According to the tenure of our last conference, we have begun to reduce our College to the Statutes of the University and to the order of other Colleges, as you may perceive by the testimony enclosed. I pray you signify the same to our Chancellor. As we are desirous in all things to keep a good conscience towards God, so are we most unwilling to show the least disobedience to our superiors.

A certificate was enclosed:

> These are to testify that in Emmanuel College as well myself as the fellows and scholars thereof use the communion book daily, and administer the sacrament kneeling accordingly; and also use the surplice according to the statute of the University, and so have done since we were required by authority.[3]

Certificates of conformity were sent in from other Colleges during the months immediately following. Trinity Hall certified: "Here be none, but verye forward in all conformitye, requyred by the late Canons, the customs of the Universitye, and the booke of Common Prayer."[4]

On 9 January 1604/5 Dr John Cowell, the Vice-Chancellor, submitted a report to the Chancellor concerning the measure of

---

[1] *Cecil MSS.*, 136, f. 199. H.M.C., Part XVI, pp. 389–90.
[2] Ibid., 136, f. 127. H.M.C., Part XVI, p. 378.
[3] Ibid., 189, ff. 51, 189. H.M.C., Part XVI, pp. 381–2.
[4] *S.P. Dom., Jas. I*, 14, Vol. X.A, no. 72. 20 December 1604.

success achieved. He had forwarded the certificates of conformity from each College, and he had also taken a brief out of the records of the University, showing the extent of the Chancellor's ecclesiastical jurisdiction. He had, however, encountered some opposition:

> Whereas your advice also was that we should . . . make trial if we could establish by a general decree that everyone called to St Mary's pulpit should first of all be brought to subscribe to the three articles prescribed by the late Convocation; I have attempted it, by propounding a grace unto the Houses, but with hard success, divers not liking to be so restrained, especially none being called to preach there, but ministers that either have or should formerly subscribe at the time when they took their Holy Orders from the Bishop . . . Nevertheless, if I understand that I shall press your directions any further, I will, with better circumspection than before, observe some convenient time for the passing of the grace, which was lately stayed clean contrary against mine expectation.

Nevertheless, a real measure of conformity had been achieved:

> I assuredly persuade myself there is no doubt of conformity in the performance of divine service and sacraments in our body but of some few in Emmanuel College, of whose reformation there is some hope, if it be thoroughly urged; but I perceive there be very many amongst us, both old and young, that stick at subscribing to the three articles,[1] and so will do, as I suppose, except they be hard pressed.[2]

James Montagu, Dean of the Chapel Royal, congratulated Cranborne on his signal success. It was a remarkable achievement, "having brought the whole body of the University, consisting of so diverse dispositions, to be conformable to his Majesty's proceedings". The King was most gratified: "His Majesty took great contentment in perusing of it, and said it was sufficient to confute all the Puritans in the Kingdom to see so great a number of learned men in a university to consent so full in one." With disarming flattery, Montagu added:

> I was bold to tell his Majesty that if it might be without loss to his service in the state, I could wish your Lordship were a bishop for a

[1] *Lansdowne MSS.*, 157, f. 83. "The Three Articles which had to be subscribed unto by the Students at the University." These are, of course, the *Three Articles* of Canon 36.

[2] *Cecil MSS.*, 136, f. 122. H.M.C., Part XVII, p. 9.

9

while to see if you could bring the Church to as good conformity as
you have done the University; for what with . . . a multitude of
Puritans, his Majesty hath had little rest since his coming from
London.

Nevertheless, he was distressed by the necessity for these harsh
proceedings and by the hurt done to the cause of Christ:

> For the precise ministers I confess I have rather a heart to com-
> miserate their state than a tongue to speak in their case, for it is
> a lamentable thing to see that neither the religious proceedings of so
> gracious a King, nor the persuasions of so many honourable person-
> ages, nor the inducements of so many learned men by their example,
> can bring these men to any better conformity, but they run on still
> in their disobedience to the great grief of everyone that professeth
> Christ. I entreat your Lordship that such moderation may be used in
> turning them out of their places, that men of more turbulent dis-
> positions may be called out little by little, rather than all without
> difference cut down at once; for I have ever found all controversies
> in religion to gather strength by opposition, and the parties de-
> pressed to gain more by pity than ever they could by their piety.

He could "wish the sign of the Cross were left out in the liturgy,
so that this breach were made up".[1]

The authorities were determined that a strict conformity
should be enforced within the Universities. On 12 March 1609,
Bancroft declined Salisbury's request for a letter in support of
Murray's application for a Wardenship, till he "has made his
mynd fully knowen . . . towching his conformitie".[2]

On 13 February 1604/5, Bancroft secured, from "all the
Justices of England, with diuers of the Nobility", assembled in
the Star Chamber, categorical answers to a series of questions
concerning the legal powers of the bishops, in relation to deprivation. It was clear that the Puritans would use all available
means to defeat episcopal regimentation, and already the Bishop
of Exeter had found himself threatened with a prohibition. "The
Lord Chancellor, after a long speech made by him . . . concerning
Papists and Puritans, Declaring how they both were Disturbers
of the State, and that the King intending to suppress them, and
to have the laws put in Execution against them; demanded of the

---

[1] *Cecil MSS.*, 103, f. 130. H.M.C., Part XVII, p. 28. 22 January 1604/5.
[2] *S.P. Dom., Jas. I*, 14, Vol. XLIV, no. 22. Bancroft to Salisbury.

Justices theire Resolutions in three things." The Ecclesiastical Commissioners desired to know:

First, whether the deprivation of Puritan ministers by the High Commissioners, for refusing to confirm [sic] themselues to the Ceremonies appointed by the last Canons was lawfull? Whereto all the Justices answered, that they had conferred thereof before, and held it to be lawfull, Because the Kinge hath the supreame Ecclesiasticall power, which he hath delegated to the Commissioners whereby they had the power of deprivation by the Canon law of the Realme, And the statute of 1 Elizabeth, which appoints Commissioners to be made by the Queen, doth not confer any new power, but Explaine and declare the antient power, and therefore they held it clear, that the King without Parliament might make orders and Constitutions for the Gouernment of the Clergie, and might deprive them if they obeyed not. And so the Commissioners might deprive them. But they could not make any Constitutions without the King, and the divulging of such ordinances by Proclamation is a most gracious admonition; and for asmuch as they have refused to obey, they are lawfully deprived by the Commissioners ex officio without Libell et ore tenus convocati.

The second question was: "whether a Prohibition be grantable against the Commissioners, upon the Statute of 2. H: 5. if they do not deliver the Copy of the libel to the party", to which the judges replied: "that that Statute is intended where the Ecclesiasticall Judges proceeds ex officio et ore tenus." Thirdly, the Commissioners asked

whether it was an offence punishable, and what punishment they deserved, who framed Petitions and collected a Multitude of hands thereto, to prefer to the King in a public cause, as the Puritans had done, with an intimation to the King, That if he denyed theire sute, many thousands of his subjects would be discontented? Whereto all the Justices answered, That it was an offence fineable at discretion, and very near to treason and Felony in the punishment. For they tended to the raising of Sedition, Rebellion and discontent among the people. To which resolution all the Lords agreed. And then many of the Lords declared, that some of the Puritans had raised a false Rumor of the King, how he intended to grant a toleration to Papists: which offence the Justices conceiued to be heinously fineable by the Rules of the Common Law, either in the Kings Bench, or by the King and his Councell, or now since the Statute of 3. H: 7 in the Star Chamber.

This judgement was of inestimable importance. The bishops could now proceed without fear of let or hindrance. The King, in the course of a letter to Matthew Hutton, Archbishop of York, reviewing his proceedings in the furtherance of the Protestant religion, urged the Archbishop to be forward in the matter of enforcing conformity. He was fully empowered to proceed to deprivation by the unanimous judgement of the judges of the realm:

> for the better satisfaction of you the Archbishop, and of the Bishops of your Province, We have thought good to signifye to you that whereas many of the Ministers of that sort haueinge been of late deprived by their Bishops for their disobedience, as persons sismaticke haue given out that the Ecclesiasticall proceedings against them weare not warrantable by Law, and the Bishops subiect to danger for their doings, and some of them vppon a sentence lately given by the Bishop of Exceter within two days after came with their Counsell to our Bench before our Judges then sittinge and demanded a Prohibition. That motion of theirs hath given occasion to a consultation amonge the whole Judges of our Realme, whoe with one consent haue likewise delivered their iudgments, that noe prohibition doth lye in that case against the Judges Ecclesiasticall, That the Bishops proceedinge to deprivation for not conforminge to the booke of Comon prayer and ceremonyes of the church is warranted by Law, and they neither will nor are to releve any man seekinge to them in such casse, but suffer the Ecclesiastical authority to haue his full execution; which evasion beinge now taken from the ministers disobedient, We doubt not will reduce a great many of them to temper.

The King hoped that the Archbishop would press on with the enforcing of conformity: "If you shall vse such diligence and constancye as we desire in your proceedings against the disobedient, we hope that in short time all our subiects shalbe reduced to one Vniformity in matter of Religion."[1]

In the southern province Bancroft urged the bishops to the diligent enforcement of the canons. There was to be no relaxing and no relenting. On 12 March 1604/5, he wrote again: "I haue written to your Lordship before concerninge your proceedinge with your factious ministers, and that you shoulde not desiste by deprivinge one, two, or three at once, untill you have purged

---

[1] *S.P. Dom., Jas. I,* 14, Vol. XII, no. 87.

your diocesse of them." The King, however, was anxious that the severity of punishment should be mitigated by a merciful and compassionate concern for shelter and provision:

> After I had written this letter, I receiued uppon occasion this direction from his Maiestie, that when your Lordship depriueth any of your factious ministers for their obstinacie, you shoulde take such order with the next Incumbent, as that the partie soe depriued may haue two or three monthes libertie to remaine still in the Parsonage or Vicaredge house, if he haue no other of his owne, that so he may haue that tyme to provide for him selfe, and not be thrust out into the streetes uppon a sodaine.[1]

[1] *Bancroft's Register*, f. 129 b. 12 March 1604/5. *S.P. Dom., Jas. I*, 14, Vol. XIII, no. 25.

5

PURITAN RESISTANCE

THESE DETERMINED measures were met by a clamorous outcry of aggrieved protest. "The people neere adjacent vnto the towne of Roiston", on behalf of their "faithfull Pastors", declared that, by the harsh and stern enforcement of a rigid conformity, "worthy lightes", by whom they had "bin taught and brought from darknes vnto light, and from the power of Satan vnto god", had been "in part extinguished", and that they were "heauily threatned to be depriued of the Remnat" that were left. They earnestly interceded for their "worthy guides", and prayed that they might be preserved from "Idle Shephards" or "careless Shephards who aime wholy at the gaine of the fleece and neglect the safety of the flocke". Their spiritual welfare was dependent on the continuance of their faithful ministry: "alas, through the want of them the soules of vs and posteritie are exposed to certain and inevitable Ruine."[1]

This petition was alleged to represent the views of two hundred yeomen of Essex. A later endorsement on the petition states: "one of ye cheefest of them, viz. Mr Hildersham, stuard to Sir Francis Barington, ys bound over therupon to appeare before ye Counsayle when he shalbe called; some 3 other at ye first stayed were after dismissed". On 25 November Sir Thomas Lake wrote to Cranborne: "about the petition at Royston, his Majesty would have all that could be gotten out of Hildersham, who he says is apparently guilty".[2] Hildersham, whose activity in connection with the Hampton Court Conference we have previously noted, was subsequently deprived.[3]

Many petitions, for reasons of self-protection, were anonymous.[4]

---

[1] *Harleian MSS.*, 677, f. 44. 6 November 1604. *Egerton MSS.*, 2,877, f. 166 b; *Additional MSS.*, 38, 492, f. 6. The endorsement of this copy is dated 20 November.

[2] *Cecil MSS.*, 189, f. 42. H.M.C., Part XVI, p. 368.

[3] See below, pp. 183–6.

[4] *S.P. Dom., Jas. I*, 14, Vol. X, no. 81; *Harleian MSS.*, 677, f. 44.

In a letter to Cranborne, dated 22 November 1604, James mentioned a petition he had recently received:

> I doubt not also but ere this time ye have received the puritans' catholic petition, for it neither names county, parish, nor pastor; what such an universal complaint deserves I need not inform you, but I deceived their expectation by dismissing the multitude in fair terms, only that knave that was framer of the petition, and drawer of them together deserving some correction, I would have been sorry that this three thousand should have boasted me, but he is so near kin to Emmanuel as I shall distrust that race the more while I live. I heartily require you that with all convenient speed that knave may receive some public correction either in the Star Chamber or otherwise, since ye see I have daily more and more cause to hate and abhor all that sect, enemies to all kings, and to me only because I am king. But, above all let him first be shrewdly and well examined.[1]

The identity of "the knave" is unknown.

In London, twenty-two preachers, in a petition to the King, protested "that the said ceremonies, and many thinges else in those bookes, are repugnant to the word of God". They would conform, if convinced by the testimony of Scripture and sound reason:

> Our exceptions[2] . . . haue not bin answered, nor any one sufficient reason given, according to your Majesties proclamation, to prove the lawfulness of the thinges imposed: we haue herd and doe beleue, that your Majestie hathe often said, that yf any can shewe the thinges Required to be vnlawful, your Highnes will not haue them vrged, and except we be able, by the evidence of the scriptures to proue the same, we will presently yeld to conformity required.[3]

They pleaded for toleration:

> We haue bine brought vp, and taken degrees in the vniuersities; we and many of vs become grey heded in the seruices of god, and of his churche, hauinge preched the gospell, some of vs ten yeres, some twenty yeres, some thirty and some more, and diuers of vs in this

---

[1] *Cecil MSS.*, 134, f. 53. H.M.C., Part XVI, p. 363.

[2] *Additional MSS.*, 29, 975, f. 14. "The exceptions of the 22 london ministers to the booke of common prayer, which they cannot subscribe vnto itt." The exceptions are the mistranslation of Scripture, the reading of the Apocrypha, the wording in some of the Collects, the use of ceremonies, the wearing of the surplice, and the sign of the cross.

[3] *Harleian MSS.*, 3,791, f. 153; *Sloane MSS.*, 271, f. 35; *Egerton MSS.*, 2,877, f. 163 b.

Citty aduenterid our lyues by prechinge, in the tyme of the late infection: nether are we so fewe as is pretended: to say nothing of our bretherine which yeld with mvch grefe and sorowe of harte: we haue wyues and children, kindfolkes and frends dependinge vpon vs, whoe are vndone, yf we be displasid. . . .

In the diocese of Lincoln, thirty ministers, under the leadership of John Burgess, petitioned the King concerning ceremonies and subscription.[1] The problem was Canon 36 requiring subscription to the Three Articles:

The first of these articles none of us ever refused to subscribe unto. To the other two we cannot: because we are perswaded that both the Booke of Common prayer and the other bookes to be subscribed by this Canon (of which yet in some respects we reverently esteem) containe in them sondry things which are not agreable but contrary to the Word of God.[2]

This petition was published early in the following year: *An abridgment of that Booke which the Ministers of Lincoln Diocess delivered to his Maiestie upon the first of December last. Being the First Part of an Apologye for Themselves and their brethren that refuse subscription, and conformitie which is required. Wherevnto is Annexed, a Table of Sondry Poynts not handled in this Abridgment, which are other exceptions they take to the subscription requyred, and shalbe the Argument of the second part of their Apology.*

Twenty-seven Warwickshire ministers presented a petition describing their unhappy plight: "We . . . are allreadie for the most part suspended from the former use of our ministerie and doe all expect presentlie to be fully deprived not onelie of our functions but of all meanes to live by, without anie regard either of our age or charge of familie and Children." They were suspended

---

[1] *S.P. Dom., Jas. I*, 14, Vol. X.A, no. 81. 1 December 1604. Cf. The memorandum found on Melancthon Jewell: "Twoe and thirtie ministers of Lincolne Diocesse beinge upon the pointe of deprivation exhibited a petition to the Kinge, by the hands of three of them the laste of November with a booke of reasons, which his Majestie haveinge reade required them to sett downe vnder theire hands, viz:

1. What are the things that are made worse nowe by the alteringe of the booke of Common prayer and the Canons than weare before.
2. What things are desyered to be releived in, and which being graunted, they will reste in."

[2] *Lambeth MSS.*, 43, pp. 100–79.

neither for error in Doctrine, whereof we are not charged: nor scandall in life; nor thorough [sic] any complainte for breach of Law: neither yet for the absolute refusall of subscription and vse of the booke of common prayer; but for not yielding to that strict manner of subscribing now so streightlie required, which for diuers reasons commen to vs with our brethren in other places likewise suspended and depriued we cannot in conscience yeild vnto: but are in our hearts perswuaded that in so doing we should sinn against God, against our owne Consciences, against our most religious and best affected people ... Wherefore we most humblie beseech your Majestie in the bowells of Christ Jesus to take some pitie and compassion vppon this our miserie.[1]

A long petition[2] was also presented from Lancashire: "The humble Petition of sundrie Gentlemen, Justices of Peace in Lancashire, for his Majesties favour, to continue to them sundrie of their godly Ministers, who haue longe lived, and laboured amongest them painfully, profitably, and peaceablie, to the furtherance in godly knowledge of themselues, and manie thowsands of his Highnes loyall and true herted subiectes."[3] They certified "that they stand meeralie uppon their Conscience therein, and not uppon any wilful stiffenes, affectation of noveltie, or humour of disobedience". "Wee greatlie feare, That yf these godly ministers shalbee depriued of their places, It will bring exceeding much greef to all the godly, Too great reioycing to the common adversaries, and further endaunger the progresse of Religion in these partes." Furthermore, "the poore wyues and Children of these faythfull Preachers" were "likely to Fall into greate extremitie and Beggery".

---

[1] *S.P. Dom., Jas. I*, 14, Vol. XII, no. 68. December (?) 1604. Concerning Canon 36: "To the .1. article towching your Majesties Supremacie we offer to subscribe most willinglie and ex animo as is required. To the .2. Article we humblie desire to be forborne subscription to the bookes mentioned: the strict obseruation of the booke of common praier and vse of the Ceremonies for diuers reasons vs neerlie concerning in conscience; So doe we promise to vse in the administration of the Sacraments and praier the booke authorized by the Kings Majestie, and that onelie and none other, and to carrie our selues peaceable in our places and respectfully to authoritie. To the .3. we willinglie offer to subscribe according to the Statute in that behalf provided. .A.13, Eliz: cap. 12."

[2] "This day Dec. 7. a petition was exhibited to his Majestie by certaine gentlemen of Cheiswate of Lancashire in behalfe of their ministers." *S.P. Dom., Jas. I*, 14, Vol. X.A, no. 81.

[3] Ibid., Vol. X.A, no. 61. December 1604. *Additional MSS.*, 38,492, f. 96.

James read the petition with testy displeasure. Francis Morice, writing to Sir Basingbourn Gawdy from Westminster on 10 December 1604, said: "A petition sent in on Friday from Lancashire gentlemen and justices on behalf of their ministers who are not conformable is said to have been taken very ill by the King ... the bishops are enjoined to enforce conformity themselves, not commiting the matter to their officials or chaplains."[1]

The arrogant autocracy of the bishops was mercilessly assailed. It was claimed that the bishops, "being vyse in thair generation, haue left no stonne vnrolled for the vpholding of thair ruinous and lettering kingdome", and have, "from tym to tym, not only Reuiled and Disgraced, but in pulpitt, and in print, theise vhom they call their brethrene fellow servants of Jesus Christ". The deprived ministers had acted out of "a fervent zeall of the glorie of God, and a perfitt detestation of poperie". Nevertheless, they had been "suspended, depryued, degraded, and imprisoned ... yea ... turned out of house and home, denyed ... all benefitt of Law, and vsed with suche contempt and contumelie, as if they bee not worthie to Liue vponn the face of the earth".[2] Only one conclusion was possible: "Metropolitans, Primates, Archbishops, Diocessans ... come out of darkness and from the Deuill ... the lordly estate of prelates is the cause of all mischeife in the Churche."[3]

Certain "Gentlemen of Leicestershire" addressed a petition to Viscount Cranborne, seeking his powerful mediation:

> The impression we have of the sundry grievances which the learned and painfullest ministers of this county of Leic [ester] sustain in the execution of their functions, and the doubt to be deprived of the spiritual comforts we have long enjoyed by their godly labours, besides the distress that would befall them ... if either their mouths should be stopped, or they deprived of their livings, whereby the increase of ignorance, atheists, papists, and secret enemies of God's truth would ensue, doth move us to become petitioners to your Lordship to interpose your powerful mediation to his excellent Majesty that this poor county may enjoy ... comfort by the continuance of their ministries ... without molestation for such matters

---

[1] *Gawdy MSS.*, Part 1, no. 613. H.M.C., *Report on the Gawdy Family*, Part 1, p. 97.

[2] *Gibson MSS.*, Vol. V, 933, f. 23 (Lambeth Palace Library).

[3] *Lambeth MSS.*, 113, f. 235. 1605.

as yet in their conscience, and by the word of God, they cannot be persuaded to yeild unto.[1]

A fortnight later the Bishop of Lincoln informed him

that many of the knights . . . have set their hands to a petition unto his Majesty in the behalf of some ministers not conformable, wherein they justify the denial of those ministers to conform themselues unto the Church of England, and condemn the most of the ministers in Lincolnshire. . . . If you do not take some course to deal with some of these maintainers, neither will any of the ministers conform themselves, neither shall we have any peace in our churches.[2]

Cranborne firmly declined to intervene on behalf of the deprived ministers. He did not deny that many of them were men of blameless rectitude and exemplary life, but the granting of toleration was incompatible with the achievement of uniformity:

For the request you make, that I shall interpose my mediation in favour of divers ministers that show themselves unconformable to the ordinances of the church . . . this . . . I must say, that for the religion which they profess I reverence them and their calling; but for their unconformity I acknowledge myself no way warranted to deal with them, because the course they take is no way safe in such a monarchy as this, where his Majesty aimeth at no other end than where there is but one true faith and doctrine preached, there to establish one form that a perpetual peace may be settled in the church of God . . . [These men] by this singularity of theirs, in things approved to be indifferent by so many reverend fathers of the church, by so great multitudes of their own brethren . . . do daily minister cause of scandal in the Church of England, and give impediment to that great and godly work towards which all honest men are bound to yield their best means . . . namely, to suppress idolatry and Romish superstition. How can you plead ignorance, or any of you, that the learned judges and fathers of the law have delivered in open Courts direct censures against those that gather hands and hearts in favour of this disobedience, and how his Majesty and the Council have dealt with other petitioners upon the like occasions? Let me entreat you now to . . . interpose your private authorities over these poor men (who are easily carried by your breath in things indifferent) as they may not be found ready to strain the gnat and swallow the camel, nor wilfully to stop their own mouths from instructing those of whom they profess to take so great care, but

[1] *Cecil MSS.*, 103, f. 100. 7 January 1604/5. H.M.C., Part XVII, p. 7.
[2] Ibid., 103, f. 139. 24 January 1604/5. H.M.C., Part XVII, p. 34–5.

rather to conform themselves to the ordinances of the church, to which they owe obedience, seeing we so fully agree in one true substance of faith and religion, and ought all to strive in a brotherly course to maintain the bonds of unity and conformity, for the advancement of God's glory and furtherance of our own salvation.[1]

Cranborne added a postscript: he had examined the messenger, to discover whether there was any justification for interceding with the bishop of the diocese for a further period of forbearance. The result of the interview was entirely unsatisfactory: "I must say, that in my life I have never spake with any of whose absolute profane curiosity I took so great distaste."[2]

The leaders of the Puritan cause resorted to their former method of procedure: they encouraged the preparation of petitions and diligently solicited signatures. Sir Richard Holland, being examined before the Lords of the Council, explained how he had come to sign a petition:

Upon the publication of the late proclamation for conformity of the church's ministers to the ceremonies therein now established, very many well affected to the preaching of the gospels, both of better and meaner calling in this county, seeing the increase of Popish religion and looseness of life, were much dismayed, and feared lo [ss] of the preachers whose life and doctrine were so mu[ch] approved amongst us. These thoughts falling into men's minds, there was brought unto my house by Mr Gosnell, preacher at Boulton in the Moors, a draft of a petition to his Majesty on behalf of the preachers by such justices of the peace as would subscribe the same, which he had framed. . . . After some alteration, using the advice of Mr Burne of the Felowes, preacher at Manchester, who was then with me, I delivered it back to Mr Gosnell to be engrossed; and, after this was done, he sent it to me to subscribe. This I did, meaning no offence or opposition to the proclamation, but having heard that unto the like suit made by Mr Chatterton, Master of Emmanuel College, Cambridge, on behalf of the ministers of that county, at the late conference, his Majesty vouchsafed a very gracious answer . . . This petition by me subscribed was carried or sent by Mr Gosnell to the rest of the gentlemen, who readily subscribed it without more solicitation, as the most part of them, as Randle Barton, esquire, now sheriff of this county, Sir Nicholas Mosseley, Sir Edmund Trafford, Sir Richard Ashton, knights, James Asheton, John Howlt, and John Bradshaw, esquires, have acknowledged. It was then given to Mr.

[1] Ibid., 110, f. 117; 193, f. 45. April 1605. H.M.C., Part XVII, pp. 165–6.
[2] Ibid., 114, f. 128. H.M.C., Part XVII, p. 166.

Mudgeley, the younger, now vicar of Rochdale,[1] to procure it to be presented unto his Majesty by such person as he could entreat to undertake the delivery thereof, for whose furtherance I wrote to my son-in-law, Mr Reddiche, that if the bearer, meaning Mr Mudgeley, did acquaint him with his business, I trusted he would yield him his best furtherance, as far as I now remember.[2]

The agitation, both spontaneous and inspired, reached a climax with the presentation of a petition from the justices and gentlemen of Northamptonshire. It was drawn up by Sir Francis Hastings, that doughty Puritan fighter, signed, among others, by Sir Richard Knightley (whose association with the Marprelate Tracts was widely suspected) and presented by Sir Edward Montagu on 9 February 1604/5. They had "iust cause to feare the losse of manie a learned and proffittable Minister, yf the Execution of this late Decree for subscription and Conformitie should proceede (as in parte it is begunn) to the Depriuation and suspension of menie of our most learned and proffitable Teachers". They prayed that the hand of the King might

> be stretched out to moderate the Extremitie of this Decree, which otherwise is like to depriue vs and Thowsands of your loyall and trewe hearted people of the labours of manie faithfull preachers whoe . . . out of the tendernes of their Consciences, and feare to offend the Kinge of heauen . . . make scruple to vse the Ceremonies, and yeeld to the subscription inioyned.[3]

The King was entirely unsympathetic. He peremptorily ordered the petitioners to be placed in custody. On the following day, sitting in Council, the King observed[4] that both he and his mother had been haunted from their cradles by a "Puritan Divell", and

---

[1] Joseph Midgley/Mudgeley was deprived. See below, p. 214.

[2] *Cecil MSS.*, 104, f. 24. 15 February 1604/5. H.M.C., Part XVII, pp. 56–7.

[3] *S.P. Dom., Jas. I*, 14, Vol. XII, no. 69 (1). *Sloane MSS.*, 271, f. 33. "The Petition of the Justices and Gentlemen of the Dioces of Peterborough for their ministers."

[4] John Chamberlain, writing to Sir Richard Winwood (26 February), said: "The Ringleaders . . . Sir Richard and Sir Valentine Knightly, Sir Edward Montague, with some three or fourscore Gentlemen more . . . were convened before the Councill, and told what danger they had put themselves in by these associations; and that thus combining themselves in a Course, against which the King had shown his Mislike both by publick Act and Proclamation, was little less than Treason, and that the Subscription with so many Names were Armatae preces and tended to Sedition, as had been manifestly seen heretofore, both in Scotland, France, and Flanders in the beginning of those Troubles." Sir R. Winwood, *Memorials*, Vol. II, p. 48.

he feared it would not leave him till his grave.[1] The Lord Chancellor, examining Sir Francis Hastings, said: "There is a Petition deliuered ... which you haue drawne, which is mutinous, seditious, malitious, factious, tendinge to rebellion, by the Combination of manie hands against lawe." To this Hastings replied: "My Lords, I doe Confesse the drawinge of the Peticion ... but that it was eyther mutinous, seditious, etc. I protest it was farr from my intencion, and more than I can apprehend." The Lord Chancellor, sentencing Hastings, said:

> Nowe you must sett downe vnder your hande this affirmacion, that the ministers you haue petitioned for, they are not worthie of peticion to be made for them, for that they be seditious, factious, and disobedient against the lawe and the Kinge, and Disturbers of the Churches peace. And also you must sett downe vnder your hande, that Peticions cominge by Combination of vnder the hands of manye, are mutinous, seditious, and Contrarye to Lawe.

Hastings protested that this was grossly untrue:

> I beseech you geve me leave to speake boldelie and playnelie; If the Ministers did refuse the Ceremonyes vppon a humour and disposicion to disobaye and not vppon Conscience; none shoulde be more opposite to them then myself. But seeinge it is throughe the tendernes of theire Conscience, lett not me laye a blott vppon them, beinge free and innocent, for that my self haue some experience of the tendernes of Conscience, neyther do I desire to live to see the Kinge so dishonored, or his Subiuects so preiudiced, that it shoulde be vnlawfull to peticionate with many or fewe hands to him who hath power to graunt or to denye.

The Council, however, was unbending: "It is theire Honors Pleasure that you shoulde retyre to your owne howse in the Countrye, and desist from all dealinge in matters concerninge the Kings service; and this is done to you in fauer; and if it were any other, he shoulde lye by the heeles."[2]

A week later, on 17 February, the petitioners agreed to frame an apology to the King. The apology was written out in full and signed in the Lord Chamberlain's Chamber, and then delivered to the Lords of the Council for transmission to the King. James complained that it was not sufficiently unambiguous, and it was

---

[1] *Baker MSS.*, M.m. 1, 43, f. 167. 14 February 1604/5.
[2] *S.P. Dom., Jas. I*, 14, Vol. XII, no. 87. February 1604/5.

given to them to frame anew. Sir Edward Montagu said that if they could not agree to one common apology, each man should make his own submission. This was agreed to. Montagu subsequently related: "I resolved not to yield any more to the like in writing . . . I submitted myself to his Majesty's mercy, and their Lordships' good pleasure . . . Then I was censured to be put out of all commissions for his Majesty's service and to depart into the country."[1] Sir Valentine Knightley was similarly censured by the Council. The King was well pleased by these proceedings. The Earl of Worcester, writing to Cranborne, reported:

> I received your letter of the 25th February, with which I acquainted his Majesty. Your proceeding with the young Knightley he very well allows of and thinketh it very fit that gentlemen of his quality should not be allowed to depart without some note of his obstinate and peevish humour, for from such fountains springs the water that infecteth the humour of the perverse ministers. [2]

Sir Francis Hastings, for his part in drawing the petition, was put from the Lieutenancy of the shire, and the Justiceship of the Peace. Sir Dudley Carleton informed a friend that the "rest upon Acknowledgment of a Fault have no more said to them".[3] Among the latter were Sir Richard Knightley and Sir William Lane, who wrote a joint letter soliciting the King's pardon for their action. In extenuation, they explained that it was "the pitifull relacion" they had received of "the deprivacion of many learned and godly Ministers" who were "dutyfull . . . (except their conformitye to matters of order of the Churche)" that had moved them to support the petition. They promised dutiful obedience for the future: "We shall ever bee readye to vse a best indeuor for the effecting of that conformity which wee well knowe your Majestie affecteth out of a religious hart."[4] Sir Edward Montagu, wearying of his banishment, secured, through the instrumentality of his brother, the Dean of the Chapel Royal, an audience with the King. He "had lived as a dead man" ever since he had incurred the King's displeasure, and he humbly prayed that he might be restored to favour again. James, speaking on the "profession of Religion", inveighed against "the papists, saying

---

[1] *Beaulieu MSS.*, H.M.C., p. 45. 18 February 1604/5.
[2] *Cecil MSS.*, 104, f. 50. H.M.C., Part XVII, p. 72.
[3] Sir R. Winwood, op. cit., Vol. II, p. 48.
[4] *S.P. Dom.*, *Jas. I*, 14, Vol. XII, no. 94. February 1604/5.

that he had rather die than they should increase in his days, and for ceremonies . . . [they] should rely on him". The King required Montagu to write a letter for his further satisfaction, and this secured his pardon.[1] Erasmus Dryden supplicated Cranborne, craving release from prison, "as the Northamptonshire petition was only a testimonial of the godliness of the preachers".[2]

The task of propaganda was continued through the medium of pamphlets and tracts, dealing not only with matters of subscription, but also with matters of ceremonies and Church government. They traversed familiar ground. According to the author of *Certayne considerations why ye Ministers should not be removed for subscription*, it was on the ground of conscience and conscience alone that ministers refused to subscribe: "Towching ye matters in question it is evident to God and their owne consciences that they refuse not of any wilfulness or peevishnes, much les of any contempt of authoritie, but only because they are perswaded that in yelding they would sinne against God." Many had indeed submitted to the ceremonies but only because they felt that it was better to yield than to incur suspension and deprivation to the injury of their flocks: "Ye greatest parte by farre of resident and paynefull preachers among our selues, for though [they] . . . rather choose to yelde then to leave their lyvings and ministery, yet is there hardly any one who had not rather thei were remooved then receyued."[3]

Thomas Hutton published replies to the arguments advanced by the ministers of Devon and Cornwall before the Bishop of Exeter: *Reasons for Refvsal of Svbscription to the booke of Common praier, vnder the hands of certaine Ministers of Devon and Cornwall, word for word as they were exhibited by them to the Right Reverend Father in God, William Coton, Doctor of Divinitie, L. Bishop of Exeter. With an Answere at Severall times returned them in publike conference and in diverse sermons upon occasion preached in the Cathedral Church of Exeter . . . And now published at the very earnest entreatie of some especiall friends for a farther contentment of other the Kings Maiesties good and loyall Subjects* (1605); and the following year: *The Second and Last Part of Reasons for Refusall of Subscription of the Booke of Common*

---

[1] *Ibid.*, Vol. XII, no. 95. February (?) 1604/5.
[2] *Beaulieu MSS.*, H.M.C., p. 47.
[3] *Additional MSS.*, 38,492, f. 10.

Prayer, vnder the hands of certain ministers of Deuon. . . . He quoted the ministers as saying:

> We may not subscribe, because we see not how it may agree with Scripture to commit the body of a notorious wicked man, dying without tokens of repentance, to the earth, in sure and certaine hope of resurrection. . . .[1] We cannot subscribe, because we know not how it agreeth with Gods word to desire him to grant anything, which our prayers dare not presume to ask. . . .[2] The worde Priest is often giuen to the Minister of the worde and sacraments as the name of his office, which is neuer found in the New Testament giuen to any minister, but to Christ. . . .[3] That this day we fall into no sinne.[4] There is no warrant in God his word to pray so. Therefore we may not subscribe unto it.

There is little novelty in these objections. They are the familiar stuff of Puritan propaganda. *A Defence of the Ministers Reasons, for Refusall of Subscription to the Booke of Common Prayer, and of Conformity against the severall Answers of T. Hutton, Bachiler of Divinity, in his two Bookes against the Minist: of Dev. and Cornwell. Wiliam Covel, D. of Divinitie, in his Booke against M.I.Burges Tho: Spark: D. of Divinitie, in his Brotherly Perswasion to Unitie and Uniformitie* . . . appeared anonymously in 1607.[5] The author advanced a

[1] Quoted from the Burial Service. *The Second and Last Part of the Reasons for Refusall* . . ., p. 1.

[2] Quoted from the Collect for the Twenty-third Sunday after Trinity. Ibid., p. 20.

[3] Ibid., p. 37.

[4] Quoted from the Third Collect for Morning Prayer. Ibid., p. 46.

[5] There is some uncertainty about the identity of the author. The British Museum ascribes it to Thomas Hutton, but this is manifestly absurd as the writer is attacking one of Hutton's books. There is an illuminating note in a seventeenth-century hand on the fly-leaf of a copy in Dr Williams's Library: "This was written by old Mr Sam. Hieron of Modbury in Devon. It was printed in Holland, and sent over packed up in the goods of an eminent Merchant of Plimouth, Mr T. Sherwil. . . . So the Author was never discovered to his Enemies or the Collectors of his Works." Samuel Hieron was a prolific writer: he also published anonymously: *The Seconde Parte of the Defence of the Ministers Reasons for refusal of Subscription and Conformitie to the book of Common Prayer. Against the several Answers of* . . . 1608. *A Dispute upon the Question of kneeling, in the Acte of Receiving the Sacramentall bread and wine, proving it to be unlawfull. Or the Third Parte of the Defence of the Ministers Reasons, for refusall of the subscription and Conformitie requyred. Against the severall answers of* . . . 1608. *A Short Dialogue proving that the Ceremonyes, and some other Corruptions now in question, are defended, by none other Arguments then such as the Papists haue heretofore used; And our Protestant writers haue long since answered. Whereunto are Annexed, Certayne Considerations why the Ministers should not be removed for the Subscription and Ceremonies,* 1605.

variety of specious reasons why ministers should not be required to subscribe: they "are in all other things of peacable carriage and refuse these things of meere conscience.... The refusers of subscription might be spared being few. ... There are 270 at least. ... The supply of sufficient men is doubtful. ... It is hard recompence after long service. ... The papists insult and grow audacious."[1] Again, it was argued (by another writer) that since "the Bishops have borne with Non-residents and Idoll Ministers, who live as Caterpillers and droanes, devouring the fruits of the earth doing noe good but to their owne bellies", they should bear with ministers who "seeke not themselves nor their owne profitt but of meere conscience refuse the ceremonies".[2] It would appear, the writer said, that ceremonies

> are more ernestlie vrged and inforced vpon men, then the most especiall duties of the Commandements of God. proof hereof, for that if a minister will submytt himself to these thinge, be he neuer so negligent, neuer so vnskillful and vnable to dischardge the duties of his Callinge, he is not onely borne withall, but greatlie comended: whereas on the contrarye, he that for Conscience sake doth refuse them, if a Mynister be neuer so skilfull, so painfull in his callinge, and effectuall in procuringe repentance and the salvation of men by the pure preachinge of the Gospell, he is hated and persecuted ... which seemeth to vs a sufficient reason, whie we should refuse these ceremonies as not indifferent.[3]

It was a highly anomalous situation: "It is Contradictory in the government to command the preaching of the ghospell and to vrge such frivolous and vnprofitable things which necessarily keepe out and drive out the best preachers and in their stede bringe in evill men, yea Simonaryes and such lyke."[4]

The debate concerning ceremonies was renewed.[5] In *A Scholasticall Discovrse Against Symbolizing with Antichrist in Ceremonies:*

---

[1] *Egerton MSS.*, 2,877, f. 166 b. "Certaine Reasons why it seemeth that ye preachers who refuse the subscription and ceremonies vrged, should not for that their refusall be removed from their chardges, or inhibited to preach, humbly offered to consideration." Printed, *A Defence of the Ministers Reasons, for Refusall of Subscription to the Booke of Common Prayer, and of Conformitie.*

[2] *Additional MSS.*, 38,492, f. 15.

[3] Ibid., 38,492, f. 7.

[4] *Additional MSS.*, 38,482, f. 15. "Reasons politicall for the freedome of the Ministers from subscription and ceremonyes."

[5] E.g., W. Bradshaw, *Twelve General Arguments, prouing that the Ceremonies imposed upon the Ministers of the Gospel in England, by our Prelates, are unlawful;*

especially in the Signe of the Crosse,[1] R. Parker described "the idolatrie of the Crosse"; "the Superstition of the Crosse"; "the Hipocrisie of the Crosse"; "the impietie of the Crosse"; "the injustice of the Crosse"; and "the soule murther of the Crosse". The cross, he vehemently insisted, is "a part of the deuill worship".[2] "The vsing of the Crosse is but an idle apishe toye, and lighter than the surplice, which is also too light."[3] The use of the cross, he declared, is detrimental to a true Christian faith: "the Crosse evacuateth and polluteth Faith".[4] "The special hypocrisie of the Crosse", he sneered, "is evidently declared in the lyfe and conversation of those that did beare it."[5]

There was the vexed subject of kneeling. Samuel Hieron, in *A Dispute upon the Question of Kneeling, in the Acte of Receiving the Sacramentall bread and wine proving it to be unlawfull*, wrote: "It is a bowing downe in the act of divine service, before a consecrated creature, out of a religious respect and reverence of it, and so against the 2 commandement."[6] It is, he claimed, a relic of Roman idolatry. "It was, for the worshipping of a forged and breaden Messiah, first brought into practise in the Church by that Antichrist of Rome, aboue 1200 yeares after Christ, and still used for that purpose by him and his members, and therefore in divers respects cannot lawfully be intertayned by the true professors of the Gospell." Accepted custom was defended by T. Rogers in *Two Dialogues, or Conferences . . . concerning kneeling in the very act of receiving the Sacramental bread and wine, in the Supper of the Lord* (1608). He had succeeded, so he proudly informed his readers, in bringing the Reverend Thomas Seffray[7] to a better frame of mind: "though he disliked, yea, and depraued our kneeling at the holy Communion, as much as any man could do . . .: yet notwithstanding after friendly and brotherly conference had with him thereabout, altered his mind, allowing that which before hee condemned."

There was the perennial problem of providing "Learned

---

and therefore, That the Ministers of the Gospel, for the bare and sole omission of them in Church-Service, for conscience sake, are most unjustly charged of disloyalty to his Maiestie, 1605. *A Short Treatise of the Cross in Baptism. A Proposition on Concerning Kneeling in the very act of receiuing*, 1605.

[1] Published 1607. [2] Op. cit., p. 7. [3] Ibid., o. 135.
[4] Ibid., p. 153. [5] Ibid., p. 163. [6] Ibid., p. 51.
[7] See below, p. 203.

preachers, graue and discreet elders, and faithful distributing Deacons". On the one hand, men could see "the pompouse and lordly estates of Bishops", on the other hand, "the horrible abhominations of the vnpreaching Ministery".[1] The Puritans bitterly complained that the bishops encouraged the evil by their own greedy pluralism. It was a situation of notorious scandal, and it lent itself to satire. "The humble petition of vs the vnpreach-able Ministers of England, to our good King" has become a classic.

Good King. Now that the heate of all other Supplicants is well quenched, we that have long bin dumb and silent, and yet can say little, have resolved to set down our homely petition to your good Majesty, trusting that, althowgh we tremble to come neare your roiall person, because they say your Grace is admirably learned; yet that somebody or other will bestow the tendering of it to your Graces hands in the behalfe of vs, a company of the most wretched Subjects that serve in your Graces dominions. Alas (our good leige King) what shall become of vs; who in your gratious Sisters dayes lived alwayes in feare, though not greatly hurt; and now much more have occasion to be disquieted, seeing we are daily more despised, rated, and threatened by our fellow ministers and the Sermon-sick people of all sortes then ever before. Shall there never be any Injunction made to stop their mouths that call vs (being men and Christians) Domme dogges, Idol Ministers, vnsavory salt, asses yoked with oxen, clouds without raine, Pittes without water, Spottes and blurres instede of starres, blinde Guides, and a thousand such wicked names? Why? What a mischiefe? God forgive vs for being in a choler . . . on all hands we are sought to be shuffled out and discarded; which cannot chuse but grieve vs that faine wold live at ease, howsoever we beare it out in company and set a good face vpon a bad matter.[2]

The deepest cause of difference and dissension was not the validity of ceremonies and the remedy of abuses, but the question concerning the apostolic form of Church government. In the ultimate analysis, this was the fundamental matter at issue. From time to time, in the tedious and interminable discussions con-cerning ceremonies, the basic issue was raised.

The case for presbyterianism was set out in *An Assertion for True*

---

[1] *Lambeth MSS.*, 113, f. 235. 1605.
[2] *Rawlinson MSS.*, B.151, f. 14.

and Christian Church-Policie. Wherein certaine politike obiections made against the planting of Pastours and Elders in every Congregation are sufficiently aunswered. And wherein also sundrie projects are set downe, how the Discipline by Pastors and Elders may be planted, without any derogation to the Kings Royal prerogatiue, any indignitie to the three Estates in Parleament, or any greater alteration of the laudable Lawes, Statutes, or Customes of the Realme, then may well be made without damage to the people. Published anonymously towards the end of 1604, the author was probably Thomas Stoughton. Episcopacy was refuted as unapostolic:

> I can not but marueile, that a disciple of the Apostles doctrine, and a successor in the Apostles Chayre should bee drawne by humane reasons, not to like of the Apostles gouerment, not to tread in the steps of the primitive church. . . . The gouerment of the church, by Archbishops, Bishops . . . now already planted and like of, was not practised by the Apostles, and primitiue church.[1]

There were differences of judgement. William Bradshaw and Henry Jacobs argued that the apostolic form of Church government was congregationalism or independency. According to Bradshaw:

> Euery Companie, Congregation, or Assemblie of man . . . is a true visible church of Christ . . . all such Churches or Congregations . . . are in all Ecclesiastical matters equall, and of the same power and authoritie, and that by the word and will of God they ought to haue the same spirituall priuilidges, prerogatiues, officers, administrations.

No Church has any pre-eminence over any other:

> Christ Jesus hath not subiected any Church or Congregation of his, to any other superior Ecclesiasticall Iurisdiction then unto that which is within it self . . . noe other Churches or Spirituall Church officers haue (by warrant from the word of God) power to censure, punish, or controule the same: but are only to counsell.

As there is no superiority among Churches, so there should be no superiority among ministers:

> The Pastors of particular Congregations are, or ought to be, the highest Spirituall Officers in the Church, over whom, (by any divine Ordinance) there is noe superior Pastor but onelie Iesus Christ. . . . No Pastor ought to exercise or accept of any Civill

[1] Op. cit., p. 5.

publique Iurisdiction and authoritie, but ought to be wholly imployed in spirituall offices and duties to that congregation over which he is set.[1]

The views of Bradshaw were supported by Henry Jacobs:

All offices and Ministeries in the Church which are found in the scripture as instituted by God, are in the affirmative parte of this second Commandment. Which are of 2 sorts: either temporary; or perpetuall and ordinary. The temporary were Apostles, Prophets, Euangelists; which are Ministeries generall and unlimited, immediatly called of Christ, and infallible in doctrine. Howbeit since the first planting of the Churches, these by the hand of God him selfe have ceased and are gone, as having attained the end and fulfilled that use for which they were given. Neither are we by any meanes to presume that we have any of them, or to looke for them now. But alwaies now the ordinary Ministeries viz. Pastors, Teachers, Elders, and Deacons to particular Congregations, are to remaine both as only lawfull, necessary, and sufficient for us.[2]

The true Church, "instituted in the Scripture and commended unto us and practised by the Saints", has certain characteristics, "such as these, Ioyning by willing consent into a visible Church, the Churches like consent in making of Ministers, Excommunicating the impenitent offenders with in, keeping forth of the malicious and untractable without, preaching, reading, hearing of the Scriptures, Administring and receaving of Sacraments. . . ." All offices, actions, signs, and ceremonies, "whether inward or outward, Divine or Humane ordinances . . . are very parts of Gods speciall worship instituted, true or false: they are matters of doctrine, matters of Faith, matters of substance in religion, yea matters of salvation, and necessary more or less either to be used or refused".[3]

---

[1] W. Bradshaw, *English Puritanisme Containening the maine opinions of the rigidest sort of those that are called Puritanes in the Realme of England*, 1605.

[2] *A Plaine and cleere Exposition of the Second Commandement*, 1610.

[3] Cf. H. Jacobs, *Reasons taken out of Gods Word and the best humane Testimonies proving a Necessitie of Reforming our Churches in England. Framed and applied to 4. Assertions wherein the foresaid purpose is contained*, 1604. *The Divine Beginning and Institution of Christs True Visible or Ministeriall Church. Also The unchangeableness of the same by men; vis. in the forme and essentiall constitution thereof*, Leyden, 1610. *An Attestation of many Learned, Godly, and famous Divines, Lightes of Religion, and pillars of the Gospell, justifying this doctrine, viz. That the Church governement ought to bee alwayes with the peoples free consent. Also this, That a true Church under the Gospell contayneth no more ordinary Congregations but one . . .*, 1613.

Cranborne, at the instigation of the King, requested Thomas Bilson, Bishop of Winchester, to reply to the pamphlet.

> There is lately come to his Majesty's hands a pamphlet against the ecclesiastical government by one Jacob. And because you have had some dealings with him lately, and have formerly (to your great commendation) handled that argument in your book of the perpetual government of the church, his Majesty is desirous that you should frame some short answer unto the said pamphlet.[1]

The Bishop readily agreed:

> I received your letters . . . signifying his Majesty's desire that a pamphlet by one Jacobs against ecclesiastical government of this realm might be answered by me. I am not unwilling to take any pains which my years may bear. . . . The man is only a man of a bold face, and his book a packet of words grounded on his own good liking, having neither sap nor substance worth the answering, yet am I so well acquainted with his humour of much prating and little proving that I forsee what a world of words the cause will come unto.[2]

Jacobs was a man of astonishing industry. His activities as agitator and organizer have already been noted. He was also a man of literary fertility and no mean pamphleteer. He was responsible for *A Christian and Modest Officer of a Most Indifferent Conference, or Dispvtation, abovt the maine and principall Controversies betwixt the Prelats, and the late silenced and deprived Ministers in England: Tendered by some of the said Ministers to the Archbishops, and Bishops, and all their adherents*. His object was a conference on the subject of Church government. He was supremely confident that such a conference would win a favourable verdict for independency:

> And if by such an indifferent Conference as is heere tendered, we shall not make it as cleere unto your Maiestie as the Sunne at Noone-day, that the Gouernement of the Churches of Christ by Pastors, Teachers, and Elders, is much more agreeable to the State of a Monarchy, then is the present Governement by Archbishops, bishops, Archdeacons, Commissaries, and the rest of that Romish Hierarchy, let us then finde no favor in your Maiesties eyes.[3]

---

[1] *Cecil MSS.*, 109, f. 82. H.M.C., Part XVI, pp. 421–2. N.D.
[2] Ibid., 97, f. 139. H.M.C., Part XVII, p. 5. 4 January 1604/5.
[3] *Gibson MSS.*, Vol. V, 933, f. 23 (Lambeth Palace Library) "A Petition presented to K. James I by some of the late silenced and deprived ministers." Printed, 1606, p. 2.

In the meantime, he urged that ministers

> may be exempted from the jurisdiction of the Prelats, the Ministers
> restored agayne to their Ministerie from which they haue been
> unjustly deprived, freed from the Conformitie and subscription
> requyred, and may (with their Elderships and Churches) be subject
> only to the authoritie and jurisdiction of the Civill Magistrate.

He was persuaded that they would conform "themselues . . . in
all things" with the saving proviso: "always so farre as they
may with a good conscience".[1]

Jacobs was impenitent and unabashed. In a book published at
Leyden, he expressed his grieved surprise that "they expressly
refused at Lambeth a most equall and umpartiall tryall offered
unto them, in the presence of sundry silenced and imprisoned
Ministers, being called about that little printed booke which was
then newly published even for that purpose".[2]

Different pamphleteers, in terms of varying scurrility, attacked
the monstrous regiment of bishops. An anonymous petitioner
complained that James had "been all moste three yeares Kinge
of Ingland", and yet had "nott abollished the false waies of
antichriste yet Remaininge withe false worshippe and false
officers thereof with their maintenance". He urged James to
finish what Henry VIII had begun:

> Doubtles if the lord had suffred him to have seene further he would
> have abollished further. As to abollish the rest of that brood as lord
> archebishop, lord bishop, lord chaunceler, archdeacon, decons,
> priestes, half priestes, withall that rable that cam out of the bottomless
> pit; the antichristian lord bishops, or as I maie trulie saie, false
> christes, because they set forth theire own popish lawes, for men to
> observe contrarie to christes lawes, as the pope of lambeth hath set
> forth his canons.[3]

The ecclesiastical jurisdiction, according to another writer, was
an usurped jurisdiction:

> There is noe Doctor nor prelate of them all, that can proue him
> selfe to haue a iuste and lawfull Christian calling by Christ and his

---

[1] Op. cit., pp. 5–6.

[2] *The Divine Beginning and Institution of Christes True Visible or Ministeriall
Church, Also The Unchangeableness of the same by men; viz. in the forme and essentiall
constitution thereof*, Leyden, 1610. Preface.

[3] S.P. Dom., *Jas. I*, 14, Vol. XVII, no. 75. 1605.

holy Disciples, or to haue any power giuen of Christ to him, whereby to vsurpe any office of tyranie and oppression, vexation and murder of vs, who are the electe belieuers and Sainctes by calling of our holy lord and King Jesus Emmanuel Christ.[1]

It was apparent, according to another, that "the present Ministerie of the Church assemblies of England, whatsoever it professe in word, yet is in deed the ministerie of Christs apostacie".[2]

An Humble Supplication for Toleration and libertie to enioy and observe the ordinances of Christ Iesus in th'administration of his Churches in lieu of humane constitutions appeared in 1609. We are fortunate to possess the King's annotated copy, now preserved in Lambeth Palace Library. Arguing that "the present Conformitie and Subscription should in politique discourse and reason determine and not further be pressed", the petitioners claimed that "the remedie, prepared to cure the disease of the State, doth in the application thereof augment and strengthen the maladie".[3] The King's laconic comment is: "Ye alleadge and conclude quhat ye liste, but the contraire positions to all these will ever prowe trew." The authors declared that "the observed experience of sundrie yeares under your Majestie and your predecessor Queen Elizabeth, doth witnes and proclayme to the world, that for freeing the church from the sickenes of Division and Faction, the urging of the said Conformitie is no receipt of any soveraine vertue in that behalf".[4] James indignantly noted: "The too great toleration of you in quene Elizabeths tyme hath made you now to be prickkels in oure sydes."

James adhered firmly to the doctrine "No bishop; no King". He distrusted the political implications of Puritanism: "I have learned of what cut they have been, who, preaching before me, since my coming into England, passed over, with silence, my being Supreme Governor in causes Ecclesiastical."[5] He needed no warning, he confessed, about "proud Puritanes, claiming to

---

[1] The Pamphlet in Dr Williams's Library has this note; *A Common Apologie of the Chvrch of England: Against the vniust Challenges of the oueriust Sect, commonly called Brownists,* by T. H[all].

[2] *Certayne Reasons and Arguments Proving that it is not lawfull to heare or have any spirituall communion with the present Ministerie of the Church of England,* 1608, p. 39.

[3] Op. cit., p. 32.

[4] Ibid.

[5] Quoted, C. H. McIlwain (ed.), James I, *Political Letters,* p. xc.

their Paritie, and crying, Wee are all but vile wormes, and yet, will iudge and giue law to their King, but will be iudged nor controlled by none".[1] The Puritans were greatly distressed about these charges. They protested their loyalty: "We . . . the ministers . . . neither hold in opinion nor intertaine in practise any matter either preiudiciall to your royall State, Supremacie and Preroga-tives."[2] They denied revolutionary intent. William Bradshaw, in *A Protestation of the Kings Supremacie. Made in the Name of the afflicted Ministers, and opposed to the shameful Calumniations of the Prelates,*[3] reiterated their obedience to the laws of the State. It was true that they disagreed about the form of ecclesiastical government, but they found no fault with the civil government. The "Discipline by Pastors and Elders" might be planted, according to the testimony of another writer, "without any derogation to the Kings Royal prerogatiue, any indignitie to the three Estates in Parleament, or greater alteration of the laudable Lawes . . .".[4] It was a wilful and malicious distortion of the truth to make "kinges and princes . . . beleeue that their state could not endure nor their Kingdome stand if these thinges should be reformed".[5] They were ready at all times to take the oath of supremacy.

> Som Ordinaryes in their publike sentences, haue most uniustly charged some Ministers [a marginal note adds: "The Bishop of Lincolne against the Ministers of Leicestershire "] with denyall of the oth to the Kings supremacy: which notwithstanding, divers tymes before, they had willingly sworne unto, and which at the very instance of pronouncying the sentence, they offred before their Ordinary to sweare unto agayne.[6]

Bancroft was unmoved by these professions and protestations of innocence. He secured a further commission on 9 February 1605/6, authorizing him to reform abuses and disorders in the

---

[1] James' *Works*, p. 175.
[2] *An Humble Supplication for Toleration and libertie to enioy and observe the ordin-ances of Christ Iesus in the administration of his Churches in lieu of humane constitu-tions,* 1609, pp. 17–18.
[3] Published anonymously. *Egerton MSS.,* 2,877, f. 170. 1605.
[4] [W. Stoughton] *An Assertion for True and Christian Church-Policie,* 1604.
[5] *Lambeth MSS.,* 113, f. 235. 1605.
[6] *A Myld and Ivst Defence of Certeyne Argvments, at the Last Session of Parliament directed to that most Honorable High Court, in behalfe of the Ministers suspended and deprived, etc.: for not Subscribing and Conforming themselues . . .* 1606, p. 79.

Church, to repress seditious books, and to enforce conformity.[1] He was not slow to use the power thus conferred on him. In *A Discourse of the Abuses now in Question in the Churches of Christ. Of their Creeping in, Growing up, and flourishing in the Babilonish Church of Rome. How they are spoken against, not onely by the Scriptures, but also by the ancient Fathers, as long as there remained any face of a true Church maintained by publique authority. And likewise by the lights of the Gospell, and blessed Martyrs of late, in the midst of the Antichristian darkness,* Thomas Whetenhall had, with aggressive and offensive bluntness, asserted:

> If the Lords and Bishopes . . . would ioyne together and first crie unto God for the saluation of their soules, and then on their knees to desire his Maiestie to pardon their former offence, and . . . to take from them their great liuings and pompous estate and unlawful superioritie ouer the Churches . . . his Maiestie would surely say; now it is euident to all men . . . that you seeke Gods glory and not your owne.[2]

Bancroft promptly caused a warrant to be directed "unto Richard Browne, a Messenger, to search the sayd Mr Whetenhall's House, for all suche of the sayd Bookes, as may be founde either there or in the Lodging of Josyas Nichols". He "likewise entreated Doctor Cover's paines, to assist the sayd Messenger". Writing to Sir Francis and Sir George Fane, the Archbishop said: "I do verry hartilie pray you, that you will gyue them your best helpe and direction in this busynes as there shalbe occasion, and as you shalbe moved by vertue of the sayd warrant."[3]

The confiscation and destruction of Puritan literature, however, was not always so easily accomplished. Many works were published abroad. Writing to Sir Ralph Winwood, Bancroft said:

> I suppose it is not unknown unto you, that sundry factious and schismatical persons, who have cut themselves off from the communion of our Church, and are thereupon departed out of the land, have planted themselves in divers towns of the Low Countries, where they have liberty, without impeachment or contradiction, to publish in print many dangerous books and pamphlets in English, to the maintenance of such their anabaptistical opinions, and to the slander of the Ecclesiastical Government established here in England.

[1] *S.P. Dom., Jas. I.,* 14. Vol. XII, no. 66.
[2] Op. cit., p. 226.
[3] *Additional MSS.,* 34,218, f. 187 b. 24 January 1606/7.

Which their insolency being lately made known to his Majesty, he willed me to give notice thereof unto Sir Noell Caron, that he might write unto the States for redress of the same. ... Wherefore ... deal with the States, not only for the stay of the said books in Amsterdam, but likewise for the suppressing and restraining of all other such English books which shall be, at any time hereafter, offered to be printed in any of the cities or towns under their government.[1]

In this work of censorship and suppression Bancroft had the ready assistance and collaboration of powerful friends. Salisbury succeeded in intercepting a book, which he forwarded to the Archbishop. Bancroft gratefully replied:

My verye good Lord. I thanke your Lordship with all my harte for the booke sent unto me. I never sawe it before. ... It seemeth by your Lordships letter that many bookes of this sort are come over: and therfore I pray your Lordship to doe what you can for the intercepting of them, or that you wil be pleased to direct me howe I may meete with them.[2]

The Puritans failed in their attempt to frustrate and defeat the enforcement of the canons. Bancroft, armed with fresh powers of censorship and coercive discipline, was determined to proceed to the deprivation of the refractory and recalcitrant.

[1] Sir R. Winwood, op. cit., Vol. II, p. 195. 9 February 1605/6.
[2] *S.P. Dom., Jas. I*, 14, Vol. XLVIII, No. 86, 6 October 1609.

6

DEPRIVATION

THERE HAS always been a measure of uncertainty concerning the actual number deprived. On the one hand it has been asserted that at least three hundred of the most "painfull, discreet, learned, grave and godly ministers" were deprived; and on the other that only a few, and they the least learned, suffered.

Towards the end of 1605, a Puritan pamphleteer reported:

> I heare a very pitifull and generall complainte of well disposed people for the suspending, depriuing and silencinge of theyre preachers, especiallye in Northamptonshire, where very many haue bine soe proceeded with . . . that the number of such as are deprived, silenced, suspended, and admonished, amounts to some of 275. at the least.[1]

Sir Christopher Yelverton protested to the Archbishop that "the storme hath fallen and thrust owt .300".[2] According to the testimony of another Puritan

> the names of those that haue bene alredy remoued, restrained, or refused to be admitted, togither with those that stand under the censure of admonition, (and therefore may be remoued or restrained when the Bishops will) their nams I say, being taken the first of November 1605 amounted to 270. and upward (And yet there were 8. Bishopricks whereof it could not yet be learned what had bene done in them).[3]

---

[1] Anon. *A Short Dialogue proving that the Ceremonyes, and some other Corruptions now in question, are defended, by none other Arguments then such as the Papists have heretofore used . . . and our Protestant writers have long since answered. Whereunto are annexed certayne considerations why the Ministers should not be removed for the subscription and Ceremonies* (Amsterdam?), 1605, p. 1.

[2] *Lambeth MSS.*, 445, p. 424.

[3] *Egerton MSS.*, 2,877, f. 166 b. Published anonymously. *Certaine Reasons why it seemeth that ye preachers who refuse the subscription and ceremonies vrged, should not for that their refusall be remoued from their chardges, or inhibited to preach, humbly offered to Consideration*, 1605, p. 57. It appears to be the work of Samuel Hieron.

Neal, the Puritan historian, placed the number at three hundred,[1] but Brook affirmed that it was even greater: "by these oppressive measures, four hundred ministers were suspended and cast out of their livings".[2] A contemporary writer, describing the situation in London, referred to "aboue 260. godly Preachers depriued, suspended, interdicted, not admitted, admonished, imprisoned, degraded or excommunicated, and of many more (for the conscience can not be compelled) looking for like seuerity".[3] Another contemporary averred that

> a third or fourth part of three or foure hundred painfull, discreet, learned, grave and godly ministers, within lesse then sixe monethes ... suspended, deprived, or deposed, some from their offices, and some from their benefices; not for the commission of the least of the grossest of sinnes, but only for omission of the least of the commaundements and traditions of men.[4]

When Yelverton asserted that three hundred had been thrust out, the Archbishop sharply replied: "not above .60. ... and ... those .60. were factious". By contrast there were ".10000." who were conformable.[5] John Spotiswood, Archbishop of Glasgow, wrote: "I was afterward told by Richard Bancroft ... that when the Rolls were brought in of those that stood out and were deposed, which was some years after, they were found to be forty-nine in all England, whereas the ministers of that kingdom are reckoned nine thousand and above."[6]

It is not difficult to explain these discrepancies. Before the deprivations took place, the Puritans feared that they might run

---

[1] D. Neal, *The History of the Puritans*, London, 1773–8, Vol. II, pp. 37 ff.

[2] B. Brook, *The Lives of the Puritans*, London, 1813, Vol. I, p. 64.

[3] Anon. *A Suruey of the Booke of Common Prayer, By way of 197. Quaeres grounded upon 58. places, ministring iust matter of question, with a view of London ministers exceptions. All humbly propounded, That they may be syncerely answered: or els Offences Religiously remoued,* 1610, p. 4.

[4] Anon. *Certaine Considerations drawne from the Canons of the last Sinod, and other the Kings Ecclesiasticall and statute law, ad informandum animum Domini Episcopi Wigorensis, seu alterius cuiusuis iudicis ecclesiastice, ne temere et inconsulto prosiliant ad depriuationem ministrorum Ecclesiae: for not subscription, for the not exact use of the order and forme of the booke of common prayer, heeretofore provided by the Parishioners of any parish Church, within the Diocese of Worcester, or for the not precise practise of the rites, ceremonies, and ornaments of the Church,* 1605.

[5] *Lambeth MSS.,* 445, p. 424.

[6] *History of the Church of Scotland,* Edinburgh, 1655, p. 479.

to many hundreds.[1] John Burgess wrote to the King that "six or seauen hundred of the ablest ministers in the land are like to be put out".[2] After conformity had been enforced, contemporary writers estimated that about three hundred had been "suspended, deprived, admonished, or excommunicated".[3] Subsequent writers concluded that three hundred had actually been deprived.[4]

An independent judgement can be arrived at by a careful study of extant episcopal Registers, Act Books, episcopal Court Books, and Visitation Books. Details of Bancroft's Archiepiscopal visitation from May to October 1605, when the Archbishop deprived eight clergymen, are to be found in Bancroft's Register in Lambeth Palace Library. Some of the diocesan Registers have perished, and, of those that remain, some are in a sad state of decay. Nevertheless, sufficient evidence remains to enable certain conclusions to be drawn. The evidence of these conclusions must first be adduced.

THE LONDON DIOCESE

In the proclamation dated 16 July 1604, the Council intimated that those with conscientious scruples and difficulties would be granted a period of grace for the purpose of further conference and reflection. On 7 December it was reported:

This daie allsoe the ministers of London weare befoe the Archbishop elected, whoe hath deprived or suspended none, but referred them over to the Bishop that shall succeede hime. He tolde them that they

[1] Cf. the statement made by Bishop Rudd in the Convocation House that the Puritan ministers were "diuers hundred in number". 23 May 1604. *Harleian MSS.*, 677, f. 41.

[2] *S.P. Dom., Jas. I*, 14, Vol. VIII, no. 85; *Harleian MSS.*, 3,791, f. 176.

[3] Cf. *Cotton MSS., Titus*, F.IV, f. 167; *Journals of the H. of C.*, Vol. I, pp. 384-5.

[4] It is worth noting the divergent estimates of two more recent scholars. On the one hand, Dr S. R. Gardiner: "it has been calculated that about three hundred of the clergy were ejected"; and in a footnote, "the number has been estimated as low as forty-nine; but the arguments in Vaughan's *Memorials* . . . seem to me conclusive in favour of the larger number." *History of England*, London, 1883, Vol. I, p. 213. On the other hand, Dr R. G. Usher: "It became clear that about sixty men were at first deprived, but that, in 1609, when the final returns were given in by the bishops, the number certified was forty-nine . . . The bishops could hardly be charged with carrying matters to an extreme." *Reconstruction*, Vol. II, pp. 6, 10.

weare deceived that thought the ministers refusinge conformitie weare by vertue of the proclamacion to be deprived immediately after November; sayinge, that it was only to publishe a cessation of Lawes formerly made, and in force againste refusers to conforme theimselves vntill such a daie, after which they should be lyable to the lawe as they weare before.[1]

However, on 12 December the Council pointed out that the time of grace allowed had expired, and on 22 December Bancroft informed the bishops that they were to proceed to the enforcement of conformity. Sir Thomas Hoby wrote in alarm to Cranborne that "my Lord of London that now is[2] (I fear by his Grace's speciall directions) has since proceeded so far as that upon Wednesday next no small number of his Majesty's faithful subjects are likely to be scattered as so many sheep without a shepherd".[3] Both the Archbishop and the Bishop of London held public disputations with the Puritans,[4] but these were without effect, and the first deprivations took place at the beginning of February, 1604/5.

Robert Smith was one of the first to suffer deprivation. He matriculated from Trinity College, Cambridge, in 1587; graduated Bachelor of Arts in 1592/3, Master of Arts in 1595, and became a Fellow in 1593.[5] He was instituted Rector of St Nicholas Acon on 7 May 1600, on the presentation of Queen Elizabeth.[6] He was deprived at the beginning of 1605, Henry Bird being presented to the living on 11 February 1604/5.[7] The cause was

---

[1] *S.P. Dom., Jas. I*, 14, Vol. X.A, no. 81. Books and papers found on "Melancthon Jewell, schismatic Puritan of Exeter".

[2] Richard Vaughan, Bishop of Chester, was elected to the bishopric of London on 11 December, the royal assent was given to the election on 18 December, and the temporalities were restored on 24 December. Bancroft's Register, f. 9; *Patent Roll*, 2 Jas. I, 31, c. 66, no. 1661.

[3] *Cecil MSS.*, 188, f. 53. 28 January 1604/5. H.M.C., Part XVII, p. 38.

[4] Ibid., 104, f. 19. 12 February 1604/5. H.M.C., Part XVII, p. 52. "Jo.Co." to Thomas Wilson.

[5] C. H. & T. Cooper, *Athenae Cantabrigiensis*, Cambridge, 1858, Vol. II, p. 479; J. & J. A. Venn, *Alumni Cantabrigienses*, Cambridge, 1922, Vol. IV, p. 107.

[6] "Septimo die mensis Maij anno domino 1600 Robertus Smithe presbiter artium magister admissus et institutus fuit ad Rectorian et ecclesiam sancti Nicholai Acon." Exchequer of First Fruits and Tenths, Bishops' Certificates, London, E.331/8.

[7] "Decimo tertio die mensis Februarij anno domino 1604/5 Henricus Bird presbiter artium magister admissus et institutus fuit ad rectoriam sancti

presumably nonconformity, for later in the year he was licensed to the curacy of Trinity Minories, where he remained for three years.[1]

William Jackson,[2] who had been instituted to the rectory of St Swithin on 15 August 1587, on the presentation of John Hart, citizen and alderman of London, also suffered deprivation at the same time as Smith,[3] Richard Cook being instituted to the rectory on 7 June 1606.[4] The Vicar-General records that the fruits of the rectory were sequestered because of the lawful deprivation and removal of "William Jackson presbyter last Rector and Incumbent of the same", who had been deprived by the royal commissioners for not observing the canons, nor the rites and ceremonies of the Church of England.[5] Nothing is known of his subsequent career.

During the following months, Robert Johnson, who had been instituted to the rectory of Braxted-Parva on 27 November 1602,[6] was also deprived;[7] and Thomas Parker was instituted to his place on 20 December 1605.[8]

Nicholai Acon, Civi. London." Exchequer of First Fruits and Tenths, Bishops' Certificates, London, E. 331/9. Unfortunately, the Bishops' Certificates do not as a rule indicate the cause of the vacancy in the living. The presentation was made by "Henry Byrde" on 11 February 1604/5, *Patent Roll*, 2 Jas. I, 29, c. 66, no. 1659.

[1] G. Hennessy, *Novum Repertorium Ecclesiasticum Parochiale Londinense*, London, 1898, pp. lxxxi, 144; R. Newcourt, *Repertorium Ecclesiasticum Parochiale Londinense* London, 1708, Vol. I, p. 505.

[2] This may be the same Jackson that was connected with the London Classis. See, R. G. Usher, *Presbyterian Movement in the reign of Queen Elizabeth*, London, 1905, p. xxviii.

[3] G. Hennessy, op. cit., p. lxvi.

[4] Exchequer of First Fruits and Tenths, Bishops' Certificates, London, E.331/9. Newcourt gives the date of Cook's institution as 31 May 1605. Op. cit., Vol. I, p. 543.

[5] *Liber Vicarii Generalis.* Stanhope, 1601–5, no. 9, p. 195. London. 26 March 1605.

[6] Exchequer of First Fruits and Tenths, Bishops' Certificates, London, E.331/8. Newcourt gives the date as 26 November. Op. cit., Vol. II, p. 93.

[7] His deprivation was certainly later than April 1605, and was probably later than October 1605. In the Visitation Books of the Archdeacon of Colchester there are these entries:
"April 1604 . . . Braxted-parva. Mr. Johnson Rector"
"October 1605 Braxted Parva, Mr. Johnson Rector
                    Mr. Petrus Barlowe Rector"
D/ACV. 4. Essex Record Office.

[8] Exchequer of First Fruits and Tenths, Bishops' Certificates, London, E. 331/9.

Nicolo Molin, Venetian ambassador in England, reported to the Doge and Senate on 2 March 1604/5, that the contentions between the bishops and Puritans

> present new difficulties every day, for the Puritans are firmly resolved not to submit to the Bishops. Their attitude causes his Majesty and the Council much anxiety, all the more that their number is very great, and they are led by chiefs of great position. His Majesty has been occupied every day in Council upon this subject, and pays attention to nothing else.

He related that:

> Recently, eight days ago, in Saint Paul's, the Cathedral Church of this city, the Archbishop of Canterbury, the Bishop of London, and other Bishops, held a meeting, and summoned to their presence all the Puritan Ministers and preachers. They called upon them to swear to observe the Constitutions recently published by the Bishops, and to promise to recognise the Bishops as their superiors. As the Puritans resolutely and boldly refused, the more audacious were deprived of their benefices, and ordered to leave the Kingdom within a month, others have been suspended, others granted twenty days to make up their minds. This has caused a great turmoil in the city which is full of people who belong to the Puritan sect. Daily meetings are held in private houses. The party shows a determination not to yield, but to take every step for the preservation of their freedom and authority. The King thinks of nothing else than of humbling the pride and audacity of this party; but he meets with much opposition, for among his Council are certain members of the sect, who while seeking to protect their fellows, point out to the King that it is unwise to raise such a hubbub about a matter of so small moment, for after all it is merely a question of ceremonies, such as the wearing of the biretta and the cotta, the use of the cross in baptism, and such like points. . . .

He reported that the King "is resolved to proceed against the Puritans and their ministers, who refused to conform and swear obedience to the Canons, and to deprive them of their benefices and expel them from the Kingdom".[1] John Chamberlain, writing to his friend Sir Richard Winwood, gave a report of events:

> Our Puritans go down on all Sides; and though our new Bishop of London proceeds but slowly, yet at last he hath deprived, silenced,

---

[1] *C.S.P.*, *Venetian*, 1603–9, Vol. X, no. 347.

or suspended all that continue Disobedient, in which Course he hath won himself great Commendations of Gravitie, Wisdom, Learning, Mildness, and Temperance, even among that Faction; and indeed is held in every way, the most sufficient Man of that Coat; yet those that are deprived wrangle, and will not be put down, but appeal to the Parliament, and seek Prohibitions by Law; but the Judges have all given their Opinions that the Proceedings against them are lawful and so they cannot be relieved that way.[1]

According to an observer "the King commends the industry of the Bishop of London, with the diligence of the recorder and other inferior ministers, hoping that it will be a means to stop the mouths of calumniating persons".[2]

The Bishop of London continued the slow work of deprivation. The Rector of Great St Bartholomew, David Dee, was deprived towards the end of the same year. He was educated at St Mary's Hall, Oxford, graduating Bachelor of Arts on 19 November 1568, and Master of Arts on 12 July 1572.[3] He was Vicar of Sherborne, Dorset, in 1580, and held the prebend of Consumpta per Mare in St Paul's Cathedral in 1598, but resigned it after six months.[4] He was instituted to the rectory of Great St Bartholomew, West Smithfield, on 15 June 1587, but was deprived in 1605, when Thomas Westfield was instituted on 18 December.[5]

Next year, Thomas Stoughton, sometime Fellow of Queens' College, Cambridge, was deprived of the living of Coggeshall, Essex. He graduated Bachelor of Arts in 1576/7, Master of Arts in 1580, and was ordained deacon and priest by the Bishop of Lincoln on 13 February 1581/2.[6] He was a member of the Dedham Classis, and he succeeded Newman, a Puritan, when he was instituted to the vicarage of Coggeshall on 22 December 1600.[7]

---

[1] Sir R. Winwood, *Memorials*, Vol. II, p. 48. 26 February 1604/5.
[2] *Cecil MSS.*, 104, f. 50. H.M.C., Part XVII, p. 72.
[3] J. Foster, *Alumni Oxonienses*, 1892, Vol. I, p. 391.
[4] *D.N.B.*, Vol. XIV, p. 270.
[5] R. Newcourt, op. cit., Vol. I, p. 206. Cf. *Harleian MSS.*, 6,955, f. 70. "Transcripts from the London Registers by Dr Matt. Hutton:" "18 Dec. 1605 Tho. Westfield S.T.B. admissus ad rectoriam Sancti Bartholomew Smithfield per privationem David Dee."
[6] J. & J. A. Venn, op. cit., Vol. IV, p. 172.
[7] "Dec. 22 1600 Thomas Stowghton presbiter in artibus magister admissus et institutus fuit ad vicariam de Coggeshall." Exchequer of First Fruits and Tenths, Bishops' Certificates, London, E.331/8. Newcourt gives the date as 12 Dec. Op. cit., Vol. II, p. 160.

On his deprivation, Ralph Cudworth was instituted on 8 April 1606.[1] Stoughton was in trouble before the High Commissioners in 1604 according to the testimony of the churchwardens who presented him, "For that he did not walk the bounds of the parishe for that he was the same weeke before the Highe Commissioners".[2] There was an active group of Puritans at Coggeshall: in July 1604 "Eduard Tyler de Coggeshall" was presented "for that he hathe had a child of vj weeks ould not yet baptised because he wold not acknowledg the Churche of England to be the Churche of Christ, and our minister to be a Lawful minister";[3] and in the same month, another parishioner, "Johannem Awbert de Coggeshall", was presented because "he hathe a Childe thre or fower yeares ould and not yet Baptised".[4] The churchwardens presented "Johannem Bushe de Coggeshall/his daughter had a Child and tendered often to the Minister to have had yt Baptized and as yet ys not baptized", and a marginal note records, "Vicar Mr Stoughton". The next entry concerns another parishioner who "hath a Child a yeare ould and not yet baptized".[5] Most of these presentments occur again,[6] although in the case of "Eduard Tyler" it is reported that he "hathe deliuered his Childe to be baptized according to the book of Comon Prayer".[7] Stoughton, however, was not silenced by his deprivation, for in June (the new Vicar having been instituted in April), it was reported that "Mr Stoughton de Coggeshall, being deprived of his benefice and function doeth often expound the Word in his deske".[8] The churchwardens presented "that yt hathe not bene usual of long tyme in our parishe that the Women haue Comen to give thanks in suche forme as the boke of Comen prayer setteth downe";[9] and they further presented a certain parishioner who "will not abid in the Churche when the Minister putteth on the surplice but goeth [out] of the Churche".[10] The churchwardens

---

[1] Exchequer of First Fruits and Tenths, Bishops' Certificates, London, E.331/9. "8 Aprilis 1606 Rodolphus Cudworth, presbiter sacre Theologie Baccalaureus admissus . . ." The London Register gives the date 4 April 1606. (*Harleian MSS.*, 6,955, f. 70 b.) Cf. R. Newcourt, op. cit., Vol. II, p. 160; Visitation Books, Archdeacon of Colchester. D/ACV. 4.
[2] Act Books, Archdeacon of Colchester, D/ACA, no. 27, f. 124.
[3] Ibid., f. 127.   [4] Ibid., f. 131 b.   [5] Ibid., f. 131 b.
[6] Ibid., f. 138.   [7] Ibid., f. 131.
[8] Ibid., D/ACA, no. 30, f. 196.
[9] Ibid.   [10] Ibid., f. 199.

complain that the burial of the dead has not been conducted according to the Prayer Book. In July 1607 William Bird "ys muche complayned vpon for buring the dead being a meare laye mann"; and being examined, he admitted "that he hathe buried manye deed bodys in the parish of Coggeshall but hathe not redd the forme of buriall sett forthe in the book of Comon prayer neither was ther anye minister present".[1] Again, in September 1606, "Johannem hopper taylor de Coggeshall/did saye that he wold not putt of his hatt when the book of Comon prayer was in reading and that the Bishopes ought not to be prayed for at service and sermon, and that the book of Comon prayer was nothing but mingell mangell";[2] and in March 1608/9, another person was presented "for refusing to bringe witnesses when his child was baptized the xv th of Januarij and ther did disturbe the minister and the Congregation in verye arrogant words hauinge ij other Children then to be baptised".[3]

The career of Peter Ferman or Firmin[4] presents some unusual features for he appears to have been deprived from one living, and at the same time to have kept possession of another. He was later restored to the other living. He matriculated from St John's College, Oxford, on 20 November 1581, and according to Foster, became a Fellow at the age of eighteen in 1580.[5] He graduated Bachelor of Arts on 28 November 1584, Master of Arts on 23 May 1588, and Bachelor of Divinity on 9 February 1594/5.[6] On 20 June 1595, he was instituted to the living of St Clement, Eastcheap,[7] and on 1 October 1602, he was instituted "ad vicariam de Hillingdon cum Capella de Uxbridge eidem annexa".[8] He was deprived from the rectory of St Clement in 1606, Hamlet Marshall being instituted on 1 December; but apparently he was later restored and died there in 1610.[9] He kept

[1] Ibid., f. 203.
[2] Ibid., f. 113 b.
[3] Ibid., D/ACA, no. 32, f. 37.
[4] His name is variously spelt Firmyn, Firmin, Fermyn, Fermyne, Fermin, Ferman, and Fyrmin.
[5] J. Foster, op. cit., Vol. II, p. 541.
[6] Ibid.
[7] Composition Book, P.R.O.
[8] Exchequer of First Fruits and Tenths, Bishops' Certificates, London, E.331/8.
[9] G. Hennessy, op. cit., pp. 129, 221.

possession of the living of Hillingdon until 1609, when he resigned it,[1] and was instituted "ad vicariam de Alvethly alius Alveley".[2]

During 1607 Erasmus Cooke was deprived from the living of St Michael, St Albans. He graduated Bachelor of Arts from Trinity College, Cambridge, in 1584/5, and was appointed Vicar of St Michael's in 1591.[3] He was soon in trouble, but in 1593 a certificate of his conformity was sent to the Chancellor of the Bishop of London, Dr Stanhope:

> Mr Cooke, our vicar, did upon the ... day of October, being Wednesday, in the time of morning service in our parish church, read the book of prayer appointed to be used at public fastings and at the same time did preach a sermon in which he exhorted them that were present unto moderation of diet for that day, and charitable alms to the poor.[4]

Anthony Bacon wrote a covering letter:

> I request you most earnestly to accept this his certificate which I send. He hath protested unto me that if there has been on his part any omission, it was through his mistaking his duty at the first, which he will be ready to repair. Let me entreat you to excuse what is past, and to exempt him from further trouble.[5]

The following year a report of the parish was forwarded to the Bishop: "St Michael's Vicarage, patron, the lady Anne Bacon, widow, valued at £10. 15. od. Erasmus Cooke, the incumbent, Bachelor of Arts, resident, a preacher. Communicants about 260. Men of special note. No recusants."[6] In 1605 Cooke was examined before the Attorney-General, Sir Edward Coke, who declared

---

[1] Ibid., p. 221. Exchequer of First Fruits and Tenths, Bishops' Certificates, London, E.331/9: "March 5 1609 (10) Thomas Awsten clericus collatus et admissus fuit ad vicariam ecclesiae parochialis de Hillingdon cum Capella de Uxbridge eidem annexa."

[2] Exchequer of First Fruits ... London, E.331/9. 5 March 1609/10. Visitation Books, Archdeacon of Essex, D/AEV, no. 4, f. 149 b; R. Newcourt, op. cit., Vol. II, p. 23.

[3] J. & J. A. Venn, op. cit., Vol. I, p. 381.

[4] This was signed by the churchwardens and sidesmen of the parish of St Michael's on 3 October 1593. *Lambeth MSS.*, 649. Quoted, W. Urwick, *Nonconformity in Herts, being lectures upon the Nonconforming Worthies of St Albans, and Memorials of Puritanism and Non-conformity in all the Parishes of the County of Hertford*, 1884, p. 117.

[5] Ibid., p. 117.

[6] Ibid., p. 157.

that he found Cooke "weak and simple".[1] In 1606 it was noted that "Erasmus Cooke, Bachelor of Arts, has provided his habit according to the Canon".[2] But besides strictly ecclesiastical offences, he was also charged with incontinency, and the testimony of his wife was given in this connection. He was declared contumacious for not attending the Archdeacon's Court, and his successor, Zephaniah Besouth, was instituted on 8 December 1607.[3]

Thomas Ravys, Bishop of Gloucester, who was elected to the bishopric of London in 1607, was responsible for further deprivations. William Buckley, who graduated Bachelor of Arts in 1582/3, and Master of Arts in 1586, from Emmanuel College, Cambridge,[4] was deprived from the vicarage of Little Leighs in Essex in 1609. There is an entry in the Act Books of the Archdeacon of Colchester, dated 9 March 1607/8: "Leighes parva Mr William Buckley vicariam ibidem presentat for not wearinge the surplice at anie tyme to our knowledge, and for not vsinge the signe of the crosse in baptizme and alsoe for administeringe the sacrament to those that doe not receyue the same kneelinge."[5] The actual date of his institution to Little Leighs is not known, but it must have taken place some time in the year 1595. The name of Robert Dyxon appears for each of the preceding years in the Visitation Book, and the name of "William Bucklie" after that date.[6] He was deprived at Lambeth on 20 March 1608/9, together with three other Puritans, by the High Commissioners, and on the following day an order was given for the sequestration of the fruits of the benefice into the hands of the churchwardens.[7] On 22 March 1608/9, the Vicar-General records that "Little Lees"

---

[1] *Cecil MSS.*, 104, f. 108. H.M.C., Part XVII, p. 107. 25 March 1604/5.
[2] Act Book of the Archdeacon of St Albans. Quoted W. Urwick, op. cit., pp. 117–18.
[3] Ibid., p. 118.
[4] J. & J. A. Venn, op. cit., Vol. I, p. 248.
[5] Act Books, Archdeacon of Colchester, D/AEA, no. 24, f. 142.
[6] Visitation Book, Archdeacon of Essex, D/AEV, no. 3.
[7] London, *Liber Vicarii Generalis*, Crompton, 1607–11, no. 10, p. 57: "22 Marche. 1608. that this daye was delyvered to James Parkes 4 intimacions dated the 20 of this instante Marche directed to the patrons of these Churches following, viz. Stanbridge voyd by the deprivacion of Ezekiel Culverwell Leigh voyd by the deprivacion of Wm. Negus Little Lees voyd by the deprivacion of Wm. Buckley Fange voyde by the deprivacion of Cam. Rusticen All 4 the same day 20 of Marche deprived at Lambeth by the highe Commissioners."

is "voyd by the deprivacion of Mr Buckley Clerke late vicar there",[1] and on 4 August 1609, his successor Henry Greenwood, was instituted to the living.[2]

Ezekiel Culverwell had a career in some respects similar to that of Peter Fermin, for he suffered deprivation, but he eventually conformed and was reinstated. He graduated Bachelor of Arts in 1573, and Master of Arts in 1577 at Oxford,[3] and was incorporated Master of Arts at Cambridge in 1578.[4] He was suspended for nonconformity in 1583,[5] and was a member of the Braintree Classis in 1587.[6] A Puritan document, dated about 1586, mentions that "Mr Culverwell, pastor of Felsted", was one of "the painfullest ministers in Essex, whom the Bishop threateneth to deprive, sayinge, we shalbe white with him, or he wilbe blacke with us".[7] He was instituted to the rectory of Great Stanbridge in Essex in 1592.[8] He did not repudiate his Puritan views, for he was presented on 25 June 1606, "for not wearinge the surplice, and not vsinge the crosse".[9] According to *State Papers Domestic*, "Mr Culverwell, parson of Great Stanbridge. Disliketh to Compromise himself to the Canons of the Church, and will give up his Livinge".[10] He was deprived by the High Commissioners at Lambeth at the same time as William Buckley. On 22 March 1608/9, the Vicar-General records that Stanbridge is "voyd by the deprivacion of Ezechiell Culverwell".[11] His successor, William Sutton, was

---

[1] Ibid., p. 56. 22 March 1608/9. The Visitation Book of the Archdeacon of Essex, under date May 1609, has the following entry: "Leighs parva Mr Willimus Buckley/vicariam ibidem." The words, "deprivatus est" have been added in a different coloured ink. D/AEV, no. 4, f. 122 b.

[2] Exchequer of First Fruits and Tenths, Bishops' Certificates, London, E.331/9. Newcourt gives the date as 3 August. Op. cit., Vol. II, p. 388. The Visitation Book, under the date April 1610, has this entry: "Leighes parva Mr Willimus Buckley vicariam ibidem", with the name of Buckley erased, and the name "Henr. Grenewood" substituted. D/AEV, no. 4, f. 138.

[3] J. Foster, op. cit., Vol. I, p. 362.

[4] J. & J. A. Venn, op. cit., Vol. I, p. 432.

[5] *D.N.B.*, Vol. V, pp. 288–9.

[6] R. G. Usher, op. cit., p. xxix.

[7] *The Seconde Parte of a Register*, 245. Ed. A. Peel, op. cit., Vol. II, p. 261. This document may be wrongly dated, as Culverwell was not instituted to Felstead till the beginning of the following century.

[8] J. & J. A. Venn, op. cit., Vol. I, p. 432. Archdeacon of Essex, Visitation Book, D/AEV, no. 3.

[9] Act Book, Archdeacon of Essex, D/AEA, no. 23, f. 337.

[10] *S.P. Dom., Jas. I*, 14, Vol. X.A. no. 48.

[11] London, *Liber Vicarii Generalis*, Crompton, 1607–11, no. 10, p. 57.

instituted on 27 March 1608/9,[1] but he himself was later instituted to the vicarage of Felstead.[2] Culverwell was a convinced Calvinist. Archbishop Ussher forwarded "to the worshipfull his dear brother Mr Chaderton, Master of Emmanuel College", a manuscript by Culverwell, entitled: "On the generall offer of salvation made to mankind by God in Christ and of the restraint of its effect to the elect, with a summary of views held thereon."[3] In 1623 he published a *Treatise on Faith*, which reached a seventh edition after his death in 1631.[4]

William Negus, who graduated Bachelor of Arts from Trinity College, Cambridge, in 1577/8,[5] was deprived at the same time. In 1582 he became a member of the Dedham Classis, continuing in it until at least 1586.[6] He was first suspended in 1583/4 for refusing the *Three Articles*. He recounts the cause of his suspension:

> The cause of my suspension was only this. Beinge convented before the Bishop of Wittham, and there by him beinge demaunded whether I had worne the surplice since my comminge to Lee, My answere was that I had not worne yt, so I had never refused yt, for there was none offered, nor any in the parish to be worne. He further asked me if I would weare yt if it were provided. My answere was, I desired his favoure that I mighte proceede in my ministry untill such time as there were a surplice made and that he knewe I refused to weare yt. He, not satisfied with this answere . . . concluded thus: Seeinge yow will not promise to weare yt, we will suspend yow till yow will.[7]

In October 1584 he informed the meeting of the classis that the Bishop had proceeded against him contrary to law, "and that he might preach again". In February 1584/5 he "took his journey to London for his restoring to liberty in his calling, and

<hr>

[1] R. Newcourt, op. cit., Vol. II, p. 542. *Harleian MSS.*, 6,955, f. 71b. Transcripts from the London Registers: "27 March, 1609, Willimus Sutton A.M. admissus ad ecclesiam de Stanbridge magna Com. Essex per privationem Ezekiel Culverwell ad presentationem Thomas Sutton armigeri." The Visitation Book, under date May 1609 has this entry: "Stambridge Mr Ezechiel Culverwell rect. ibidem deprivatus est. Mr Sutton Rect. ibidem"; the latter part of the entry being written in different coloured ink. D/AEV, no. 4, f. 126.

[2] J. & J. A. Venn, op. cit., Vol. I, p. 432.

[3] *Rawlinson MSS.*, C. 849, f. 282.

[4] *D.N.B.*

[5] J. & J. A. Venn, op. cit., Vol. III, p. 529.

[6] *The Minute Book of the Dedham Classis*, 1582–9.

[7] *Seconde Parte of a Register*, 172. Ed. A. Peel, op. cit., Vol. I, p. 274; cf. Vol. II, pp. 164, 261.

he was at that time restored to his public ministry again".[1]
He settled at Ipswich on a year's agreement with the people,
probably as assistant to Dr Robert Norton, common preacher
there. Trouble arose between the two, and Negus seems to have
displaced Norton. He was instituted to the rectory of Leigh in
Essex on 31 March 1585, where he remained until he was deprived on 20 March 1608/9, by the High Commissioners at
Lambeth.[2] The inhabitants of Leigh were grieved at the loss of
their venerable pastor, and urged him to conform.

> It is our great griefe that your mouth is shutt up, and that we are
> deprived of our spirituall comforte, for wee knowe that in time, if it
> continue, yt wilbe our ruine. Wee do also understand that your
> libertie maye be redeemed only by wearinge the surplice at some times,
> and that you shall not be urged any further. It is a thing which we
> wishe with all our harts . . . were removed. But yet we take yt not
> to be a matter of such weighte as that to the hazarde of our souls
> and losse of our spirituall comforte, the not wearinge of yt should
> deprive us of your ministerye, for then we looke to have such an
> one thrust upon us, that we shall be constrained to beare with
> greater things then the surplice, and want our godly instruction.
> We wishe rather to beare with that, and to have your teaching, then
> to beare not only that, but much more, and to be without your
> teachinge. We do therefore intreat yow, as you tender our souls,
> and as yow regarde that accounte which you must make unto God
> for them, not to forsake us for such a trifle.

The twenty-eight signatories termed themselves, "your hungrie
sheep".[3] Negus refused to compromise, and, on 3 August 1609,
John Simmes was instituted to the rectory of Leigh.[4]

At the same time Camillus Rustren or Rustian also suffered
for his nonconformity. He was admitted a pensioner of Corpus
Christi College, Cambridge, in 1558, and matriculated on 27 May
1559, but he does not appear to have taken a degree.[5] After his
ordination he was suspended for eight weeks for not subscribing,

[1] D.N.B.
[2] London, Liber Vicarii Generalis, Crompton, 1607–11, no. 10, p. 57. Visitation
Book, Archdeacon of Essex, D/AEV, no. 4, f. 125. May 1609: "Lee Mr
Willimus Negoose Rect. ibidem./deprivatus."
[3] Seconde Parte of a Register, 172 (1). Ed. A. Peel, op. cit., Vol. I, p. 275.
[4] R. Newcourt, op. cit., Vol. II, p. 384.
[5] C. H. & T. Cooper, op. cit., Vol. III, p. 18.

but was then restored.[1] On 23 May 1581, he was instituted to the rectory of Vange.[2] In 1583 or 1584 he associated with several other Puritan clergy in a supplication to the Lords of the Council: we are (they said)

> in great heavines, some of us being allreadie put to silence, and the rest living in fear, not that we have bene, or can be, as we hope, charged with false doctrine or slaunderous life, but for that we refuse to subscribe that there is nothing contained in the booke of Common praier and of ordaining bishops, priests, and deacons, contrarie to the worde of God.[3]

In a survey of 1586 "of the sufficient, painfull, and carefull prechers and ministers in Essex, who have bene sundrie times molested and vexed, partlie for not wearing the surples, and omitting the Crosse in Baptisme, and such like", the name of "Camillus Rusticus" appears as "pastor of Fange, suspended 8 weeks or ther about for not subscribing and being restored, hath bene of late suspended againe for the same cause".[4] He was deprived on 20 March 1608/9,[5] Richard Taylor being instituted in his stead on 27 April 1609.[6]

A like fate overtook Richard Scott, who was instituted to the rectory of Bushey on 16 July 1584.[7] He probably matriculated from Merton College, Oxford, in 1581, but did not take a degree.[8] There is a report of the parish in the year 1584: "Bushey, a parsonage. The late patron, Henry Hickman is dead, and I know not who hath the patronage. Valued at £18. 2. 1. Richard Scott, clerk, incumbent, a preacher, resident. Communicants

---

[1] T. W. Davids, *Annals of Evangelical Nonconformity in the County of Essex from the time of Wycliffe to the Restoration; with Memorials of the Essex Ministers who were ejected or silenced in 1660–1662* . . ., London, 1863, p. 121.

[2] R. Newcourt, op. cit., Vol. II, p. 613.

[3] *Seconde Parte of a Register*, 143. Ed. A. Peel, Vol. I, p. 225.

[4] Ibid., ed. A. Peel, Vol. II, p. 165.

[5] London, *Liber Vicarii Generalis*, Crompton, 1607–11, no. 10, p. 57. 22 March 1608/9: "Fange voyd by the deprivacion of Camillus Rusticen Clerke, late parson there." The Visitation Book of the Archdeacon of Essex describes him as Rector in October 1608. In May 1609 he is again described as Rector, but another hand has added, "vacat". (f. 121.) In April 1610, the Rector is given as "Camillus Rusticius", which has been erased, and the name "Tayler" substituted. (f. 156.) D/AEV, no. 4.

[6] R. Newcourt, op. cit., Vol. II, p. 613.

[7] Ibid., Vol. I, p. 816.

[8] J. Foster, op. cit., Vol. IV, p. 1,325.

about 240 . . . No recusants."[1] He was deprived about the beginning of the year 1609,[2] and on 8 May William Westerman was
instituted in his place.[3]

On 10 July 1609 Robert Baker was deprived from the vicarage
of Chrishall in Essex, by Bishop Ravys and other commissioners.[4]
He graduated Bachelor of Arts in 1603/4, and Master of Arts in
1607, from Christ's College, Cambridge,[5] and was instituted to
the vicarage of Chrishall on 5 October 1605.[6] He was frequently
presented for non-residency,[7] until he was deprived on 10 July
1609, Abraham Jenne being instituted on 22 September following,[8] and John Griffin on 16 November of the same year.[9]

The last Puritan to suffer at this time was John Spencer, who
was instituted to the chapel of Hoddesdon on 16 September 1592,
and was deprived towards the end of 1609.[10]

THE LINCOLN DIOCESE

Shortly after the promulgation of the canons, William Chaderton, Bishop of Lincoln, held his triennial visitation.[11] The Bishop
desired information about the precise observance of the Prayer
Book and the wearing of the surplice:

> I praye you also informe your selfe of suche good meanes as you
> can devise what ministers they be which doe not conforme them
> selves exactlie to observe the booke of common prayer bothe in
> Service, Sacraments and Ceremonies, and in the wearinge the
> Surplisse and other apparell prescribed by Lawe, for if they continue

[1] Quoted, W. Urwick, op. cit., p. 393.

[2] London *Liber Vicarii Generalis*, Crompton, 1607–11, no. 10, p. 59.

[3] Exchequer of First Fruits and Tenths, Bishops' Certificates, London,
E. 331/9. Newcourt gives the date as 6 May. Op. cit., Vol. II, p. 613.,

[4] *S.P. Dom., Jas. I*, 14, Vol. XLI, no. 24. "Sentence of Deprivation of
Robert Baker, Vicar of Chrishall, diocese of London."

[5] J. & J. A. Venn, op. cit., Vol. I, p. 72.

[6] Exchequer of First Fruits and Tenths, Bishops' Certificates, London,
E.331/9.

[7] London, *Liber Vicarii Generalis*, Crompton, 1607–11, no. 10, p. 57. 20
March 1608/9.

[8] R. Newcourt, op. cit., Vol. II, p. 196.

[9] Exchequer of First Fruits and Tenths, Bishops' Certificates, London,
E.331/9.

[10] R. Newcourt, op. cit., Vol. I, p. 813.

[11] The MS. is dated 1602 but this is plainly an error, as the "Kings Majestie"
is mentioned in the context of the letter.

in their obstinacie the Kings Majestie will have them proceeded
with all without any further tolleration, for so he hathe signifyed
vnto vs the Byshopps when we parted from him: and hath notifyed
also his good pleasure by his publique proclamation (July 16).
Wherefore they must be inquired after bothe by your selfe privatelie,
and publiquelie by the Church wardens and swornemen at the
Visitation, that I may then be certified of theire names and proceede
with them accordinge to his Majesties prescription.[1]

These questions were specifically included in the Visitation
Articles:

Whether you haue in your Church or Chappell all things necessarie
and requisite for Common Praier, and administration of the holy
Sacraments, specially the booke of Common praier lately set forth
by the Kings Maiesties authoritie . . . the Bible of the largest volume
. . . and a comely large surplesse with wide sleeues. . . . And whether
your minister at all times vpon sundaies an [sic] holidaies doe weare
in time of Diuine seruice and administration of the Sacraments, the
surplesse, yea or no, or do suffer any other to saie the common
praier or minister either of the sacraments in your church not
wearing the same . . . and whether doth your minister in the baptizing of children, obserue the orders, rites, and ceremonies appointed
and prescribed in the Booke of Common praier, without any addition, omission, or other innouation.[2]

The *detectiones*[3] reveal more breaches of church order than
any other visitation record at Lincoln. On 3 October 1604 ninety-
three men were cited to appear in the church of St Benedict to
answer to Articles charging them with not wearing the surplice,
and also in some cases, with not using the sign of the cross in
baptism. The Bishop charged those who appeared to subscribe
and conform. Some did so at once, or at the courts held within
the next few weeks; others craved time for deliberation, and this
was granted them.[4]

There were a number of ministers, however, who stubbornly
refused to abandon their nonconformity. On 3 October it was
reported to the Bishop that Alexander Cooke "will rather lose

[1] Correspondence of William Chaderton, Bishop of Lincoln, Cor/B/2, f. 36.
Lincoln Diocesan Record Office.
[2] Quoted, C. W. Foster, *The State of the Church*, Lincoln Record Society,
1926, p. lxvi.
[3] The churchwardens' answers to the Bishop's Articles.
[4] C. W. Foster, op. cit., p. lxix.

his livinge than wear yt" (the surplice).[1] Several others indicated that they were prepared to suffer deprivation rather than conform.

In November 1604, twenty-eight Huntingdonshire laymen presented a petition in favour of the ministers who stood in danger of deprivation,[2] and in the following month thirty ministers of the diocese, under the leadership of John Burgess, presented to the King their reasons for not conforming.[3] They declared

> very many of the learned, fruitfull, and best experienced ministers in the land, dead and aliue, haue iudged these things either so unlawful or inexpedient that they haue chosen rather to endure any outward trouble then to yeeld to the use of them; and we doubt not to affirme that the greatest number of resident able and godly ministers in the land at this day (yea even of such as are drawn to yeeld unto the use of them) doe in their Consciences dislike them, and iudge them needles and unfit.[4]

The Council wrote to Archbishop Bancroft on 12 December concerning the enforcement of conformity, and we have seen that the Archbishop forwarded this letter to the diocesan bishops on 22 December. The Bishop of Lincoln, in the meantime, had not been inactive. In a letter to Dr Montagu, Dean of the Chapel Royal, he reported:

> The unconformists of my diocese, being about 30, appeared before me at Huntingdon, who stand all stiff in their former resolution, viz, that they could not yield either to conformity in apparel, or the Cross in baptism, or subscription; for I examined them particularly, poll by poll, in these three points, unless they might be satisfied in those reasons which in a book they delivered to his Majesty at Hichingbroke.

He had hesitated to proceed to extremities, in the absence of any explicit directive.

> I thought not good to deprive any of them, for I received letters this day from Mr Bullingham, my principal register, signifying

---

[1] Episcopal Court Book, 1602–9, Cj 14, f. 65 d.
[2] *Harleian MSS.*, 677, f. 44.
[3] Published: *An Abridgment of that Booke which the Ministers of Lincoln Diocess delivered to his Maiestie upon the first of December last, 1605* [sic] *Being the first part of an Apologye for themselves and their Brethren that refuse subscription, and conformitie which is required*, 1605.
[4] Ibid., p. 51.

that his Grace of Canterbury could not as yet send any certain direction for my proceedings against them; but as soon as they should be resolved upon, he would send them, neither was there any other Bishop that had as yet censured any of the obstinate ministers with sentence of deprivation, neither yet with three admonitions, as I have done, according to our agreement in Convocation. . . . I gave some four or five of them who had received but two admonitions before, by reason of their bad dealing with me . . . their third, and to all the rest a fourth admonition *in virtute juramenti de praestanda Canonica obedientia in omnibus licitis et honestis Domino Episcopo Lincolniensi et Successoribus suis;* assigning to 8 of the chief the 16th. day of January (for till then judicial days are expired). And to the rest, who are thought altogether to depend upon the other, the 30th day of the same month, *ad audiendam finalem sententiam,* hoping that before that time some sound course of proceeding against them will be resolved upon by my Lord of Canterbury, or the Lords of the Council, taking the opinion of the best lawyers in that behalf, and notified to all the Bishops of our Church, that we may all join in the execution thereof at one time, without prejudice one of another, for it would be a great grief and reproach to us all if we should attempt to do that which is not warrantable by law, or which being done should be reversed by law.[1]

At the beginning of January, the King met the Bishop, and learnt that he had not yet proceeded to deprivation. James was considerably provoked. Sir Thomas Lake wrote to Cranborne that

his Majesty . . . having had long conference with the Bishop of this diocese about the disobedient ministers, his Highness finds in the end that the Bishop draws back in the execution, pretending sometime that he has received no express directions from any public authority, sometime that he has no example of any others' proceedings within their dioceses, namely, of my Lord Archbishop of Canterbury, of whom he says that it were fit that he should show the way to the rest; both because his place is most eminent, and having more access to the King and his Council, his actions would be counted to be the actions of the State. Which fearfulness the King much mislikes, and did think that upon like doubts put by him at his Majesty's last being here, whereof my Lord of Canterbury was advertised, there had been some order given him to proceed, as my Lord of Canterbury did by his letter to his Majesty signify that the Judges had resolved that by law they were deprivable.

[1] *Cecil MSS.,* 108, f. 22. H.M.C., Part XVI, p. 379. 12 December 1604.

The King desired Cranborne to consult with the Council and the Archbishop with a view to immediate orders being issued to the Bishop:

> For his diocese being large and comprising the countries most suspected to be favourers of these men, and many being within his jurisdiction, and he aged and fearful, he had need to have a daily spur, for in effect his Majesty says he has done nothing, neither is about to do. I am to recommend this matter to your care; for I perceive his Majesty takes his credit to be engaged in it, and this Bishop is old and weak.[1]

The charges were unfounded. The very day on which Sir Thomas Lake wrote to Cranborne, the Bishop deprived two notorious nonconformists, John Burgess and Alexander Cooke.

John Burgess was one of the most eminent of the Puritan leaders. He was born at Peterborough,[2] and graduated Master of Arts from St John's College, Cambridge, in 1587.[3] He subsequently graduated Doctor of Medicine at Cambridge in 1612, being incorporated from Leyden, and in 1627 he was incorporated Doctor of Medicine at Oxford.[4] He was "admitted preacher and presbyter by the Bishop of Norwich",[5] and was appointed Rector of St Peter's, Hungate, in Norwich, in 1590.[6] From the very beginning of his ministry he revealed Puritan sympathies. He regarded the ceremonies as not in themselves unlawful and sinful, but as simply inexpedient. If they caused any to stumble, he would not use them; if they caused no offence, he would use them for the sake of peace, for in themselves they were things "indifferent". Burgess was therefore prepared to abide by the judgement of his congregation at Norwich: if they were agreeable to his wearing the surplice and using the ceremonies, he would conform; but if their consciences would be offended by his conformity, he would not. His congregation said that if he wore the surplice "they would never profit by his ministry". and, in

---

[1] Ibid., 188, f. 44. H.M.C., Part XVII, p. 15. 16 January 1604/5.
[2] The Presentation Deed for the living of Waddesdon in 1601 states: "Born at Peterborough. Aged 40." Presentation Deed, 1601, no. 20.
[3] J. & J. A. Venn, op. cit., Vol. I, p. 257.
[4] J. Foster, op. cit., Vol. I, p. 213.
[5] Endorsement on the Presentation Deed, 1601, no. 20.
[6] J. & J. A. Venn, op. cit., Vol. I, p. 257.

obedience to their judgement, he resigned his living.[1] Burgess then removed to the diocese of Lincoln, and in 1601, it being reported that he was not beneficed elsewhere, he was presented to the rectory of the third part of Waddesdon.[2]

Whilst the canons were being debated in Convocation, Burgess was commanded to preach before the King at Greenwich on 19 June 1604. He preached from the text, "For my brethren and companions' sakes, I will now say, Peace be within thee; Because of the house of the Lord our God I will seek thy good", Ps. 122.8–9. He likened the ceremonies to Pollio's glasses, which are "not worth a man's life or livelihood".[3] The King was greatly incensed, and committed him to the Tower. From prison Burgess sent a transcript of his sermon to the King, together with two letters of apology: one to James and one to the Lords of the Privy Council.[4] In the letter to the King, Burgess wrote:

I doe upon my knees confesse unto your most excellent Majesty, that by Pollios glasses, I did intend to notifie the Ceremonies for which this Church of God hath bin in vexation above fifty yeeres. And though they be small things, yet have they caused great troubles; as light exhalations breed great tempests; and the course of Religion hath bin much hindered by them, as in the way of a ship in the sea, by the little fish Remora as Plinie writes. Things (which I confesse) I hold not impious, but needlesse and scandalous, of some so extreamely hated, of others so superstiticiously affected, as a good man cannot tell, whether to please himself best, in pleasing or displeasing others. Many hundred worthy Ministers thinke them unlawfull, and

[1] *D.N.B.*

[2] There are two different Presentation Deeds: "Presented by Q. Elizabeth, by lapse, of John Burges, Master of Arts to 3rd portion of the rectory of Waddesdon vacant. Westminster. 15 July. 43 Eliz." "Presented by Francis Goodwin of Windindon, county of Bucks, Esq. of John Burges Master of Arts to 3rd. of Waddesdon vacant by death. 27 July. 43 Eliz. 1601." Presentation Deeds, 1601, nos. 19, 20. The latter presentation has a detailed endorsement, giving details of the career of Burgess to that date.

Burgess was instituted to the living on 7 August 1604. Exchequer of First Fruits and Tenths, Bishops' Certificates, Lincoln, E.331/2.

In the *Liber Cleri* for 1603 there is this entry: "Wadsden, 3rd. portion Q[uality of benefice] parsonage prop [not appropriate nor impropriate] V[alue] 15 l. P[atron] Sir Francis Goodwin I[ncumbent] John Burges. D[egree] Bac: of diu: Pr[eacher] non L[icenciatus] R[esident] est. Comm [municants] 140." Quoted, C. W. Foster, op. cit., p. 273.

[3] *Rawlinson MSS.*, D.353, f. 36.

[4] *Cecil MSS.*, 187, f. 145. H.M.C., Part XVI, p. 238. "John Burges to Lord Cecil."

12

would surely dye, rather then use them; some others will much
more willingly perform their subjection to your Majesty, in bearing
the penalty, then suffer by their occasion so many to fall off to
Brownisme on the one hand, and others to rise up in scorne, and
contempte of their lightnesse, on the other. This is the state of the
poore Ministry, like that of the Britons, betwixt the sword of the
Saxons, and the sea: in which case, most noble Prince, I protest to
God, I durst not but speak (by way of supplication) before your
presence, more then ever I spoke before the people, for what knew I,
whether God had brought me thither for that time?[1]

Shortly after this, Burgess was required to answer certain
questions concerning his attitude to the discipline and ceremonies
of the Church and subscription. He replied:

1. I doe thinke and belieue touching the government of the
Church by Bishops, as with vs in England: or by ruling of Elders
as in other Churches of God, That neither of them was prescribed
by the Apostles of Christ, neither of them is repugnant to the Word
of God, but may well and profitably be vsed, if more fault be not in
persons then in the Callings themselves.

2. I doe hold and am perswaded of the Crosse and Surples that
as our Church vseth them, they be not vnlawfull, though in some
men and places soe inexpedient, as that I thinke no mans Ministerie
likelie to doe so much good, as some mens sodaine vse of them might
doe hurt.

At this point Burgess added a marginal note: "I prayed the
Deane to enterpret my selfe for one of those vnto his Maiestie."
As regards subscription:

3. ffor the subscription to the Articles of 1562 as the law requireth
it, and to his Majesties supremacy, I approve yt, without any
Exception or qualification; And touching the third article about the
booke of Common Prayer, and Booke of ordination, doe hold, That
how soever they have some things in them which cannot be allowed,
as false translations &c yet considered in the purpose and intention
of the Church of England and reduced to the doctrines which it
publiquely professeth, they Conteine nothing contrarie to the

---

[1] *S.P. Dom.*, *Jas. I*, 14, Vol. VIII, no. 85. 2 July 1604. *Harleian MSS.*,
3,791, f. 176; *Rawlinson MSS.*, D.353, f. 43 b. The sermon and letters of apology
were published in 1642: *A Sermon preached before the late King James his Majesty
at Greenwich, the 19. of July, 1604. Together with two letters in way of Apology for
his Sermon: The one to the late King James his Majesty; the other to the Lords of his
Majesties then Privie Councell.* This pamphlet dates the sermon 19 July, but all
the MS. sources give the date 19 June.

Word of God. And in witnes that this is my unfeigned iudgment to the premisses I have sett my name the second of Julye 1604.[1]

A week later, 9 July, Burgess was called before Bancroft, still Bishop of London, and Montagu, Dean of the Chapel Royal, and received "many sharp rebukes". He was ordered to subscribe to the *Three Articles*. Burgess related:

> wee stood a tyme in cleereing some exceptions then taken: At last I prayed leave to write downe the same limitation, which I had written to his Majestie and then read before them, which being denied as idle and needelesse to be expressed, because yt was alwaies implied and vnderstood (I takeing them both and God to witnesse) That I did subscribe in the same sense and with the same limitation which I had written to his Majestie, did then subscribe.

Bancroft was concerned, not only with subscription, but also with conformity. Burgess replied that although he did not object to the lawfulness of the ceremonies, he had once resigned his living rather than use them, so that he could not now yield to conformity until he had done what he could "to prevent offence". In a letter to the Bishop of Lincoln, Burgess said:

> Two daies after this I was called againe before the Bishop [of London] to bee discharged for imprisonment by order from his Majesties Counsell, at what tyme the Bishop exhorted mee to conforme my selfe and perswuade other men for Conformitie. I besought his Lordship not to expect it at my hands, nor to say I doubled with him yf I performed it not so long as the feare of scandall should constreine mee, adding, that his Lordship might gayne great honor to himselfe and peace to the Church by sheweing Compassion vpon the Ministers in a few light things, when their hearts were enclined to peace.[2]

On 3 October 1604 Burgess appeared before the Bishop of Lincoln for not wearing the surplice nor conforming himself to the use of the ceremonies of the Church in the celebration of divine service, and was admonished to conform and subscribe. The Bishop of Lincoln subsequently declared that Burgess, in the presence of all the other ministers, had acknowledged:

---

[1] *Rawlinson MSS.*, D.353, f. 46.
[2] Ibid. Much of this material is also found in *Harleian MSS.*, 3,791, ff. 167–77. It is in chaotic disorder. It can be sorted out by comparing it with *Harleian MSS.*, 677, f. 49, and with *Rawlinson MSS.*, D.353, f. 36 ff.

1. that the ceremonies of the Church were lawful;
2. that they ought to be used, seeing they were established by the Church and commanded by the magistrate;
3. that he himself would use them after the day specified by his Majesty's proclamation;
4. that he desired time to confer with his fellow ministers to persuade them, and that he might also confer with his own people to induce them, lest if he should change upon the sudden, they would fall away from him. . . .[1]

Burgess had previously subscribed four times, but he now wrote unto the Bishop: "I present vnto you my determinate Answere, and therein my refusall of such subscription as your Lordship and the late Canons do require." He was not being inconsistent: "ffirst . . . I have fower tymes subscribed to the booke of Common Prayer, with limitation and reference of all things therein conteined vnto the purpose and doctrine of the Church of England. And this limitation I either wrote downe, or protested before witnesse."[2] The Bishop of Lincoln reported: "Burges continues his former refusall, alleging . . . that he did never subscribe but with a protestation and an interpretation of his meaning (which I assure you is untrue, for he did simply subscribe before me when he was admitted to Waddesden)."[3] Burgess replied: "I never promised present conformity in practise howsoever I confessed the Ceremonies not simply vnlawfull, as I did also since before your Lordship." The Canons had materially altered the basis of subscription:

Now because it may seeme a part of dishonesty or levitie now to refuse the Conditions soe oft accepted I beseech your Lordship to weigh this mine answere; That forasmuch as the purpose (if not doctrine) of our Church, to which I referred my Subscription appeareth vnto mee by the late Cannons, booke of Conference and some speeches of your Lordship, and some others to be varied somewhat from that which I before (not without reason) tooke yt to bee, I hold myselfe to be where I was, but the state of subscription to bee Chaunged from it selfe, partly in the end of requiring subscription, partlie in the things subscribed vnto. I ever tooke our

[1] *Cecil MSS.*, 108, f. 22. H.M.C., Part XVI, p. 379. 12 December 1604. Bishop of Lincoln to the Dean of the Chapel Royal.
[2] *Rawlinson MSS.*, D.353, f. 46.
[3] *Cecil MSS.*, 108, f. 32. H.M.C., Part XVI, p. 379.

subscription to import an admission of things as so farre tolerable (taken in the Churches intention) That men not otherwise prejudiced might lawfully vse them being imposed. This Conceipt the words of the subscription (in which wee acknowledge the booke such as may lawfully be vsed) did breede in mee. And the ordinary speeches of your Lordshippe and other Bishopps did strengthen, as namely that the Ceremonies were trifles, Raggs, beggarlie rudiments . . . which if it pleased the King to remove they would bee glad. All which are pleas for tolleration, rather then approbation of them. . . .

But now I perceive by the Clause of the third Article of subscription, wherein ex animo wee must professe to subscribe to all things conteined in any of the three Articles, And by the sixt Cannon, where the approbation of the rights and Ceremonies is provided for as well as the vse, and by the whole tenure of the Cannons which doth apparantly condemne and preiudge all Clayme made or to be made for any alteration.

Now my Lord if this be the intention of our Church in requiring subscription, I Cannot yeald thereto.[1]

He had not revoked his former subscriptions "but onely refused a new". "I had reason for that which I did and that which I doe . . . the interpretation of ambiguous things maketh good or evill . . . it is neither straunge nor vnfitt to chaunge the iudgment as the evidence chaungeth." He had now reached the end of his public ministry in the Church he had loved and served:

For the rest I will now speak as a dyeing man, counting my selfe after xx tie yeares ministry (painfully, I thank God, peaceably, as his Church knoweth, would God I could adde fruitfully) spent in the Churches service, vtterly cast out of service and of all meanes of maintenance, charged with a wife and x Children in a poore Estate . . . and would God you would think that our labour in the Church might doe more good in one yeare than the Ceremonies while the world standeth. . . . As for mee, I shall praye alwaies for the Kings Majestie, and the State, for you and the Church of God, and henceforth striue to live as a peaceable private member of that Church, in which I was not soe happy to live a publique though an honest and peaceable minister.[2]

This moving letter, with its defence of past practice and present resolution, proved so persuasive that Dr Covell, later sub-dean of

---

[1] *Harleian MSS.*, 3,791, f. 173.
[2] *Rawlinson MSS.*, D.353, f. 46.

Lincoln Cathedral, was charged to prepare an answer.[1] Burgess disclaimed responsibility for its publication and dissemination: "that writing which was private became public without my knowledge of it; but no man can truly say that in that book I say anything at all to prove these ceremonies unlawful to be used, whatever there be said against the urging of them."[2] He was prepared, so he informed the King, to resign his living rather than conform. The ceremonies were inexpedient: "they seem slight, but if their derivation be from Antichrist, they are hatefull. If the simple vse of them be considered, they are shaddowes, but yf the late abuse (which is hardly severed from the things) they are gyants, but if there vse not so, while the Papists insult, the zealous mourne."[3]

On 31 October 1604 Burgess failed to appear before the Bishop, and was pronounced contumacious, and on 12 December he, together with others, received a third admonition "in virtute juramenti de praestanda Canonica obedientia in omnibus licitis et honestis Domino Episcopo Lincolniensi et Successoribus suis", being assigned until 16 January.[4] On the latter day, Burgess, according to his own account, offered to subscribe in the same sense in which he had previously subscribed,[5] but he was deprived for not conforming himself "after four admonitions".[6] According to the Episcopal Court Book he appeared

[1] W. Couell, *A Briefe Answer vnto Certaine Reasons by way of an Apologie deliuered to the Right Reuerend Father in God, the L. Bishop of Lincoln by Mr Iohn Bvrges: wherein he laboureth to prooue, that hauing heretofore subscribed foure times, and now refusing (as a thing vnlawfull) that he hath notwithstanding done lawfully in both,* London, 1606.

[2] Quoted, *D.N.B.*

[3] *Rawlinson MSS.*, D.353, f. 46. The *D.N.B.* has treated the letters to the Bishop of Lincoln and to the King as identical. The two letters, alike in substance, are different in form. A transcription of the letter to the King is printed in the Appendix p. 564.

[4] *Cecil MSS.*, 108, f. 22. H.M.C., Part XVI, p. 379. Cf. "A briefe . . . of the L: B: of Lincoln his proceedinge against those ministers in his diocesse which were presented vnto his Lp. for not conforminge. . . ." Printed, C. W. Foster, op. cit., p. 363.

[5] *Rawlinson MSS.*, A.419, f. 48 ff. "A Particular of those Interpretations of some things Questioned in the matter of subscription, with which I had satisfied my selfe in former times, and with which I offered to subscribe the same day wherein I was deprived for not subscribing, which were presented to his Maiesty by the Bishop of Winchester, and after to his Lo: Grace of Canterbury, vpon which I was restored to my ministry."

[6] C. W. Foster, op. cit., p. 364. Cf. "A note of vnconformed ministeres in

et fatetur that he hath not yet conformed himself nor hath anie certificate according to the admonicion given to him. And further saith that he will not now conforme himself niether can he doe yt for such reasons and consideracions as he hath delivered in writinge vnto the Kinges most excellent Majestie.[1]

Burgess's subsequent career is revealing. After his deprivation, he retired to Leyden, where he graduated Doctor of Medicine about 1611, and then returned to England. He was incorporated Doctor of Medicine of Cambridge University,[2] whereupon James complained that he had been admitted without first subscribing to the *Three Articles* in Canon 36, and branded him as "one who upon a humour or spirit of faction or schism apostatizing from his orders and ministry, hath betaken himself to the profession of physic".[3] As a consequence of this, the University passed a statute that none should be admitted to a doctorate in any subject without first subscribing. Burgess practised his profession of medicine at Isleworth, where he was very successful. In June 1616 Bacon wrote to Villiers suggesting that he should intercede for Burgess with the King as he was now willing to subscribe, and as a consequence he was offered and accepted the living of Sutton Coldfield in Warwickshire. Subsequently he preached at St Paul's Cross, and in 1620 he accompanied Sir Horatio Vere as chaplain in the war of the Palatinate. In January 1625, Bishop Morton collated to him the prebendal stall of Wellington in the Cathedral of Lichfield. He continued to reside at Sutton Coldfield until his death on 31 August 1635, being "held in much respect among the godly". Shortly before his death he testified: "I have parted with more profit by taking up Conformity and a Benefice than any man in England hath done by his Inconformity

---

the Dioces of Lincoln whoe haue had some 3. or 4. admonic'ones and stand vpon their depriva'on." 18 January 1604/5: "Jo: Burges bach: in divinity R: de Waddesden 3 ae partis deprived at Huntingdon 16. Januarij. 1604." The third part of the rectory of Waddesden was vacant through Burgess's deprivation, 10 June 1605. Chaderton's Register, xxx, f. 258 d. His successor was instituted in July of the same year. Exchequer of First Fruits and Tenths, Bishops' Certificates, Lincoln, E.331/3.
[1] Episcopal Court Book, 1602–9, Cj 14, f. 77.
[2] J. & J. A. Venn, op. cit., Vol. I, p. 257.
[3] *D.N.B.*

and loss of his benefice; therefore it was not a benefice that drew me on."[1]

Alexander Cooke, who also suffered deprivation on the same day as Burgess, was born at Beeston in Leeds in 1564.[2] He was educated at Leeds Grammar School, and then entered Brasenose College, Oxford, in Michaelmas term, 1581, where he graduated Bachelor of Arts in 1585. He was elected to a Percy Fellowship at University College, Oxford, in 1587, proceeding Master of Arts in the following year, and Bachelor of Divinity in 1596.[3] He was ordained presbyter by the Bishop of Gloucester about 1593, and was admitted preacher by the University of Oxford.[4] On 22 January 1601, he was presented to the vicarage of Louth,[5] being inducted into the vicarage by virtue of letters mandatory from the Bishop of Lincoln on the presentation of the Queen.[6] According to the *Liber Cleri* of 1603 the value of the parsonage was "36*li.* 5*s.* 4*d.*", and of the vicarage "12*li.*",[7] which was considerably more than that of most parishes. The communicants numbered 1,400. Cooke was chosen as one of the select preachers on the King's accession, and represented the deaneries of Louthesk and Ludborough.[8] On 3 October 1604 he was charged by the Bishop with not wearing the surplice, it being reported that

> he will rather loose his livinge then weare yt. He appeared, and being interrogated whether he will weare the surplisse or no he saith yf he haue reason for yt he will not. Whereupon my lord admonished him for the first time, to conform himself before 31 October, and then to appear and subscribe; and further my lord injoined him to deliuer a coppie of his sermon preached on Wensday [*sic*] last vnder his hand before 31 October and to forbeare preaching against the lawes and ceremonies of the churche and booke of common praier.[9]

[1] *An Answer Rejoyned to that much applauded Pamphlet of a Namelesse Author, bearing this Title, viz.* 'A Reply to Dr Norton's General Defence of three nocent Ceremonies . . .' Published by his Majesties special command, London, 1631.
[2] A. A. Wood, *Athenae Oxonienses*, London, 1813–20, Vol. II, p. 535.
[3] J. Foster, op. cit., Vol. I, p. 319.
[4] Presentation Deeds, 1600, no. 38. Endorsement.
[5] Exchequer of First Fruits and Tenths, Bishops' Certificates, Lincoln, E.331/2.
[6] *Lansdowne MSS.*, 984, f. 120. Quoted, *D.N.B.*, Vol. XXI, p. 75.
[7] Printed, C. W. Foster, op. cit., p. 323.
[8] Brown Book, 1580–1618, ff. 182 d–184. Lincoln Diocesan Registry.
[9] Episcopal Court Book, 1602–9, cj 14, f. 65 d. Quoted, C. W. Foster, op. cit., p. cvi.

On 31 October the Bishop admonished him, under canonical obedience, to deliver a copy of his sermon before 30 November, on which day he appeared and produced his sermon, and was again admonished to conform and subscribe. On 12 December the Bishop objected articles against him, *ex officio*, and charged him by his oath to answer faithfully. Cooke objected to a sermon of Mr Eland, the Bishop's chaplain and Archdeacon of Bedford, who was reported "to haue preched a verie dangerous and heretical sermon at Lincoln and said that there wer 4. sortes of men in the church but one of the church and thereby excluded all such as stick at theis ceremonies".[1] Cooke was admonished to specify his objections against Mr Eland's sermon, which he did on the following day. Eland answered them in the negative, and Cooke was assigned to prove them at the next Court.[2] On 16 January 1604/5, Cooke appeared before the Bishop and said "that he hath not yet conformed himself accordinge to his admonicion, neither doth certifie. And further that he cannot conforme himself without further reasons especiallie to the crosse and surplisse. . . ."[3] The Bishop pronounced a sentence of deprivation against him,[4] and admonished him to undergo examination in respect of the objections against the sermon before he withdrew from the town.[5]

As a last resort, and a measure of self-defence, some of the deprived clergy appealed to the common law judges to obstruct by means of prohibitions the disciplinary actions of the bishops. Cooke resorted to this device. On 24 January 1604/5 the Bishop of Lincoln, in the course of a letter to Cranborne, said:

it is full time some strict course be used against them for what bold speeches would they not use at other times when as Cooke, late of Lowth, dares say, since his return to Lincolnshire, that he makes small account of your proceeding, as not in his case competent judge, and that he has appealed from you accordingly. Whereupon

[1] Ibid., ff. 67 d, 74. Quoted, ibid., p. lxx.
[2] Ibid., f. 74. Quoted, ibid., p. cvi.
[3] Ibid., f. 76 d. Quoted, ibid., p. cvi.
[4] "A briefe . . . of the L: B: of Lincoln his proceedinge against those ministers in his diocese which were presented unto his Lp. for not conforminge. . . ." Printed, C. W. Foster, op. cit., p. 364. "Alexander Cooke and John Burgesse were deprived for not conforming themselves after four admonitions." Chaderton's Register, xxx, f. 246. Cf. Exchequer of First Fruits and Tenths, Bishops' Certificates, Lincoln, E.331/3.
[5] Episcopal Court Book, 1602–9, cj 14, f. 76 d.

as he says, he looks hourly for an inhibition to be served upon you, and he hopes that there will be such a curb put into the jaws of your Lordship and my Lord of Peterbourghe for these proceedings against him and others, as upon the same shame will ensure to you both; whereof though I had no understanding from himself, but from some others of credit, I thought good to let you have knowledge.[1]

On 23 February 1604/5, James Montagu, Dean of the Chapel Royal, informed the Archbishop that "one Cooke of Louth" was "very forward to trouble the King. He is deprived by the Bishop of Lincoln, and his suit is to have his living again, which his Majesty says he shall have if he will be conformable; but I see no such disposition in him."[2] The following day Montagu addressed a letter to the Bishop of Lincoln:

> my verie good Lord. Mr Cooke hath by earnest suite to his Majestie, procured that I should write to your Lordship in his name, that hee may enioy his howse and liuinge, with all commodities thervnto belonginge, vntill the first of August, and if in case the partie instituted and inducted into his place by your Lordship will not heerunto condiscend, that then your Lordshipp should write vnto the highe sheriff of the Countie to putt Mr Cooke into the place for so longe a tyme, not that Mr Cooke should therby claime anie Interest or possession in his place by this Course, but that hee may haue somewhat to releiue himsealf by, vntill hee bee ether otherwise mynded, or better prouided; his Majestie is willinge to haue all fauor shewd vnto him, and therefore doubteth not of your Lordships forwardness.[3]

From the evidence of the *Comperta* it is clear that in Louth a number of parishioners continued to profess Puritanism.[4] Alexander Cooke served as curate to his brother, Robert Cooke, Vicar of Leeds. On the death of his brother he was collated to the vicarage of Leeds by the Archbishop of York on 30 May 1615, without a subscription being required of him.[5] He was a

---

[1] *Cecil MSS.*, 103, f. 139. H.M.C., Part XVII, p. 34.
[2] Ibid., 104, f. 39. H.M.C., Part XVII, p. 65. 23 February 1604/5.
[3] *S.P. Dom.*, *Jas. I*, 14, Vol. XII, no. 90. 24 February 1604/5.
[4] A certain Spendlowe and John Marshall and others were presented, "the said Spendlowe for that hee did leave his owne parishe churche, and came to Ludburghe churche the second daie of August, and the others for the like, they being all of Lowthe". Ludborough was a centre of Puritan activity. Episcopal Visitation, 1607, Vj 19, ff. 148 b, 150.
[5] R. Marchant, *The Puritans and the Church Courts in the diocese of York, 1560–1642*, London, 1960, p. 34.

prolific writer of anti-Roman tracts.[1] He died at Leeds on 23 June 1632.[2]

Towards the end of the month of January 1604/5, two more nonconformists suffered deprivation at the hands of the Bishop. George Pike (or Piek) was educated at Trinity College, Cambridge, where he graduated Bachelor of Arts in 1582/3, Master of Arts in 1586, and was elected a Fellow in 1585.[3] He was presented by Queen Elizabeth to the vicarage of Donington in Holland on 20 December 1592,[4] a living valued at " 13*li*. 17*s*. 3*d*. *obulus*" with 600 communicants.[5] Pike was a preacher, but not licensed. He was presented at the Bishop's visitation in August 1604, for not wearing the surplice nor signing with the sign of the cross.[6] He appeared before the Bishop again on 3 October, 1 November, and 1 December, and was admonished to conform himself.[7] By 18 January 1604/5, "George Pike Master of Arts vicar de Donnington" had received four admonitions.[8] On 30 January he appeared before the Bishop and answered "that he cannot yet conforme himself bicause he cannot be satisfied neither will he now conforme *sed expresse renuit et recusauit*", whereupon the Bishop decreed a definitive sentence of deprivation upon him after four admonitions.[9]

After Pike's deprivation,[10] William Moone was instituted to the

---

[1] *Pope Joane. A dialogue betweene a Protestant and a Papist, manifestly proving that a woman called Joane was Pope of Rome*, London, 1610. *More Work for a Mass-Priest*, London, 1621. *Yet More Work for a Mass-Priest*, London, 1622.

[2] A. A. Wood, op. cit., Vol. II, p. 535.

[3] J. & J. A. Venn, op. cit., Vol. III, p. 363.

[4] "Presentation by Queen Elizabeth, of George Picke, Master of Arts, to the vicarage of Doyngton vacant by death. Westminster, 20 Dec. 35 Elizabeth." Presentation Deeds, 1592, No. 71.

[5] "Donington. Quality. Parsonage appropriate endowed with a vicarage. Value vicarage 13*li*. 17*s*. 3*d*. *obulus*. Patron the Kings Majestie. Incumbent George Piek. Degree Master of Arts. Preacher non Licenciatus. Communicants 600." *Liber Cleri*, 1603. Printed, C. W. Foster, op. cit., p. 313.

[6] Visitation Book, 1604, p. 48.

[7] Episcopal Court Book, 1602-9, Cj 14, ff. 65, 73 d. Cf. "A briefe of . . . the L:B: of Lincoln his proceedinge against those ministers which were presented . . . for not conforminge . . ." Printed, C. W. Foster, op. cit., p. 363.

[8] "A Note of vnconformed ministeres in the Dioces of Lincoln whoe haue had some 3. some 4. Admonic'ones . . ." Printed, C. W. Foster, op. cit., p. 365.

[9] Episcopal Court Book, 1602-9, Cj 14, f. 78. Quoted, C. W. Foster, op. cit., pp. cxi-xii.

[10] The benefice was vacant by Pike's deprivation on 1 February 1604/5. Chaderton's Register, xxx, ff. 245 d, 249 d.

vacant benefice on 14 March 1604/5.[1] In the meantime Pike
thought better of his nonconformity, and he appeared before the
Bishop on 29 March, and submitted himself, subscribing to the
Articles in Canon 36, and promising conformity according to the
Prayer Book and the royal proclamation; whereupon the Bishop
absolved him from the sentence of suspension, and restored him
to the execution of his office wherever he might be admitted
within the diocese. The churchwardens certified to his present
conformity.[2] Consequently, on 15 May 1605, Pike was reinstituted
to the same living from which he had been deprived.[3] He died
towards the end of 1610, and on 7 January 1610/1, William
Symonds was presented "to the vicarage of Donington, vacant
by the death of George Pike".[4]

Anthony Nutter was deprived the same day as George Pike.
Nutter was an unlicensed preacher, who was ordained by the
Bishop of Lichfield and Coventry on 29 September 1578.[5] He was
presented to the rectory of Fenny Drayton on 26 September
1582,[6] and was soon in trouble for his Puritan views. The *Liber
Cleri* of 1585 records that "Sir Anthony Nutter rector" was "bred
in the schools", and that he had not exhibited his letters testimonial of subscription to the Articles.[7] He was a member of the
Dedham Classis in 1589, and in 1591/2 he was before the High
Commission with Cartwright and others on a charge of trying to
establish the Book of Discipline. Bancroft discovered that Nutter
was one of the Puritans who had subscribed to articles at one of
the classes.[8] In 1593 Nutter turned Queen's evidence,[9] and
testified:

They . . . perused the Book of Common Prayer, to satisfy themselves

[1] William Moone was presented to the living on 15 February 1604/5.
Patent Roll, 2 Jas. 29, c. 66, 1659. He was instituted on 14 March 1604/5.
Exchequer of First Fruits and Tenths, Bishops' Certificates, Lincoln, E.331/3;
Chaderton's Register, xxx, f. 249 d.
[2] Miscellaneous Correspondence, 1604, 4.
[3] Chaderton's Register, xxx, f. 255 d; Exchequer of First Fruits and Tenths,
Bishops' Certificates, Lincoln, E. 331/3.
[4] Presentation Deeds, 1611, no. 44.
[5] *Liber Cleri*, 1585. Printed, C. W. Foster, op. cit., p. 112.
[6] Presentation Deeds, 1582, no. 17.
[7] Printed, C. W. Foster, op. cit., p. 112.
[8] *Dangerous Positions*, p. 86.
[9] *Minute Book of the Dedham Classis, 1582–9*. Printed, R. G. Usher, *The
Presbyterian Movement in the Reign of Queen Elizabeth*.

how far it is to be yielded unto for their ministeries sake: also, by what godly means authority might be moved, to establish the discipline in question. ... Which meetings were begun and ended with prayer for God's direction, for her Majesty, and the authority under her. They did also approve the discipline in question.

He further revealed that "they agreed and subscribed certain articles in approbation of the discipline, and promised to observe the same".[1] The *Liber Cleri* of 1603 gives the number of communicants at Fenny Drayton as ninety, and records the fact that Nutter was resident and hospitable.[2] He appeared before the Bishop, with other nonconformists, on 3 October and 30 November 1604, to answer for not wearing the surplice.[3] On 30 January 1604/5, he appeared again and answered "that he hath not yet conformed himself neither will now conforme himself, and saith that whatsoever ys the invention of man ys not to be allowed in the service of god"; whereupon the Bishop passed sentence of deprivation upon him for not having conformed himself after four admonitions.[4] Nutter dissented from the judgement as null and void, and appealed to the Court of Arches. Edward Lynne was instituted to the living on 9 August 1605,[5] but Puritan practices were still in evidence in 1607, when thirteen people were presented for that they "haue not receaued the communion at Easter last and the Reason is because they refuse to take the same kneeling".[6]

Another nonconformist was Richard Sherwood, who graduated Bachelor of Arts from Merton College, Oxford, in 1581.[7] He proceeded Master of Arts at some date unknown, and was presented to the rectory of Thurlaston on 27 December 1587, being

---

[1] J. Strype, *Whitgift*, Vol. III, pp. 276–7.
[2] *Liber Cleri*, 1603. Printed, C. W. Foster, op. cit., p. 298.
[3] Episcopal Court Book, 1602–9, Cj 14, ff. 67 d, 75. Cf. "A briefe of the manner and times of the L:B: of Lincoln his proceedings against those ministers in his diocesse which were presented ... for not conforminge. ..." Printed, ibid., p. 363.
[4] Episcopal Court Book, 1602–9, Cj 14, f. 78 d.
[5] Chaderton's Register, xxx, f. 264 d; Exchequer of First Fruits and Tenths, Bishops' Certificates, Lincoln, E.331/3. The Presentation Deed says: "Presentation by George Lurefey esquire of Eduard Linn, clerk to the rectory of Fennie Draiton vacant by the deprivation of Anthony Nutter, 6 July 1605." Presentation Deeds, 1605, no. 8.
[6] Episcopal Visitation, 1607, Cj 19, f. 27.
[7] J. Foster, op. cit., Vol. IV, p. 1,350.

instituted on 4 January 1587/8.[1] The *Liber Cleri* for 1603 states
that the value of the benefice was "13*li*. 9*s*. 7*d*.", that the communicants numbered 120, that Sherwood was licensed as a
preacher by the Bishop of Norwich, and that he was resident and
hospitable.[2] He was cited to appear before the Bishop on 3
October 1604 to answer for that he "neither signeth with the
crosse, and omitteth diuers thinges in the booke of common
praier, twoe surplisses haue bene tendered him, which he reteyneth at his howse, sayeing he tooke them thither to see what
condicion they were of". He appeared on that day and on
30 November and 16 January 1604/5.[3] By 18 January he had
been admonished no less than five times.[4] The episcopal *Court
Book*, under date 6 January 1604/5 records that

> John Hackett hathe confessed yt he hathe not Communicated at his
> parishe Churche at Glenfield or Chapell of Bramston synce mid-
> somer was twelve moneth, Because he mislyked the behauiour of
> the Minister at Bramston, and not at Glentfeilde because he neuer
> went there in his liffe. But hathe communicated with Mr Sherwood
> parson of Thurleston twyse synce mydsomer last. And saith further
> that he repayreth to heare Common prayer sometymes to Thurleston
> aforesaide and sometymes to St Martyns . . . where Sermons are.[5]

On 10 April 1605 Sherwood appeared and said that he could not
be resolved to be conformed, and prayed right and justice;
whereupon the Bishop pronounced sentence of deprivation, in the
presence of Sherwood, who dissented and protested against it as
void and unjust and contrary to the statutes and ecclesiastical
laws of the kingdom, and appealed to the Archbishop in his Court
of Arches.[6] The Bishop assigned 29 May for him to follow up his

1 Presentation Deed, 1587.
2 *Liber Cleri*, 1603, Printed, C. W. Foster, op. cit., p. 294.
3 Episcopal Court Book, 1602–9, Cj 14, ff. 67, 74 d, 77.
4 "A Note of vnconformed Ministeres in the Dioces of Lincoln whoe haue
had some 3. some 4. Admonic'ones. . . ." Printed, C. W. Foster, op. cit., p. 365.
5 Episcopal Court Book, 1603–6, Cj 15, f. 80. The sentence was that "Johannem Hackett yt he Communicate and receyve the holie Communion with and
at the hands of the Minister of Bramston for the time beeinge at the next
Communion to be celebrated there, viz. in and vpon the firste Sondaye in
Lent next followinge and to certifie within 14. days nexte insuinge vnder the
hands of the saide Minister and Tho: ffoster Churchwarden there".
6 "A briefe of the manner and times of the L:B: of Lincoln his proceedinge
against those ministers in his diocesse which were . . . not conforminge themselves. . . ." Printed, C. W. Foster, op. cit., p. 366. Thomas Wood was

appellation and to certify,[1] on which day he produced the certificate.[2] There is no further evidence concerning his appeal.

The Archbishop was desirous that the places of those deprived should be filled as speedily as possible, so that scandal might be avoided and the people not lack spiritual ministrations.[3] In accordance with this request, the Bishop of Lincoln, in a letter to the clergy of the parishes contingent to Thurlaston,[4] wrote:

Mr Sherewood parson of Thurleston being deprived of his benefice hath made request vnto me that vntill such time as there may be an incumbent established, the cure may be sufficientlie provided for, by some of the neighbour ministers, and withall hath commended you vnto me in this behalf, which request of his being agreable to the directions I haue received from the Arch: of Cant.' his G: I doe therefore pray and require you, and by theis my lettres doe aucthorize you and euerie of you, that vntill further order may be taken herein, you doe take some extraordinarie paynes (without preiudise to your owne charge) to preache the worde, Read divine Service, and administer the sacramentes, and the Rites, and the Ceremonyes of the Church of England there accordinge to the booke of Common [Prayer], that the people may not altogether be deprived of those . . .[5] that belonge vnto them, and you shall not fayl . . . [5] the like kyndnes of other your neighteboures . . . [5] mynsters when you shall haue any just occasion to . . . [5] see and provide that the Cure of sowles of the parishioners of Thurleston aforesaid be well and sufficientlie discharged. And theis my lettres shalbe your sufficiente warrant in that behalf.[6]

Sherwood's advice, however, was not disinterested. The men he

---

instituted to the rectory of Thurlaston on 20 September 1605, which was vacant through Sherwood's deprivation. Chaderton's Register, xxx, f. 264 d; Exchequer of First Fruits and Tenths, Bishops' Certificates, Lincoln, E.331/3.

[1] Episcopal Court Book, 1602–9, Cj 14, f. 87.
[2] Ibid., f. 87 a.
[3] Cf. The Council to the Archbishop: "We desire you to acquaint them all with another point of his Majesty's pleasure, which is that when they are deprived from the benefice, their lordships presently take such order with the neighbour preachers that their places may be conveniently by their charitable pains supplied. . . ." Cecil MSS., 108, f. 43. H.M.C., Part XVI, pp. 416–17.
[4] "To my lovinge Freinds Mr Browne parson of Loughborowe Mr Wood curate there Mr White parson of Broughton and Mr Sampson preacher at Leicester and everie of them."
[5] The MS. has been damaged at various points.
[6] Correspondence of William Chaderton, Bishop of Lincoln. Cor/B/2, f. 38. 24 April 1605.

recommended were Puritan nonconformists,[1] and, by arranging
for them to minister at Thurlaston, he was furthering the cause!
At the episcopal visitation in 1607 Agnes Wallen was presented
"for goinge out of the parishe to bee deliuered of child because it
should not bee baptized with the signe of the crosse and not bee
churched after the booke of common prayer". Another member
of the same family, Thomas Wallen, was presented "for not
receavinge the communion these .2. yeares last past in their
parishe but hath taken it at other parishes, the reason is because
hee will not receaue it kneelinge". "Elizabeth, wief of the sayd
Tho: Wallen" was presented "for the like". There were almost
a dozen other people who were all presented "for the like",[2]
and at the visitation in the following year most of them were
presented again for the same thing.[3] These presentments vividly
indicate the perpetuation of a vigorous Puritan tradition among
the laity of the parish.

Within four months the Bishop of Lincoln had deprived four
men from their benefices, and had admonished many others. In a
letter to Cranborne dated 12 April 1605, the Bishop lamented
that the Puritans stood out so obstinately over such inconse-
quential trifles:

It is no small grief to me (as to others of my brethren) to see
men of great learning, pains and fruit breed such a grievous schism
in the church as they have done for matters of ceremony, wherein is
reposed no substance of religion or godliness, other than decency,
order and obedience, which having a good interpretation may be
easily endured, without any just scandal of their consciences. I am
fully persuaded the most part of them would not stand so
obstinately in these terms were they not encouraged by their
favourers, and were they not unwilling to be brought into any disgrace with their people. But it is a great grief to us all (if there were
any other remedy) to remove them from their livings, by reason
whereof their wives and children who have given no cause of
offence, neither are able to shift for themselves, should be distressed.
I will by the grace of God use all the best means I can devise by
conference and brotherly exhortations with mildness and discretion
to win them.[4]

[1] The parish of Loughborough was frequently mentioned in the visitation
records as a centre of nonconformity. Vj 20, f. 14 d; Vij 11, f. 117 d, etc.
[2] Episcopal Visitation, 1607, Vj 19, f. 24.   [3] Ibid., Vj 20, f. 97.
[4] *Cecil MSS.*, 110, f. 74. H.M.C., Part XVII, p. 133.

Nevertheless, in spite of the Bishop's pious intentions, circumstances forced him to proceed to another deprivation at the end of the month.

Arthur Hildersham was born on 6 October 1563, and after being educated at Saffron Walden in Essex, entered Christ's College, Cambridge, where he graduated Bachelor of Arts in 1580/1, and Master of Arts in 1584.[1] Both his parents were papists, his mother being a niece of Cardinal Pole, and they designed him for the priesthood of the Church of Rome. He was disinherited because of his convictions, but was supported by a distant kinsman, Henry Hastings, Earl of Huntingdon. He was invested by his relatives with the impropriated tithes of the parish of Ashby-de-la-Zouch.[2] He was made a Fellow of Trinity Hall in 1584, and became lecturer at Ashby-de-la-Zouch in 1587 before his ordination. In 1588 he was in trouble with the Archbishop for preaching without a licence. His "recantation" is dated 10 January 1587/8:

I confesse here that I have rashly and undiscreetly taken upon mee the office and function of a preacher, and have preched abroad, nether beinge admitted into orders, nether licensed by any authoritie, and contrarie to the orders and lawes of this church of England, contrary to the example of all antiquitie in the primitiue churche, and contrary to thexample and direction of the apostles in the Actes, and thereby have given great and just offence unto manye. And this rashenes I have made more greveous and offensive in that I have uttered in my foresaid sermons and prechinges certaine impertinent and very unfitt speaches for the auditory, as moveinge their mindes rather to discontentment with the state, than tendinge to any godly edification. For which my presumption and undiscreetenes, I am very hartily sorye, and desire you to beare witnesse of this my confession and acknowledgeinge of my seid offences.

By me *Arthur Hildersham*[3]

In 1591 he was before the High Commissioners with Cartwright and others, but was released "upon his Petition and other ecclesiastical considerations".[4] His relative, the Earl of Huntingdon,

[1] J. & J. A. Venn, op. cit., Vol. II, p. 368.
[2] W. Haller, *The Rise of Puritanism, 1570–1643*, New York, 1938, p. 55.
[3] *Morrice MSS.*, M, no. viii. *Seconde Parte of a Register*, 244. Ed. A. Peel, op. cit., Vol. II, pp. 259–60.
[4] *Beaulieu MSS.* H.M.C., pp. 33–4.
13

presented him to the rectory of Ashby-de-la-Zouch on 5 July 1593,[1] and there he became one of the most ardent Puritan agents, especially in connection with the Millenary Petition.[2] With other nonconformists he appeared before the Bishop on 3 October, 31 October, and 30 November 1604, to answer for not wearing the surplice and not signing with the cross.[3] A memorandum in the Court Book, dated 12 December states: "vpon a monicion from his Majestie for some of the ministers to conferr with my Lord and Mr d: Mountacute deane of the kinges chappell Mr Hildersham said they would not come to be borne downe with countenance and scoffs."[4] On the same day the registrar noted in the Court Book: "Dominus tradidit mihi librum canonum editorum in vltima Convocatione et perlecta .54. caput dominus monuit ministros sequentes tunc presentes to take notice thereof at their perills."[5] Canon 54 provides that if any licensed preacher, after being admonished by the bishop does not conform himself within the space of a month, his licence shall be void. A note about the "vnconformed ministeres in the dioces of Lincoln" records that by 18 January 1604/5 Hildersham had received five admonitions, and "John Brinsley Curate of Ashby delazouche" three admonitions, as well as suspension from his curacy on 1 December 1604.[6] On 24 April 1605 Hildersham again appeared before the Bishop, when he said that "he doth not nor can conforme himself for manie causes".[7] The Bishop thereupon deprived him for not conforming himself after five admonitions,[8] Hildersham himself being present, dissenting, protesting that it was of none effect, and appealing to the Archbishop in his Court of Arches.[9] He failed to prosecute his appeal.[10]

---

[1] Presentation Deeds, 1593, no. 27: "Presentation by Henry, earl of Huntingdon, of Arthur Hadersbye clerk. . . ."
[2] See above, pp. 51, 62.
[3] Episcopal Court Book, 1602–9, Cj 14, ff. 67, 74 d.
[4] Ibid., f. 74 d. Quoted, C. W. Foster, op. cit., p. cxxix.
[5] Ibid., f. 73 d.
[6] Printed, C. W. Foster, op. cit., p. 365.
[7] Episcopal Court Book, 1602–9, Cj 14, f. 87.
[8] Ibid., f. 89 a. Cf. "A briefe of . . . those ministers . . . not conforminge. . . ." Printed, C. W. Foster, op. cit., p. 366. The vicarage of Ashby-de-la-Zouch was vacant through his deprivation, and Richard Jarfield was instituted on 18 October 1605. Chaderton's Register, xxx, f. 268 d; Exchequer of First Fruits and Tenths, Bishops' Certificates, Lincoln, E. 331/3.
[9] Episcopal Court Book, 1602–9, Cj 14, f. 89.   [10] Ibid., f. 91.

Hildersham was a loveless and intransigent Puritan.[1] On one occasion Richard Spencer came to Hildersham's curate, and desired him to publish and demand in the church the return of some money which had been taken out of Spencer's house when it was burned to the ground:

> Mr Brinsley [the curate] answered, nay, nay, the crosse hath lighte on the, and a wors judgement hangeth ouer thy head, thow wilte have thy children baptised with the crosse and the said Spencer answered that yf he had anie more children he would haue them baptised with the signe of the crosse according to his Majesties lawes and Mr Brinsley asked, yf not godes lawes, and Spencer said that his Majesties lawes was godes lawes.

Hildersham adopted an attitude of like uncharity:

> Afterwardes Mr Hildersham in his sermon said that there was three dwelling houses burned and .2. of them were Chrestians and the third meaning the said Spencer, he could not tell what to make of him. Also Mr Hildershams wife came to a widowe woman where the fire began and told her Jone to be of good comforte iiij*l.* will build vpp thy howse againe, and as for Spencer the crosse hath lighte on him, let him beware the surplesse or other wordes to the like effecte.[2]

Hildersham remained an impenitent Puritan to the end of his days.[3] Shortly after his deprivation Bishop Overton of Coventry and Lichfield licensed Hildersham, and, in conjunction with William Bradshaw, Hildersham conducted two weekly lectures at Burton-on-Trent, Staffordshire, and Repton, Derbyshire. Bishop Barlow of Lincoln restored him to Ashby-de-la-Zouch on 1 January 1608/9, whereupon a weekly lecture was re-established there. Neile, the new Bishop of Coventry and Lichfield, suppressed the lectures at Burton and Repton in November 1611, and on 22 April 1613 Hildersham was suspended by the High Commissioners. In 1615, for refusing the oath *ex officio*, he was imprisoned for three months in the Fleet and the King's Bench. Next year, at the instance of Hacket, who had succeeded him as Vicar at Ashby-de-la-Zouch, he was prosecuted in the High Commission Court as a schismatic, chiefly on the allegation that

---

[1] See sermon by Hildersham, *Sloane MSS.*, 598, f. 8.
[2] Miscellaneous Correspondence, 1601–43, Cor/M/2, f. 38.
[3] The following facts are largely taken from the *D.N.B.*, Vol. IX, p. 833.

he had refused to receive the Holy Communion kneeling. On 28 November 1616 he was sentenced to be imprisoned, degraded, and fined £2,000. He compounded for the fine, and escaped imprisonment by remaining concealed. He was invited to the pastorate of the English Church at Leyden, but declined it because of his wife's aversion to crossing the sea. On 20 June 1625 the Vicar-General of the Archbishop gave him a licence to preach in the dioceses of London, Lincoln, and Coventry and Lichfield, and on 3 August he resumed his work at Ashby-de-la-Zouch. Five years later he was again suspended for not using the surplice, but five months later was restored. His last sermon at Ashby-de-la-Zouch was preached on 27 December 1631, and he died on 4 March 1631/2.

Lawrence Bott, who suffered deprivation a few months after Hildersham, was a non-graduate, but a licensed preacher. He was presented to the benefice of Cadeby on 28 March 1587, and instituted on 19 June.[1] The *Liber Cleri* for 1585 records that "Sir Lawrence Boote, rector" was ordained priest by the Bishop of Lincoln.[2] The rectory of Cadeby was a place of no great importance: its value was only "*4li. 10s. 2d. obulus*", and the communicants numbered seventy-two.[3] He appeared before the Bishop to answer for not wearing the surplice on 3 October, 31 October, 30 November, 12 December 1605,[4] and by 18 January 1604/5 had received five admonitions.[5] He was cited at numerous subsequent dates, but each time he was respited until some later date.[6] Finally, he was deprived on 18 September 1605 "for not conforming himself after many admonitions".[7]

Another nonconformist was Oliver Perkins (or Parkins) who

---

[1] Presentation Deeds, 1578, no. 47.

[2] *Liber Cleri*, 1585. Printed, C. W. Foster, op. cit., p. 113.

[3] Ibid., 1603. Printed, ibid., p. 297.

[4] Episcopal Court Book, 1602–9, Cj 14, ff. 67 d, 75, 77, 89. Cf. "A briefe of . . . those ministers . . . not conforminge. . . ." Printed, C. W. Foster, op. cit., p. 363.

[5] "A note of vnconformed ministeres in the dioces of Lincoln. . . ." Printed, C. W. Foster, op. cit., p. 365.

[6] "A briefe of . . . those ministers . . . not conforminge. . . ." Printed, ibid., pp. 366–7.

[7] Ibid., printed, C. W. Foster, op. cit., p. 367. The benefice was vacant by his deprivation, and Nathaniel Wood was instituted on 27 November 1605. Chaderton's Register, xxx, f. 271; Exchequer of First Fruits and Tenths, Bishop's Certificates, Lincoln, E. 331/3.

graduated Bachelor of Arts in 1587/8, and Master of Arts in 1591, from Christ's College, Cambridge. He was ordained deacon and priest by the Bishop of Peterborough in 1596.[1] He was instituted to the vicarage of Offley in 1603,[2] a benefice valued at "9*li.*" with seventy-eight communicants.[3] On 3 October he was cited to appear before the Bishop for not wearing the surplice. On 1 December he did not appear and was excommunicated by the Bishop for his contumacy,[4] but on 13 December, having promised to obey the law of the Church, he was absolved.[5] On 10 January, he said, "that (he doth) not vse the crosse in baptisme nor weareth the surplisse in celebracion of divine service neither can he yet be perswaded to vse the crosse nor surplisse".[6] He continued to desire time for further deliberation, and was respited from time to time,[7] but on 19 June, when he craved time for further deliberation, he was suspended from his office.[8] On 23 October he again refused to conform, and the Bishop, because of his growing contumacy, in not appearing before him, and not obeying his monitions, excommunicated him; and, further, enjoined him to provide for the cure of souls in his parish to be served by a fit minister.[9] His vicarage was vacant because Perkins had not paid his tenths, and Fulk Roberts was instituted on 5 December 1606, in his place.[10] The Bishop declared that "Mr Perkins . . . mighte have bene absolved yf he would have submitted himself and taken the oath".[11]

The final deprivation for nonconformity in the diocese of

[1] J. & J. A. Venn, op. cit., Vol. III, p. 347. The ordination certificate reads "Olibrius Perkinson".

[2] The Presentation Deed is no longer extant.

[3] *Liber Cleri*, 1603. Printed, C. W. Foster, op. cit., p. 280.

[4] Episcopal Court Book, 1602–9, Cj 14, f. 69.

[5] Ibid., f. 76.

[6] Ibid., f. 77 d.

[7] Ibid., ff. 78, 89. "A briefe . . . of those ministers . . . not conforminge. . . ." Printed, C. W. Foster, op. cit., p. 366.

[8] Episcopal Court Book, 1602–9, Cj 14, f. 91 d. "A briefe of . . . the ministers . . . not conforminge. . . ." Printed, ibid., p. 367.

[9] Episcopal Court Book, 1602–9, Cj 14, ff. 92, d, 102 d, 125. Cf. "A briefe of . . . the ministers . . . not conforminge. . . ." Printed, ibid., p. 368.

[10] Chaderton's Register, xxx, f. 296 d; Episcopal Court Book, 1602–9, Cj 14, f. 113 d; Exchequer of First Fruits and Tenths, Bishops' Certificates, Lincoln, E. 331/3.

[11] "A briefe of . . . the ministers . . . not conforminge. . . ." Printed, ibid., p. 369.

Lincoln was that of Thomas Heape. He graduated Bachelor of Arts from Christ's College, Cambridge, in 1583/4,[1] and was ordained priest by the Bishop of Chester and licensed preacher by the Bishop of Lincoln.[2] He was presented to the vicarage of Little Marlow on 20 September, and was instituted the following day.[3] The value of the benefice was estimated in 1603 as "8*li*." (the value in the King's book being "8*li*. 5*s*. 10*d*."), and Heape himself was described as resident.[4] He was cited to appear before the Bishop to answer for not wearing the surplice on 3 October 1604, and he appeared again on 30 November, when he alleged "that there are diuers scandalous ministers in Buckinghamshire and nothing done against them", whereupon the Bishop admonished him to bring in their names before 30 November.[5] He wrote asking that his attendance might be excused:

> Good Mr Chancilir, these are to signifie vnto youe, that having bene syke, I feare my personall appearanc' would have bene with some hazard of my lyffe and so I ame homble to crave to be excused. And doe by these presentes acknowledge that as yet I cannot be resolued to conformitie (as youe cale it) but do willingly by these presentes submit my selffe to the sensure of a second admonition if it so please my lord and your worshipe so to proceed with vs. And thus with my humble commendation and dutie to your worshipe I take my leave commitinge yow to the protection of the Almightie this 12 of November 1604. Lytle Marlowe. Your humble petetioner
>
> Thom. Heape[6]

In response to this request, the judge "of his grace" granted him till the last day of November. He appeared several times, and on 16 January 1604/5 his attendance was excused because of the plague, and he was respited until 27 March.[7] On 19 June

---

[1] J. & J. A. Venn, op. cit., Vol. II, p. 344. In the Presentation Deed to the vicarage of Little Marlow in 1596, and the *Liber Cleri* of 1603, he is described as "Master of Arts".

[2] Endorsement on the Presentation Deed, 1596, no. 43. *Liber Cleri*, 1603. Printed, ibid., p. 275.

[3] Presentation Deed, 1596, no. 43.

[4] *Liber Cleri*, 1603. Printed, ibid., p. 275.

[5] Episcopal Court Book, 1602–9, Cj 14, ff. 69, 71 d.

[6] Miscellaneous Correspondence, 1604/2. Quoted, C. W. Foster, op. cit., p. cxxi.

[7] Episcopal Court Book, 1602–9, Cj 14, ff. 75 d, 77. "A briefe of . . . the ministers . . . not conforminge. . . ." Printed, ibid., p. 364.

1605, "Heape not conforminge, was suspended in respect of punishment".[1] On 2 October he appeared and answered:

> that he cannot yet conforme himself And saith further that since his suspencion his cure hath beene some holie daies vnserved *contra monicionem* etc. and some daies the cure hath bene served by Mr — [blank] Tice schoolmaster at Henley Mr Wade master of Stoke hospital and one Mr — [blank] Evans of Cloke lane in London preched there .2. sabbaths and Mr Robertes vicar of Wooborne baptised another at Great Marlowe both which were borne in the parish of Little Marlowe: And saith further that there hath not bene anie communion celebrated in the said parish churche of Litle Marlowe since his said suspencion. *Unde dominus monuit dictum* Heape that before the feast of All Saintes nexte he do provide a sufficiente curate and presente him to the said reuerend father or other competent judge to be admitted according to law *et ad certificandum proximo sessione sequenti sub manu judicis predicti Et vlterius dominus denuo monuit eum ad conformandum et certifcandum 9. Novembris proximo in ecclesia de Buckden inter horas .6. et 11. ante meridiem.*[2]

The Bishop decreed that Tice, Wade, Robertes, and Watson, should be cited to answer before the Chancellor concerning the premisses. On 6 November, after preconization, Heape did not appear or certify about the provision of a curate, and the Bishop declared him contumacious and excommunicated him.[3] On 4 December 1605 Heape appeared, and answered that he had not conformed nor did he intend to conform, and the Bishop pronounced sentence depriving him of his benefice, Heape renouncing the benefit of appeal.[4] An entry in the official record, under the date 15 January 1605/6, states that Heape

> was .5. times absent before he was excommunicate and yet he was not excommunicate for his absence onelie, but also for not providing a Curate to discharge his Cure, and the rather bicause (at the

[1] Episcopal Court Book, 1602–9, Cj 14, ff. 87, 89, 91 d, 92 d, 124 d. Cf. "A briefe of ... the ministers ... not conforminge. ..." Printed, ibid., p. 367.
[2] Episcopal Court Book, 1602–9, Cj 14, f. 100. Quoted, C. W. Foster, op. cit., p. cxxi.
[3] Ibid., f. 125. "A briefe of ... the ministers ... not conforminge. ..." Printed, C. W. Foster, op. cit., p. 367.
[4] Episcopal Court Book, 1602–9, Cj 14, f. 106. The vicarage of Little Marlow was vacant through his deprivation, when Thomas Buckley was instituted on 14 May 1606. Chaderton's Register, xxx, f. 282; Presentation Deeds, 1606. no. 28.

Courte before) he confessed that he would not suffer anie minister
to celebrate anie divine service in his church, but such as would doe
as he had done before, and for that cause was at last deprived. That
he was not deprived for not subscribinge appeareth by the sentence
which ys onelie for not conforminge himself to the orders and ceremonies of the church being lawfully admonished.[1]

In a document entitled, *A Briefe of Greevances in the Ecclesiasticall
Iurisdiction delivered by the Lower House of Parliament at a Committie
with the Lords of the Vpper House*, exhibited in April, 1606, the case
of Heape is cited as an example of

peaceable ministers [who] are often called to theire extreame trouble
and chardge, though for the avoidance of both, they haue desired
to be soner deprived—Instance hereof: Mr Heape who was called
14 times and at last deprived . . . the same ministers are deprived
for not subscribinge contrarie to the lawe ˙and canon made the last
Convocation.[2]

In reply, it was pointed out that

as for Mr Heape he was spared manie times for his appearance and
at the last for his contumacie being factiouslie disposed and having
made manie publicke invectives against the state of the church
and the booke of common praier, and not suffering anie minister to
say divine service, preache, or administer the sacraments, in his
churche, but those that were of his faction, allthoughe he did per-
mitte other irregular persons to doe the same he was deprived: And
as for his excommunication yt was denownced against him not
onely for not appearinge, but for not providinge that his Cure might
be served, allthoughe he was divers times admonished thereof:
From the which he mighte have bene released yf he would have
submitted himself and taken the oathe *de parend' iuri* etc. according
unto lawe.

And in answer to the grievance that ministers were deprived
simply for not subscribing, the statement is made that

This ys alltogether untrue for the ministers were not urged with
subscripcion neither anie one of them deprived or suspended
bicause they would not subscribe, but onelie shewinge themselves
otherwise to be factious and troublesome after manie charitable
admonitions they were deprived.[3]

[1] Episcopal Court Book, 1602–9, Cj 14, f. 106. "A briefe of . . . the ministers
. . . not conforminge. . . ." Printed, C. W. Foster, op. cit., p. 368.
[2] "A briefe of . . . the ministers . . . not conforminge. . . ." Ibid., pp. 469–70.
[3] Printed, C. W. Foster, op. cit., p. 370.

Despite Heape's deprivation, Puritanism continued to flourish at Little Marlow. Of Thomas Buckley, Heape's successor, it was reported: "The minister doth administer the communion to those that sitt givinge the cup at one end of the seat with the words of benediction and soe it is deliuered from the hands of one of them to the other. And vsually christen without the signe of the cross."[1]

There were many other presentments for nonconformity in the Lincoln Diocese, but no further cases of deprivation. Some of the ministers never conformed, but as they were quiet and peaceable, they were permitted to retain their benefices. Thus

yt appeareth that some of the unconformed ministers (who seemed to be most stubborne) were suspended and deprived so soone as they could be convenientlie by lawe, tempered with mercie, and the rest spared longer (for the most parte upon their owne erneste suite and their freinds letters) in hope of their conformitie, havinge an example of others their deprivacion to drawe them thereunto.[2]

THE CHICHESTER DIOCESE

In 1603 the Puritans of the diocese of Chichester drew up a petition praying "the King to ease the ministry of the burden of that subscription heretofore imposed otherwise than the laws of the land require, and of these ceremonies which press the conscience of many of God's servants, and hinder the execution of their ministry". The petitioners were earnest for the establishment of "a learned, godly, and resident ministry, with sufficient maintenance", and the setting up "among them that ancient form of the church's censures as agreeable to his word". Concerning the state of the ministry they stated that

the number of churches in their country is about 300, of which the impropriations are 108. The insufficient maintenances are many, and of them 23 not above 16*l.* by the year, and some of 4*l.* or 5*l.* Double beneficed men about 50. Single and yet non-resident 6. Non-preaching 100. negligent in preaching about 60. Of all these many are scandalous for corrupt life or doctrine.[3]

---

[1] Episcopal Visitation, 1607, Vj 19 b. July 13, 1607.
[2] "A briefe of . . . those ministers . . . not conforminge. . . ." Printed, C. W. Foster, op. cit., p. 368.
[3] *Cecil MSS.*, 103, f. 64. H.M.C., Part XV, p. 390.

Letters were sent from the Privy Council on 18 October 1603 directed to Anthony Watson, Bishop of Chichester, Dr Drury, Sir Thomas Bishop, and Mr Henry Shelly, to inquire of and examine the framers of this petition.[1] It was discovered that the "makers of the ministers' petition [were] Samuel Norden, a parson of Hamsey, [who] made the first draft at Walter Doble's, there being assembled Mr Goldsmith, Mr Healie, Mr Knight, Mr Porter and Mr Frewen, giving their approbation thereof". Further, it was revealed that the "principal carriers and procurers of subscription to the same [were] Mr Norden, Mr Goldesmith, Mr Lister, Mr Postlethwait, Mr Vinall, Mr Goodacre"; and that the "travellers to the Court about the business [were] Mr Frewen, Mr Erburie, Mr Healie, Daniel Hanson". Six of these ministers were subsequently deprived. The examiners also discovered that the friends of the petition at Court were "Mr Gallowaie, Mr Pickeringe", and that divers ministers supported the petition with money. Some of these Puritans were associated with another petition called "the commonalty's petition", of which John Peerson confessed "that he drew the petition at Thomas Collen's house in Brightlinge, where were assembled Messrs Norden, Goldesmith, Healie, Bingham, Porter, Boys, Attershall, Frewen, and Goffe, ministers". This petition was signed by 2,285 hands, and that of the ministers' by forty. Subscriptions had been obtained "sometimes at meetings at sermons, sometimes after evening prayers in church, where the petition was read unto the people, much by private solicitation, sometimes by a constable, and at one time by an officer or sergeant". The chief "conventicles" were listed:

Hoo, Wartlinge, at Mr Healie's.
Brightlinge, at Tho. Collen's.
Arlington, at Mr Knighte's.
Hellingslie.[2]
Hamson, at Mr Norden's.
Thakeham, at Walter Doble's.
Yapton, at Mr Carussie's.
Wullavington, at Mr Stoughton's.
Hunstone, at Mr Lister's.

[1] Ibid., 101, ff. 160–1. H.M.C., Part XV, pp. 262–3. 1603.
[2] The vicar was Warren, who was subsequently deprived.

The examiners deduced that

> it is plain that the petition, not only of the ministers but also of the commonalty, was devised, made and dispersed by the fore-named ministers, and the people under a blind zeal of reformation, drawn only by them to this presumptuous practice.

They added:

> the most base agents of those ministers, viz., Norden, Frewen, Healie, Goldesmith, Goffe, and Erbury, their general, having intelligence that the Lords had sent commission to examine their enterprises, fled from the messenger to the Court. They also denied before the Privy Council to have any hand in the commonalty's petition, by which denial they obtained to the Bishop of Chichester the Council's letters for favourable dismission.

Concerning these men, the commission of inquiry commented:

> sundry of these hot reformers and learned ministry never saluted any university, some of them departed thence with the lowest degrees and continue Bachelors of Arts, and the best of them in Sussex is but Master of Arts, yet they dare control degrees, orders and ordinances.[1]

Little information is available about the course of events during the following year, but Bishop Andrewes' Register in 1605 gives "the names of ye preachinge Ministers" who were "deprived at Eastgreensted ultimo Aprilis A.D. 1605".[2] These deprivations were not the work of Lancelot Andrewes, who was not consecrated Bishop of Chichester until 3 November 1605,[3] but were carried out by Bancroft during the vacancy of the see. Those deprived were

Mr Norden parson of Hamsey
Mr Goldsmith parson of Kingston Bowsey
Mr Knight Vicar of Arlington alias Erlington
Mr Boyse parson of Easthoathly
Mr Warren Vicar of Hellingly
Mr Heeley Vicar of Wartling alias Whartling

---

[1] *Cecil MSS.*, 101, ff. 160–1. H.M.C., Part XV, pp. 262–3.

[2] Bishop Andrewes' Register, f. 56. There are accurate transcripts by E. H. W. Dunkin from bishops' Registers, Act Books, and other ecclesiastical documents in the Chichester Diocesan Registry, *Additional MSS.*, 39,406–39,465.

[3] The royal licence to elect was given on 10 October 1605 (*Patent Roll*, 3 Jas. 28, c. 66, 1690); the royal assent was given on 29 October (*Patent Roll*, 3 Jas. 1, c. 66, 1663); and the temporalities were restored in November (*Patent Roll*, 3 Jas. 28, c. 66, 1690).

Mr Stephen Goughe parson of Bramber with vicarage of Buttolphes
Mr Vinall Vicar of Stayninge
Mr Beda Goodacres parson of Ashurst
Mr Brian Lister Vicar of Hunston.[1]

On 19 November 1583 Samuel Norden was ordered to subscribe to the *Three Articles*, but "Mr Norden ... and some others,
required further respite to consider the 2nd Article, because in it
were many braunches and diverse things which oughte not
lightlye to be passed over or subscribed unto". He subscribed in
the form, "S.N. Subscribit primo et tertio articulis, de secundo
deliberationem petit", whereupon he was given three admonitions.[2] The Archbishop undertook to answer the objections of
Norden and others, and on 6 December they appeared before him
alleging

> that there were certain rubrics in the said book, wherein there was
> contained some ambiguity or doubt; which moved them to inquire
> of the said most reverend Father ... the interpretation of the said
> rubric, Which being made and given ... and signified unto them,
> that touching the rubrics ... their subscription was not required
> unto any other sense than such as was not against the Word of God,
> and agreable unto the substance of religion, now professed in this
> Church of England, and by law established, and according to the
> analogy of faith. And that their subscription is not to be extended
> to any thing not expressed in the said book. And hereupon they did
> voluntarily subscribe.[3]

The date of Norden's institution to Hamsey is not known, but in
1603, "Hamson, at Mr Norden's" was mentioned as one of the
"places where conventicles were held". He was one of the prime
movers in the petitions of 1603, and was described as one who had
both drawn up drafts and obtained subscriptions to them.[4] In a
Puritan list of representatives for the Hampton Court Conference,
he was suggested as one of "the ministers for the Conference".[5]
The following return was forwarded from the parish of Hamsey
in 1603:

[1] Andrewes' Register, f. 56; *Additional MSS.*, 39,406, B.
[2] *Seconde Parte of a Register*. Ed. A. Peel, op. cit., Vol. I, pp. 209 ff.
[3] J. Strype, *Whitgift*, Vol. I, pp. 256–7.
[4] *Cecil MSS.*, 101, ff. 160–1. H.M.C., Part XV, pp. 262–3.
[5] *Beaulieu MSS.*, H.M.C., pp. 33–44.

1. The nomber of Communicants are about. . . .[1]
2. We haue no recusant man or woman to my knowledge.
3. Their be none that refuse to receiue the Communion.
4. The minister hath one benefice, he is a Master of Arte,[2] the parsonage is valued at xvij pownds in the Kings Booke.
5. The benefice is not impropriat but paieth a pencion of xvij*s.* yearly to the King. the minister hath bine allwayes resident and serueth it himself.
6. The liuing is a parsonage, and hath no vicaredg indowed.
7. The Patrone for his life time is Sir Edward Lewcknor,[3] after Mr Edward . . .[1] sford.[4]

Norden was deprived from the rectory in April 1605,[5] Edward Wood being instituted on 25 September.[6] The following entry appears in the parish register: "one the first day of february was buryed Mr Samuell Norden", 1608/9.[7] Apparently Norden remained in the parish after his deprivation till his death.

Christopher Goldsmith was another who was prominent in the agitation of 1603, being described as one of "the most base agents".[8] He was recommended as one of the Puritan representatives for the Hampton Court Conference.[9] He graduated Bachelor of Arts in 1581/2, and Master of Arts in 1584, from Merton College, Oxford,[10] and was instituted Rector of Kingston-by-Sea in 1588. He was deprived in April 1605,[11] John Postlethwaite being instituted on 26 September 1605.[12] The new Rector, Postlethwaite, was also a man of Puritan sympathies, for in

[1] The MS. has been eaten away in places.
[2] There is no record of the University from which Norden graduated. His name is not listed by Venn or Cooper.
[3] "Sir Edward Lewcknor" was an earnest Puritan layman. He was patron of a number of livings to which he was careful to appoint Puritan ministers. In the Townshend Papers there is a document by "Sir Edward Lewkenor of Denham" about the plans of the Puritans. *Additional MSS.*, 38,492.
[4] Register of the archdeaconry of Lewes. Transcript, *Additional MSS.*, 39,455, f. 10.
[5] Andrewes' Register, f. 56.
[6] Bancroft's Register, f. 206 b; Exchequer of First Fruits and Tenths, Bishops' Certificates, Chichester, E.331/3.
[7] Parish Register Extracts, Chichester Registry, Transcript, *Additional MSS.*, 39,465, f. 6.
[8] *Cecil MSS.*, 101, ff. 160–1. H.M.C., Part XV, p. 262.
[9] *Beaulieu MSS.* H.M.C., pp. 33–44.
[10] J. Cooper, op. cit., Vol. II, p. 579.
[11] Andrewes' Register, f. 56.
[12] Bancroft's Register, f. 207a; Exchequer of First Fruits and Tenths, Bishops' Certificates, Chichester, E.331/3.

1603 he was described as one of the "principall carriers and procurers of subscriptions" for the petitions.[1] He evidently confirmed
and continued the Puritan tradition, for other Puritans continued
to resort to "Kingston Bowsey". In 1607 the parish register
records that the rector "baptized the tenth of May, 1607, Samuell
Goffe, the sonne of Mr Stephen Goffe".[2] The latter had been
deprived in April 1605 from the vicarage of Bramber.

William Knight, perpetual Vicar of "Arlington alias Erlington", also played an important part in the activities of 1603, his
vicarage being mentioned as one of the "places where conventicles were held".[3] The value of the living in 1604 was "x*l.*
vij*s. id.*"[4] He was deprived with his *confrères* in April 1605,[5]
when William Smith was instituted to the living on 5 October
1605.[6] The latter must have soon resigned it, for Caleb Burdell
was instituted on 24 November 1605,[7] "per deprivationem
Guliel Knight" on the presentation of "Thomas Pelham de
Easthothleigh".[8] The patron may have had Puritan sympathies,
because the Rector at East Hoathly was also deprived at the same
time as Knight. The Rector of East Hoathly was John Boyse, who
had played a minor part in the petitions of 1603. He may be the
same John Boyse who graduated Bachelor of Arts in 1589/90, and
Master of Arts in 1593, from St John's College, Cambridge.[9] On
his deprivation, Marmaduke Burton was instituted to the living
on 9 October 1605.[10] Of Warren, who was deprived from the
vicarage of Hellingly, there is practically no information, except

---

[1] *Cecil MSS.*, 101, ff. 160–1. H.M.C., Part XV, p. 262.
[2] Parish Register Extracts, Chichester Registry. Transcript, *Additional
MSS.*, 39,465, f. 169.
[3] *Cecil MSS.*, 101, ff. 160–1. H.M.C., Part XV, pp. 262–3.
[4] *Plea Roll*, E.337/13, no. 14. "Erlington."
[5] Andrewes' Register, f. 56.
[6] Bancroft's Register, f. 205 a; Exchequer of First Fruits and Tenths,
Bishops' Certificates, Chichester, E. 331/3. He was exonerated from the payment of his first fruits, *Plea Roll*, E.337/13, no. 14.
[7] Exchequer of First Fruits and Tenths, Bishops' Certificates, Chichester,
E.331/4. There are two separate returns, one 9 October 1605 and the other
24 November 1605.
[8] Andrewes' Register, f. 38 b. The transcript in *Additional MSS.*, 39,406 B,
is dated "24 Nov. 1607". This is plainly an error, and, as a comparison with
the Bishops' Certificates shows, should be "24 Nov. 1605".
[9] J. & J. A. Venn, op. cit., Vol. I, p. 195.
[10] Bancroft's Register, f. 205 b; Exchequer of First Fruits and Tenths,
Bishops' Certificates, Chichester, E.331/3.

that Hellingly was reputed in 1603 to be a place where there was a "conventicle".[1] Shortly after his deprivation, the church-wardens were presented because they wanted "a fflagon pott for wyne to furnishe the communicants".[2] The judge admonished them to get a "standing pott" before Michaelmas.

On 25 June 1602 Thomas Healy[3] was instituted to the vicarage of Wartling.[4] Wartling soon became notorious as the location of a "conventicle". and Healy himself became known as one of the "most base agents" of the Puritan party.[5] His Puritanism was of long duration, for in 1583 he refused to subscribe to the Three Articles and was suspended. In a dispute before the Archbishop, Healy protested: "My Lord, if we subscribe to the booke, do we not subscribe to the translation of the bible which that booke appointeth to be read? And that translation is faultie in many places, yea, and very corrupt. . . ." The Archbishop patiently explained the sense of subscription, and then he "did voluntarily subscribe".[6] He was deprived from Wartling in April 1605,[7] and the fruits of the living were subsequently sequestered.[8] John Peryn was instituted to the living on 20 July 1605.[9]

Stephen Gough (or Goffe) graduated Bachelor of Arts in 1583 from Magdalen College, Oxford,[10] and Master of Arts at some unknown date.[11] He was ordained deacon and priest by the Bishop of Sarum in 1600,[12] and was instituted by the Bishop of Chichester to the vicarage of Bramber and Botolphs on 12 June 1603, on the presentation of the president of St Mary Magdalen, Oxford.[13] The church was in a sad state of dilapidation: six

[1] *Cecil MSS.*, 101, ff. 160–1. H.M.C., Part XV, pp. 262–3.
[2] Act Book, 1605, Chichester. Transcript, *Additional MSS.*, 39, 446, f. 42.
[3] Variously spelt Helie, Heeley, Healie, or Healy.
[4] Exchequer of First Fruits and Tenths, Bishops' Certificates, Chichester, E.331/3.
[5] *Cecil MSS.*, 101, ff. 160–1. H.M.C., Part XV, pp. 262–3.
[6] J. Strype, *Whitgift*, Vol. I, pp. 255–7. *Seconde Parte of a Register.* Ed. A. Peel, op. cit., Vol. I, pp. 214 ff.
[7] Andrews' Register, f. 56.   [8] Bancroft's Register, f. 225 b.
[9] Ibid., f. 204 a; Exchequer of First Fruits and Tenths, Bishops' Certificates, Chichester, E.331/4.   [10] J. Foster, op. cit., Vol. II, p. 590.
[11] He is certified as having graduated Master of Arts in the *Liber Exhibitorum*, Chichester Diocesan Registry.
[12] *Liber Exhibitorum*, Chichester Diocesan Registry. Transcript, *Additional MSS.*, 39,459, f. 247 b.
[13] Ibid., Exchequer of First Fruits and Tenths, Bishops' Certificates, Chichester, E.331/3. This gives the date of the institution as 3 June 1605.

months previously it was reported that "the chauncell [is] sum-what ruinous, the walles within are vnwhited, the windowes vnglased, and it hath no seats in it".[1] One of the churchwardens certified: "The Churche hath many defects the roofe in the cealinge the walles within want whitinge and bewtifying the flower is vnpaved the seats very ruinous the communion Table not decent the place for the redinge of publicke prayer not decent the pulpitt wanteth a deske the font not decent there is but one bell and it hangeth inconveniently in the chauncell xxv th. die Sept. 1602."[2] Gough, in the examination before the commission of inquiry in 1603, was described as one of the "most base agents" of the Puritan agitation.[3] He was deprived in April 1605,[4] Nathaniel Vertue being instituted on 9 October 1605.[5] It was Stephen Gough who had his son, Samuel, baptized by the Puritan minister of Kingston-by-Sea on 10 May 1607.[6] Robert Goffe, Vicar of Litlington, possibly a brother or other relative of Stephen Gough, was presented on 27 August 1605 "for not vsinge the crosse in baptizing of Children". The judge admonished him to use all things in the Book of Common Prayer.[7] Nothing further is known of the subsequent career of Stephen Gough.

Stephen Vinall graduated Bachelor of Arts in 1579/80 from St John's College, Cambridge,[8] and was ordained deacon on 8 July and priest on 2 August 1592 by the Bishop of Chichester.[9] He was instituted to the vicarage of Steyning on 8 November 1599 on the presentation of John Shurley.[10] In 1602 it was reported of his church that "the Chauncell within is very ruinous and hath not bin occupied of longe time by reason the windowes are vnglased the walles vnpurgited and vnwhited the roofe is vnsealed

---

1 *The Book of the Reparations, 1602.* Chichester Diocesan Registry, 11 December 1603. *Additional MSS.,* 39,454, f. 152.

2 Ibid.

3 *Cecil MSS.,* 101, ff. 160–1. H.M.C., Part XV, p. 262.

4 Andrewes' Register, f. 56.

5 Bancroft's Register, f. 206 a; Exchequer of First Fruits and Tenths, Bishops' Certificates, Chichester Registry. *Additional MSS.,* 39,465, f. 169.

6 Parish Register Extracts. Chichester Registry. *Additional MSS.,* 39,465, f. 169.

7 Act Book, 1605. C. 18. Transcript, *Additional MSS.,* 39,446, f. 42.

8 J. & J. A. Venn, op. cit., Vol. IV, p. 303.

9 *Liber Exhibitorum,* Chichester Diocesan Registry, Transcript, *Additional MSS.,* 39,459, f. 252.

10 Ibid.

and the fflower vnpaved lyinge very vndecent So that it is now a common haunt for pigiens". The report of the churchwardens, John Rochester and Philip Bennett, was equally depressing :

> The roofe of the Churche in the cealinge is faultie in sundrie plases whereby it often rayneth down in to the Churche, the walles are not well whited and bewtified within but in some places are vnpaynted. The hiest windows on the north side of the Churche are vnglased and in divers other windowes the glasse here or there broken the seats are the most part of them ruinos and badd the flower is in sundrie places vnpaved. The pulpit olde and badd the founte wantethe a decent cover and the south dore is not good . . . xvj Oct. 1602.[1]

Vinall was active soliciting and securing signatures for the petitions of 1603.[2] He was deprived in April 1605,[3] at the same time as other Puritan nonconformists, and John Michael was instituted in October 1605.[4] A legal point was raised in connection with the manner in which the actual sentence of deprivation was pronounced :

> An injustice is, because some acts and sentences have been made and given in some private chamber of some common Inne or Taverne, and not *in publico et competente foro*, in any publike or competent seate, of Ecclesiastical justice, As M. Vinall and M. Warren, in the Diocesse of Chichester, were deprived, in a common Taverne, viz. at the signe of the Ounce and Ivy Bush in Grensted.[5]

Beda Goodacres was ordained deacon on 10 October 1573 and priest on 21 October 1574 by the Bishop of Exeter.[6] He was instituted by the Bishop of Chichester to the vicarage of Ashurst on 20 March 1580/1 on the presentation of Thomas Sherley.[7] This church was also dilapidated, the churchwardens reporting on 6 November 1602: "The vpper wall ouer the Chauncel is

---

[1] *The Book of the Reparations*, 1602. Chichester Diocesan Registry. Transcript, *Additional MSS.*, 29,454, f. 152.

[2] *Cecil MSS.*, 101, ff. 160–1. H.M.C., Part XV, p. 262.

[3] Andrewes' Register, f. 56.

[4] *Liber Exhibitorum*, Chichester Diocesan Registry. Transcript, *Additional MSS.*, 39,459, f. 90 b.

[5] *A Myld and Ivst Defence of Certaine Argvments . . . in behalfe of the Ministers suspended and deprived*, p. 82.

[6] *Liber Exhibitorum*, Chichester Diocesan Registry. Transcript, *Additional MSS.*, 39,459, f. 252.

[7] Ibid.

not decent but wolde be better pargeted and trimed the seats are most of them very ruinos and badd the flower is vnpaved the font is very badd and ruinos and standeth in a very inconvenient [place] out of the face of the Churche and sight of the greatest [part] of the congregation."[1] Goodacres, like Vinall, was an energetic procurer of subscriptions to the Puritan petitions in 1603, and he, with Vinall, suffered deprivation for his nonconformity in April 1605.

Brian Lister graduated Bachelor of Arts in 1578/9, and Master of Arts in 1582, from Trinity College, Cambridge, being elected a fellow in 1581.[2] He was ordained priest by the Bishop of Lincoln on 19 August 1587,[3] and was instituted to the vicarage of Hunston by the Bishop of Chichester on 29 September 1587.[4] He was deprived in April 1605, and the living apparently remained without a Vicar until Thomas Emerson was instituted on 2 September 1608, when it was described as vacant "per deprivationem Briani Lister", last incumbent of the same.[5]

There were no further deprivations during the following two years. Richard Robinson, however, was deprived from the rectory of St Clement's, Hastings, about the middle of the year 1608. We possess his answers to the articles of inquiry of the Archbishop in 1603:

The answere of Richard Robinson parson of saint Clement in Hastings.

1. The number of them that do receyue the Communion is about six hundrethe.

2. Theis not any recusant.

3. Theis not any but ye are willinge to receyue.

4.5. this dothe not concerne me but my benefice is valued in the Kings books at xxiij*li*. which is more than its worth by yeare.

6. Ther is ye castell parishe which is worthe xx*li*. by yeare and ye lady Mountague farmers do geue me but x*s*. by the yeare for ye— thereof but whether it be an impropriat or a parsonage with cure I

---

[1] *The Book of the Reparations*, 1602. Chichester Diocesan Registry. Transcript, *Additional MSS.*, 39,454, f. 153.

[2] J. & J. A. Venn, op. cit., Vol. III, p. 89.

[3] *Liber Exhibitorum*, Chichester Diocesan Registry. Transcript, *Additional MSS.*, 39,459, f. 234 b.

[4] Ibid.

[5] Ibid., *Additional MSS.*, 39,459, f. 222; Andrewes' Register, ff. 39 b, 37; *Additional MSS.*, 39,406 B.

know not. And theis ye Maudlin parishe, saint Leonardo and saint
Maryes and saint Michell all which parishes do come to our churche
and pay litell or nothinge for ther seruices but I know not whether
they be impropriat or not.

    7. Sir George Browne is patron of ye parishe of saint Clemens by a
grant maid from his mother ye Lady Montague.

per me Richardum Robinson[1]

On 28 July 1607, the fruits of the rectory of St Clement's were
committed into the hands of the churchwardens,[2] and on 14
September 1607, William Kippis was instituted to the rectory
"per deprivationem Richardi Robinson", last incumbent of the
same.[3]

    John Packe, who graduated Bachelor of Arts in 1572/3 from
Jesus College, Cambridge,[4] was ordained deacon and priest by
the Bishop of Leighlin in Ireland on 3 July 1597, and was instituted to the rectory of Iping and Chithurst on 23 June 1602.[5]
John Packe's name appears in "a note of the Ministers in Medhurst
Deanry" (1603): "a preacher one that hath done exercise before
the Lo: Bisshopp of Winton he is well commended."[6] Of the
church itself it was reported (23 October 1602) that "the Chauncell walles and partition" of the church at Iping are "vnwhited
the glasing and pavinge at reparations"; and again (10 December
1602) "the walles vntrimed the pavinge broken the seats vndecent
iij littell windowes vnglased j bell broken the flower and the
Church porche at Reparations".[7] The condition of the chapel of
Chithurst was little better: "the Chaunsell walles glas windowes
flower and north doore at reparations." The churchwardens
presented: "the cealinge glasinge seats and flower are at defalte
the walles vntrimed the communion table insufficient there is no
bell the porche is at reparations."[8] On 30 January 1608/9 Ed-

---

  [1] *Additional MSS.*, 39,455, f. 30.
  [2] Act Book, 1607. Bishop's Registry, Chichester, C. 20. *Additional MSS.*,
39,447, f. 36.
  [3] Andrewes' Register, f. 38.
  [4] J. & J. A. Venn, op. cit., Vol. III, p. 293.
  [5] Episcopal Visitation, 1606. Transcript, *Additional MSS.*, 39,459, ff. 81,
241 b.
  [6] Parcel 1,348, Bishop's Registry, Chichester. Transcript, *Additional MSS.*,
39,427, f. 80.
  [7] *The Book of Reparations*, 1602. Transcript, *Additional MSS.*, 39,454, f. 168.
  [8] Ibid., *Additional MSS.*, 39,454, f. 168 b.

mund Gray was admitted "ad rect. Ipinge cum capella de Chithurste eidem annex. per deprivac. Johannis Packe, cler. ult. rect."[1]

The only other person to be deprived in the diocese of Chichester was Ringe, Rector of Albourne. His answers to the Archbishop's inquiries in 1603 are extant:

The answere of John Kinge [sic] Clerke Parson of Alborne: made the Second daie of August, 1603.

1. To the first he answereth, That there are Communicants in his parishe fourescore, or thereabouts:

2. To the second, he answereth There is no Recusant man or woman in his parishe.

3. To the third, he answereth: That euerie one Receaveth the Communion, which by the Lawes of this Land are bound to receave and fitt:

4. To the fourth: he answereth, he is onelie parson of Alborne and hath no other benefice: his parsonage is valued at vij*li*. x*s*. in the Kings Booke: and is litle more worth:

5. To the fifth: he answereth: That within the parishe there is a prebend called the prebend of Busshoppshurst in the Cathedrall Church of Chichester, the land is worth foure score poundes by the yeare, and payeth onelie to the parson for his tiethes thereof xiij*s*. iiij*d*. yearelie.

6. To the 6: yt is answered before:

7. To the vij th: he answereth: That the Ladie Aburgavennie is patronesse.

John Kinge[2]

He was in trouble for the dilapidated state of his church and parsonage: on 24 September 1605 he was cited before the Bishop's Court "for that the parsonage is at reparation", and the judge admonished "him to repair the parsonage house before the feast of Nativity".[3] Again, on 16 February 1607/8 he was cited because "some parte of the stone cealing of the Chauncell is broken downe and lyeth open, the flowre of the Chauncell very vneyen and vndecent. The parsonage howse Decayed in the timber walles and Roof." He was ordered to repair this before the feast of St

---

[1] Andrewes' Register, f. 41 b; Bancroft's Register, f. 160 a.

[2] *Additional MSS.*, 39,455, f. 24.

[3] Act Book, 1605. Bishop's Registry, Chichester, C. 18. *Additional MSS.*, 39,446, f. 42.

John the Baptist.[1] One of the churchwardens, John Fowle, presented that "the covering of the Roof of the Church many of them vnboorded and very vnseemly, in the glasse windowes of the Church there are some defects, one pannell of the fence of the Churchyard is faulty".[2] Ringe was deprived during the year 1609, and on 26 September John Moore was admitted "ad Rect. Arborne alias Alborne per depriv. John Ring, cler. ult. incumb."[3] This deprivation brought the total number who suffered in the diocese of Chichester to thirteen.[4]

THE NORWICH DIOCESE

The number of deprivations in the diocese of Norwich can only be arrived at from a study of the various entries in the Institution Books, for other information is almost entirely wanting.

James Harrison, who graduated Bachelor of Arts in 1592/3, and Master of Arts in 1596, from St John's College, Cambridge,[5] was ordained deacon and priest by the Bishop of Peterborough on 18 March 1596/7, and instituted to the rectory of Breesworth on 8 April 1601 on the presentation of William Colman.[6] After his deprivation, John Hill was presented by the same patron to the living on 26 May 1605.[7]

Thomas Seffray[8] was instituted to "Depden alias Debden" on the presentation of Sir John Jermyn on 5 October 1588,[9] and was deprived during the early months of 1605, John Plaifere (or Playford) being instituted on 25 June on the presentation of the same patron.[10] It is possible that Seffray ultimately reconciled

---

[1] Ibid., C. 20. *Additional MSS.*, 39,447, f. 38.

[2] Ibid., C. 20.

[3] Andrewes' Register, f. 44; *Additional MSS.*, 39,406 B.

[4] Usher erroneously states that there were six deprivations in the diocese of Chichester (op. cit., Vol. II, p. 6). He indicates that he arrived at this figure from a study of the Institution Books of the diocese, but it would appear that he relied on the figures given in Bancroft's own Register, which only records the deprivations made *sede vacante*.

[5] J. & J. A. Venn, op. cit., Vol. II, p. 315.

[6] Institution Book xx, f. 391 d. Diocesan Registry, Norwich.

[7] Ibid., xxii, f. 7 d.

[8] Otherwise spelt Seffraie or Sefferey.

[9] Institution Book, xx, f. 167. According to another entry, the date of the institution was 23 April 1589, xx, f. 173.

[10] Ibid., xxi, f. 18 d; xxii, f. 7 d.

himself to the discipline of the Church, for Rogers, in the preface
to his pamphlet *Two Dialogues*, declares that

> M. Seffray, who . . . disliked yea and depraued our kneeling at the
> holy Communion, as much as any man could do . . . chusing rather
> to abide the censure of authority . . . then somuch as bend his knees
> at the receiuing that most blessed and heauenly Sacrament: yet
> notwithstanding, after friendly and brotherly conference had with
> him thereabout, altered his mind, allowing that which before he
> condemned.

He has shown his change of mind, Rogers declares, by "his late
orderly and submissiue kneeling in the very act of receiuing the
sacred bread and wine at the Communion the last Easter"; he
prays that Seffray may "doe the like in other things ceremoniall".
Rogers testifies that if he had only conformed, ". . . he had still
enioyed a sweete and competent liuing (to the singular refreshing
of many a Christian soule, hauing a very good gift in preaching;
and to the temporal benefiting of himselfe and his) which he hath
forgone . . . chusing rather to leaue it, then to condemn his
vanities". Further evidence is wanting concerning his subsequent
conformity.

Robert Allen graduated Bachelor of Arts in 1575/6, and Master
of Arts in 1579, from Trinity College, Cambridge, and was
ordained priest by the Bishop of Norwich in 1584.[1] He was
instituted to the living of Culford on the presentation of Sir
Nicholas Bacon on 3 March 1596/7.[2] After his deprivation,
William Knight was instituted to the living on 7 August 1605
on the presentation of the same patron.[3]

William Hall graduated Bachelor of Arts in 1580/1, Master of
Arts in 1584, and Bachelor of Divinity in 1591, from St John's
College, Cambridge,[4] being elected a fellow in 1587, and in-
corporated at Oxford in 1584. He was ordained priest by the
Bishop of Norwich in 1587, and was instituted to the vicarage of
Redgrave and Botesdale on 4 August 1597 on the presentation of
Sir Nicholas Bacon.[5] He was deprived, and Henry Mihill was
instituted on 7 August 1605.[6]

---

[1] J. & J. A. Venn, op. cit., Vol. I, p. 19.
[2] Institution Book, xx, f. 249 d.
[3] Ibid., xxii, f. 7 d.   [4] J. & J. A. Venn, op. cit., Vol. II, p. 289.
[5] Institution Book, xx, f. 254 d.   [6] Ibid., xxii, f. 7 d.

George Hulkes, who probably matriculated sizar from Corpus Christi College, Cambridge, in 1580,[1] was instituted to the vicarage of Kenton on 13 May 1594.[2] He was deprived towards the end of 1605, and Thomas Gurrey was instituted on 10 December 1605, the patron being the King, by reason of the minority of Frammingham Gawdie, his ward.[3] Information concerning his nonconformity is contained in the Visitation Book, April 1608:

> Kenton. Mr. Hulkes cler. vic. ibidem. (Deprivatus ante detectionem) he hath not redd the Cannons. he doth not vse the signe of the Crosse in baptisme he doth not vse the prescribed forme of Common Prayer neyther doth obserue the orders rights and ceremonies Commaunded. he doth not weare the surples nor such apparell as is appoynted.[4]

In May of the same year it was reported that Hulkes, "deprived from his benefice" is "preachinge once in a moneth", at the church of Wickham Markett "not knowne to be licensed".[5]

Ralph Furness, who graduated Bachelor of Arts in 1579/80, Master of Arts in 1583, and Bachelor of Divinity in 1590, was elected a fellow of St John's College, Cambridge,[6] and was ordained deacon on 28 March and priest on 9 July 1583 by the Bishop of Peterborough.[7] He was presented at the Archdeacon's visitation in 1604, for "that he doth not obserue the book of common praier both in the reading the devine service and in ministration of the sacraments". It was also certified "that in the readinge of devine service and ministration of the sacraments he doth not weare the surplisse". The church itself was in a state of disrepair: "the Chauncell in diuers places thereof is vnpaved and the place where the highe altar stood vnpaved and lieth verie vndecentlie. It raineth into the church in diuers places thereof."[8] Furness was deprived, and William Armistede was instituted on 3 March 1605/6.[9] Merston was again mentioned in

[1] J. & J. A. Venn, op. cit., Vol. II, p. 428.
[2] Institution Book, xx, f. 230.
[3] Ibid., xxii, f. 10. *Patent Roll*, 3 Jas. 11, C. 66, 1673.
[4] Visitation Book, 1606. Diocesan Registry, Norwich.
[5] Visitation Book, 1606. Diocesan Registry, Norwich.
[6] J. & J. A. Venn, op. cit., Vol. II, p. 186.
[7] Institution Book, xx, f. 247.
[8] Archdeacon's Visitation Book, 1604. The Muniment Room, the Castle, Norwich.
[9] Institution Book, xxi, f. 25 b; xxii, f. 10 d.

the Visitation Book for 1606. An entry states that "magister Radulphus ffirnies Clericus depriuatus ... hath not reade the booke of Cannons. he doeth not signe with the signe of the Crosse in Baptism. he wereth not the surples. he doeth not reade service according to the booke of Common prayer."[1]

Robert Swett graduated Bachelor of Arts in 1565/6, and Master of Arts in 1571, from Corpus Christi College, Cambridge, being a fellow from 1571 to 1579, and bursar in 1572.[2] He was ordained deacon on 21 December 1574 by the Bishop of Ely, and was instituted to the vicarage of Weybread on 7 May 1579.[3] According to the Visitation Book "there is no devine service red in the church neyther on sondayes nor holidayes, he hath procured diuerse straungers to preach in the said church, and the church-wardens Commaundinge to se their licenses Mr Sweet said he had aucthority to procure them".[4] He was deprived at the beginning of 1606, and John Chatteris was instituted on 3 March 1605/6.[5]

William Bendes, who was instituted to the rectory of Little Wenham on 19 April 1597,[6] may have been the same William Bendys who matriculated from Peterhouse, Cambridge, in 1584.[7] He was deprived from the rectory of Little Wenham, Oliver Armerod being instituted on 25 February 1605/6.[8]

THE PETERBOROUGH DIOCESE

Information about individual Puritans in the diocese of Peterborough is tantalizingly meagre, apart from a few scanty facts in letters of the Bishop of the diocese, Thomas Dove.

All except one of the deprivations took place on 16 January 1604/5.[9] Early in the month, the Bishop gave an account of his proceedings to the Lords of the Council:

---

[1] Visitation Book, 1606. Diocesan Registry, Norwich.
[2] J. & J. A. Venn, op. cit., Vol. IV, p. 191.
[3] Institution Book, xx, f. 36.   [4] Visitation Book, 1606.
[5] Institution Book, xxii, f. 10 d.   [6] Ibid., xx, f. 250 d.
[7] J. & J. A. Venn, op. cit., Vol. I, p. 131.
[8] Institution Book, xxii, f. 10 d. Cf. Visitation Book, 1606. "Wenham Parva. Chappman clericos Curate he seruethe and hath serued the cure of Wenham euer since the depriuation of Mr Bends vicar there. . . ."
[9] Sir Thomas Lake to Cranborne, 16 January 1604/5: "This day the Bishop of this diocese [Lincoln] has given sentence against Burgese and one other of

Touching the unconformable ministers of my diocese, I have laboured to win them to obey the laws established in the church for good order; I have exposed myself to disputations both privately and publicly and many have yielded themselves. The rest I pitied and begged to pity themselves, and then monished them by myself or such as were far off by my deputies; and when nothing would prevail, in the anguish of my soul, I suspended nine or ten, and deprived one only, telling them all that if they still remained disobedient, I should proceed in like manner against the rest.

He would not have proceeded to further extremities had not the Council, by their letters forwarded through the Archbishop, insisted on more stringent procedures:

There I ceased and meant so to have done still, but that letters came from you, that it was the King's pleasure that I and the rest of my brethren should at once remove such as were obstinate. Such were mine who had conspired, as I think, to make unto me one and the same answer, namely that they would never conform themselves. I prayed to demand time for further conference, that I might conceive some hope of their submission; they answered that if they should do so, they would seem to be doubtful in those things wherein they were resolved never to yield; and that they had as leif be deprived at first as at the last, then enforced by their own obstinacy I deprived fourteen more, ten of whom were formerly suspended.

By way of explanation, the Bishop added:

Your lordships wonder at the number and so do I, but I am informed that my diocese has been from time to time the nest and nursery of factious ministers. Here they have held their classes, hither have repaired from other parts the most fiery and disorderly preachers of the whole kingdom.

Whereas complaint is now made that their places are unfurnished of preachers, your lordships will understand that it is not my fault but theirs, for they have all appealed from my sentence, and *pendente appellatione*, I have nothing to do with their benefices; yet I have written to the preachers near to the void places to supply their defects.[1]

On 16 February 1604/5 the Bishop addressed a further letter to Cranborne, his previous letter not having arrived: "I wonder where the fault may be, seeing that I returned answer immediately

---

the ministers, and the Bishop of Peterborough has given like sentence against fifteen." *Cecil MSS.*, 103, f. 114. H.M.C., Part XVII, p. 17.

[1] Ibid., 104, f. 1. H.M.C., Part XVII, p. 46. 4 February 1604/5.

upon receipt of the letters by the messenger, Dickinson, who brought them to me." The Bishop's further letter, with its "summary repetition" merits quotation:

> The number of disorderly ministers I cannot justly tell, because my Register, who keeps the records, is now in London. But to my knowledge I deprived 13 or 14. The rest by me suspended are curates and mercenary readers. The most of them have taken no degree or schools, some are bachelors of arts, a few are masters of arts, but all are extremely wilful. I gave them three several admonitions, those near me I admonished myself, those far off I admonished by my officers.

> I exposed myself to all kinds of conference both private and public. In private conference I have reclaimed more than I have deprived.

> In my public conference, which lasted two whole days in the cathedral church, in the hearing of two hundred people, I took on me the place of respondent and answered all objections propounded by the factious ministers of my diocese from morning till night. When nothing would prevail, I prayed them to ask further time, that by conference with other men they might dispose themselves to submit; they answered out of a premeditated confederacy, as I take it, that thus they should dissemble, for they were resolved never to yield. Hereupon I deprived one, a principal ringleader of that band, and suspended 9 or 10, the most whereof were mean men and curates. The rest I respited until another time, before which date I received letters from your lordships, encouraging me to proceed against those who were obstinate.

> At their next appearance I entreated them by my best skill, and not prevailing, out of my duty I deprived 13 or 14, men of such invincible obstinacy, as never any Bishop met with; who in matters of mere order and decency have shown as much stomach as any other men can do in the highest points of our redemption.

> As to the placing of other men in their rooms, they have all appealed from my sentence, during which appeal they must take care of their own cures themselves; yet have I written unto the preachers of my diocese, that as they dwell conveniently nigh to those benefices which are vacant, they shall employ their labours diligently to the comfort of the people there. And this is well performed, saving at Northampton, where Mr Catline has locked up the pulpit door and will suffer no one to preach. But my hope is that if these men prevail not upon their appeal the patrons of the vacant churches will supply men of good conformity.[1]

---

[1] Ibid., 104, f. 30. H.M.C., Part XVII, p. 58.

Of the character and learning of the deprived clergymen, there is little independent information. "Mr Catline", who resisted the efforts of others to preach from his pulpit, was formerly a prominent member of the Northamptonshire Classis, and an organizer of Puritan petitions in preparation for the Hampton Court Conference. The Puritan leaders had agreed, 21 July 1603,

> that a survaye of the ministrye be taken, and of all the chiefe grevances of the courtes candide, with the handes and witnesses of such as doe complaine. . . . That men [*sic*] bringe his true knowledge of all such matters in writinge to Mr Catelyne, Mr Stone and Mr Barbone, and they to communicate one with another, and This with all possible speede, and yf it may be by this day 3 weekes.

They had further resolved "that for these supplications, Mr Cateline, Mr Stone and Mr Barbon take order with the advise of the brethren to procure their supplications in readines, and also yt they kepe true copies, and Registers of all that they doe".[1] Catline was presumably deprived with the others on 16 January 1604/5. On 21 January 1604/5 the mayor and aldermen of Northampton wrote to Cranborne, praying

> for the restoration of Mr Robert Gatelin [*sic*], their minister, who had been deprived of his living for not conforming himself to the use of the ceremonies (in that church omitted and grown out of use for nearly 40 years), of whom about 1500 Communicants felt the want.[2]

Catline strenuously resisted these measures to silence him. On 26 February John Lame wrote to Dr Neile:

> Good Mr Dr Neale, the deprivinge of our factious ministers . . . hath put out our puritanes into greate discontentment, and now more particularly in Northampton, the Cheife fountaine of that humor, by the disturbance that Mr Catlin made on Sunday Last in kepeing the pulpitt doore against my Lorde of Peterburgh his appointment. . . .[3]

At this point Cranborne intervened. Writing to the patron of the living, Mr Stanley, he said that he had hope of Catline's ultimate conformity, and, in the meantime, asking him to postpone further action:

[1] *Sloane MSS.*, 271, f. 20 b.
[2] *Cecil MSS.*, 103, f. 124. H.M.C., Part XVII, p. 26.
[3] *S.P. Dom., Jas. I*, 14, Vol. XII, no. 96.

Although it is far from me to be an encourager of any that withstand the ordinances of the Church, or show any spirit tending towards faction in this so happy government of his Majesty's, yet where I find unconformity accompanied with earnest profession to receive satisfaction in scruple to the intent to obey, my desire in such is to recover as the last work I wish should be to punish: and yet to that shall I as willingly consent as this, when I am satisfied that there is no other remedy. To be short, therefore, I understand that you are patron of a living, whereof one Mr Cathelin was incumbent, by whose deprivation the right of presentation is in you. I have by conference with him found some appearances of future conformity, for which purpose he will omit no means to work in himself a conscionable resolution, the lack whereof he protesteth to be the sole cause of his aversion from the orders imposed. I have thought good to entreat you (the rather to keep an entry open to his former residence, if he shall hereafter conform) to forbear, at my request, to present any new until there may [be] some further proof, and yet no longer than to prevent any injury to yourself by any default, for that supply which the law prescribes. Herein I desire your answer, that I may be certain what to promise him. . . .[1]

Tantalizingly, we have no knowledge concerning subsequent events.

We can identify two more of the deprived clergymen: one was Richard Baldocke, who graduated Bachelor of Arts in 1574/5 from Queens' College, Cambridge,[2] and was deprived from the vicarage of Brigstock, having been instituted in 1585. George Sharpe succeeded him. In a letter to Cranborne, dated 24 February 1604/5 Sharpe describes his welcome by the parishioners:

As by your goodness I was presented to Brixtoke, so by my Lord of Peterborough instituted, by the parishioners kindly entertained, and by the late incumbent nothing at all resisted. I find all the chief of the parish, with many of the inferior sort on both sides depending, to consist of puritans, I hope something conformable, and of papists, I fear refractory and obstinate. . . .

He provides additional information about the parish and discusses his personal plans:

The value of the living is 40l. to be farmed, but this year scarce anything, as Mr Baldock the late incumbent has sown all the land

---

[1] *Cecil MSS.*, 109, f. 48. H.M.C., Part XVI, p. 420.
[2] J. & J. A. Venn, op. cit., Vol. I, p. 73.

and must reap the benefit. In regard whereof, and intending to take
the degree of Bachelor of Divinity this year at Cambridge, I beg to
continue in the University till Midsummer. I have provided for the
discharge of the cure till then.[1]

The other nonconformist of whom we have knowledge is Robert
Travell, who graduated Bachelor of Arts in 1589, and Master of
Arts in 1592, from Magdalen Hall, Oxford.[2] and was instituted
to the rectory of Weston Favell in 1593. He and his heirs were
discharged from the payment of first fruits of the parsonage of
Weston, "to which parsonage he was heretofore presented and
admitted by the Bishop of Peterborough, and lately deprived
thereof because he would not conforme himself to the Canons in
that behalf".[3] The Patent Rolls state that at the beginning of
1605 the vicarages of "Morton Pinckney" and "Lilborne"
were vacant because of the deprivation of the previous incumbents but the names of the previous incumbents are not recorded.[4]

OTHER DIOCESES

Owing to the fact that many Institution Books and episcopal
Registers are no longer extant, particulars concerning deprivations in other dioceses are difficult to discover.

During 1605 Bancroft held his first metropolitical visitation.
He filled a number of benefices which were vacant through
deprivation. In the diocese of Chichester he was responsible for
the majority of the deprivations where he was acting *sede vacante*.
The archiepiscopal Register also gives information about a
number of deprivations elsewhere.

In the Canterbury diocese there were at least three deprivations. Anthony Field, who graduated Bachelor of Arts in 1582/3,
and Master of Arts in 1586, from Jesus College, Cambridge, was
ordained deacon by the Bishop of London on 27 June 1587 at the
age of twenty-five.[5] He was instituted to the rectory of Chillenden
in Canterbury diocese in 1588, and also to the rectory of Knolton

---

[1] *Cecil MSS.*, 127, f. 5. H.M.C., Part XVII, p. 67.
[2] J. Foster, op. cit., Vol IV, p. 1,503.
[3] *S.P. Dom., Jas. I*, 38, Vol. VIII, 18 May 1605. Docquet.
[4] *Patent Roll*, 2 Jas. 29, c. 66, 1659. Ibid., 3 Jas. 29, c. 66, 1659.
[5] J. & J. A. Venn, op. cit., Vol. II, p. 135.

in 1591.[1] He was deprived from the former towards the end of 1607, when Samuel Carrington was instituted to the living on 18 December[2] and from the latter benefice in the following year, when Robert Ewell was instituted on 19 April 1608.[3] About the same time, Walter Jones, who graduated Bachelor of Arts in 1576/7, and Master of Arts in 1580, from Trinity College, Cambridge, and who was elected a fellow in 1579, was deprived from the vicarage of Benenden in Kent, to which he had been instituted in 1586.[4] On his deprivation, V. Hussam was instituted to the living by the Archbishop on 29 April 1608.[5] It is possible that Jones later conformed, for there is a writ for the appearance of Walter Jones, "vicar of Starton" in the diocese of Peterborough, in the Court of Arches, on 8 January 1609/10,[6] but the name is a common one. Benjamin Solly graduated Bachelor of Arts in 1590/1, and Master of Arts in 1594, from Queens' College, Cambridge, and was instituted to the vicarage of Bekesbourne in Kent in 1597.[7] After Solly's deprivation, John White was instituted to the living on 29 April 1608.[8]

In the diocese of Oxford, the Archbishop was responsible for two more deprivations. Robert Clever[9] was deprived from the rectory of Drayton and Richard Smyth was instituted in March 1606/7.[10] John Dod, an intimate friend of Clever's,[11] graduated Bachelor of Arts in 1575/6, Master of Arts in 1579, and was a fellow of Jesus College, Cambridge, from 1578 to 1585. He was ordained deacon by the Bishop of London on 16 April 1579, and

---

[1] Ibid.

[2] *Patent Roll*, 5 Jas. 27, c. 66, 1747. Bancroft's Register, f. 282 a.

[3] Bancroft's Register, f. 283 b. Exchequer of First Fruits and Tenths, Bishops' Certificates, Canterbury, E.331/5.

[4] J. & J. A. Venn, op. cit., Vol. II, p. 488.

[5] Bancroft's Register, f. 284a. Exchequer of First Fruits and Tenths, Bishops' Certificates, Canterbury E.331/5.

[6] *S.P. Dom., Jas. I*, 14, Vol. XLIII, no. 10.

[7] J. & J. A. Venn, op. cit., Vol. IV, p. 121.

[8] Bancroft's Register, f. 283 b. Exchequer of First Fruits and Tenths, Bishops' Certificates, Canterbury, E.331/5l

[9] This may be the same person as Clevely, described by Bancroft as one of the Puritan leaders in *Dangerous Positions*, p. 86.

[10] Bancroft's Register, f. 279 b.

[11] Dod and Clever published several books jointly: *Two Sermons on the 3rd chap. of the Lamentations of Jeremie; preached at Hanwell, by J. D[od] and Richard Cleaver*, 1602. *A Plaine and Familiar Exposition of the Ten Commandments with a . . . Catichism*, 1604.

priest by the Bishop of Ely on 16 April 1580. He was a University preacher in 1585, and in the same year was instituted to the rectory of Hanwell in the diocese of Oxford.[1] He was a member of the Oxford Classis, being a diligent minister, preaching twice each Sunday and, in conjunction with four others, setting up a weekly lectureship at Banbury.[2] While at Cambridge he met frequently to read and expound Scripture with William Fulke, Master of Pembroke, Laurence Chaderton, Master of Emmanuel, and William Whitaker, Master of St John's. With Hildersham he took charge of Cartwright's papers after the latter's death, preaching the funeral sermon.[3] He was mentioned in one of the first drafts as one of the Puritan ministers to attend the Hampton Court Conference.[4] A little later he was deprived from the rectory of Hanwell, L. Yate being instituted in his stead in March 1606/7.[5] He preached for some time at Fenny Compton, Warwickshire, and then at Canons Ashby, Northamptonshire, where he was silenced by Archbishop Abbot at the instigation of the King, on 24 November 1611.[6] On the death of James I, he was presented by Richard Knightley—a successor of the Sir Richard Knightley who sheltered the Marprelate Press at Fawsley in Northamptonshire—to the rectory of Fawsley, where he remained until his death in 1645.[7]

In the diocese of Worcester there was one deprivation, William Meacocke being deprived from the rectory of Hasley, and Samuel Watson being instituted in August 1605.[8] In the diocese of Coventry and Lichfield there was another: Richard Ward was deprived from the rectory of Sustocke, and Joseph Harrison was presented to the vacant benefice on 19 July 1605,[9] and instituted in August of the same year.[10] Bancroft's Register also records that there were two deprivations in Lancashire, and to both these benefices the Bishop of Chichester was nominated by Bancroft.

[1] J. & J. A. Venn, op. cit., Vol. II, p. 50.
[2] R. G. Usher, *Presbyterian Movement in the Reign of Queen Elizabeth*, p. xxxix.
[3] W. Haller, op. cit., p. 56.
[4] *Beaulieu MSS.*, H.M.C., pp. 33–44.
[5] Bancroft's Register, f. 279 a.
[6] *D.N.B.*, Vol. V, p. 1,050.
[7] W. Haller, op. cit., p. 56.
[8] Bancroft's Register, f. 188 b.
[9] *Patent Roll*, 3 Jas. 11, c. 66, 1673.
[10] Bancroft's Register, f. 199 a.

The first was the vicarage of Blackburne, from which Edward Welsh was deprived in 1606.[1] A report on the parish in 1604 states: "Blackburne. A Viccaridge; the Patron, the Lord Archbishop of Canterbury. The Incumbent, Mr Welsh, a Preacher. The Farmor, Sir William Fleetwood, Knight."[2] The other deprivation was that of Joseph Midgley from the vicarage of Rochdale in 1606.[3] He graduated Bachelor of Arts in 1584/5, and Master of Arts in 1588, from Magdalene College, Cambridge, and was instituted to Rochdale in 1595.[4] He evidently had strong Puritan sympathies, for he took an active part in the presentation of petitions in 1604/5. Sir Richard Holland, in his evidence before the Council, spoke of his association with Midgley in connection with the presentation of a petition:

> It was then given to Mr Mudgeley the younger, now vicar of Rochdale, to procure it to be presented unto his Majesty by such person as he could entreat to undertake the delivery thereof, for whose furtherance I wrote to my son-in-law, Mr. Reddiche, that if the bearer, meaning Mr Mudgeley did acquaint him with his business, I trusted he would give him his best furtherance.[5]

Both Midgley[6] and Welsh sent a letter to the Archbishop of York extenuating their nonconformity. Many, they explained, are

> caryed into scandall at these thinges, which soe greatly are drawn into abuse by the papists, that plainely many of them would in sundrie places Leave vs and our ministration, yf wee should bee brought vnder the same. Whome to grieue in anie thing of that kinde, it may seeme no small matter to such of their pastors (especially) by whome they haue been reclaimed from papistrie and brought to the gospel.

In a marginal note the Archbishop makes the comment: "It ought to seeme a greater matter to greeue the whole state of the church." Their nonconformity had previously been condoned, "and therefore sith our Latter dealinges haue not altered from

---

[1] Ibid., f. 278 b.
[2] *MSS. of Lord Kenyon,* no. 14, 1604. H.M.C., Fourteenth Report, Appendix Part LV, p. 9.
[3] Bancroft's Register, f. 278 b.
[4] J. & J. A. Venn, op. cit., Vol. III, p. 185.
[5] *Cecil MSS.,* 104, f. 24. H.M.C., Part XVII, p. 57.
[6] The letter is signed "Richard Mougley Pastor of Rachdale". Presumably Joseph Midgley is the same person as Richard Midgley.

the former ... we trust your good Lordship ... will not varie from the former fauourable proceedinges, which hitherto haue beene taken with vs". The Archbishop stated bluntly that it was "a small commendation for anie in auctoritie to winck at the busines of the church", and he gave them the choice of conformity or deprivation.[1] They chose deprivation.

Lists of presentations to various livings are recorded in the Patent Rolls. The cause of the vacancy is generally recorded (*per mortem naturalem, per cessionem, per resignationem*, or *per deprivationem*), but the name of the previous incumbent is seldom given. Not only did the Crown have extensive rights of patronage, the Crown also claimed the right to present to all livings in the gift of a diocesan, during the vacancy of the see. The Patent Rolls, therefore, provide a certain amount of supplementary information. In the diocese of Worcester, Francis Horsepoole was presented on 26 February 1609/10, to the rectory "de Comberton parua per deprivationem" of the last incumbent of the same.[2] It is probable that the person deprived was Robert Hale, who was instituted to the living on 20 May 1607.[3] In the diocese of Sarum, Francis Dalton was presented on 1 June[4] to the rectory "de Manyngford Bruce per deprivationem" of John Jesopp last incumbent of the same, being instituted on 28 June 1605.[5] Again, in the Oxford diocese, Paul Salisbury was presented to the rectory of "Lillingston Lovell per deprivationem" of the last incumbent of the same on 22 April 1605,[6] and was instituted on 18 May 1605,[7] the living being valued at "viij*l*. ix*s*. iiij*d*.".[8] In the diocese of Gloucester, Peter Small was presented to the rectory of the parochial church of St Michael's in the city of Gloucester, through the deprivation or removal of Richard Maunsell, the last incumbent of the same.[9]

---

[1] *Rawlinson MSS.*, C.167, f. 62 b.

[2] *Patent Roll*, 7 Jas. 43, c. 66, 1831.

[3] Exchequer of First Fruits and Tenths, Bishops' Certificates, Worcester, E. 331/1.

[4] *Patent Roll*, 3 Jas. 11, c. 66, 1673.

[5] Exchequer of First Fruits and Tenths, Bishops' Certificates, Sarum, E.331/5. Francis Dalton was exonerated from the payment of his first fruits. *Plea Roll*, E.337/13, no. 91.

[6] *Patent Roll*, 3 Jas. 11, c. 66, 1673.

[7] Exchequer of First Fruits and Tenths, Oxford, E.331/3.

[8] Exchequer of First Fruits and Tenths, Composition Book, E.336/5.

[9] *Patent Roll*, 3 Jas. 12, c. 66, 1674.

15

In the Winchester diocese Emmanuel Hodges was presented on 15 August 1606, to the vicarage of Chortsey through the deprivation of the last incumbent of the same,[1] the value of the benefice being "xiij*l*. xiij*s*. iiij*d*.".[2] In the Exeter diocese, John Haycroft was presented on 5 May 1610[3] to the vicarage of Abbotts Kerswell through the deprivation of the last incumbent of the same, being instituted on 3 June 1610.[4] A contemporary states that "the Bishop of Exeter hath lately silenced 23 of the reverend preachers within Devon and Exeter and thereby quenched the light of a great parte of these countyes".[5] Another list "of resolute Puritane ministers . . . in the Dioceses of Exeter, whoe for the moste parte were conformable and subscribed" mentions thirty-five names, of whom three—Holmes,[6] Burton, and Cleye—are said to have been deprived.[7]

There are a few other items of miscellaneous information concerning one or two other deprivations. The Act Book of the Dean and Chapter of Chichester states that William Thorpe was presented on 23 June 1606 to the vicarage of "Anna Porta alias Amporte", with the chapel of "Appleshawe et Cholderton" annexed to the same, which was vacant through the deprivation of the last incumbent, George Goldeman.[8] In the diocese of Bath and Wells, Philip Martyn and Thomas Jones were deprived. Martyn was instituted to the vicarage of St John the Baptist, "Keinsham", on 18 January 1594/5 and was deprived in 1606,

---

[1] Ibid., 4 Jas. 17, c. 66, 1707.

[2] Exchequer of First Fruits, Composition Book, E.336/5. January 1606/7.

[3] *Patent Roll*, 8 Jas. 59, c. 66, 1897.

[4] Exchequer of First Fruits and Tenths, Bishops' Certificates, Exeter, E.331/5.

[5] *Additional MSS.*, 38,492, f. 43.

[6] Is this the same John Holmes, who figured prominently in Puritan activities about 1586? John Holmes was ordained by the Bishop of Exeter, and by him presented to Ken, a living of his own. Here Holmes instructed and catechized his parishioners in a more thorough manner than even the Bishop had done. He reproved the "grosse vices and disorders" of his flock, and, being complained of to the Bishop, he was removed. He was presented to the living of Telcott, but the Bishop declared that Holmes was an obstinate maintainer of schism and unfit for the living. (*Seconde Parte of a Register*. Ed. A. Peel, op. cit., Vol. II, pp. 27–8.) In November 1586, "one Mr Holmes, a good preacher, presented, was refused for not subscribing or such like cause. . . ." Ibid., Vol. II, p. 87.

[7] *S.P. Dom., Jas. I*, 14, Vol. X.A. no. 81.

[8] Act Book, A. 1545–1618, f. 134; *Additional MSS.*, 39,409, A.

Thomas Smith being instituted on 27 February 1606/7.[1] Jones was instituted to the benefice of Sutton Bingham on 22 February 1592/3 and was deprived about 1609, William Gollop being instituted in his place on 23 January 1609/10.[2]

CONCLUSION

The evidence is necessarily incomplete. Nevertheless, certain conclusions may be drawn. It is clear that there were at least eighty deprivations in fifteen different dioceses. It is possible that there were some ninety deprivations altogether.[3] This figure[4] means that there were more deprivations than Bancroft admitted, but considerably less than the Puritans claimed. Some of the deprived clergy later conformed. If the proportion in the dioceses of London and Lincoln is typical, about one-fifth of those who were deprived later conformed.

It has been claimed that the Puritan clergy were "few in numbers and by no means highly educated as a whole",[5] but it is doubtful whether this can be maintained. In the diocese of London, nine of the fourteen deprived clergy had a Bachelor or a Master's degree, one was a Bachelor of Divinity, and two were fellows of Colleges. In the diocese of Lincoln, of nine deprived, seven were graduates (including one with the degree of Bachelor of Divinity, another who later took the degree of Doctor of Medicine, and two others who were fellows of colleges). In the diocese of Norwich, of eight deprived, five were graduates, and two were also Bachelors of Divinity. An examination of the Institution Books reveals that those who were instituted to fill the

[1] *Additional MSS.*, 30,279, f. 90. "Register of institutions of incumbents to churches in the county of Somerset." *Harleian MSS.*, 6,967, f. 111 b.

[2] Transcripts from the Registers of the Diocese of Bath and Wells by Dr Matthew Hutton.

[3] Dr Usher's figures are unduly cautious and conservative. He concludes: "a further tabulation of the institutions in London, Norwich, Lincoln, Peterborough and Canterbury (the diocese) shows that no other than sixty deprivations is consistent with the general trend of ecclesiastical administration". Op. cit., Vol. II, p. 7. But Usher's figures need correction. E.g., there were fourteen in London, not five or six, nine in Lincoln, not eight; three in Canterbury, not one.

[4] This figure includes four deprivations for the diocese of York. For further details, see R. Marchant, op. cit., p. 149.

[5] R. G. Usher, op. cit., Vol. II, p. 13.

places of the deprived clergymen were little better qualified academically than those whom they replaced.[1] Some of the deprived men were authors and scholars. Of them it is probably true to say that academically they were neither better nor worse educated than the average conformist.

A study of the various deprivations indicates that only the most stubborn and intransigent were actually deprived. Many, who never conformed, were nevertheless allowed to retain their benefices, and only those who refused both to conform and subscribe were in fact deprived. It was claimed that "certain Ministers in the Dioceses of Oxford and Lichfield" were deprived "for none other cause, then only for not subscribing to the 3 Articles, mentioned in the 36. Canon. And this wrong hath been openly in Parliament acknowledged to be a wrong by the Archbishop himself, and the Iudges and advocates of his owne Courts".[2] The charge was repeated in *A Briefe of Greevances in the Ecclesiasticall Iurisdiction delivered by the Lower House of Parliament at a Committie with the Ll. of the Vpper House* in April 1606.[3] This was denied: "This ys alltogether untrue for the ministers were not urged with subscripcion neither anie one of them deprived or suspended bicause they would not subscribe, but onelie shewinge themselves otherwise to be factious and troublesome after manie charitable admonitions they were deprived."[4] The bishops generally appear to have acted with reasonable restraint in circumstances of difficulty and complexity. They were genuinely reluctant to proceed to extremities, and several of them made unavailing personal efforts to induce a better mind. The Bishop of Peterborough

---

[1] Canon C. W. Foster has prepared an analysis indicating the proportion of graduates to non-graduates in the various archdeaconries of the Lincoln diocese in the year 1603; in the archdeaconry of Lincoln and Stow there were 350 non-graduates out of 560 clergymen; in the archdeaconry of Bedford there were 28 non-graduates out of 115; in the archdeaconry of Buckingham there were 43 non-graduates out of 178; in the archdeaconry of Huntingdon there were 38 non-graduates out of 143; and in the archdeaconry of Leicester there were 79 non-graduates out of 188. For the whole diocese there were 538 non-graduates out of a total of 1,184 clergymen. Cf. C. W. Foster, op. cit., p. 454.

[2] *A Myld and Ivst Defence of Certeyne Argvments . . . in behalfe of the Ministers suspended and deprived &c: for not Subscribing and Conforming themselues . . .*, 1606, p. 82.

[3] Printed, C. W. Foster, op. cit., p. 469.

[4] Ibid., p. 360.

declared that it was only when "nothing would prevail", that, in the anguish of his soul, he proceeded to deprivation. He was willing and desirous that the nonconformists should have more time for deliberation and conference, but they rejected this, protesting "that if they should do so, they should seem to be doubtful in those things wherein they were resolved never to yield".[1] The Bishop of Lincoln on 12 April 1605 promised that he would, "by the grace of God use all the best means" that he could devise, "by conference and brotherly exhortations with mildness and discretion to win them", and subsequent events show that he redeemed his promise.[2] No one was deprived in the diocese of Lincoln until he had been respited several times, and had received at least four admonitions. This is the spirit which appears to have animated the bishops in the fulfilment of their invidious and unhappy task.

[1] *Cecil MSS.*, 104, f. 1. H.M.C., Part XVII, p. 46. 4 February 1604/5.
[2] Ibid., 110, f. 74. H.M.C., Part XVII, p. 133.

7

CONFORMITY AND SUBSCRIPTION

ON 29 JULY 1605 Simon Bradstreet, the nonconforming Vicar of Horbling, wrote to the Bishop of Lincoln:

Right reverend father, as I have soe doe I still whollie committ my selfe to your Lordshipps favour, for which you shall fynd me as thankfull as a poore Minister may be. ... Concerning my conformitie I beseech your LL. giue me leave and leysure to goe somwhat slowly that I may goe the more suerly. I have and doe still desire and indevour the Lord his good direction for the good of his Church and the lawfull contentment of my superiours.[1]

Bradstreet had never worn the surplice since his institution in 1596, although he had been admonished many times.[2] On 23 October 1605 the Bishop, because of Bradstreet's labours for God's Church and its dignity, and of his peaceable and honest behaviour, dismissed him in hope of his conformity, until he should be cited again.[3] At the Bishop's triennial visitation in 1607 he was presented because he did not wholly conform himself to the orders and ceremonies appointed in the Prayer Book and Canons, refusing to use the sign of the cross or to wear the surplice. In the *Liber Cleri* for 1611 it was reported that he is of good behaviour "saving hee is not conformable".[4]

The case of Bradstreet is typical. He never conformed; nevertheless, he was not deprived. He was permitted to continue in the exercise of his ministry in hope of his ultimate conformity. There were many others in a like situation. A number of nonconforming clergymen were cited before the Bishop of Lincoln on the occasion of his triennial visitation (August 1604). He charged those who appeared to subscribe and conform. Some did so at once, or at

---

[1] Correspondence of William Chaderton, Cor/13/2, f. 19.
[2] Episcopal Court Book, 1602–9, Cj 14, ff. 64, 73 d, 78, 86, 91.
[3] Ibid., Cj 14, f. 102.
[4] *Liber Cleri*, 1611, f. 2.

one of the courts held within the next few weeks. There were others, however, who were unwilling either to subscribe or conform. Some of those who were willing to conform were not prepared to subscribe to the Articles, while others craved time for deliberation which was granted them.

Further illustrative cases may be quoted: John Jackson, Vicar of Bourne, was cited before the Bishop for omitting the surplice. On 10 April 1605 he informed the Bishop that "he cannot yet be resolved to conform himself, and craves time".[1] He continued to be presented at subsequent visitations, and in the *Liber Cleri* for 1611 was reported as of good behaviour, "saveing that he nowe stands suspended being presented for vnconformytie".[2]

Thomas Cotton, Rector of Laughton, appeared before the Bishop on 3 October 1604 to answer for not wearing the surplice and not observing the Prayer Book.[3] On 30 January 1604/5 he refused to conform or subscribe, and craved time. On 19 June 1605 the Bishop gave him time to confer with Mr Sacheverill, but on 23 October, on exhibition of letters of William Turpin and Basil Brook, knights, touching Cotton's peaceable and quiet behaviour, the Bishop, in hope of his conformity, dismissed him until he should be cited afresh, provided that in the meantime the ceremonies of the Church should be observed by him or by another fit minister there approved by lawful authority.[4] At the episcopal visitation in 1607 he was presented because "he doth not read the holy service neither morninge nor eveninge prayer noe further then the second lesson nor weareth the surplice",[5] but on 20 January 1607/8 he certified that he had now conformed, and was dismissed.[6]

On 3 October 1604 John More, Rector of Knaptoft, appeared before the Bishop, sitting in his court, to answer for not wearing the surplice. He craved respite when the Bishop admonished him to conform and to subscribe and to certify touching his conformity.[7]

---

[1] Episcopal Court Book, 1602–9, Cj 14, ff. 78, 86.
[2] *Liber Cleri*, 1611, f. 1.
[3] Episcopal Court Book, 1602–9, Cj 14, f. 67 d.
[4] Ibid., f. 67 d. "A briefe of the manner ... of the L:B: of Lincoln his proceedinge against those ... not conforminge. ..." Printed, C. W. Foster, *The State of the Church*, p. 363.
[5] Episcopal Visitation Book, 1607, Vj 19, f. 29 d.
[6] Ibid., Vj. 19, f. 70 d.
[7] Episcopal Court Book, 1602–9, Cj 14, 78 d.

On 30 January 1604/5 he appeared and alleged "that he hath considered of those reasons which moved him to stand against conformitie, and he ys still more and more confirmed in his opinions and therefore hath not yet conformed himself neither can he now conforme himself".[1] Later in the year he alleged that he was conferring with Mr Sacheverill, and on 23 October the Bishop dismissed him on the same terms as he did Thomas Cotton.[2]

A spirit of patient forbearance was also exercised in the case of Henry Wilkinson, Rector of the first and second parts of Waddesdon, who was first cited for nonconformity on 3 October 1604.[3] On 12 December he alleged "that he hath a curate who doth conform himself and therefore he being freed by the canon ought not to be compelled vntill a yeare be expired".[4] On 15 January 1605/6, in hope of his conformity, he was granted till the next Wednesday fortnight after the end of the session of Parliament then pending.[5] He never conformed and he died in possession of his benefice.

Where there was some hope of ultimate conformity, the bishops appear to have deferred proceeding to extremities. David Allen, Rector of Ludborough, was presented by his churchwardens in 1604 because he omitted part of Common Prayer, did not wear the surplice, nor use the order of the book in the sacraments, nor use the sign of the cross—and whether he omitted or changed anything, they had not been able to observe.[6] On 6 November 1605, he appeared before the Bishop, and "vpon conference had with him the said reuerend father thoughte good to graunte him a further time of reading and conference &c till the Wensday fortnighte after the end of this session of parliament".[7] On 6 June 1606, he appeared, and stated "that he hath not yet conformed himself neither can he yet satisfie himself therein, but will indevor to satisfie and conform himself therein according to the law".[8]

The evidence makes it clear that many sturdy nonconformists were permitted to continue in the exercise of their ministry in

[1] Ibid., Cj 14, f. 78 d.
[2] Ibid., Cj 14, f. 102.
[3] "A briefe of . . . the L:B: of Lincolne his proceedinge against those . . . not conforminge . . . ." Printed, C. W. Foster, op. cit., p. 363.
[4] Episcopal Court Book, 1602–9, Cj 14, f. 75 d.
[5] Ibid., Cj 14, f. 107.
[6] Episcopal Visitation Book, 1604, Vj 18, pp. 106–7.
[7] Episcopal Court Book, 1602–9, Cj 14, f. 100.
[8] Ibid., f. 108.

consideration of their peaceable behaviour or hope of their later conformity.

Nevertheless, the significance of outward conformity must not be exaggerated. There were a number who conformed on the cogent ground that conformity was a lesser evil than deprivation. This was the view adopted by Thomas Cartwright during the previous reign: "As touching that point whether the minister should wear it [the surplice], although it be inconvenient; the truth is, that I dare not be author to any, to forsake his pastoral charge for the inconvenience thereof."[1] William Bedell, subsequently Bishop of Kilmore and Ardagh, was of the same mind. The wearing of the surplice, he wrote,

> ys commanded by ye Bishopes and ye Magistrate: so now ye Cere-monyes haue force from them both. In which case, me thinckes yf the comandement be not contrary to ye Law of god, there ys obedience to be yeilded not only for feare but for conscience sake. ... As for relinquishing ye Ministry, yf nothing impious be required at our handes I dare not approue yt for all ye inconveniencyes in ye world. sith both to minister and people that which ys so necessary should me thinckes swallow all inexpediencyes.

Obedience was due to those in authority:

> this course especially seemeth necessary yf ye Magistrates should require a Minister to doe some thing without which he could not be suffered to exercise his Ministry. In which case ye preaching of ye Gospell should sway more than all our desire of euen our owne liberty.[2]

Reynolds, who was one of the Puritan spokesmen at the Hampton Court Conference, indignantly denied saying that the ceremonies were unlawful and such as might not be used:

> I am advertised by a Gentleman of credit, that of late when the King was at my Lord Sayes house, my Lord told his Highness that I denyed at Banbury to Mr Dodd[3] and others, that ever I said in the Conference, that Cap and Surplice were things indifferent, nor ever would be brought to say so, and (as far as the Gentleman who was present remembreth) that I dehorted them from wearing the same too: A thing most untrue, for proof whereof, I might say to cleer

---

[1] *Rest of the Second Reply*, p. 262.
[2] *Tanner MSS.*, 75, f. 176.
[3] Dodd was deprived. See above, pp. 212-3.

mine innocence, as Job did, my witness is in heaven and my Lord on high, unless the very absurdity of the thing convinced it, that I, who by continual wearing of the Cap and Surplice (which I never refused) do show I think them indifferent and lawfull to be worn, should against mine own speech made in such a presence, deny I said it or ever would: yea the Crosse it selfe (the most offensive Ceremony) which as in Conference with Hart, I thought that Ezechias breaking the brazen serpent directed men of like Authority what to do with, soe did I in that great Conference because of the superstitious conceit that Papists have of it . . . yet the use of the Cross I say after Baptisme, with that signification and sense alone, in which our Gratious King requireth it, I have rather might men to yeild unto for obedience then to leave their charge.[1]

This was the point of view adopted by many Puritans: they regarded the ceremonies as things indifferent, and, being enforced by authority, were prepared to use them. They agreed that it was better to yield the ceremonial points in dispute than to incur deprivation to the injury of the flock. It was a coerced conformity: "Ye greatest parte by farre of resident and paynefull preachers amoung our selues", one Puritan wrote, "rather choose to yelde then to leave their lyvings and ministery, yet is there hardly any one who had not rather thei were remooved then receyued."[2] Thomas Sparke, who had also been one of the Puritan disputants, in *A Brotherly Perswasion to Unitie*, wrote: "I am not ignorant . . . that I haue and doe vndergoe already the hard censure of many for conforming my selfe as I haue to the orders of the Church, and that I am like to endure harder for the writing and publishing of this Treatise." He subscribed to the view that men should conform for the sake of the ministry. The ceremonies, he wrote,

> were rather to be yealded vnto, being but of the nature they are, and being vrged no otherwise then in deed and truth they be, by our Church, then that any minister should for his refusing conformity thereunto, suffer himself to be put from the vse of his gifts, place and ministry, for such a necessity is laid vpon vs that be in the ministery . . . to preach the Gospell, that woe is to vs if we do not so. I Cor. 9.16.[3]

[1] *Gibson MSS.*, Vol. I, 929, f. 121. 5 August 1605. Dr John Reynolds to William Herbert, Earl of Pembroke.

[2] *Additional MSS.*, 38,492, f. 10.

[3] *A Brotherly Perswasion to Unitie, and Uniformitie in iudgement, and Practise touching the Received and present Ecclesiasticall government, and the authorised rites and ceremonies of the Church of England*, 1607.

Men's motives are always mixed, and we are all swayed, to a greater or lesser extent, by personal considerations. Were those Puritans who conformed animated by a spirit of calculating self-interest? Was their chief concern the continued opportunity to preach the gospel, or a more human and less worthy one: an understandable desire to continue in the enjoyment of the emoluments of ecclesiastical office? Archbishop Laud was emphatic that their motives were sordid and self-seeking. Their conformity, he said, was a hypocritical device to enjoy the rewards of the ministry:

> Others . . . that they might saue their repuatacion and yet contynue in their places, invented a new course, which ever since the said Conference at Hampton Court, they haue put in practice, and haue yeilded to a kind of Conformity; not that they thought any whit better of the things, but for that they held them (though in themselues vnlawfull) not to be such as for which a man ought to hazard (not his lyving, that might savour of covetousnes, but) his Mynisterie, and the good which gods people might by that meanes receaue.[1]

Laud was not only cynical but uncharitable. He was unable to understand the way in which they sought the will of God in these circumstances of peculiar complexity and difficulty. This is not to deny that they were exposed, like all men, to a variety of pressures. No doubt they were swayed by prudential considerations. But the final and overriding consideration was the will of God. In their agonized perplexity they sought to discover the divine will by prayer and fasting. Whatever other charges may be levelled against them, they were not restless and ambitious place seekers; they were men of deep piety and earnest faith. The overriding question which weighed with them was their responsibility to the flock; ought private scruples to hinder the continued exercise of their ministry to the injury of the Church?

There was no infallible and certain answer. For some of the Puritans the answer was clear and unambiguous: they declined to conform, and they paid the price in deprivation or suspension; for others, the answer was less plain: they chose the painful path of reluctant obedience and unhappy conformity.

The matter of subscription was also a cause of anxious debate.

---

[1] *Tenison MSS.*, 731. *A Briefe Suruey of the Tymes and Manner of Reformacion in Religion of the Churches of England and Scotland; and of the Liturgie, Rites, Ceremonyes and Discipline therein vsed or controuerted.*

John Reynolds refused to subscribe in the form prescribed in the canon, though he conformed. In a letter to the Archbishop of Canterbury, he explained his scruples

> Right Reverend, myne humble duty remembered. Although your affection appearing other towards me the last year then the former, disheartened me, when I could not subscribe with peace of conscience, to write thereof to your Grace, as some friendly wished me, yet on their advise and request, assuring me your honourable favour, have I yeilded thereto. . . . I cannot in Conscience undergoe the forme of the subscription to the three Articles required; for out of the books of Judith and Wisdom, there are some observed . . . which being . . . publickly read . . . yeild in my opinion scruples . . . and Besides divers things my selfe have noted, who have not yet examined all that falleth within the compass of subscription (more necessary employments have hindered me therefrom) by others have I heard of certainly which I find true and of consequence weighty as namely that the Booke of Ordering Bishops, Priests, and Deacons set forth in King Edwards time, hath the oath of the Kings Supremacie with this clause, so help me God, all Saints and the holy Evangelists, whence it would ensue . . . it impiously imparteth to creatures Gods own honour through Invocation of them.

He would be affirming "a known untruth", if he subscribed to the article which declared that there was nothing in the book of Common Prayer contrary to the Word of God:

> But these, I hope, albeit there were no more, will seem sufficient in your Graces eyes to prove, it is in truth the care of conscience before God, as well as the credit before men, that moveth me, which yeilded willingly to conformity, not to yeild to subscription.[1]

A month later, after his refusal to subscribe,

> the Lord Treasurer by the King's command willed D. Abbot his Vice-Chancellor to set him a certain day within which, unless he subscribed, he should be expulsed from the University. Abbot urged him to read some authors on the " Apocrypha-places ", his chiefest scruples, to prove he stood not obstinate in his own conceit.[2]

Reynolds sought Salisbury's mediation with the King:

> He hopes his suit will not seem importunate to the King, whose mildness, thinking religious men of moderate spirits may be borne

[1] *Gibson MSS.*, Vol. I, 929, f. 121. 5 August 1605.
[2] *Cecil MSS.*, 191, f. 44. H.M.C., Part XVII, pp. 422–3. 12 September 1605.

with for disobedience to the lawful ceremonies of the Church, promises him more favour that is obedient thereto, and wishes others also to yield to conformity.[1]

There was an important difference, he said, between conformity and subscription. He denied that he "had promised the King at Hampton Court to subscribe, and thence offended, now refusing it". His attitude to subscription was the same now as at the Conference.

> I assure myself that, since I had no private speech there with his Highness, but am said to have promised it in the conference publicly, his wise discerning of the difference between subscription and conformity, this latter only then urged, as sundry of that audience too can testify (to omit that the note which, upon his royal commandment, I exhibited of errors in the Apocrypha, did mention them as just cause why to forbear subscription, yea, the same approved by some correction of the book therein afterward) will suffice to acquit me from it.[2]

It is not surprising that some, for conscience' sake, only subscribed with explicit provisos. One Puritan explained to Bancroft that he subscribed with this qualification:

> To the third Article which is that there is nothing conteyned in the booke of Common Prayer, the booke of ordination of Bishops, Preists and deacons, or two bookes of Homilyes, contrary to the word of god, I doe also willingly subscribe: so as I may be allowed to interpret the things in the fayrest sense which the words of subscription and things subscribed vnto may beare. . . .

In an additional note, he enlarged on the significance of this reservation:

> I take not the booke to impose vpon any, wearing of that very surplice which hath beene vsed in Idolatry, neither doe I thinke it to be imposed as an holy vestment . . . nor as a thing necessary to the worship of God, or any part thereof, neither take I it to be enjoyned as any Sacramentall Signification, but only for order and vniformity sake.[3]

Another Puritan explained:

[1] Ibid.
[2] Ibid., f. 46. H.M.C., Part XVII, p. 431. 23 September 1605.
[3] *Harleian MSS.*, 3,795, f. 58.

I do not so take subscription as if it did imply a generall and absolute allowance of all thinges within the bookes subscribed vnto as in euery poynte agreeing to the worde, but I do vnderstande the nature of it by end of it, viz. to draw men into a vniformity of the worship of god, which as I conceiue may be effected without an exact approbation of eyery misplaced worde, incautelous phrase, inexpedient ceremony, not so well ordained on the churches behalfe. Now thus to take it I am further induced in that to affirme the sayde bookes to haue no taynture of blemish were to giue to the authors of them a possibility of making their constitutions voyde of error, which themselues deny.

"The bar omission", he argued, "of som hard incongruous speach or a ceremony in some congregatione offensiue is not forbidden." Subscription did not imply unreserved approbation of all particulars:

I do confesse and holde, that howsouer that authority of the Magistrate, shall not by gods helpe force me to call euel good, nor yet my liberty in my ministery cause me to giue my approbation of any thinges simply wicked, nor yet the peace of the church driue me to betray any iota of gods truth, yet all of them togither shall and as I conceiue oughte to preuayle so farre with me as rather to yeeld to an inconvenience, an vnequall yoake, an vnnecessary constitution, then ether by disobedience to spurne against authority or by a relinquistration to forsake my ministery or vnseasonably to trouble the peace of the Church. . . . So then if Paul became all thinges to all men by vertue of Christian liberty, to the Jewes as a Jew, to them that were without law as if he had ben without law, I thincke he yielded to somme inconveniences, vnmeete ordinances and rites, rather then he would ether be contentious or breake of the course of his ministery.[1]

William Bedell explained that he did not "find any great difficulty" in subscribing, for

truth that is there be other thinges euen in the reformed book subject to doubt but where they will giue them all . . . a comodious interpretation what reason haue I to be witty in anothers meaning against my selfe and not to giue yt to their wrightinges, which I would to be giuen to mine owne.[2]

---

[1] *Harleian MSS.*, 828, f. 29. "Positions touching Subscription and Conformity submitted with reuerence vnto the iudgement of the godly learned."
[2] *Tanner MSS.*, 75, f. 176.

He was ready and willing to place the best construction on the wording of the Articles. Thomas Sparke adopted the same point of view: some things might be misconstrued, but they were not matters of sufficient importance to justify refusal of subscription:

> I must needes say ... I haue thought certayne things therein so set downe ... unlesse they bee fauourably vnderstood, they seem to carrie some shew of contrarietie to the word of God, yet in verie deede, I neuer thought any therein, or within the compasse of the required subscription such, but that the same by such a charitable and fauourable construction, and that also but well standing with the professed and publikely established doctrine of our Church, and with the best and true meaning of the Bookes themselues where the obiections to the contrarie did seeme to arise, might with a good conscience for the peace and good of the Church be quietly yealded vnto.[1]

Other Puritans sought to evade the embarrassing and exacting requirements of the canons in the accommodating shelter of a lectureship. The canons only required a lecturer to read divine service twice during the course of a year.[2] Arthur Hildersham, who was deprived from the vicarage of Ashby-de-la-Zouch in 1605, secured appointment as a lecturer at the same place in 1609, although still a nonconformist. As a lecturer he contented himself with preaching, engaging a curate to read the statutory services. On 26 November 1604 William Bedell wrote to Samuel Ward seeking a conforming assistant for John Knewstubs:

> I am to entreate you to prouide for Mr Knewstub yf you may any young man that would be his Curate and teach in his parish that would ware ye surplice. He should haue 10*l.* yearly and his Table and yf he taught (as he were like to for yf he would) ye children of any borne out of ye Towne what he could gett for them. I pray send me worde by your Letter what you can doe heerin, but deale not perfunctorily in yt.[3]

Sir Thomas Hoby, writing to Cranborne (28 January 1604/5) extenuated the nonconformity of Stephen Egerton on the ground that he was only lecturer at Blackfriars in London and an assistant duly observed the Prayer Book: "there is another minister duly

---

[1] *A Brotherly Perswasion to Unitie.*
[2] Canon 56.
[3] *Tanner MSS.*, 75, f. 180.

observes the book and ceremonies; so as Mr Egerton is but a
lecturer there and is not bound by any statute to use the book,
nor by the canons themselves, is tied to any conformity but twice
in the year, which as yet is not half expired." In spite of this fact,
Egerton was being threatened with suspension:

> My lord of London that now is (I fear by his Grace's special direc-
> tions) has since proceeded so far as that upon Wednesday next no
> small number of his Majesty's faithful subjects are likely to be
> scattered as so many sheep without a shepherd by Mr Egerton's
> suspension. Amongst which number finding myself included, and
> having some probable reasons to think that your lordship is the only
> remedy left to relieve so many hundreds of religious distressed hearts,
> I have presumed to be a humble suitor for your letters unto my Lord
> of London to suffer Mr Egerton to continue his ministry (which he
> has now enjoyed twenty-two years without detection), until either in
> his life or doctrine he be justly tainted; or that he be duly convicted
> of factious or turbulent preaching against the Church government.[1]

Sir Thomas Hoby, together with many others, was dismayed at
the threatened termination of Egerton's ministry through suspension.

A similar situation existed in many other places. It created a
spirit of unhappy concern which found expression in the presentation of petitions and the collection of subscriptions. A newsletter,
dated February 1607/8, describes a collection at Manchester:

> For Manchester news, there is non but this. Dr Batts brought a
> preacher from Chester . . . who preached two sermons on the last
> Sunday, and, at Dr Batts' request, they got him a collection. The
> collectors were Mr George Tipping, Humfray Booth, Christopher
> Downes, Robert Atkinson, and others, and as it is reported, my
> Lady Boweyer gave 25s., Mr Holland of Denton 20s., Sir Edmund
> Trafford 10s., the College 6s. 8d., the rest they gathered of the
> townsmen. His whole collection was 9l. odd moneye. The collectors
> came unto [the] parson of Shuters Brooke . . . and he tould them
> hee durst give no moneye, because the preacher would not subscribe
> unto the King's lawes. And I did heare that he came from about
> Northampton[2] and lost his benefice, because he would not subscribe,
> and is going to Ireland. . . .[3]

---

[1] *Cecil MSS.*, 188, f. 53. H.M.C., Part XVII, p. 38.
[2] Possibly Robert Catline. See above, pp. 208-10.
[3] *MSS. of Lord Kenyon*, no. 19. H.M.C., Fourteenth Report, Appendix,
Part IV, p. 14.

A striking instance of this practical concern for the deprived is to be seen in the will of Mrs Sarah Venables, widow of Richard Venables, merchant taylor of London. In a will dated 23 July 1606, she bequeathed a substantial proportion of her property "for the benefitte and releife" of "distressed ministers within the realme of England". She explicitly directed:

> The residewe of all and singuler my goodes, cattailes, plate, Juells, Implements, househould stuffe, apparell, and whatsoeuer els to mee belongeth, I will shalbe sold to the vttermost and when it shall appeere what the somme of Monie thereof proceedinge ... then my will is that a great care be had for the distributinge and disposinge thereof according to the true meaninge of this my will, which is that it shold be distributed vnto and amongste such poore ministers which I see are greevouslie distressed.

The amount allocated to each necessitous and deserving minister was to be determined by the executors. Furthermore, the corpus was not "to be distributed ... all at one instant or in one year but ... the same distribucion made yerelie by Fyve hundreth pounds in the yere so longe as the same will last".

> My will and minde is that such of the said ministers as shall receive a porcion of this my said guifte one yere maie notwithstandinge if their be cause be lyable to receave a further porcion thereof there next yere the which I do referre to the discretion of my said executors.

Two Puritan clergymen were appointed executors of the will:

> For the execucuion of this my present Testament and last will I do institute ordaine and appointe my approved trustie and good freinds Mr Anthoni Wotton minister, and Mr Edward Buckland minister ... to be Executors and for their paynes takeinge herein I do bequeath vnto Mr Wotton and to Master Buckland to eache of them the somme of fortie poundes.[1]

The relatives of Sarah Venables, however, contested the will, affirming that "there sisters slender regard towards them did not procede of anie vnnaturall loue or neclecte of dutye towards there said deceased sister But out of the inordinate zeale the which she did beare vnto the said ministers". They testified that "this her Will was made even at the instant of the deprivation of the

---

[1] *S.P. Dom., Jas. I*, 14, Vol. XXXVII, no. 113 (i).

ministers being inticeed therevnto by diuers of them who did repaire vnto her to that purpose without the knowledge of anie of the said Brothers and sisters".[1] On 9 June 1608 the Court of the Exchequer made a decree setting aside Anthony Wotton and Edward Buckland as Executors of the said will: "It is therevpon ordered by the right honorable the lord Treasurer Chauncellor and Barons of this Court that the sayd Anthony Wotten and Edward Buckland being ministers non-conformable shall not intermeddle in the execucion of the said will."[2]

Puritanism enjoyed powerful lay patronage and support. Within the House of Commons influential laymen marshalled their forces to protect those now threatened by the rigid enforcement of conformity and subscription. The Elizabethan pattern of events was to be repeated in a new setting under new conditions.

[1] Ibid., no. 113 (iv).
[2] *S.P. Dom., Jas. I*, 14, Vol. XXXVII, no. 113 (v).

8

PURITANISM AND PARLIAMENT

DURING THE latter years of Queen Elizabeth's reign the House of Commons had grown rapidly in political responsibility and independence. The Queen peremptorily forbade Parliament to meddle in ecclesiastical affairs—she adopted the view that she was supreme Governor of the Church, and that Convocation was the proper sphere for the discussion of ecclesiastical matters—but this view was steadily resisted in the House of Commons. They argued that the Reformation had been effected by the King in Parliament, and that Parliament had a proper responsibility for ecclesiastical affairs. The manner in which the Elizabethan settlement had been established supported their contention. It had not been possible to work through Convocation, and the religious settlement had been the work of the Queen in Parliament. Puritan members therefore believed that they had the constitutional right to initiate and frame ecclesiastical legislation. Elizabeth denied this: she insisted that petition was the proper method of procedure.

On 17 July Bishop Horne of Winchester, in a letter to the eminent Swiss Reformer, Rudolph Gualter, spoke of the forthcoming session of Parliament. Concerning the ornaments Rubric in the Act of Uniformity, he confessed: "we certainly hope to repeal this clause of the act."[1] After matters concerning the succession had been lengthily debated, the radicals introduced a bill for "the Sound Christian religion". Other Bills concerning the quality of ministers, non-residence, corrupt presentation to livings, simony, and pensions paid from benefices, were also introduced. The first Bill, after receiving three readings, was stopped by the Queen, who "disliked the manner of putting it forth".[2] She took the view that matters of religion were the proper concern of Convocation, and that, as supreme Governor,

---

[1] *Zurich Letters*, Vol. I, p. 143.
[2] *Parker Correspondence*, p. 292.

such matters might not be introduced into Parliament without her knowledge and consent. Despite the intercession of the Archbishops, Elizabeth refused to lift her veto, and Parliament was dissolved.

In 1571 a new Parliament met. It met in a mood of national indignation after the Northern Rebellion and the proclamation of the Papal Bull of Excommunication. A Bill was promoted "concerning coming to church and receiving the Communion". It was an attempt to make the reception of the Sacrament a test of political loyalty. It violated Elizabeth's principle of avoiding any "inquisition or examination of conscience", and she therefore vetoed it.

Other ecclesiastical Bills were read, including the one which had failed five years previously, but further action was prohibited by the Queen. Concerning a Bill about the Articles, the Queen transmitted a message that "she liketh very well of them, and mindeth to publish them, and have them Executed by the Bishops, by direction of her Highness Regal Authority of Supremacy of the Church of England, and not to have the same dealt in by Parliament".[1] This was the position she consistently adopted: on 22 May 1571 the Speaker signified "her Highness' pleasure, that from henceforth no more bills concerning religion shall be prepared or received into this House unless the same should be first considered and liked by the clergy".[2] In the Parliament of 1576 the Puritans promoted a petition concerning various abuses in the Church: an interesting departure from previous attempts at direct action in Parliament. The Queen was exceedingly jealous of the royal prerogative and she continued to remind her faithful Commons that proper procedure was to petition the sovereign for the remedy of abuses, not to frame legislation. It was the prerogative of the Government to initiate ecclesiastical legislations. During the last decade, however, Parliament refrained from aggressive action in deference to the wishes of the aged Queen.

The conflict was renewed in intensity with the accession of the new sovereign. A proclamation for a new Parliament was issued in January 1603/4. The Puritans were anxious to secure the

---

[1] Sir S. D'Ewes, *Journals*, p. 180. See above, p. 15.
[2] Ibid., p. 213.

maximum representation possible and strenuous endeavours were made to achieve this. One Puritan writer described how

> notwithstandinge the Non-conformists had been Depressed . . . yet they continued their petitions and desiers for a learned godly Ministry . . . they and their friends laboured the more for the discharge of their duty, Whatsoever the issue should be; to choose Members well affected to the Reformation to serve in the next Parliament, and very many such were chosen.[1]

The Puritans were rewarded for their labours by securing a majority in the Lower House.

The first session of the new Parliament was held on 19 March 1603/4 when the King, discussing differences in religion, pointed out that Puritans could not be suffered in the Commonwealth, because they were "ever discontented with the present government, and impatient to suffer any superiority, which maketh their sect unable to be suffered in any well-governed commonwealth".[2]

The Commons were determined to debate the state of the Church. They desired that ministers who scrupled at certain ceremonies should be indulged, and that measures should be taken to secure a resident and preaching ministry. On 23 March 1603/4 Sir Edward Montague of Northamptonshire moved that "Three main Grievances" should be remedied, among which grievances he included "the Suspension of some learned and grave Ministers, for matters of Ceremony, and for preaching against Popish Doctrine".[3] Introducing the motion, he said:

> I know my own weakness in judgment and mine infirmities of speech, both which as you may well perceive, makes me in fear to speak before this grave, wise and honourable presence. Yet I had rather submit myself to your wise censures and brave your patience than be silent in matters so straightly enjoined me by the County for which I serve.[4]

A committee was thereupon appointed to consider the motion.

In April 1604 Sir Francis Hastings moved for a committee to

---

[1] *Morrice MSS.*, G. f. 549.
[2] James' *Works*, p. 485. Printed, G. W. Prothero, *Select Statutes*, p. 282.
[3] *Journals of the House of Commons*, Vol. I, p. 151; *Cotton MSS., Titus*, F.IV, f. 4 b.
[4] *Beaulieu MSS.* Notes on the First Parliament of James I, taken from Sir Edward Montagu's Journal. H.M.C., p. 42.

consider how religion might be strengthened and a learned ministry increased. On 16 April James asked the House, before proceeding further, to confer with Convocation:

> Mr. Speaker publisheth to the House, that he understood by Message from his Majesty, that he had taken knowledge . . . of their Desire to treat, touching a Reformation of Matters of religion. Before they intermeddle with these things, he wished, they would confer with the Members of the Convocation House.[1]

This request caused much heated controversy: "it was then propounded that the conference should be with the Convocation, which the House utterly refused to consent to."[2] The point was made "that there was no Precedent of any Conference with a Convocation". The Commons declared that "they would be ready to confer of any Matter of that Nature with the Bishops, as Lords of Parliament; and wished, that so much might be made known to his Majesty".[3] The following day the matter was raised again, and after further dispute, the same reply was sent: it was "thought fit, and so ordered, to have Conference with the Bishops, as Lords of the Upper House, touching these matters".[4]

In the meantime, Bancroft, as President of Convocation, appointed a committee of bishops to confer with the Speaker and others of the House of Commons about complaints brought before them against the clergy, "et ad enarranda coram oratore et membris domus inferioris parliamenti gravamina clericorum contra laicos".[5] On 18 April the King informed the Lower House of Parliament that "he had given Power by his Letters Patent to the Members of the Convocation House, to debate, consider and determine" certain "Matters of Religion and Government ecclesiastical". Concerning his initial request that the Commons should consult with Convocation, James declared that he "would make no new Precedents"; that he would protect the Lower House in their privileges; and that he wished they "would confer (as was assented) with the Bishops, as Lords of Parliament".[6] The following entry appears in the *Journals of the House of Lords*:

[1] *Journals of the H. of C.*, Vol. I, pp. 172–3.
[2] *Beaulieu MSS.*, H.M.C., p. 44.
[3] *Journals of the H. of C.*, Vol. I, pp. 172–3.
[4] Ibid., Vol. I, pp. 175–6.
[5] Quoted, E. Cardwell, *Synodalia*, Vol. II, p. 584.
[6] *Journals of the H. of C.*, Vol. I, p. 176.

Mr Secretary Herbert delivered another Message to the Lords, from the Common House to this Effect, That, Whereas they had received Signification of his Majesty's Pleasure ... for Conference by them to be had with certain of the lords the Bishops, Concerning the Reformation of certain Matters and Rites of the Church (whereof some complaints had been made), and for the better Correspondence to be holden betwixt the Commonalty and the Clergy; they were willing to have such Conference with some select Number of the Bishops; but so as they might confer with them as Lords of the Higher House of Parliament, and not in such Condition and Quality as they are of the Convocation House. . . .[1]

On 19 April the Lords approved the arrangement, and appointed a committee of thirty Lords, to represent them at the Conference with the Commons.[2]

The committee of the House of Commons proceeded to draw up a series of Articles or Heads to be handled in Conference with the Lords. Sir James Perrot expounded the details to the House.[3] The first Article concerned the controverted question of subscription:

that the Articles only concerninge the doctrine of faith and of the sacraments, Whereunto the Ministers ought to subscribe by the Statute of the xiij yeare of the Reigne of the late Queene Elizabeth, may be explained, perfected, and established, by parliament. And that no contrary doctrine may bee taught within the realme and that all Maisters of Houshoulds may be compelled to subscribe vnto the same articles as well as the Ministers.[4]

This was a device to modify the stringent requirements of Canon 36. The second article was an attempt to secure official authorization of the Lambeth Articles, thereby securing for the Church the profession of a rigid Calvinism:

that the nyne Articles agreed vpon before the Lord Archbishop of Canterbury and others at Lambeth A.D. 1595, may bee proposed to the Lords as things proceeding from some of them selues to bee so farre added to the rest of the aforesaid articles as they shall thinke meete.

The Lambeth Articles defined the doctrine of predestination in its

---

[1] *Journals of the H. of L.*, Vol. II, p. 281.
[2] Ibid., Vol. II, p. 281.
[3] *Journals of the H. of C.*, Vol. I, pp. 199–200.
[4] *Additional MSS.*, 38,139, f. 38 b; *Journals of the H. of C.*, Vol. I, pp. 199–200.

most uncompromising form ("Deus ab aeterno praedestinavit quosdam ad vitam et quosdam ad mortem reprobavit"). The Lower House was divided about the wisdom of including this article, and, after considerable discussion, it was determined not to press this point. Sir James Perrot explained that the other Articles were concerned with the reform of abuses in the existing ecclesiastical system. In regard to clerical learning it was resolved to press

> from henceforth none other bee admitted to be ministers of the Word and Sacrament then suche as are at the tyme of their admittance Bachellors of Arts or of a higher degree in schooles, haueinge testimony from the Vniuersitie or Colledge whereof hee was, of his abilitie to preache. . . .

It was agreed that they should work for the abolition of non-residence and pluralities by providing

> that from henceforth noe dispensation or tolleration shall bee allowed to any to haue or retaine twoe or more Benefices with Cure of Sowles or to bee non resident; and that suche as nowe haue double benefices or bee non resident shall giue sufficient allowance yearely to maintaine a Preacher in their absence. And that for this purpose the incombent shalbee allotted to make his residency in one of his Personages to th'intent that in the other Church a certen and constant minister maye bee maintained and kept.

Further, that they should urge the increase of ecclesiastical incomes:

> yt is thought meete where the lyuinge of the Vicar or Curat is vnder xx*l.* by the yeare that for the better maintenance of the Vicar or Curate (beinge a Preacher) there may bee some increase made of his lyuinge as shalbee thought conuenient.

Finally, they stressed the need for easing the requirements of subscription:

> Yt is humbly desired that the Lords would conferre with vs touching a Petition to bee conferred to the Kings Majestie that by his gracious fauor such order bee taken that no minister bee forced to subscribe otherwise then to the Articles Concerninge only the doctrine of faith and Sacraments, whereunto by the said Statute made in the xiij yeare of the Reigne of the late Queene Elizabeth they are appointed to subscribe.

Above all, the needs of the threatened Puritan ministers were not to be forgotten: the committee was charged

> to conferre with the Lords that such faithfull ministers as duetifully carrye themselues in their functions and callings, teachinge the people dilligently may not bee depriued, suspended, scilenced, or ymprisoned for not vsinge of the Crosse in Baptisme or the Surplice, which tourneth to the punishment of the people.

On 15 May 1604 Anthony Erbury presented a Bill "For the Declaration of certayne practises of the Bishops of London to be treson".[1] He accused Richard Bancroft of having "lately enterteyned and ... complotted with seminaries and priests", and having "caused to be published in print, certen trayterous bookes". Erbury earnestly petitioned that

> his courses and practises, may be by th'assent of your Majestie, and by the said Lords and Commons in this present Parliament assembled, declared to be high treason, and the saide Richard Bishop of London to be a traytor ... and that he, the said Richard Bishop of London, doe and may therefore suffer as in case of high treason.

This hostile attack was not allowed to pass unnoticed, and the Speaker, Sir Edward Phelippes, examined Erbury, who confessed "that himself drewe and framed the Bill exhibited into the parliament howse against the Busshopp of London".[2] He was confined to prison, from whence he wrote a petition to Cecil, confessing that if he "had conceaued that yt would haue offended your Lordships and the State, [he] woulde not haue medled in yt".[3]

The Conference between the Committees of the two Houses took place on 17 May 1604. The King assured them, with great fervour and sincerity, that he was implacably opposed to the Papists, and that "so long as his Heart was in his Body, he would ever continue this [present] Religion".[4] He desired the Lord Chancellor "to provide against Atheists, Papists, and such as refuse to receive the Sacrament", and he "wished the Lords and

---

[1] *S.P. Dom., Jas. I*, 14, Vol. VIII, no. 21. *Journals of the H. of C.*, Vol. I, p. 210.
[2] *S.P. Dom., Jas. I*, 14, Vol. VIII, no. 24. 16 May 1604.
[3] Ibid., Vol. VIII, no. 25. May (?) 1604.
[4] *Journals of the H. of C.*, Vol. I, p. 214.

Commons to think of Laws to hem them in". He was equally determined concerning the Puritans: "touching refractory Ministers, and Reformists, let them consider of the Book of Common Prayer."

A week later Sir Francis Hastings conveyed a report of the proceedings at the Conference to the Commons. He said that the Committee of the Commons proposed "An Act for planting a learned Ministry", and also expressed the desire "to proceed with the Bill against Pluralities". They had decided to defer the proposed Act touching the Articles of Religion to the next Conference.[1]

A second meeting was held on 4 June 1604.[2] The Commons again agitated for a learned ministry and for the removal of pluralities. Convocation, however, greatly resented this initiative on the part of the Commons. "The Bishop of London read a letter of writing from the Convocation inhibiting the Bishops to confer with the House of Commons."[3] The Instrument of Inhibition made it clear that Convocation utterly misliked "that the House of Commons should deal in any Matters of Religion",[4] since the King had granted to Convocation "letters patent".[5] Convocation also disliked the Conference of the Bishops with the Commons, as "it prejudged the Liberties of the Church",[6] and threatened, "that, if the Bishops would not desist, they would appeal to the King, who had given them Authority to deal only in these Matters".

Sir Francis Hastings' "Report of the Meeting and Conference of the Sub-committees of both Houses at Whytehall" aroused the House of Commons to indignant protest, and sundry proposals were made. Since the bishops were inhibited from joining with them, the Commons decided to proceed with a petition, dealing with "all Matters induced into the Church, savouring of Popery". The Instrument of Inhibition was discussed at length: some members favoured sending for it at once, so that it could be mentioned in the petition; others recommended waiting until it

---

[1] Ibid., Vol. I, p. 224.
[2] Ibid., Vol. I, p. 235.
[3] *Beaulieu MSS.*, H.M.C., p. 44.
[4] *Journals of the H. of C.*, Vol. I, p. 235.
[5] *Beaulieu MSS.*, H.M.C., p. 44.
[6] *Journals of the H. of C.*, Vol. I, p. 235.

was known "whether it was the Fault of the Convocation".[1] It was suggested that an Act of Protestation should be made against the bishops, since the Commons were also called to consult of matters for the Church and Commonwealth. The House was reminded that "Papists get too much Encouragement out of the Convocation House". The urgent matter was the relief of the suspended and deprived clergy. It was decided to draw a petition, begging "mercy for the Ministers threatened by the Bishops, and inhibited to preach, for not using fruitless Ceremonies". With an eye on the objectionable Instrument of Inhibition and the needs of the Puritan ministers, the House resolved:

1. That the great Committee shall select a Sub-committee amongst themselves, to search, view, and consider, of all such Precedents, as have warranted, or may warrant, this House to intermeddle with Matters ecclesiastical.
2. To consider of the Frame of a Petition to be exhibited to his Majesty, for Dispensation with some learned and faithful Ministers, in Matters indifferent, and of Ceremony. And if they shall not think it meet to be done by way of Petition, to report their Opinion to the House.[2]

Five days later the House of Commons passed a Bill dealing with the perennial problem of a learned and godly ministry.[3] According to the provisions of the Bill, every ordinand was to be a graduate: "none shalbe made minister of Gods holy Word and Sacrament vnles hee shall haue accomplished the age of fower and twenty yeres at the least and if hee haue been resident in one the vniversities of this Realme [and] shall haue first taken the degree of Bachilor of Arts or some higher degree . . .", and capable of preaching: he "shall bringe a Testimoniall to such Bishopp as shall make him minister . . . of his abilitie to Preach and instruct

---

[1] The Instrument of Inhibition from Convocation continued to rankle. On 21 June it was "Resolved to pray Conference touching the Instrument read by the Bishops at the late Conference, taxing the Intermeddling of this House in matters of Religion". (Ibid., Vol. I, p. 244.) On 2 July the Instrument was read at the Conference between the Commons and the Lords, and Sir Francis Hastings reported to the Commons that "the Bishop of London said, they conceived the Privilege of Parliament to stand upright; therefore wishes, there might be no more ado made of it . . .". (Ibid., Vol. I, p. 251.)

[2] Ibid., Vol. I, p. 235. 8 June 1604. *Beaulieu MSS.*, H.M.C., pp. 44–5.

[3] *S.P. Dom., Jas. I*, 14, Vol. VII, no. 66. 9 June 1604. *Journals of the H. of C.*, Vol. I, p. 236.

the people in sound and whollsome doctrine of faieth". To achieve
this laudable end, it was further provided that "if any person or
persons ... be made minister after the end of this Session of
Parliament not soe qualified, commended, and approved as
aforesaid ... then every such admission, institucion, collacion,
and induction, shalbe utterly void". The Bill was sent to the
House of Lords with an accompanying note emphasizing that it
was "especially recommended from the Lower House to the
Lords".[1] The Bill was subsequently mentioned several times in
the *Journals of the House of Lords*,[2] but it failed to reach the statute
book.

On 13 June Sir Francis Hastings gave a report on the sub-
committee's investigations into the precedents touching the
propriety of the Commons intermeddling in ecclesiastical affairs.[3]
Sir Francis, having informed the House that many precedents
and laws existed, then submitted "a Petition for Dispensation
with some Ministers in Matters indifferent", which had been
drawn up by the committee.[4] It was agreed that the Lords should
be invited to join in the same petition, which dealt with

> the pressing the Use of certain Rites and Ceremonies in this Church;
> as the Cross in Baptism, the Wearing of the Surplice in ordinary

---

[1] *Journals of the H. of L.*, Vol. II, p. 316.

[2] Ibid., Vol. II, pp. 318, 406, 408.

[3] A reply is to be found in *Cotton MSS.*, *Titus*, F.IV, f. 174. "An Answeare
to certaine arguments raised from supposed antiquitie and practise, by some
Members of the Lower House to proue ecclesiasticall lawes oughte to be
enacted by temporall men." The document begins: "What besides self
regard, or sidinge faction, hath byn the mayne reason of the lower laye howse
labour in Parliament to deale with lawes of the Church: the mylder members
haue yielded a right which they would maynteine by former president raisinge
the same from primytiue vse, wyde practise, and vninterrupted Contynuance,
professinge the same warranted by the lawes of the Roman Empre...."

[4] For an early draft of this petition, see, *Additional MSS.*, 38,492, f. 17.
"Forsomuch as ther be very many godly, able and painfull ministers and
preachers in this lande, who for and by the space of many yeares past have
forborne to vse some of the rytes and Ceremonies prescribed in the booke of
Common prayer, as by name the surplice, the Crosse in baptisme, and kneeling
at the Communion, out of scruple and tendernes of their owne Consciences,
or of the weake Consciences of their Congregations, wher the same things
have beene longe discontinewed and distasted, or sometymes out of feare to
scandalize such as professe to put holynes, religion, and necessitie in the said
Ceremonies, rather then out of any contentious humour or affectation of
opposition to the state ... [who] doe stande inhibited or suspended from their
ministry for not vsinge the same ... it might please your Majestie ... that
... none may be vrged ... to promise his conformity to the same...." 1604.

Parish Churches, and the Subscription required of the Ministers, further than is commanded by the Laws of the Realm; Things which, by long Experience, have been found to be the Occasions of such Difference, Trouble and Contention, in this Church, as thereby divers profitable and painful Ministers, not in Contempt of Authority, or Desire of Novelty, as they sincerely profess and we are verily persuaded, but, upon Conscience towards God, refusing the same, some of good Desert have been deprived, others of good Expectation withheld from entering into the Ministry . . . to the great Grief and Discomfort of many of your Majesty's most faithful and loyal subjects. . . .[1]

The petition was warmly supported. One member of the House referred to the many "ministers that haue bene here to procure some releefe for the Church at this time, aswell those of the Citie, as also those that are sent vp from sundry parts of the land", who declare that they "do discerne nothing of greater importance for the procuring and contynewance of a learned and fruitfull ministery" than the removal of ceremonies.[2] They testify (he reported) that "the continewance of them will breed extreme daunger to the Church, for many more able Ministers wilbe thereby thrust out of the Church, besides very many that wilbe discouraged from entring the Ministry then many yeares have or can breed". Other consequences will follow, particularly the spiritual impoverishment of the people. A member interjected: "in .3. parishes in Lancashire 1,400 communicants fewer this Easter than heretofore." This was no time for dilatory debate. What was required was prompt and immediate action since Parliament might be "very shortly either dissolved or adiourned, so that vnlesse this cause be first dealt in, It shalbe vtterly neglected". There were other compelling reasons for decisive measures: "it is necessarie that the Ministers ease from these burthens be provided by law, neither is it safe to rest vpon any promise, Considering what experience the house hath formerly had in this case".

Another member stressed that the time must not be "lett slipp so yt the cause of god should be slowen", and members of the House were earnestly exhorted "to be carefully present att all meetings that nothing be varied in evill sort or any good bill

---

[1] *Journals of the H. of C.*, Vol. I, p. 238.
[2] *Additional MSS.*, 38,492, f. 63.

overthrowen". "Great Wisedom and resolutenes both in the cause of freedome of subiects and also in the freedome of the gospell and the ministers thereof" was needed, and members were urged to "hazard ther whole estats then leaue ther prosterity to perpetuall thraldome". The dire consequences of failure were underlined: "if there be not obtained some act for the freedome of the ministers in ceremonies and superscription at this tyme lett them looke for nothing but miserie, for the papists will surely encrease vpon us, and the Lord our god wilbe revendged that his servaunts have no better entertaynment." It was important that every effort should be made to secure toleration for the Puritans, while taking great care "that the lawes made agaynst papists be not mitigated".[1]

On 20 June the Commons prepared an important defence of their proceedings.[2] They dealt, first of all, with fundamental matters of constitutional principle. They regretted that the King had been misinformed as to certain matters, namely, that the privileges of the House were of grace, not of right, renewed every Parliament on their petition. Their privileges were their due inheritance, no less than their lands and goods, and these privileges had now been more dangerously impugned than at any former time. There were ominous overtones of coming conflict. "The prerogatives of princes may easily, and do daily grow: the privileges of the subject are for the most part at an everlasting stand. They may be by good providence and care preserved, but being once lost are not recovered, but with much disquiet." In regard to ecclesiastical affairs, the Commons disclaimed revolutionary intent: "We have not come in any Puritan or Brownish spirit to introduce their parity, or to work the subversion of the state ecclesiastical as now it standeth." On the contrary, "their desire was only peace": to discover "now this lamentable and long-lasting dissension amongst the ministers, from which both atheism, sects, and all ill life have received such encouragement and so dangerous increase, might at length, before help come too late, be extinguished". Their earnest wish was that "such laws may be enacted, as by the relinquishment of some few ceremonies of small importance, or by any way better, a perpetual uniformity

[1] Ibid., f. 42.
[2] Printed, G. W. Prothero, op. cit., p. 286.

may be enjoyed and observed". They prayed that "the land might be furnished with a learned, religious, and godly ministry", and, for the maintenance of such a ministry, the Commons would willingly have "granted no small contributions" if they had "found that correspondency from others which was expected".

The Apology, though completed and read in the House, was never formally presented to the King. It was indicative, however, of the fact that an alliance had already been cemented between the Puritans and the House of Commons, an alliance that was to challenge and finally to destroy the whole concept of royal absolutism. By his tactless arrogance and extravagant pretensions James had succeeded in provoking an opposition far more determined than anything his predecessor had known. Further debate was precluded by the prorogation of Parliament on 7 July 1604. During the session, several Bills on ecclesiastical affairs had been read, but none became law.

At the next session of Parliament, after the initial scare associated with the Gunpowder Plot, ecclesiastical questions were again to the fore. On 15 March 1605/6 certain grievances were delivered by Mr Fuller, "touching the restoring of deprived ministers", and a conference with the bishops was suggested. Sir Francis Hastings suggested that they should proceed, as in the last Parliament, by way of petition, but that they should repudiate any desire for "Innovation" or "Presbytery". Mr Wentworth spoke movingly about the poverty of the clergy, some of whom had as many as ten children. Sir George Moore sensibly suggested the desirability of a thorough investigation to discover whether they were "justly deprived", but Sir Nathaniell Bacon replied that the facts were not in dispute: there were "260 Ministers deprived". Sir George Moore thereupon moved "that they be suffered to preach again, and that there may be no more any such Course taken by the Bishops hereafter". Mr Hoskins sententiously observed: "he hath a dull Spirit, that hath no feeling in this Cause", adding, "we ought to be Intercessors for such as are Intercessors for us to God".[1]

Members were urged to renewed endeavours by the receipt of further communications from their friends. Typical of this kind of Puritan propaganda is a document entitled, "Certain arguments, to perswade and provoke the highe court of Parliament,

[1] *Journals of the H. of C.*, Vol. I, p. 286.

nowe assembled, withall the State therein . . . to provoke and advance the syncere ministerie of the gospell, as also zealouslie to speake for the ministers . . . nowe degraded, depriued, silenced or admonished, or afterward lik to be called in question for subscription, ceremonies, strict observation of the booke of common praier, or for other conformitie. . . ."[1] The Commons agreed that they should confer with the Lords, before proceeding to petition the King. The Lords assented to a conference but required particulars; whereupon the Commons submitted the following heads:

1. Touching the deprivation, suspension, and silencing of ministers.
2. Touching the multiplicity of ecclesiastical Commissions.
3. Touching the form of citations.
4. Touching excommunications.

On 10 April the Commons appointed a committee of fifty-three persons for a Conference with the Lords. The Lords appointed a committee, consisting of the Archbishop, the Bishops of London and Ely, and certain lay peers, to consider the proposed subjects for the Conference. On 8 April they appointed a committee of forty-four of their number, including the Archbishop of Canterbury and fourteen bishops, with lawyers to attend them, in order that they might meet together with the committee of the Commons on Monday 14 April in the Painted Chamber near Parliament.

The Conference having assembled, the representatives of the Commons spoke at length on the subject matter of other various grievances.[2] Touching deprivations, they complained that

1. Peaceable ministers are often called to theire extreame trouble and chardge, though for the avoidance of both, they haue desired to be soner deprived—Instance hereof: Mr Heape who was called 14 times and at last deprived.[3]
2. The same ministers are deprived for not subscribinge contrarie to the lawe and canon made the last Convocation.

Regarding the multiplicity of ecclesiastical Commissions, they are abused and made

---

[1] *Cotton MSS., Cleopatra*, F.II, f. 281.

[2] "A Briefe of Greevances in the Ecclesiastical Iurisdiction delivered by the Lower House of Parliament at a Committie with the Ll. of the Vpper House." Transcribed, C. W. Foster, *The State of the Church*, p. 469.

[3] See above, pp. 188–91.

contemptible bycause
1. They call men for litle and trifeling causes. . . .
2. The L: Bishoppes doe sitte in theire private houses.
3. The L: Bishoppe is assisted but with a small number, and those but his shadowes, vs. his Chauncellor or Commissarie and Chaplains.

Concerning citations *ex officio* their complaint was that "they doe not specifye the cause in theire citations", and "they name not the partie at whose instance the parties cited are sent for". Fourthly, they charged that excommunication was pronounced "for little or noe cause at all". A further meeting with the committee of the Commons was arranged for the following Thursday in the Painted Chamber.

In the meantime, the bishops considered what answers should be made to the four heads.[1] Speaking in the House of Lords, Bancroft said that the bishops recommended that the articles should be handled by certain of their number:

1. The silencing of ministers, by the archbishop.
2. Concerning the multiplicity of commissions, by the Bishops of Winchester and Exeter.
3. Touching citations, by the Bishops of Bath and Wells, Carlisle, and Ely.
4. Concerning excommunication, by the Bishops of St Davids and Hereford.
With liberty reserved to the archbishop to speak upon any of the points.

This was agreed. The Lords also agreed that no decision should be taken at the Conference about joining in a petition without further reference to the Upper House in full session.

On 29 April 1606, Sir Francis Bacon gave a report to the Commons about the Conference. Bancroft, he said, had made a long speech touching the deprived ministers, describing the proceedings which had been taken against them. He rejected the

---

[1] The answer of the Bishop of Lincoln to the Brief of Grievances is entitled: "A Briefe of the manner and times of the L:B: of Lincoln his proceedinge against those ministers in his diocesse which were presented unto his Lordship for not conforminge themselves to the Ecclesiasticall orders of the Church of England in the administration of common praier of sacraments and of other rites and ceremonies of the said church by lawe established." Printed, C. W. Foster, op. cit., p. 363.

17

demand for their restoration. He quoted the precedent of the Reformed Churches, all of whom required subscription. He explained that kneeling at the Sacrament was "like All-hayle to Christ"; the cross in baptism was "like Broth at the Sacrament"; the surplice was "like a Coat with many patches" it was simply a "Coat with four Elbows". Bancroft instructed the Commons "to leave off Connivence", and urged them to "fall to execution".[1]

Five days later Yelverton gave an expanded report:

> We sayde in the name of the howse that Religion was the grounde of pollicie. ... We went to approch his Maiestie for these men, by assistance and countenance of there Lordships. But this course was verie clowdy, and therefore needed to be verie well clered lest scattering suspicion layd vpon a few might be fastened vpon all, and therefore
> 1. We protested against parity and presbiterie.
> 2. We excluded owt of this peticion all men led by heate or humor.
> 3. We cam as wayving the benefit of law, and craving mercie, for that many things lawfull were not expedient.
> 4. We said these men were not the onely and principall men, but acknowledged that the church is furnished with many other verie Lerned and sufficient men.[2]

Yelverton "protested against parity and presbiterie", but the Archbishop replied that "he could not tell what to make of it. He looked they should be Patrons of Conformitants", and yet "they spoke for Schismaticks".[3] The Archbishop irritably observed that "these men had set owt .11. bookes, and soe their humor yet continued". Yelverton countered: "The storme hath fallen and thrust owt .300."[4] Bancroft hotly denied that 300 had been deprived, and said that there were "not above .60. and against them opposed .10000. and that those .60. were factious". He insisted that "where noe Ceremonies are there is no Church".[5] Yelverton assured the Archbishop that the Commons only spoke "for som, who were onely affrayde to communicate with vs in ceremonies, for feare of syn".[6] Yelverton further reported:

---

[1] *Journals of the H. of C.*, Vol. I, p. 302.
[2] *Lambeth MSS.*, 445, p. 424. "Notes of Mr Yelverton's Report concerning the depriving of ministers."
[3] *Journals of the H. of C.*, Vol. I, p. 304. 3 May 1606.
[4] *Lambeth MSS.*, 445, p. 424.
[5] Ibid.
[6] Ibid.

Afterwards we petitioned there Lordships to ioyne with vs in this peticion to his Maiestie, because of the necessitie of there Ministerie . . . and showed fower causes to move the stay of punishment herein.

1. When the falt is not much seene, leste the Corne with the teares shold be pulled vp.
2. When the falt is of informitie and for fear of Sinne. . . . We wished the Parliament shold acknowledge the Ceremonies to be decent and indifferent, but yet that these Offences shold not be soe sharpely punished.
3. An Offence withowt contempt is not to be punished as an Offence of malice.
4. It were good in policy to permit them to escape, when the Offences can not be remedied withowt greate preiudice to many, which .300. allredie have felt, and it is much feared that many more may doe the like.[1]

At this point (Yelverton reported) Bancroft interjected, with some asperity: "His Grace marveiled that our affections shold be soe strong for these men who accompted vs Reprobates." The Conference, at this stage, "tasted not of swete brede, but of som tartenes". The discussion inevitably reached the difficult problem of subscription. Yelverton argued that the statute "13 Elizabeth Ordered that the Ministers shold subscribe only to the Articles of Faith and Sacraments", and that it excluded, by implication, subscription to the ceremonies. It follows (he said) that "noe subscription to the Boke of Common prayer is warranted by the Law, for it is owt of .13. Elizabeth". In his report to the Commons, he said:

We said that manie of these deprivacions were *coram non Judice*, .9. in Oxfordshier for not subscribing to the 36. Canon, because that Canon giveth no such subscription or punishment. This spirit of error rested not there but proceded into the Diocese of Coventry and Lichfield where (an old man who had bin a precher .46. yeres) near Oxenbridge, was also deprived for not subscribing to that Canon . . . We said . . . that all there proceedings since the last Session of Parliament are not warranted by the Law . . . his Grace hastened over the businesse, and cam to the point of Law vpon the Stat. 13. Eliz: and where we saide, *fides* was taken *pro fide Religionis*, His Grace said, Sacraments were Ceremonies and Ceremonies were Religion. his Grace confessed that for divers of the Deprived Ministers the proceedings were *Coram non Judice*, as those in Oxfordshere, and

[1] Ibid.

that there Lordships cold vrge subscription to no Ministers who are
allredy admitted. Soe therein we had the Victorie. . . . To our speech
that those men kept the people warme: his Grace said, they kept
them warme in vndiscretion; our good opinions of them made them
the worse, and yf we will lett our peticion fall this Session, they will
all subscribe . . . his Grace also said, that the punishment of those
men, even for a Ceremonie, is proportionable, and that there is no
Religion, where there are no Ceremonies, the hands and the knees
must be affected besides the harte. His Grace wisshed we wold
affect vniformitie. And his Graces conclusion was, that for those
men there is no hope of mercy, withowt hope of their Conformitie.[1]

A detailed report of the conference was forwarded by Salisbury
to the King. He was exceedingly pleased by the outcome. Sir
Thomas Lake wrote to Salisbury that "his Majesty seems to hope
by the success of that day's work that all the controversies about
these Church causes will either die, or be weakly pursued . . ."[2]

The House of Commons continued its zealous endeavours on
behalf of those Puritans threatened with ecclesiastical censures.
Several Bills were promoted for the more due execution of ecclesiastical government,[3] and for the restraint of ecclesiastical canons
not confirmed by Parliament. The latter Bill was read twice in
the House of Lords, when it appears to have been dropped.[4] "An
Act touching the Restraint of Excommunication in Ecclesiastical
Courts" was read twice in the House of Lords on 19 May and
again on 22 May,[5] but was rejected on the same day by the House
of Commons "with much Distaste".[6] The session closed without
any ecclesiastical Bill having been made law.

Parliamentary activity was renewed on 9 March 1606/7,
when a Bill against non-residence and pluralities of benefices
was read three times in the Commons and passed. This Bill was
sent up with others to the Lords by the hand of Sir Francis
Hastings, who returned and related to the Commons that he had
presented five Bills, and had "especially commended the first

---

[1] *Lambeth MSS.*, 445, p. 424. Cf. *Journals of the H. of C.*, Vol. I, p. 304.
[2] *Cecil MSS.*, 116, f. 24. 6 May 1606.
[3] *Journals of the H. of C.*, Vol. I, p. 274. 25 February 1605/6. Ibid., Vol. I,
p. 290. 26 March 1606.
[4] *Journals of the H. of L.*, Vol. II, pp. 425, 429. 6 May 1606. H.M.C. Appendix
to the Fourth Report, p. 118.
[5] *Journals of the H. of L.*, Vol. II, pp. 436, 438.
[6] *Journals of the H. of C.*, Vol. I, p. 311.

Two, touching Canons and pluralities, to their Favour and Passage; urging, the Abuse sought to be redressed by those Bills, was a great Scandal to the Church, and the greatest hindrance to the instruction of God's people".[1] Although several Bills were read in the Lords, none became law. A petition against recusancy and non-residence was stopped by order of the King.[2]

The Commons were nothing daunted by these recurrent rebuffs, and on 18 June 1607 they presented another petition to the King for the more rigid enforcement of the laws against Jesuits and priests; praying that the "Judges both civill and ecclesiasticall maie be quickened and stirred vp to a more full and due execution of theire authorities ...; and that diligent and frequent serch and care [may] be enioyned for the findings and apprehendinge of them". Their desire was that unqualified men be excluded from the ministry, and that negligent clergymen be disciplined:

> That therefore the Bishoppes maie be by your Highnes commanded to vse all good meanes in theire power aswell for the easinge of the Church of ignorant Curates and Ministers alreadie crept in, as also to keepe the Doores of the Church better closed (a thinge absolutelie in theire power) against the entrie of the like hereafter. And that the like course to be taken touchinge Ministers scandalous and offensive in liffe.

They had made repeated but unsuccessful attempts to secure the passage of Bills for the prevention of non-residency, an evil condemned by Convocation in the reign of Queen Elizabeth as "foedum in se, odiosum in vulgus, et perniciousum ecclesiae Dei". Their desire was that men might not be preferred who "haue lived in that pernicious course ... as holdinge them vnworthie to be made rulers ouer much, who haue beene found vnfaithfull in a littell". Their immediate concern, however, was the relief of the deprived clergy: "Wee are inforced once againe to be most humble petitioners vnto your most excellent Maiestie touching the late deprived, suspended, and silenced Ministers, that they maie be restored to the vse of theire Ministerie." They interceded on behalf of "tender consciences": "Wee sue for none but such

---

[1] Ibid., Vol. I, p. 350.
[2] Ibid., Vol. I, p. 384. 16 June 1607.

of them as are readie to cleare vppon theire oathes that their
refusall of these Ceremonies proceedeth onlie from Conscience,
and feare to offend god, and not from anie contradictions of
malignent humor." The faithful service of these men deserved
consideration: "theire greate painfulnes in theire callinges, and
theire contentment with small mainetanunce amonge other
virtues not Common, worke in vs great commisseration, especially
on the Churches behalf."[1] According to a note in the *Journals of
the House of Commons*:

> In the Dispute touching the Petition, it was, by occasion, delivered,
> that in England there were, 8000 Parish Churches.
> Not 2000 resident Preaching Ministers.
> Not 1000 that preach once a Month.
> Not 500 single beneficed.
> 300 deprived, suspended, or silenced.
> 400 Jesuits and Seminaries in England.
> 40 single people converted in a Year by One Jesuit.
> 300 convicted Recusants in a Shire, at the Queen's death, now 800.[2]

James personally prepared a draft answer to this petition. He
was greatly incensed by their unwearying pertinacity:

> Since I persaue by this youre petition, that my last speache unto
> you anent matters of religion hath so littil openid youre under-
> standing as not only ye nou moue me againe in those uerie pointes
> quhiche I directlie discharged you to meddle with at that tyme for
> the waithtie reasons then alleadgit by me, but ye are euen comed to
> that heicht of forgetfulnes as in the uerry first wordis of youre petition
> to alleadge my comande for youre warrande to entir into consultation
> upon causes of that nature, quhairas by the plaine contrarie I not
> only directlie dischairged you to medle any further in these pointis,
> and did especiallie name unto you suche pointis as I uolde haue
> hadd you to consulte upon, but also ordained that youre consulta-
> tion upon these pointis that I named unto you shoulde not be into
> your house, but by a priuat conference of some few of youre nomber
> ioined with some few of the upper house, theirfore in consideration
> heirof and that my former trauellis and reasonis haue so littil
> praeuailed with you I can nou giue no other ansoure to youre
> petition then by repeating shortly those reasons that I formerlie
> alleadgit unto you.

---

[1] *Cotton MSS., Titus,* F.IV, f. 167.
[2] *Journals of the H. of C.,* Vol. I, pp. 384–5.

A setlid ordoure in a setlid churche must aither be uniformlie
obeyed uithout any exception, or ellis the dispensing thairwith to
certaine particulaire personis can not but surelie promeise a confusion to the quhole state of the churche, for aither are these ceremonies indifferent, or ellis against Scripture and not indifferent
if they be not indifferent then are all the memberis of the conformable
Church of englande that practise thaime haeretikes, and I ame the
archihaeretike that maintaine thaime, and quhen euer any man
alyue is able by uorde or uritte to proue those caeremonies to be
contraire to the worde of god, then shall I be content for my pairt to
make a publique recantation, but if thay be indifferent as surelie
they are, then can it not be denyed that these painfull. . . . Ministeris
by disobedience to the Kings authoritie and ordinances of a setlid
churche in indifferent things do proue thaimselfis to be nothing ellis
indeid but seditiouse schismatikes, and thairfore my counsall is
hearafter ye medle only in suche things are ar within the reache of
your capacity *noli altum sapere*.[1]

Parliament was in session during 1610 from February to July.
The Puritans used the opportunity to promote a number of Bills,
but they failed to reach the statute book. There was evident a
more resolute determination on the part of the Commons to
legislate in ecclesiastical affairs, which was matched by an equal
determination on the part of the King to oppose such parliamentary interference.

In this session, a Bill for the restraint of canons not confirmed
by Parliament, was read in the House of Commons three times,[2]
and was then sent up to the Lords, by whom it was read and
committed.[3] On 24 April the Commons discussed the preparation
of another address to the King for the redress of ecclesiastical
grievances. There was much discussion over the form of the
address. Sir Dudley Diggs said that they should have the names
of those ministers they desired to have relieved, and set them down
by way of petition and not of grievance. Sir Francis Hastings
agreed. Sir Richard Spencer, however, was entirely opposed to
either procedure: he saw "no Reason, but, without Offence to
God, or to their own Consciences, they may subscribe". There
was much debate whether they should seek relief for the ministers,

[1] *Cotton MSS., Titus*, F.IV, f. 169.
[2] *Journals of the H. of C.*, Vol. I, p. 417. 31 March 1610. Ibid., Vol. I, p.
421. 26 April 1610. Ibid., Vol. I, p. 422. 28 April 1610.
[3] *Journals of the H. of L.*, Vol. II, p. 584. 30 April 1610.

or their restoration. It was finally agreed that they should proceed by way of petition.[1]

The Commons prayed, first of all, that the King's "naturall Clemencie" might retire itself, and give place to justice, so that there might be a more strict enforcement of the laws against popish recusants. They urged the King, through his ecclesiastical and civil judges, to enforce more stringently and consistently "the lawes made against Jesuites, Seminarie pristes, theire Recevors, and mayntainers and abettors, and all other popish Recusantes, of what kinde, degree, and sex so ever". Secondly, they desired the restoration of:

> divers paynfull and learned preachers, that haue long travailed in the worke of the Ministerie with good frute and blessinge of theire laboures (who weare ever readye to perform the legall subscription appoynted by the Statute xiij Eliz. which onlye concerneth the confession of the true christian faythe and doctrine of the Sacraments), yet for not conforminge in some poynts of Cerimonies, and refusinge the subscription directed by the late Cannons, haue bine remoued from theire ecclesiasticall livings, (beinge their free-hold) and debarred of all meanes of maintenance, to the great greif of sundry your Maiesties well affected Subiects.

Their modest request was

> that such deprived and silenced Ministers, may, by licence or permission of the Reverend Fathers the Bishopes in their seuerall dioceses, instruct and preach vnto the people in suche parishes and places where they maye be imployed, so long as they applye themselves to theire Ministerie, to wholsome doctrine and exhortation, and live quietlie and peaceablie in theire callinges, and shall not by wrightinge or prechinge impugne thinges established by publicke authoritie.

They renewed their protests about pluralism and non-residency.

> Those that haue plurallities of such livings and non residencie, doe frame excuse of the smalenes of some livings and pretend the maintenance of learninge: yet we finde by experience that they couplinge manie of greatest livings doe for the most parte leaue the least meanlye furnished and the best as ill served, and supplyed with preachers as the meanest: And where such men heapinge many benefices into one hand doe by that meanes keepe divers learned

---

[1] *Journals of the H. of C.*, Vol. I, p. 420. 24 April 1610.

men from maintenance to the discoragement of Students, and hindrance of learninge. And the non residents (neglectinge theire pastorall charges) doe leaue the people in apparante daunger to be seduced.

They desired, if not the abolition, at least the restraint of these evils.

yt might therefore please your most excellent Maiestie for remedie of those evills in the Church, to provide that dispensacions of pluralitie of benefices with cure of soules may be prohibited, and that tolleracion of non Residencie maye be restrayned, so shall true Religion bee better vphelde and the people more instructed in devine and Civill duties.

Finally, they petitioned for some "due and fitt reformation" in the use of excommunication

which is often times exercised and inflicted vppon the Common people by sundrie subordinate officers of the iurisdiction ecclesiasticall for verie small causes in which case the parties before they can be discharged are driven to greate expence for matter of verie smalle moment to the great scandale of the Church government in the abuse of so highe a censure, the contempt of the censure it selfe, and vnspeakable greevaunce of our Maiesties poore subiects.[1]

In the meantime, on 24 June 1610, a Bill was introduced limiting subscription to the articles of religion and faith only (in terms of the Statute 13 Elizabeth, c. 12). "Advowsons and patronage of Churches are lay inheritance and freehoulde" (so the argument ran), and no fruit can "be had or enioyed otherwise then by admission and institucion of Clarkes presented to benefices". In these circumstances, it is unreasonable that the freedom of presentation should be "clogged and interrupted by Condicions, scripcions, and other points of Obligacion, added and required as necessary thereunto". Parliament, in the reign of Elizabeth, passed a Statute requiring subscription "to the Articles and Religion which onely Concerned confession of the true Christian faith and the doctrine of the Sacraments": conse-

---

[1] *S.P. Dom., Jas. I*, 14, Vol. LIII, no. 123. 24 April 1610. *Cotton MSS., Titus*, F.IV, f. 134 ff; *S.P. Dom., Jas. I*, 14, Vol. XX, no. 57. Wrongly dated "April? 1606". The Heads of the Grievances are given: *Additional MSS.*, 15,750, f. 11; *Journals of the H. of C.*, Vol. I, pp. 420–1; Printed, G. W. Prothero, op. cit., p. 300.

quently, the proposed Bill provided that "noe person or persons
... shall ... be required or enioyned to subscribe otherwise then
according to the forme and manner appointed in the said Act".
An additional clause provided that "all and euery Cannon,
Ordinance, and institution aswell heretofore made as hereafter to
be made to the Contrary, or different from the said Act, and the
Manner and Order herein lymitted and appointed, shalbe from
henceforth vtterlie voyde and of none effect".[1] After its preliminary passage through the Commons, the Bill proceeded no
further.

The Commons presented their grievances to the King on 7 July,
and three days later they attended in a body to Whitehall to
hear his Majesty's determination so far as he was then able to
answer them. His interim reply was

1. That they meddle not with the main points of government;
that is his craft "*tractent fabrilia fabri*".

2. He would not have such ancient rights, as he had received
from his predecessors, accounted grievances.

3. That they should be careful not to present that for a grievance,
which was established by a law; for it is very undutiful in subjects
to press their king wherein they are sure to be denied. Complaints
may be made unto them of the high commissioners; let the abuse
appear and then spare not; there may be errors among them: but to
take away the commission is to derogate from him: and it is now in
his thoughts to rectify it in a good proportion.[2]

The King gave his final answer, in the presence of both Houses, on
23 July. Regarding the execution of the laws against popish
recusants, he stated that he had made his mind upon this subject
sufficiently clear by his own writings, and by his proclamation
and speeches concerning this point. There was no need for him to
make a further pronouncement. Concerning the enforcement of
subscription and the deprivation of the nonconforming clergy,
he stated:

There hath never bene hitherto any particuler Church in the world
for ought that wee haue read or heard that hath allowed such
ministers to preach in ytt, as haue refused to subscribe to the doctrine

---

[1] *S.P. Dom., Jas. I*, 14, Vol. IV, no. 45. 24 June 1610. Cf. *Cotton MSS., Cleopatra*, F.II, f. 198; *Harleian MSS.*, 6,849, f. 274.

[2] *S.P. Dom., Jas. I*, 14, Vol. LIII, no. 124. *Lambeth MSS.*, no. 251, f. 177 b. 10 July 1610.

and discipline settled in ytt, and maynteyned by itt, and hereof the Reformed Churches in France doe yeild a freshe example, who haue and doe daylye require subscripcion to the Articles of the Synodes, thoughe very many in number. Neverthelesse, as in our owne Princelye iudgement, wee ever intended to make some distinction betweene the persons and disposicions of the deprived and Silenced Ministers, in regarde of better hope of Conformitye in some then in others, although they be in the same degree offenders by our Lawes, So wee shall be pleased when wee shall know the number, the names and the qualletyes of those, for whom this Peticion is made, to take such order in that behalfe, as in our princely wisedome wee shall hold most fitt and convenyent for the good and peace of the Church.

Concerning pluralities and non-residency, he had ever had a great detestation of "the Covetous and ymmoderatte heaping of many Benefices togither especially when the neglecte of the Cures is ioyned therewith", yet he felt that it was not convenient to make any change

vntill some further provision be made that the Benefices of this Realme might be made Competent Livings for godlye Ministers and Learned Preachers, and that with some difference in proporcion answerable to the guiftes and meritts.

Nevertheless he willingly agreed to

lay a streight Charge vpon the Bishoppes vnder the paine of our displeasure that such Ministers as either now haue, or hereafter shall haue, two Benefices with Cure, shall Carefully observe the 41 and 47 Constitutions Confirmed by vs Anno 1603—Whereby it is provided, that every such person, as hath two Benefices shall (when he doth not reside) mainteyne a Preacher Lawfully allowed, that is able sufficientlye to teache and instructe the people in his absence.[1]

If the bishops failed in their duty in this respect, they would experience his displeasure: "wee shall make it appeare, how much wee dislike such neglecte, and how much wee tender a Reformacion in such Cases." Concerning the abuse of excommunication, he promised amendment:

We are pleased to assure them by our Royall promise, that our Ecclesiasticall Commissions shall not be directed to singular persons,

[1] For Bancroft's letter touching these matters, see Bancroft's Register, f. 172 b. Printed, E. Cardwell, *Documentary Annals*, Vol. II, p. 120.

but to such a number of Commissioners, and them so selected as the weight of such Causes doth require, And that no definitive sentence be given or pronounced by such our Commissioners vnder the number of Seaven of them sittinge in Courte.

He would not "graunt forthe any forme of Commission extending further then to ymprisonment and reasonable fine", and he would establish such an order touching the Commission that no subjects "shalbe drawne from remote places to London or Yorke".[1] Parliament was prorogued and subsequently dissolved.

---

[1] *Journals of the H. of L.*, Vol. II, p. 658. *S.P. Dom., Jas. I*, 14, Vol. LVI, no. 39. 23 July 1610. *Cotton MSS., Titus*, F.IV, f. 150 ff. The last section of the Reply, dealing with the Commission for Ecclesiastical Causes, is given in *Lambeth MSS.*, no. 251, f. 171 b, dated 7 May 1610.

9

THE COURT OF HIGH COMMISSION

THE COURT of High Commission, in the eyes of the judges of the common law, was an upstart creation, threatening, by its reliance on the incriminating oath *ex officio*, established and accepted methods of legal procedure. The ecclesiastical authorities, however, relied heavily on the Court of High Commission for their disciplinary activity: they found it an effective and ready instrument for the discovery of evidence and the infliction of punishment.

The judges of the common law, for reasons both of prudence and of policy, were determined to curb its powers. A weapon lay ready to hand. It was sufficient to claim that the matter before the Court of High Commission concerned temporalities, and, by the issue of a writ of prohibition, to bring about a stay in proceedings.

The Puritans were quick to take advantage of this situation. They continually impeded the coercive activities of the bishops by securing the issue of prohibitions. The fundamental question became the status and authority of the Court of High Commission.

The common lawyers contended that the Court of High Commission was created by the Statute 1 Elizabeth c. 1, para. 18,[1] and that it permitted the temporary delegation to Commissioners of a limited part of the ecclesiastical authority vested in the Crown as Supreme Governor. The Act of Supremacy (1559) had given the Queen power to nominate Commissioners who should exercise supreme ecclesiastical jurisdiction under the Crown, with power to correct and amend all errors, abuses, and offences, "which by any manner of spiritual or ecclesiastical power . . . may lawfully be reformed, ordered, redressed, corrected, restrained, or amended". In the accomplishment of this task the Commis-

---

[1] The Statute 1 Eliz. c. 1, is quoted in full in *The Report of the Commissioners appointed to inquire into the Constitution and Working of the Ecclesiastical Courts*, 1883, *Historical Appendix* (XII), p. 224; H. Gee, *The Elizabethan Clergy and the Settlement of Religion*, 1558–64, Oxford, 1898, p. 9.

sioners might proceed with or without the aid of a jury, or by any other means that might appear expedient. They might compel attendance on mere suspicion, examine anyone—whether accused or witness—on oath, and punish offenders or contumacious persons by fine or imprisonment.

The ecclesiastical lawyers, on the other hand, argued that the Statute of 1 Elizabeth merely confirmed an authority already exercised by the High Commissioners since 1535. In that year a Commission had been issued to Cromwell, as Vice-Regent, investing him with the plenitude of royal authority in ecclesiastical affairs, and directing him to delegate part of it from time to time to such persons as he thought fit for the suppression of heresy.[1] In 1549 Edward VI had issued Letters Patent authorizing a general Commission. The substance and form of the Letters Patent had assumed final shape in the general Commission issued by Mary in 1557.[2] By this the Commissioners were charged to inquire into all types of ecclesiastical and religious offences, using the oath *ex officio* "to examine and compel to answer, and swear, upon the holy evangelists, to declare the truth in all such things whereof they or any of them shall be examined". It was significantly added that they were to proceed, "any of our laws, statutes, proclamations, or other grants, privileges, or ordinances, which be, or may seem to be, contrary to the premises, notwithstanding".[3] The Letters Patent issued by Elizabeth in 1559[4] were similar to those issued in 1557.

The conflict, in the first place, revolved around the question of origin: the common lawyers asserted that the High Commission was created by Statute: the ecclesiastical lawyers denied this assertion and declared that it was created by the royal prerogative, and that its continuous and legal existence dated back to the the days of Thomas Cromwell. Nevertheless, despite these divergent interpretations of origin, both parties to the controversy assumed the legal existence of the Court of High Commission, and conceded its possession of a jurisdiction and a regular procedure. Furthermore, it is clear from contemporary writers that

[1] R. G. Usher, *The Rise and Fall of the High Commission*, Oxford, 1913, p. 15.
[2] Ibid., p. 23.
[3] Quoted, ibid., pp. 24–5.
[4] For the text of the writ for the issue of the Commission, 19 July 1559, see H. Gee, op. cit., pp. 147 ff.

the Commission itself was regarded as a regular institution, rather than as a temporary delegation of authority to a few men.[1]

The first Commissions issued by Elizabeth were mainly concerned with visitation and inquiry. The Commissioners were given untrammelled authority and absolute discretion. With their broad indefinite powers, and their freedom of discretionary procedure, they were very useful to the Queen and the Privy Council.[2] But by about 1580 the Ecclesiastical Commissioners for the Province of Canterbury became transformed into the judges of a permanent ecclesiastical Court, who heard cases between party and party, and tried them by a regular procedure.[3] This transformation was facilitated and encouraged by the delegation to the Commission of the routine ecclesiastical work which the Privy Council had previously performed itself. As a result the Commissioners began to receive the petitions that had previously been directed to the Council. The efficiency and finality of the Court fostered its rapid evolution to the position of the most important tribunal for the trial of ecclesiastical offences.

The jurisdiction of the Court of High Commission was very extensive, for the Letters Patent stated

> we do give and grant full power and authority unto you and six of you ... from time to time and at all times during our pleasure, to visit, reform, redress, order, correct, and amend, in all places within this our realm of England all such errors, heresies, crimes, abuses, offences, contempts, and enormities spiritual and ecclesiastical whatsoever which by any spiritual or ecclesiastical power, authority, or jurisdiction, can or may lawfully be reformed, ordered, redressed, corrected, restrained or amended. . . .[4]

[1] Gee argues that the Court of High Commission, in contrast to the series of temporary commissioners appointed in 1558-9, was intended by Cecil to be a *permanent* body. He quotes the Letters Patent and says: "It is clear from the terms of the commission that it was intended to be more permanent. Thus the commissioners are to serve 'from time to time, and at all times during our pleasure'; and mention is made not only of offences actually committed, but of such as 'hereafter' shall arise." Op. cit., pp. 138-9.

[2] R. G. Usher, op. cit., p. 46.

[3] It was partly this rapid transformation in the functions of the High Commission, and partly the use of the High Commission for the enforcement of ecclesiastical discipline, that prompted Martin Marprelate to protest: "It was ordained for very good purposes, but it is most horribly abused by you, and turned clean contrary to the end wherefore it was ordained" (*Marprelate Tracts*).

[4] Letters Patent, 1559, quoted, G. W. Prothero, *Select Statutes*, p. 227. H. Gee, op. cit., pp. 148-9.

This covered practically every type of offence which an ecclesiastical authority could try. Besides this, the High Commission had original jurisdiction (in the strict legal sense); anyone could begin any suit in its Court which its jurisdiction permitted. The fact that the decision was final made suitors prefer this Court. The High Commission Court did not supersede any of the existing courts, but its jurisdiction tended to become concurrent with the jurisdiction of the lower ecclesiastical courts. In the eyes of the common lawyers, the Court appeared as a rival and "foreign" jurisdiction. They resented the large number of suitors who frequented it, and they were apprehensive about the Court's extending influence.

The only recognized means of formal communication between the common-law courts and the Commission were the writs of prohibition and consultation. The writ of prohibition, issued by the common-law judge, prohibited the ecclesiastical judge from continuing the trial, on the ground that it concerned temporal matters. The writ stopped proceedings in either court pending a decision as to the proper jurisdiction, which decision was awarded by the common-law judge. If the common-law judge concluded that the case contained nothing temporal, he issued a second writ or consultation annulling his prohibition and allowing the case to continue at ecclesiastical law. On the other hand, if he decided that the case did concern temporality, he allowed the prohibition to stand, which put an end to the case at ecclesiastical law.[1]

During the last decades of Whitgift's primacy, the Ecclesiastical Commissioners found that their activities were continually obstructed by prohibitions from the temporal courts.[2] The bishops made an attempt to circumvent the impasse by preparing a series of queries for the Lords and Judges concerning prohibitions, under the heading of "Certaine Pointes which the Reverend ffathers, the Bishops and others executinge Ecclesiasticall Jurisdiction . . . do desier the Lords and others the Reverend Judges of the Realme to consider, towching, the grauntinge of Prohibitions".[3] Despite

---

[1] R. G. Usher, op. cit., p. 159.
[2] J. Strype, *Whitgift*, Vol. II, p. 397.
[3] *Rawlinson MSS.*, B.202, f. 110 b. 1598; *Cotton MSS.*, *Cleopatra*, F.1, f. 112; *Harleian MSS.*, 358, f. 186.

this attempted clarification, prohibitions tended to increase in number more and more.

Despite the inconveniences inseparable from proceedings in the Court of High Commission, Whitgift was compelled to rely on it for the execution of his administrative policy. The High Commission, he said, is "the only means we have to punish and restrain sectaries and Contentious persons which refuse to observe laws and to keep order"; and "the whole ecclesiastical law is a carcasse without a soul; yf it be not in the wantes supplied by the Commission".[1] The Puritans were particularly incensed about the use of the oath *ex officio*: "This oath is to inquire of our private speeches and conference with our dearest and nearest friends, yea, of the very secret thoughts and intents of our hearts, that so we may furnish both matter of accusation and evidence of proof against ourselves."[2] It is not surprising, in these circumstances, that the Puritans made common cause with the common lawyers against the swelling powers of the Court of High Commission.

Bancroft inherited a situation of peculiar difficulty. He was compelled to rely, like his predecessor, on the Commissioners for the enforcement of his administrative reforms. The Puritans were bitter in protest and opposition.[3] Typical is a document entitled: "A briefe treatise of oathes exacted by Ordinaries and Ecclesiasticall Judges, to aunswere generallie to all such Articles or Interrogatories, as pleaseth them to propound, And of their forced and Constrayned oathes *ex officio*, Wherein is prooved that the same are vnlawfull."[4] The oath *ex officio* was sacrilegious, tyrannical, and popish:

It doth manifestlie appeare . . . that . . . the taking of these generall oathes is a prophane abusing of the holie name of God, that the exacting of oathes *ex officio* is . . . a wrong and injurie to the freedome and libertie of the subjects thereof, that the same . . . is brought in onlie by the practise of the popish Clergie to the prejudice of the publique peace and tranquilitie of this Realme, and that the same never had any good allowaunce by any law, custom, Ordinance, or Statute of this Kingdom.

[1] J. Strype, op. cit., Vol. I, p. 267.
[2] J. Strype, *Annals*, Vol. IV, app. LX.
[3] *Lambeth MSS.*, 445, f. 430.
[4] *Lambeth MSS.*, 445, ff. 452–505; *Cotton MSS.*, *Cleopatra*, F.1, ff. 50–67; *Rawlinson MSS.*, B.202, ff. 43–81.

18

The same sentiments were echoed in another pamphlet:

> The oath *ex officio*, whereby Popish and English Ecclesiastical
> Governors . . . go about to bind mens consciences to accuse them-
> selves and their friends of such crimes or imputations, as cannot by
> any direct court of law be proved against them . . . such an oath
> (on the urgers part) is most damnable and tyrannous, against the
> very Law of Nature, devised by Antichrist, through the inspiration
> of the devil, that by means thereof, the professors and practisers of
> the true Religion, might . . . in their weakness, by perjurie, damn
> their own souls. . . .[1]

In his harassed perplexity Bancroft sought the judgement of
the judges and privy councillors of the Star Chamber, particularly
concerning the power of deprivation. They testified to the legality
of the Commission's jurisdiction. The King, they said, possesses
"the Supream Ecclesiasticall Power which he hath delegated to
the Commissioners whereby they had the power of Deprivation
by the Canon Law of the Realm". "The King without Parliament might make Orders and Constitutions for the government
of the Clergy."[2] Bancroft subsequently informed the bishops
(22 December 1604) that "the Lord Chief Justice, and Mr
Attorney generall beinge conferred with, are verie resolute, that
you may lawfully, by virtue thereof so proceede against such
obstinate persons".[3] On 18 February 1604/5 the King, in a letter
to the Archbishop of York, said that some of the Puritans had
"given out that the Ecclesiasticall proceedings against them weare
not warrantable by Law, and the Bishops subiect to danger for
their doings". He related that certain nonconforming clergy in
the diocese of Exeter who had been deprived, had come to the
judges "then sitting and demanded a Prohibition". It was a
test case. The outcome, however, had been reassuring and
heartening:

> The whole Judges of our Realme . . . with one consent haue . . .
> delivered their judgments, that noe prohibition doth lye in that
> case against the Judges Ecclesiasticall, That the Bishops proceedinge
> to deprivation for not conforminge to the booke of Comon prayer

---

[1] W. Bradshaw, *English Puritanisme Containening the manie opinions of the rigidest
sort of those that are called Puritanes in the Realme of England*, 1605.
[2] Quoted, R. G. Usher, op. cit., p. 167.
[3] Bancroft's Register, f. 127 b.

and ceremonyes of the church is warranted by Law, and they nether will nor are to releve any man seekinge to them in such casse, but suffer the Ecclesiastical authority to haue his full execution.[1]

Despite this judgement, the common-law judges continued to issue prohibitions. Bancroft appealed to the Privy Council. In October 1605 he submitted "Certain Articles of Abuses, which are desired to be reformed in granting of prohibitions . . . in the name of the whole clergy".[2] Bancroft argued that since the King united in himself both the ecclesiastical and temporal jurisdictions, prohibitions, being issued by the temporal courts to the ecclesiastical courts, were an offence and derogation to the King's ecclesiastical prerogative.[3] Bancroft pointed out that prohibitions were being issued "in all causes almost of Ecclesiasticall cognizance". The clergy, consequently, had "iust cause to complaine"; they earnestly craved the "restraint of this over lavish granting of prohibitions in every cause without respect".[4] Bancroft properly objected to "the multiplying of Prohibitions in divers causes, but of the same nature, after consultations formerly awarded". "The Temporall Judges", he said, "doe wittingly and willingly grant prohibitions, whereupon they know, beforehand, that consultations are due."[5] Furthermore, in connection with consultations, the temporal judges had issued new forms of consultations, in which the cause was not expressed. This was a breach of precedent:

> Upon the granting of Consultations, the Judges in times past did therin expresse and acknowledge the causes so remitted to be of

---

[1] *S.P. Dom., Jas. I*, 14, Vol. XII, no. 87. In April 1605 Sir Edward Coke wrote to Viscount Cranborne concerning the need for a clear exposition of the ecclesiastical statutes so that discipline might be executed on Papists and Puritans alike: "the papists . . . and the Sectarie . . . thinking the proceedings Ecclesiasticall to be popish and unlawfull. . . . It seemeth to me very necessarie that some thing were published manifesting (without any interference or bombasting) the very words of the Auncient Laws and statutes of England . . . whereby it shall appeare, what Jurisdiction Ecclesiasticall by the auncient Laws of England, appertaine to the Crown. . . . And thereby both parties, being Englishmen, may the sooner be perswaded to yeilde their obedience." *S.P. Dom., Jas. I*, 14, Vol. XIII, nos. 61, 62.

[2] *Cotton MSS., Cleopatra*, F.11, f. 319 ff. 1605; *Rawlinson MSS.*, B. 202, f.112; *Harleian MSS.*, 1299, f. 95 b; 4,282, f. 4 b. Quoted, E. Cardwell, *Documentary Annals*, Vol. II, pp. 82 ff; Sir E. Coke, *The Second Part of the Institutes of the Laws of England*, 1642, pp. 601 ff.

[3] Articles 1 and 2.   [4] Article 4.   [5] Article 6.

Ecclesiastical cognizance ... the said Temporall Judges have now altered that course, and doe onely tell us that they grant their consultations *certis de causis ipos apud Westm.* moventibus, not expressing the same particularly, according to their ancient presidents. By meanes whereof the Temporall Judges leave themselves at liberty, without prejudice, though they deny a consultation.[1]

Bancroft complained that prohibitions were being granted "upon trifling and frivolous suggestions"—"a prejudice and derision to both his Majesties Ecclesiasticall and Temporall iurisdictions".[2] The clergy pleaded that prohibitions should not be granted, except "upon due consideration of the libell". "It is a great abuse", Bancroft protested, "and one of the chiefe grounds of the most of the former abuses, and many other, that prohibitions are granted without a sight of the libell in the Ecclesiasticall Court."[3] There were further grounds for concern: "there is a new devised suggestion in the Temporall Courts ... whereby they may at their will and pleasure draw any cause whatsoever from the Ecclesiasticall Court ... under pretence, that one witnesse cannot be received in the Ecclesiasticall Court, to ground a judgment upon."[4] The common-law judges were, in effect, withdrawing from the ecclesiastical jurisdiction all cases except those of a testamentary and matrimonial nature, on the ground that these alone were matters of ecclesiastical cognizance.[5] To restrain this indiscriminate granting of prohibitions, the ecclesiastical lawyers made request that no prohibitions be granted "upon surmise onely ... either out of the Kings Bench, or Common pleas, but out of the Chancery onely". The position was scandalous and intolerable: "the Ecclesiasticall iurisdiction is oppressed with a multitude of prohibitions upon surmises onely ... through incroachment ... there are so many

---

[1] Article 7.   [2] Article 9.   [3] Article 11.
[4] Article 12.

[5] Article 13. See *Rawlinson MSS.*, B.202, f. 1. "A colleccion shewing what jurisdiccion the clergy hath heretofore lawfully vsed and may lawfully vse in the Realme of England. Wherein it is manifestly prooued that the Prelates or ecclesiasticall Judges neuer had any authority to compell any subiect of the land to an oath, vnles it were in Causes testamentary or matrimoniall or thereto apperteyning, with a Confutacion of such frivolous and vnlearned surmises as have been made for the maintenance of the Clergies vnlawfull proceedings in these dayes to the contrary, Whereby they haue sundry wayes incurred the penaltyes of the Statutes of Provision and Premunire." (There are forty-two closely written large folio pages expanding this thesis.)

several Courts, and Judges in them . . . the one Court oftentimes crossing the proceedinges of the other."[1]

The ecclesiastical judges were insistent that tithes were within their exclusive jurisdiction, and therefore "ought not to be drawne thence by Prohibitions";[2] neither should a prohibition be granted "because the treble value of tithes is used for in the Ecclesiasticall Court".[3] Statute 2 Edward VI, c. 13, explicitly gave the Commissioners the right to hear and determine all suits of tithes, and also to impose a penalty of treble value.[4]

When a case was being tried in an ecclesiastical court, Bancroft concluded, a prohibition should not be granted upon "any incident plea", for "otherwise either party in every cause might at his pleasure, by pleading some matter Temporall by way of exception, make any cause Ecclesiasticall whatsoever subiect to a prohibition".

Bancroft pointed out the scandal created by and inseparable from the present conflict: "the Kings authority in Ecclesiasticall causes is greatly impugned by Prohibitions."[5] It was the earnest desire of the ecclesiastical lawyers that no prohibition should be "granted, under pretence to reforme the manner of proceedings by the Ecclesiasticall Lawes, in causes confessed to be of Ecclesiasticall cognizance". Originally, a prohibition was

> to restraine the Judges Ecclesiasticall from dealing in a matter of Temporall cognizance, now prohibitions are awarded upon these surmises, viz: That the Libell, the Articles, the Sentence, and the Ecclesiasticall Court, according to the Ecclesiasticall lawes, are grievous and insufficient, though the matter there dealt withall be meerly Ecclesiasticall.

[1] For detailed arguments on this point see *Rawlinson MSS.*, B.157, f. 18 b, C.731, f. 48: "A breviate of the selected proofes touching prohibitions out of the Common Place, Noe record being before them. The question is, Whether the Courte of Common Pleas maye graunt prohibitions vpon surmises only, where there ys noe plea before them depending." Article 14.

[2] Article 16.   [3] Article 17.

[4] Article 19. For detailed arguments see *Rawlinson MSS.*, B.157, f. 12; B.202 f. 161; C.731, f. 56: "A breuiat of the selected proofes touching the recouerye of the treble value in the Spirituall Courte. The question is, whether yf Tythes in Kinde be not deuided and set forth, an Action maye be brought in any of the Kings Courts in Westminster by the partye greiued for treble damages grounded upon the statutes of 2 Ed. 6 cap. 13." See also *Tanner MSS.*, 280, ff. 342–417. This has Bancroft's endorsement: "A defense of Ecclesiasticall jurisdiction in point of Tithes."   [5] Article 22.

Temporal judges were now arbitrarily revoking and amending the decrees and sentences of ecclesiastical judges.[1] This procedure was in flagrant contradiction to the oath taken by the temporal judges "to defend the Ecclesiasticall Jurisdiction".[2] Both the ecclesiastical and temporal jurisdictions were legally constituted, and it was improper that one should encroach on the domain of the other. "Two meanes have been ordained . . . the censure of excommunication, and the writ of prohibition: the one to restraine the incroachment of the Temporal iurisdiction upon the Ecclesiasticall, the other of the Ecclesiasticall upon the Temporall." Thus both excommunication and prohibitions were lawfully ordained "for the mutual preservation of both his Majesties supreme jurisdiction", and both should respect this mutual relationship.[3]

These *Articuli Cleri* were exhibited by Bancroft in the name of the whole clergy in the Michaelmas term 1605 to the Lords of the Privy Council against the common-law judges. After mature deliberation the judges and the barons of the Exchequer gave their unanimous answer in the Easter term following, and delivered them to the Council. The Archbishop's articles were answered seriatim. Concerning prohibitions, they were by law "to be granted at any time to restraine a Court to intermeddle with, or execute any thing, which by Law they ought not to hold plea of, and they are much mistaken that maintaine the contrary". Therefore, "it is the folly of such as will proceed in the Ecclesiastical Court for that, whereof that Court hath not iurisdiction; or in that, whereof the Kings Temporall Courts should have the iurisdiction".[4] Concerning jurisdiction:

> None may pursue in the Ecclesiastical Court for that which the Kings Court ought to hold plea of, but upon information thereof given to the Kings Courts, either by the Plaintife, or by any meere stranger, they are to be prohibited, because they deale in that which appertaineth not to their iurisdiction, where if they would be carefull not to hold plea of that which appertaineth not to them, this needed not; and if they will proceed in the Kings Courts against such as pursue in the Ecclesiasticall Courts for matters Temporall, that is to be inflicted upon them, which the quality of their offence

---

[1] Article 23.   [2] Article 24.   [3] Article 25.
[4] *Harleian MSS.*, 827, f. 2. 1605. Sir E. Coke, op. cit., p. 602. Answer to Article 3.

requireth; and how many sentences howsoever are given, yet prohibitions thereupon are not of favour, but of iustice to be granted.[1]

They emphatically repudiated the suggestion that they were guilty of any impropriety in the issue of writs of prohibition:

> we prohibit not so generally as they pretend, nor doe in any wise deale further then we ought to doe, to the preiudice of that which appertaineth to that iurisdiction; but when they deale with matters of Temporall contracts, coloured with pretended Ecclesiasticall matter, wee ought to prohibit them with that forme of prohibitions, mentioning, that it concerneth not matter of Marriage, nor Testamentary: And they shall not find that we have granted any, but by form warranted, both by the Register, and by the Law.[2]

They replied to the submission that no prohibition should be granted except out of Chancery:

> A strange presumption in the Ecclesiastical Judges, to require that the Kings Courts should not doe that which by law they ought to doe, and always have done, and which by oath they are bound to doe! . . . by these Articles thus dispersed abroad, there is a generall unbeseeming aspersion of that upon the Judges, which ought to have been forborn.[3]

The common-law judges were not (as was implied) animated by jealous motives of hostility, and they had no malicious desire to obstruct the proper activities of the ecclesiastical judges: "We doe not, neither will we in any wise impugne the Ecclesiastical authority in any thing that appertaineth unto it."[4] (The crux of the question was, of course, what did legally "appertain unto" the Court of High Commission.) The common-law judges repudiated the suggestion that they had illegitimately intruded into the sphere of the ecclesiastical judges:

> We are assured, that none can iustly charge any of us with violating our oaths, and it is a strange part to taxe Judges in this manner, and to lay so great an imputation upon us; and what scandall it will be to the iustice of the Realme to have so great levity, and so foule an

---

[1] Ibid., p. 607. Answer to Article 10.

[2] Ibid., p. 609. Answer to Article 13. (Cf. *Cotton MSS.*, *Cleopatra*, F.11, f. 171. "Noe Judge Ecclesiastical ought to charge any Laye Partye to answeare vpon oath in any cause but only matrimoniall and testamentarye.")

[3] Coke, op. cit., p. 610. Answer to Article 15.

[4] Ibid., p. 615. Answer to Article 22.

imputation laid upon the Judges, as is done in this, is too manifest. And we are assured it cannot be shewed, that the like hath been done in any former age, and for lesse scandals then this of the iustice of the Realme, divers have been severely punished.[1]

The common-law judges had no doubts concerning the validity of their own arguments nor the rightness of their judgement: they self-righteously affirmed that their "answers and resolutions although they were not enacted by authority of Parliament ...; yet, being resolved unanimously by all the Judges of England, and Barons of the Exchequer, are for matters in law of highest authority next unto the Court of Parliament".[2]

In the meantime the Lower House of Convocation sent a petition to the King in protest against the abuse of prohibitions in the matter of tithes:[3]

Most humblie beseechen your most excellent Maiestie, your faith-full subiects, the Clergie of your Lower howse of Convocation, for themselues, and the rest of their Brethren in the ministerie: That wheras they haue bin verie much of late yeres defrauded of their Tithes, and debarred from obteyninge ther right due vnto them by your excellent Lawes of this Church, throwghe Prohibitions, pro-cured by those which wronge them, out of your Maiesties temporall Courts to your suppliants great hinderaunce, molestion, and vtter impouerishinge in tyme, if remeady be not prouided, besids the stoppinge of Justice, occasion of periurie and further wronge, and overthrowe of your Ecclesiasticall iurisdiction, as thoughe it wer an uniust vsurpation of forriene power against your Maiestie and Crowne, and not the due execution of your Maiesties owne rightfull power, and iust iurisdiction in causes ecclesiasticall: yt maie please your most excellent Maiestie vppon due notice giuen and in tender Consideration of our greevances herein, to take some speedie order

---

[1] Ibid., p. 617. Answer to Article 24.   [2] Ibid., p. 618.

[3] Prohibitions could be issued in tithe cases on the following grounds: (i) if prescription was pleaded in attempting to establish a *modus*, or where there was a written *modus*, or where the existence of a *modus* was in dispute; (ii) if the bounds of a parish were in dispute; (iii) if it was claimed that the lands were tithe-free as former monastic lands, or as reclaimed waste; (iv) if the things sued for were not tithable at common law; (v) if it was claimed that tithes had been taken after parishioners had separated the minister's tenth from the remaining nine parts—unless the suit was between two ecclesias-tics; (vi) if there had been irregular procedure in a spiritual court; (vii) if a church court disallowed proof by one witness. C. Hill adds: "It was a poor lawyer who could not get a prohibition with all those possibilities before him." *Economic Problems of the Church from Whitgift to the Long Parliament*, p. 127.

for the helpe, and release of the same in such manner, as to your highness wisdome, pietie, and Clemencie, shall seeme iust, fitt, and convenient. . . .[1]

The unanimous and emphatic rejection of the Archbishop's submissions caused the utmost consternation. The ecclesiastical judges earnestly appealed to the Archbishop to exert himself afresh. They urged a direct approach to the King. They spoke of the calamities which had "befallen vnto the church and the Jurisdiction ecclesiasticall by the multitude of prohibitions devised and framed in barr of proceedings in ecclesiasticall courtes: but especiallie" since the Archbishop's "comminge to the Sea of Canterburie"; and they pointed out what a great danger prohibitions were to the Church as a whole, and to themselves in particular, "if remedie be not obtained from his majestie therein". Otherwise,

the Church must needes susteine great detriment for the present, and we, whoe haue bin trayned vpp for the moste part of our Lives in that service, and therby unfitt now to betake our selfes to anie other course, are like vtterlie to be vndonne. . . . We therefore most humblie beseeche your Grace to commiserate our presente estats, and for the avoydinge of theise inconveniences which are presentlie greate, and likelie hereafter to increase, to be a meanes vnto our dread souereigne (before whom we prostrate our selfes in all humilitie) that some such speedie course may be taken for the releife of this declyninge Jurisdiction, in soe dangerous and violent opposition, as to his highness shalbe thought most convenient, seinge otherwise it will be indangered to be vtterlie overthrowne. The consideration whereof we humblie submitt to your Graces great wisdome and care.[2]

Forty-three Procurators of the Court of Arches signed the petition.

On 21 November 1606, the Archbishop was able to report to the Lower House of Convocation "that the King had consented to put a restraint upon prohibitions".[3]

The fact that proceedings in the Court of High Commission could be obstructed by the issue of prohibitions gave welcome and

---

[1] *Cotton MSS.*, *Cleopatra*, F.11, f. 344, 1606. *Harleian MSS.*, 827, f. 1 b. "A Copie of the Petition of the Lower Howse of Convocation to his Maiestie against Prohibitions." Quoted, E. Cardwell, *Synodalia*, Vol. II, pp. 587 ff.; D. Wilkins, *Concilia*, Vol. IV, p. 429.

[2] *Cotton MSS.*, *Cleopatra*, F. 11, f. 343.

[3] E. Cardwell, op. cit., Vol. II, pp. 587 ff.

unexpected aid to the Puritans. A barrister, Nicholas Fuller, was engaged to launch a case impeaching the High Commission itself. Fuller was a notorious Puritan. He had been a member of Parliament, in which he had shown himself to be an implacable critic of the Church. Fuller was engaged to defend Thomas Lad, a merchant, and Richard Maunsell, a preacher, who were both imprisoned for Puritan practices.[1] They both refused to take the oath *ex officio*. Fuller described the case against Lad:

> Thos Lad, a marchant of Yarmouth, in Norfolke, was brought before the Chauncellor of Norwich, for a supposed Conventicle; because that hee, on the Sabbath dayes after the Sermons ended, sojourning in the house of M. Iackler in Yarmouth, who was late Preacher of Yarmouth, joyned with him in repeating of the substance and heads of the sermons that day made in the Church, at which Thomas Lad was usually present: and was forced upon his oath to answer certaine articles touching that meeting, which he could not see untill hee was sworne; and having answered upon his oath twice before the Chauncelor there, he was brought to Lambeth before the Ecclesiasticall Commissioners, to make a further answer upon a new oath, touching the supposed Conventicle: which he refused to doe, without sight of his former answers (because he was charged with perjury) and therefore was imprisoned by the Commissioners a long time, and could not be bayled: whereupon the writ of *Habeas Corpus* was granted out of the Kings bench, to bring the prisoner to the Bar.

Richard Maunsell also declined to take "the oath *ex officio*, to answer to certaine articles, which he could not be permitted to see". Maunsell was imprisoned by the Commissioners at Lambeth, "where hee remayned very long, and could not bee bayled, and was brought to the barr upon the writ of *habeas Corpus*". Fuller procured the writs of *Habeas Corpus* for both men from the King's Bench on 30 April 1607. At the hearing on 6 May Fuller strenuously maintained that the imprisonment of his clients by the Commissioners was unlawful. He claimed that the laws of the land did not give the Ecclesiastical Commissioners the power to

---

[1] N. Fuller, *The Argument of Nicholas Fuller of Grayes Inne Esquire, in the Case of Tho: Lad, and Rich: Maunsell his Clients, Wherein it is plainly proved, that the Ecclesiastical Commissioners have no power by their Commission, to imprison, or to fine any of his Majesties Subjects, or to put them to the Oath Ex. Officio*, London, 1607. For a critical review of the case see R. G. Usher, *Reconstruction*, Vol. II, pp. 136 ff.

imprison subjects of the Crown, or to administer the oath *ex officio*.

> He did not see, how, by colour of the statute of 1. Eliz: which gave power to the Commissioners to *execute the premisses* contained in that Act, they should inlarge their Patent to enquire of offences contrary to other statutes, made thirty or fourty yeares and more after an. 1 Eliz:, which then were not dreamed of, nor meant to be any part of the premisses contained in the said statute of anno 1. Eliz: and of other civill and temporall things.[1]

He proceeded to impugne the authority of the Court of High Commission:

> But this Ecclesiasticall Commission is but a Commission executorie, by the intent of the Statute of 1 Eliz. to continue so long as should please the Queen, or King, and no settled Court: and was meant at the first to have continuance for a short time, to strengthen the authoritie of the Bishops, against whose Ordination and installment the Papists did at first except. In which cases of things done by Commissions, whatsoever the Commissioners doe, it is examinable in every Court where it shall come in question, at any time after; whether that they have persued their Commission or authority, in due forme or noe.[2]

The judges of the King's Bench reserved the case for further argument before all twelve judges.

In July the Archbishop had Fuller arrainged before the High Commission for his scandalous speeches. Fuller promptly procured from the King's Bench a prohibition, which put an end to the trial in the Commission until the prohibition could be returned to the King's Bench at the end of September. This bold move aroused the King and Salisbury, both of whom feared that it might prejudiciously affect the stability of the monarchy. On 16 September Dudley Carleton told John Chamberlain that the King had been to Lambeth to "harten" the Archbishop in his conflict with Fuller.[3] The King himself wrote to Salisbury expressing his anxiety.

---

[1] N. Fuller, op. cit., p. 29.   [2] Ibid., p. 30.

[3] *S.P. Dom., Jas. I*, 14, Vol. XXVIII, no. 51. Dudley Carleton wrote that the King was "likewise with the Archbishop at Lambeth to harten him in his conflict with Nicholas Fuller, who had procured inhibition from the Judges to the high Commission to proceede no further in that cause. but vppon better advice they have sent (as I heare) a retraction of theyr inhibition. And poore Nich is nickt as before."

I praye yow forgette not Fuller's matter that the ecclesiasticall comission maye not be sufferid to sinke besydes the euill desairtis of the uillaine, for this farre darre I prophecie unto ye, that quhen soeuir the ecclesiasticall dignitie together with the Kings gouuerne-mente thairof shall be turnid to contempte and beginne to euanishe in this kingdome, the kinges haeirof shall not long prosper in thaire gouuerment and the monarchie shall fall to ruine, quhiche I praye god I maye neuer liue to see.[1]

At the end of September (the opening of the Michaelmas term), the judges of the King's Bench took counsel with their brethren of the Common Pleas and of the Exchequer upon the rightfulness of upholding the prohibition, or the necessity of issuing a consulta-tion. Early in the following month, a consultation was issued, with additional phrases intended to save the jurisdiction of the common law over the case as it had originally appeared. By refusing to support Fuller's appeal (thus declining jurisdiction) the judges had abandoned the case. The High Commissioners convicted Fuller on 20 or 21 October, fining him £200,[2] and sentencing him to imprisonment during pleasure. Fuller's arrogant rashness had made any spectacular decision against the Commission impossible, and the real assault was consequently postponed.

The spate of prohibitions showed no signs of abating. Previously, the common-law judges argued that they had done no more than restrain the Commission to its proper jurisdiction; now they attacked both its jurisdiction and procedure.[3] They complained of the Commission's use of the oath *ex officio*, its use of fine and imprisonment, its use of its own pursuivants to arrest culprits. They therefore justified the continued issue of prohibitions from the Court of Common Pleas.

Civilian lawyers, who practised in the ecclesiastical courts, presented their own petition to the King, protesting against the

[1] *Cecil MSS.*, 134, f. 126. 19 Oct. 1607.

[2] *S.P. Dom., Jas. I*, Vol. XXXVIII, no. 8. 14 Nov. 1607. "Gift to John Patten, keeper of the King's Closet, of £200, fine lately imposed vpon Nicholas Fuller by the Commissioners for Causes Ecclesiasticall."

[3] Thomas Ridley wrote in 1607: "As things are neither jurisdiction knowes their owne bounds, but one snatcheth from the other in a maner as in a batable ground lying betweene two Kingdomes." *A View of the Civile and Ecclesiastical Law, and Wherein the practice of them is streightened and may be relieved within this Land. Dedication*, p. 3.

abuse of prohibitions.[1] This was followed, on 22 January 1608/9, by another petition, this time addressed to the Archbishop, concerning the prohibitions sent from the temporal judges, in cases of mere ecclesiastical and civil cognizance.[2] They explained that "heretofore" they had "exhibited a peticone to his Majestie" demonstrating the "manifold grevances by prohibitiones".

> Wee were bould to deduce our sensible feelings of the apparante decaye of our professione ensuinge for wante of maintenaunce, and that this decaye hath a risene of late yeares from a powere that the temporall Judges have assumed to send prohibiciones in cases of meer Ecclesiasticall and ciuell cognizances in such multitudes as (yf the recordes be serched) all the prohibiciones since the conqueste vntyle our late Queenes tyme are not halfe so manye as have swarmed within these Laste Twentie years.

Further:

> Wee did put his Highnes in remembrance of the Necessarie vse of oure professione as well abroad as at home for Negotiacone and intercourse of affaires betweene his highnes owne Kingdomes and other stats and the administracon of Justice in sundrye cases of ecclesiasticall Cognizances and Civill equitie.

They had secured the support of the Universities, who had thought good

> to ioyne their complaints shewinge how by reasone of discorage-mente given to the students of this professione they are of late become barrene of suche Childrene as they were wonte to bringe forthe, and send in greate numberes fraughte with all kinde of knowledge not inferiour to any other vniuersities in Christendom for the service of the Churche and comon welthe, and that nowe whole Colledges erected for that Studie are lyke to become desolate.

The King, who had appointed a time to hear and examine the specific grievances of the civilian lawyers, had given "ordere . . . that moderacone should be vsed in sendinge out prohibicones". In spite of this, "contrary to his Majesties pleasure", prohibitions

> have not only bene multiplyed, but also ther hath bene devised a strange and newe kynde of prohibicone against your Graces

---

[1] *Harleian MSS.*, 827, f. 1. "The Civilians Petition to his Maiestie touching Prohibitions."
[2] *Harleian MSS.*, 358, f. 184, 1608/9; *Cotton MSS., Cleopatra*, F.1, f. 107; *Rawlinson MSS.*, B.202, f. 107 b.

Courts in a case never thought of before, which, yf it bee maintained will at once, aswell cutt of [sic] all the Chiefe maintenaunce of Civilians, as give a deepe wound to your Churche of Canterbury in hir privileges hetherto inviolablye kepte for thes fowere hondred yeares and vpwards.

In the course of their petition to the archbishop, the civilian lawyers reminded the Archbishop that his courts in London, which existed "for the ease of suitores repairinge to the Cittie of London for other occasiones", had "tyme out of mynde bene in the Cittie ordinarie kepte as the fitteste place for retaining of suffitiente Counsell and shortening the course of the proceedinges in tyme and expence".

Nowe the said Judges without all former presidente . . . have pro-hibited your deane of the Arches to call origenally before him any of the dioces of London, where your said courts are Cituated, by coulor of a statute never since the makynge thereof, which is almoste fower score yeares, so interpreted, but the Contrary by vse, the beste interpretere of Statuts, evere practised and obserued.[1] Yf this succeede according to the designe, not to speake more of the ouer throwe of the Civill Lawes, our selues, and other ministeres of the Courtes, howe preiudiciall it would bee to his highnes subiects that have bene suitores in those courts by disanullinge all processes and sentences geven for thes fowerescore yeares as before Judges com-petente.

Their urgent request was for the powerful mediation and inter-cession of the Archbishop on their behalf:

Wee wholye Submitte to your graces better iudgement and doe humblye intreate your grace to contynewe your favoure and mediacone to his Majestie for redress in this the Church most iuste cause and oures, And your Suplyants shall praye for your Graces evere lastinge happines.

The Archbishop[2] deeply sympathized with the unhappy plight

---

[1] Sir Edward Coke's views on the subject are given in Cotton MSS., Cleopatra, F.11, f. 467. "The Lord Cooks arguments touching Rochesters case, upon the Stat. 23 Hen. VIII, cap. 9, that none ought to be called out of their diocese to answer before the archbishop of Canterbury in the court of Arches or Audience."

[2] Cotton MSS., Cleopatra, F.11, f. 121. 23 Jan. 1608/9. "An Answere of Arch-bishop Bancroft to the petition of the doctors and advocates of the Civil Law, in behalf of their profession which then suffered by the encroachment of the Common lawyers, and especially by prohibitions." Quoted, J. Strype, Whitgift, Vol. III, pp. 385 ff.

of the civilian lawyers, who were "contemned and vilified" by the common lawyers. He spoke bitterly and satirically of the arrogant self-righteousness of their enemies: they

> appropriate to themselues the Quintessence as it wer of all wisdome and vnderstandinge, or rather a vaine and ridiculous conceipt borrowed from the pope, as if they had the power to iudge all menn but must be iudged of none, except (saie some papists of the pope) by a generall Counsell, except (saye some lawyers for them selues) by the vpper howse of parliament.

The Archbishop wisely suggested that the petitioners be not too "prodigall" in the vse of his letter, for he had been much maligned. He urged on them the need for the greatest circumspection:

> least some occasion thereof be taken of explayninge against me, as some doe, giveinge it out very seditiouslie . . . that by my meanes a Course is entred into which tendeth to the overthrowe of the Common Lawe, and to depriue his Majesties subiects of ther Birthright; that I labour by all waies I can devise to make the Kinge belieue that he is one absolut monarch and maie *iure Regio*, do what he list, and that I am an Enimie to all the professors of the Comon Lawe.[1]

Bancroft repudiated all these malicious slanders:

> all these imputations are cast vpon mee, as god knoweth very vniustlie, and fore noe other Cause, but for that I desire that his Majesties temperall Judges, might keepe themselues in some reasonable sort within ther owne lists, and not invade as they doe his Majesties Ecclesiasticall Jurisdiction.

The common-law judges, Bancroft said, ought to beware of straining royal complaisance too far:

> if the Kinge shall take vppon him to be a Judge in these Causes, it is not vnlike, that he will hold the like Courses in all other Causes to the preiudice of his temporall Judges, who pretend for sooth in

---

[1] An incidental reference, in a letter written by John Chamberlain to Dudley Carleton, throws an interesting side-light on this matter: "The King hath had two or three conferences of late with the Judges about prohibitions . . . Which prohibitions he wold faine cut of, and stretch his prerogative to the vttermost: the iudges stand well yet to theyre tackling. . . ." *S.P. Dom., Jas. I,* 14, Vol. XXXVII, no. 53. 8 Nov. 1608. Neal, who was undoubtedly biased, and whose judgement is suspect, says Bancroft "was for advancing the prerogative above the law, and for enlarging the jurisdiction of the spiritual courts, by advising his Majesty to take from the courts of Westminster, to himself, the whole right of granting prohibitions". *History of the Puritans*, Vol. II, p. 35.

effect that they are the *Ephori* betwixt the Kinge and his subiects, and that therfore they, his saide subiects, are thereby depriued of ther Birthright.

Bancroft had every confidence in the wise exercise of the royal prerogative:

He is the fountaine of all iustice from whence whoso imediatly draweth is sure to receiue the same with all clernes and purity; whereas often tymes beinge deriued through pipes and Cesterns not soe cleane as they should be, it is tainted and looseth a great parte of the vertue it had. Did the Comons knowe howe in the practize of Lawe they are vsed, they would not be soe farr in loue with the temporall Judges as they the said Judges would pretend they are. . . .

He therefore advised them once again to petition the King direct

that he will be pleased to effect, as I doubt not that he maie, without deprivinge his subiects of ther birthright, or shewing himself to be suche a Kinge as not careinge for anie Lawes, will doe what he list.

The vexed question of rival jurisdictions added fuel to the flames. Each side was diligent in its search for precedents to support its case. In November 1606 Bancroft wrote to the Keeper of Records asking him to allow searches to be made, and copies from the records of courts and Parliament.[1] Bancroft also wrote letters to the bishops inviting them to search among their records for precedents, "concerninge prohibitions, how and in what cases they should be granted for the maintenance of the Jurisdiction and liberties of the Church".[2]

Whereas in the last session of Parliament 3 Jas I generall complaint was made by the whole clergy of the over-frequent granting of prohibitions, and whereas the King out of his princely care of the poor ministry has been pleased to take order thereupon for the good of the church, the Bishop is earnestly entreated to have search into his own records, and those of the dean and chapter, for any orders with regard to prohibitions by any former kings, and to report thereon between this and Easter; and likewise as to any proceedings taken by any ecclesiastical judge concerning the payment of tithe.[3]

[1] *Petyt MSS.*, 538,17, f. 281.

[2] *Cambridge University MSS.*, Dd. 3, 64, f. 68. 16 Feb. 1608/9. Bancroft to the Bishop of Norwich.

[3] *The Brown Book*, Register 1580–1618, f. 213 a. 10 Feb. 1608/9. Lincoln Diocesan Record Office.

Bancroft knew well the importance of the issue. The very administrative life of the Church was at stake.

The King ordered the Attorney-General, Sir Henry Hobart, to prepare briefs for fresh debates in the Trinity term, 1609. These debates commenced on 6 July at Whitehall, the Lord Chief Justice, Sir Edward Coke, opening the proceedings.[1] The following day, the Solicitor-General, Sir Francis Bacon, spoke on behalf of the ecclesiastical lawyers,[2] and argued that the Common Pleas could not issue original writs and therefore could not grant a prohibition to the ecclesiastical courts, unless the same case was also being heard at its own bar.[3] The Lord Chief Justice vehemently resisted this contention, and the debate was adjourned until the following day. On 8 July the Attorney-General defended the High Commission, and dealt with the objections made against its jurisdiction and procedure.[4] He further attacked the claim of the judges of the temporal courts to interpret the statutes of the realm.[5] He said that statutes which modified or amended part of the ecclesiastical law, having been once passed by Parliament, were as much part of the ecclesiastical law as though they had been enacted by Convocation, and were to be interpreted solely by the ecclesiastical courts.

The defenders of the Church argued "that the King hath power in his owne person to heare and determine all kinds of Causes, when it shall soe please his Majesty". Hoary historical precedents were cited: "The chiefest cause why God hath sett a kinge over anie National is to iudge the people. 1 Sam. 8.11"; furthermore: "Moses in person at first in all Causes Administered Justice, and though afterwards had delegated others, yet in *causis gravioribus* the people appealed to him, And the ancient Kinges of Israell did usuallie in person sitt in the gate to administer justice." The conclusion was irresistible: "it is absurd that the King whoe is the fountaine of all Justice, by whose

---

[1] *Lansdowne MSS.*, 160, ff. 416–15.　　　　　　　　　　[2] Ibid., ff. 414–13.

[3] *Cotton MSS., Cleopatra*, F.1, f. 215; *Tanner MSS.*, 120, f. 25. "A Breuiat of the selected proofes: prohibitions out of the Common Pleas noe Recorde being before them."

[4] *Cotton MSS., Cleopatra*, F.1, f. 128; *Stowe MSS.*, 420, f. 18. "The ground of Prohibitions to the High Commission and the aunsers vnto them."

[5] *Cotton MSS., Cleopatra*, F.1, f. 132 b; *Stowe MSS.*, 420, f. 24 b. "Prohibicions grounded vpon the posicion that the interpretation of Statutes belonge to the judges of the temporal cortes."

authorityes all Magistrates sitt, and by whose death all authorities expire, should not have power to iudge his people in his owne person." It was abundantly clear that "in all Causes Ecclesiastical the subjects may have recourse to the Kinge".[1]

The debate was inconclusive: the Lord Chancellor was instructed to look into the powers of the Court of Common Pleas and to report before the Michaelmas term. His Majesty observed that the Court of High Commission had been "impeached many waies by unfitt and uniust prohibitions", and he commanded Coke to answer in writing before the next term. In the meantime Coke was to refrain from prohibitions to that court, and if he found his jurisdiction infringed, he was to seek redress from the King. The King would have the Church flourish as the green bay tree, as long as it grew neither popish nor Puritan. Sir Francis Bacon was ordered to prepare answers "concerninge the treble valew of Prediall Tithes vpon the Statute of 2 Ed: 6: 13". In September "Mr Sollicitor" was also commanded to prepare answers on two more questions: "the one concerning the triall *de modo decimandi*, and the other touching the jurisdiction of the Courte of Common Pleas in grauntinge of Prohibitions."[2]

In obedience to the royal directions, Coke proceeded to compile from various legal sources a weighty justification for the issue of prohibitions. Bacon also prepared a long argument concerning *modus decimandi*, which he submitted to Coke during the vacation.[3]

---

[1] *Additional MSS.*, 25,270, f. 29; *Cotton MSS.*, *Cleopatra*, F.11, f. 287; *Harleian MSS.*, 1,299, f. 93, 4,282, f. 2; *Rawlinson MSS.*, B.202, f. 193 b; C. 731, f. 107; *Tanner MSS.*, 120, f. 141. "The Argument contra for the archbishoppe of Canterburye."

[2] *Cotton MSS.*, *Cleopatra*, F.1, f. 116. "A Preface to the answeres of the Judges of the Courte of Comon Pleas Vnto the Obiections and Arguments made (on behalfe of the Lorde Archbishop of Canterbury) against Prohibitions." *Rawlinson MSS.*, B.202, f. 113 b; C.731, f. 26.

[3] *Tanner MSS.*, 120, f. 72. *Rawlinson MSS.*, B.157, f. 1; B.202, f. 165 b; C.731, f. 63. "A Breuiat of the chiefe proofes selected touching *Modus Decimandi*. The Question is, Whether vpon a suite commenced in the spirituall Courte, and a prescription or custome *de modo decimande* pleaded, A prohibition maye be brought in Temporall Courte, or whether the Spirituall Courte may not trye that yssue, and soe sentence the intire cause."

The answers are to be found in: *Rawlinson MSS.*, C.731, f. 73: "An Answeare to the Chief proofes selected touching *Modus Decimandi*. . . ." *Tanner MSS.*, 120, f. 90; 280, f. 432; *Lansdowne MSS.*, 161, f. 253; 421, f. 183; *Cotton MSS.*, *Cleopatra*, F.1, f. 191; *Harleian MSS.*, 1,229, f. 56; 7,161, f. 111 b; *Additional MSS.*, 25,270, f. 4.

Coke knew that the vital question was "to whome the exposition of Statutes concerninge Causes Ecclesiasticall" appertained. The ecclesiastical lawyers did not challenge the right of the Court of Common Law to issue prohibitions: they complained of their repeated misuse.

> There haue not bene any question made whether prohibitions should be taken away, for they be as auncient and necessarie as any parte of the lawes of England and continewally allowed by all Acts: but in what cases they ought by lawe to be graunted divers questions haue bene made.

Coke produced numerous "demonstrative arguments" to show the incontestible superiority of the "lawes of England . . . over the civill and Cannon Lawes within this Realm". He argued that

> the first founders of the Common Lawes, instituted, and the wisdom of all the succeeding ages hath continued, prohibitions to the Ecclesiastical Judges commaundige them to surcease, which the prelates and Clergie haue euer hithervnto inviolably obserued and obeyed; but they could neuer prohibite the Kings Courts of record, for that they were neuer vnder their Commaundement.

This in itself demonstrated the superiority of the temporal courts, for there can be no "greater proufe of superioritie . . . then to commaund, and that the commaundment be obeyed".

Taking as a basis for his argument the Statute 24 Henry VIII, 2.12, he proved that

> the Kinge, the Lords spirituall and Temporall and Commons doe all, by Act of Parliament, acknowledge and declare that such things as belonge to Ecclesiasticall iurisdiction haue bene allowed to the Ecclesiasticall Judges by the goodnes of the princes of this Realm and by the Lawes and Customes of the same. Seinge then that they haue their jurisdiction by the allowance of the Kings and of the Lawes and Customes of England, it followeth that when they exceed that iurisdiction which the Lawes and Customes of England haue allowed them, That they should be vnder the controlement and prohibicion of the Kinges Lawes.

The Church was properly entrusted with the power of excommunication, but because the danger of abuse was always present, the temporal courts were entrusted with the power of issuing prohibitions, so that a just balance between both jurisdictions might be preserved.

There was reason that the first Law makers instituted, and that all succeeding ages continued Prohibicions to Ecclesiastical Courts, for that they haveinge that power to excommunication (*tradatur Sathane*) sought euer from tyme to tyme to encroche and vsurpe in matters of iurisdiction and authoritie vpon the Kings prerogative and the lawes, statutes, and Customes of England.[1]

The Archbishop, in the course of his original submission, had claimed that the ecclesiastical judges possessed authority to interpret the Statute 1 Elizabeth, on which the High Commission was grounded, and also all other acts of Parliament concerning ecclesiastical causes: "the interpretation of this Statute and of such others as do concerne any cause Ecclesiasticall belonge to the high Commissioners themselues, and other Ecclesiasticall Judges." Replying to this argument, Coke said:

Acts of Parliament made by the Kinge, the Lords and Commons, are parte of the Lawes of England, and are to be interpreted by the Judges of the Lawes of Englande, and not by any Ecclesiasticall Judge. And this is proued by many expressed authorits and Judgments reported in our booke, and there is no one opinion extant in any booke of Lawe that any Ecclesiasticall Judge, ought to euer pretend to interprett any Act of Parliament . . . If the end and scope of the Statute bee temporall then doth it belonge to the temporall Judges to expound and determine the same . . . though the cause be ecclesiasticall.[2]

No judgement made by any ecclesiastical court was necessarily final, since an appeal was always possible to the more original and superior temporal jurisdiction.

By the same case appeareth, that if a man imprisoned by any authority giuen or pretended to be giuen by Act of Parliament; if the partie take himself to be imprisoned contrary to the Act, he may haue his action of false imprisonmente; for the breach, or not persuinge of an Acte of Parliament, to the preiudice and damage of any man (though it concerned an ecclesiasticall Cause), is temporall, and shalbe punished in the Kings temporall Courte.

Coke referred again to the "former resolution of all the Judges of England and Barons of the Exchequer", which was "certified in

---

[1] *Cotton MSS., Cleopatra*, F.1, f. 116; *Rawlinson MSS.*, B.202, f. 113 b; C.731, f. 26.

[2] Cf. *Cotton MSS., Cleopatra*, F.11, f. 467.

writing to the Lords of his Majesties most hon: priuy Counsell in the lord Pophams tyme vpon longe and great deliberation". The Archbishop had formerly made a similar claim on behalf of the ecclesiastical judges, which the Judges and Barons had then rejected:

And for the Judges expoundinge of Statuts, that concerne the Ecclesiasticall gouernmente or proceedinges, it belongeth to the temporall Judges and we neuer hard it excepted vnto haertofore that any statute should be expounded, by any other then the Judges of the land, neyther was there euer any soe much euer-seene, as to oppose himselfe againste the practise of all ages to make that question, or to lay any such uniuste imputation vpon the Judges of the Realme, as by the said Certificate of all the Judges and Barons of the Exchequer appeareth.

Coke associated himself with this previous judgement and dismissed the claims advanced by the Archbishop:

if the authorities of our bookes in all ages, the continuall practize and experience of former tymes vnto this day, and resolution of all the iudges of Englande may giue satisfaction in a question of lawe (there beinge noe one opinion in all our bookes euer mentioned before this tyme made to the contrary) then we hope the Lord Archbishop (beinge nowe truly informed) will herewith rest satisfied.[1]

Coke conducted his own independent investigation into the authority of the Court of High Commission under the title of: "A Declaration of the true grounds of the Prohibitions to the High Commissioners and the authorities and reasons approvinge the same, with answeares to the obiections made to the Contrary, wherein amongst other things it is mainteyned and proved that the high Commissioners may in diuers cases lawfully fine, and imprison, and particularly what those cases bee. ..."[2] He ex-

---

[1] *Tanner MSS.* (Bodl.), 120, f. 180; *Lansdowne MSS.*, 161, f. 254; 421, f. 151; *Cotton MSS., Cleopatra*, F.1, f. 159; *Harleian MSS.*, 827, f. 28; 1,299, f. 128; *Rawlinson MSS.*, B.202, f. 147 b. "The second question propounded on the behalf of the Lord Archbishop of Canterbury toucheinge the exposition of Statutes Concerning ecclesiasticall Causes: Whether the same belong to the Judges of the Realme, or to the enterpretation of the Civillians and Cannonists." Cf. *Rawlinson MSS.*, C.731, f. 51, "Propositions grounded vppon this position that the interpretation of all Statutes doth belonge to the Judges of the Temporall Courts."

[2] *Lansdowne MSS.*, 421, f. 131; *Cotton MSS., Cleopatra*, F.1, f. 138; *Rawlinson MSS.*, B.202, f. 133 b; C. 731, f. 1.

pounded with legal exactitude the scope and significance of the Act
1 Elizabeth, c. 1, since "euery act of Parliament doth consist of
the letter, and of the meaninge of the makers of the act". He
proved, by means of abundant citation, that the High Commissioners could only adjudicate in certain limited kinds of cases.

> The cause of restoringe and vnitinge the aunciant Jurisdiction to
> the Crowne is lymited only for this end and purpose, viz: for visita-
> tion of the ecclesiasticall estate and persons, and for reformation and
> correction of the same, and of all mannours, errours, herisies,
> schismes, abuses, offences, contempts, and enormities, and this is
> all that is restored and vnited by this act to the Crowne; which of
> necessitie accordinge to the originall institution to be vnderstood of
> such enormous and heynous Crymes as necessity requireth a more
> speedie proceedinge then can be by the ordinary Jurisdiction, but
> extendeth not to the Common or inferiour offences, nor to any cause
> of tithes, legacies, or other Civill causes.[1]

In another substantial monograph Coke discussed the jurisdiction of the Court of Common Pleas in the matter of prohibitions.
He criticized the Archbishop's bold assertion that neither the
Court of Common Pleas nor the King's Bench could grant prohibitions. Coke, despite his pedantry, was a jurist of vast erudition:
it was not difficult for him to compile a lengthy series of precedents:
"the Court of the Common Pleas", he concluded, "is the proper
Court of the Common Lawe, for the determination of the Common
Pleas in actions reall, personall, and mixt."[2]

On 10 October 1609, the Archbishop of York wrote to Sir
Julius Caesar about the protracted and notorious strife between
Bancroft and Coke.

> For I will not importune you so farr as to craue your opinion what
> will become of the prohibitions: wherein I hope you will stande the
> Clergies frende, as in manie other respects they haue alwaies founde
> you fauourable. It greiueth me not a little, that between my Lo:
> Grace of Cant: and my lor: Chief Justice, there should be so long
> and so lowde an opposition, if it be such as some reporteth, and

---

[1] *Cotton MSS., Cleopatra*, F.11, 171; *Lansdowne MSS.*, 253, ff. 139–90.
[2] *Lansdowne MSS.*, 421, f. 213; *Cotton MSS.*, 827, f. 17; 1,299, f. 1; 6,683, f. 37.
"In what cases the Kings Court of Common Pleas may grant Prohibitions
by Lawe, and many presidents of former tymes."

blazeth abroad Terme by Terme. Whereof more at some other tyme. . . .[1]

Both parties were fighting for their respective jurisdictions. For Coke the question at issue was the supremacy of the law; for Bancroft, the survival of the Church as by law established.

In these circumstances, the publication of a book, under Bancroft's patronage, entitled, *The Interpreter*, was doubly untimely. The author, Dr Cowell, was Reader in Civil Law at Cambridge. Cowell claimed that the King of England was an absolute King, and that his prerogative included the power to make laws. His views were expressed with uncompromising vigour in the section on "Parliament", in which he argued:

> Of these two, one must needs be true, that either the King is above the Parliament, that is, the positive laws of this Kingdom, or else that he is not an absolute King. . . . And, therefore, though it be a merciful policy, and also a politic mercy (not alterable without great peril) to make laws by consent of the whole realm, because so no one part shall have cause to complain of a partiality, yet simply to binde a prince to or by those laws were repugnant to the nature and constitution of an absolute monarchy.

The House of Commons was greatly incensed by these aggressively absolutist doctrines, and immediately caused an inquiry to be instituted. On 27 February 1609/10 a message was sent to the Upper House requesting Conference:

> we, having assurance of the Conjunction of their Lordships united affections with us, in all matters that may concern the Dignity of the Parliament . . . and having of late taken understanding of some scandalous Matter, touching the Body of parliament, and of other dangerous Nature, published in a Book by one D. Cowell, called *The Interpreter*; that their lordships will be pleased to join with us in Examination of the Matter, and in Censure and Punishment of the Party, as the Cause shall deserve; and, to that End, your Lordships would be pleased to afford us Conference, at such Time and Place, and with such Number, as your Lordships shall think meet.[2]

The Upper House agreed, and appointed fifty members to meet with the Lower.[3] Salisbury, the skilful peacemaker, informed the

---

[1] *Lansdowne MSS.*, 513, f. 81.
[2] Ibid., 161, f. 269. 10 Oct. 1609.
[3] *Journals of the H. of C.*, Vol. I, p. 400, 27 Feb. 1606/10.

Commons that the King had summoned Cowell before him, and had admonished him. The King considered that the book impugned the Common Law of England, and the fundamental grounds of the constitution of Parliament, and that, in opposing the prerogative to the law, Cowell had attacked both King and Parliament together. The King acknowledged that although he derived his title from his ancestors, "Yet the law did set the crown upon his head . . . and that he was a King by the Common Law of the land." He recognized that he "had no power to make laws by himself, or to exact any subsidies *de jure* without the consent of his three estates, and, therefore, he was so far from approving the opinion, as he did abhor those that believed it".[1]

On 25 March 1610 a Proclamation castigating the author and denouncing his doctrines as subversive, was issued.[2] The author had meddled "in matter above his Reach", and had "fallen in many things to mistake". In some places he had made remarks "very Derogatory to the supream Power of this Crown"; while in other places he had spoken "irreverently of the Common Law of England, and of the Works of some of the most famous and Antient Judges therein, it being a thing utterly unlawful to any Subject to speak or write against that Law, under which he Liveth, and which we are Sworn and are resolved to maintain". All copies of the book were to be delivered up "to the Lord Mayor of London, if they or any of them be dwelling in or near the said City, or otherwise to the Sheriff of the County where they or any of them shall reside", and "the Buying, Uttering, or Reading of the said Book" was forbidden.

It is difficult to exaggerate the fear and antagonism engendered by the expanding activities of the Court of High Commission. Its arbitrary procedure, its undefined scope, its clerical composition, its reliance on the oath *ex officio*—all these things offended the lay instincts of the rising middle class as incompatible with the traditional processes of English law. Opposition found its focus in the formidable figure of the Lord Chief Justice and in certain vocal members of the House of Commons. In July 1610 the House of Commons addressed a Petition to the King for the

---

[1] S. R. Gardiner, *Parliamentary Debates in 1610*. Edited from the Notes of a Member of the House of Commons, p. 24.
[2] *Additional MSS.*, 12,515, f. 73; *Lansdowne MSS.*, 513, f. 89.

redress of grievances arising through the said Court. The preamble bluntly declared that

> whereas by the Statute 1 Eliz. cap. 1, Entituled, An Act restoring to the Crowne the auncient Jurisdiction over the State Ecclesiasticall, power was given to the Queen and her Successors to constitute and make a Commission in Causes Ecclesiasticall, the said Act is found to be of inconveniente and dangerous extent in divers respects.

The Commons complained that the scope of the original Commission had been improperly extended and enlarged:

> whereas by the intencion and words of the said Statutes Ecclesiasticall iurisdiction is restored to the Crowne, and your Highnes by that Statute enabled to give onely such power ecclesiasticall to the said Commissioners, yet vnder color of some words in that Statute, whereby the Commissioners are authorised to execute their Commission according to the tenor and effect of your Highnes Lettres Patente, and by Lettres Patente grounded thervpon, the said Commissioners to fyne and ympryson and exercise other authorities not belonging to the ecclesiasticall iurisdiction restored by that Statute, which wee conceive to be a great wrong to the Subiect, and that those Commissioners might as well by color of those words, yf they were so authorised by your Highnes Lettres Patente, fine without stint and ymprison without lymitacion of tyme, as also according to will and discretion without any rules of Lawe, spirituall or temporall, adiudge and impose vtter confiscacion of goods, forfeyture of lands, yea, and the taking away of lym and of life it self, and this for any matter whatsoever pertayning to spirituall iurisdiction, which never was nor could be meant by the makers of that Lawe.

They strenuously objected to the fact that

> every petty offence pertayning to spirituall iurisdiction is by color of the said words and Lettres Patente grounded thervpon made subiect to excommunicacion and punishments by that strange and exorbitant power and commission, whereby the least offenders not committing anything of any enormious or high nature may be drawne from the most remote places of the Kingdome to London or Yorke, which is very greivous and inconvenient.

The Court of High Commission caused confusion in the administration of the law and its activities were oppressive and unjust:

> the same men have both spiritual and temporal jurisdiction, and may both force the party by oath to accuse himself of any offence

and also enquire thereof by a jury, and lastly may inflict for the same offence at the same time and by one and the same sentence both a spiritual and temporal penalty. . . .

Wheras upon sentences of deprivation or other spiritual censures given by force of ordinary jurisdiction, an appeal lieth for the party aggrieved, that is here excluded by express words of the commission; also here is to be a trial by jury, yet no remedy by traverse or attaint, neither can a man have any writ of error, though a judgement or sentence be given against him, amounting to the takeng away of all his goods and imprisoning of him during life, yea, to the adjudging him in case of praemunire whereby his lands are forfeited and he out of the protection of the law.

For these and other cogent reasons the Commons desired the restraint and limitations of the Commission:

All which premisses . . . considered, your Maiesties most loyall and duetifull Commons in all humilitie beseech you, that for the easing of them aswell from present grievance, as from the feare and possibility of greater in tymes future, your Highnes would vouchsafe your royall assent and allowance to and for the certifying of the said Statute, and the reducing thereof, and consequently of the said Commission to reasonable and convenient Limmitts, by some Act to be passed in this present Session of Parlyament.[1]

The oath *ex officio* was the subject of a bitter attack. Originally it "crept into the Courts Ecclaesisticall by the Statute on A°2° H.4., slippinge in amonge the rable of Canonicall functions which the pope then obtruded to haue the Church here gouerned by", and later it had been "discouered from amongst them as an adder in the grasse". It "was dampned and expelled by the Statute of 25 H.8. cap. 14 as vtterly agaynst equitye and the lawe and Common Justice of the lande". The mover urged that

the Commons most humblye praye that the vnlawfullnes thereof and grievance ensuinge therby maye be Considered of, and a bindinge lawe framed and established for reformation of the abuse, for the Common lawe of the land hateth yt for divers Cawses. first, for that yt is coacted and Constrayned. Secondlye, for that yt standeth not with the Certayne knowledge of the deponent what he shall answere vnto. Thirdlye, for that yt is not finale as the oath prescribed in the Judicialls was. fourthly, for that yt is an apparent

---

[1] *S.P. Dom., Jas. I*, 14, Vol. LVI, no. 10. 7 July 1610. Quoted, G. W. Prothero, op. cit., pp. 302 ff.

occasion of periury which Carnall men will rather fall into then to submit themselues to Corporall punishement or to laye open their owne turpitude or shame. . . .[1]

Further information is lacking.

In the following year, 1611, the High Commissioners were again complaining in a Petition to the King, of the many prohibitions issued by the Court of Common Pleas. When Henry VIII broke from Rome, he assumed supreme authority in things ecclesiastical as well as temporal: no subject had power to exercise ecclesiastical jurisdiction,

> or any part thereof, otherwise then by Letters Patents from the Kinge or Queene for the time beinge. And by force of such Letters patents his Maiesties subiect, or subiects named Commissioners, may exercise so much Iurisdiction, and in such manner, as in the Letters patents is or shalbe expressed.

Commissioners, being royal appointees,

> haue had and haue authoritie to exercise all Jurisdiction ecclesiasticall, even the whole which was annexed to the crowne, without exception of any part, at their discrescions, throughout the realmes of England and Irelande.

Earlier sovereigns

> reposed themselues vppon the discressions of such worthie subiects, and of none els, for this service, contayninge the gouernment of the Church, Religion, and state ecclesiasticall of this Realme. And the sayd Commissioners for the time beinge, haue continually discharged this service accordingly; And delt only in such civile, or Criminall Causes ecclesiasticall, as the exorbitant nature of the same, or qualitie of the persons in question enforced them; leavinge the rest vnto the inferior Iudges ecclesiasticall: Insomuch that neuer any such inferor judge hath hethervnto complayned of any abridgment of his authoritie, by this vnlimited Jurisdiction of his Maiesties highe Commissioners.

Their authority, they contended, was derived directly from the King himself:

> Howbeit, the Judges of the Comon Pleas, which haue no Colour to intermedle with any Jurisdiction ecclesiasticall in any Cause

---

[1] *Harleian MSS.*, 158, f. 182. July 1610.

ecclesiasticall whatsoeuer ... doe neuerthelesse prohibite in the Kings name these Commissioners to exercise for the Kinge this Jurisdiction, as his Majesties letters patente warrenteth them.[1]

A Conference was called, on 23 May 1611, to discuss, once again, the whole vexatious matter. It was summoned by the King's special appointment. The Lord Treasurer, who presided, opened the proceedings by pointing out that the King had often been solicited by the Archbishop for the redress of certain grievances, and especially for the restriction of the issue of prohibitions by the Judges of the Common Pleas. The King's purpose in summoning both the Lords of the Council, and the High Commissioners and Judges of the realm, was "to haue amonst them all a lovinge and friendly Conference", in which the Lords of the Council were "to heare the complaints on the one side, and the answers on the other". He desired to receive "the true examination and vnderstandinge of the business, as alsoe the cause of the same, and where the same cause rested", so that

> if noe other peaceable course could be taken amongst themselues, he might at length sett downe some further or finall order therein as to Justice, and the greatnes of his place should appertaine, houldinge it noe small infortunitie to himselfe that fyndinge all things at peace att his cominge hether, and being himselfe soe much addicted to peace, And to allowe to every Court theire owne Justice and naturall Jurisdiction, he should finde these great differences to arise in this tyme betweene the States Ecclesiasticall and Temporall.

Dr Martin, the chief ecclesiastical spokesman, alleged that the temporal judges undermined the judicial authority of the High Commissioners, and encouraged the spread of licentiousness and licence throughout the country. This was the reason that there had "sprung vpp in the land ... an inundation of wicked and notorious adulteries". Apart from these deplorable practical consequences, the fact remained that the authority of the High Commission was "deriued out of the Kings authority ecclesiasticall". Dr Martin quoted Cawdry's case—a case in which Coke had himself recognized the power of the Commissioners to deprive and administer censures on the basis of the Elizabethan

---

[1] *Lansdowne MSS.*, 161, f. 252. 1611.

Statute;[1] he mentioned divers commissions made in the reigns of Henry VIII and Edward VI; and the commission granted by Elizabeth in July 1559, with power to fine and imprison; he stressed the fact that Commissioners "in all succeedinge tymes . . . haue practised this power and Authority"; he reminded the Council that "the Lord Cooke himself beinge Attorney generall hath penned divers of these Commissions, with the clauses of power to fyne and imprison, wherein himselfe hath beene a Commissioner"; he insisted that this authority of the Commissioners had never been "questioned till nowe of late years"; and he recalled the fact that "the Kinge himselfe at the last debatinge of this business expressly forbadd the Judges to graunt any more prohibitions to the high Commissioners. He therefore concluded that by the restraint of such prohibitions God would be pleased."

The Lord Treasurer called upon Sir Edward Coke to reply, and particularly to "shew the reason how and wherein by vertue of your oathes you are bound to prohibitt them",[2] and further, whether the Commissioners "may fyne and imprison or noe". The Attorney-General declared that neither the pope before the dissolution of the monasteries, nor the King after he was made Supreme Head of the Church, could make any Commission to fine and imprison the body of a free subject, but under the authority of the Act 1 Elizabeth they had the power to fine and imprison for heresies, schisms, and other enormities. Coke complained of the arbitrary powers exercised by the High Commissioners:

soe that allowe them what they desire, and then for every petty cause, they may fine a man to the vttermost dureinge his life, and the subiect hath noe remedy, whereas all errours comitted by the Judges of the Common Pleas or Corrigible, and theire Judgments, of what valewe soever, are reverseable in the Kings Bench, soe likewise are the Judgements of the Kings Bench reverseable by the Kinge and the Lords Spirituall and Temporall in the vpper house of Parliament, whereof the Bishopps make a great number . . .

Archbishop Abbott, who had been translated to the primacy on

[1] For a contemporary account of Cawdry's case, see G. Powell, *A Consideration of the Depriued and Silenced Ministers Arguments*, p. 42; and for a recent review of the case, R. G. Usher, op. cit., pp. 136-40.

[2] Cf. *Cotton MSS., Cleopatra*, F.1, f. 128. "The grounds of the Prohibitions to the Highe Commission and the aunswers vnto them."

Bancroft's death[1] replied. He said that these protracted dissensions did great injury to the Church, and that basically the

> onely point in difference is whether the Kinge by the Act of 1 Eliz: may giue authority to his Commissioners (whereof evermore the Archbishop of Canterburie for the tyme beinge, hath beene the first both in place and trust) to fyne and imprison in all Ecclesiasticall causes whatsoever without restriction or limitation.

With some acrimony he attacked Coke for granting prohibitions upon the Act 23 Henry VIII, c. 9, where a man is cited out of the diocese,[2] "sayinge that he did thereby strike att the roote of the Archbishopps Jurisdiction Ecclesiasticall, and indeavoured to overthrowe these Courts, which haue had continuance, and receiued allowance, for many Hundred yeares . . .". The Attorney-General replied with asperity that he thought this was "the first tyme that ever any Judges of the Realme haue beene questioned for deliuering theire opinions in matters of lawe accordinge to theire Conscience in publique and solemne Arguments sittinge vpon the Bench". The Archbishop reiterated the points made by Dr Martin, stressing the authority given to the Commissioners under the Act 1 Elizabeth, whereby they were permitted "first to exercise, vse, etc. any manner of Jurisdiction, privileges, and preheminences in any wise touching or concerninge any Spirituall or Ecclesiasticall Jurisdiction", and "secondlie. to exercise, vse, and execute all the premisses according to the tennor and effect of the Letters Pattents, any manner or any cause to the Contrary in any wise notwithstandinge". Coke replied by saying that "by the said Act of 1 Eliz: noe other Spirituall or Ecclesiasticall Jurisdiction is revived or transferred to the Kinge, but such onely as had been formerly lawfully exercised within this Realme".[3]

The Conference ended inconclusively. The vexed question of rival jurisdictions was not resolved, nor was the authority of the Court of High Commission redefined.

[1] Bancroft died in 1610.

[2] Cf. *Cotton MSS.*, *Cleopatra*, F.11, f. 467. "The Lord Cooks Arguments touching Rochesters case, upon the statute 23 Henry VIII, c. 9, that none ought to be called out of their diocese to answer before the Archbishop of Canterbury in the Court of Arches or Audience."

[3] *Harleian MSS.*, 1,299, f. 120. "A Conference of the Kinges especiall appointment held before the Lords of the Councell touchinge Prohibitions on the 23 of May 1611, where were present both of the Chiefe high commissioners and all the Judges of the Realme."

Bancroft need not be reproached for failure: "the creeping invasion of the common-law courts had advanced too far to be driven back."[1] His successors were equally unsuccessful. The problem was only solved in July 1641, when the Long Parliament arbitrarily declared the Court of High Commission an illegal institution.[2]

[1] C. Hill, op. cit., p. 131.

[2] 16 Charles I, c. 11.

10

STIPENDS AND PLURALITIES

"TO DESIRE that every parish should be furnished with a sufficient preacher, and to desire that pluralities be forthwith taken away", wrote Sir Francis Bacon, "is to desire things contrary."[1] So spoke the official apologist. The majority of benefices were insufficiently endowed (in 1585 Whitgift stated that half the benefices with cure were worth less than £10 in the Queen's Books),[2] and for this impropriations were chiefly to blame. A spokesman in the House of Commons in 1601 said that so far from pluralities being responsible for corruptions in the Church, it was poverty made the corruptions, which would be taken away if competent livings were given to every minister.[3]

The argument was plausible. The truth, however, was not so simple. The most notorious offenders were the bishops and deans. Preaching before the Convocation of Canterbury on 20 February 1593 Lancelot Andrewes made outspoken reference to the mercenary greed of the episcopate: "You take heed verily to the enriching of your sons and daughters. You are so careful of your heirs that you forget your successors." He spoke of duties neglected, nepotism, plurality, non-residence. He singled out the bishops for special reprobation: not only did they connive at these things, they themselves were the chief culprits.[4] It is depressing to discover that Andrewes was himself guilty of the very evils he condemned. His worthless brother was appointed, through his personal intervention, Fellow of Pembroke, Vicar of Chigwell, prebendary of Ely and of Winchester, and Master of Jesus College, Cambridge.

---

[1] *Certaine Considerations Touching the better pacification and Edification of the Church of England*, 1604.
[2] J. Strype, *Whitgift*, Vol. I, p. 371.   [3] S. D'Ewes, *Journals*, p. 640.
[4] *Concio ad Clerum in Synodo Provinciali Cantuariensis Provincial ad D. Pavili, Printed, Oposcula Quaedam Posthuma* (ed. J. Bliss), pp. 29 ff.

The Puritans knew that in attacking pluralities, they were also attacking prelacy, for the most notorious examples of pluralism and non-residence were the bishops themselves. John Preston, the Duke of Buckingham's Puritan chaplain, proposed the confiscation of dean and chapter land to subsidize preachers,[1] and, at a later date, a committee of the House of Commons listed as a grievance "the great revenues of deans and chapters, the little use of them, and the great inconvenience that came by them".[2] Thus theological prejudice lent support to the claims of those who desired to abolish pluralities and increase stipends.

Pluralism was an admitted evil: how was the evil to be solved? The Puritans insisted that the problem was capable of easy resolution: let the prelates resign their pluralities and forswear their proud estate. The hierarchy adopted a very different view: they declared that the problem was insoluble apart from the augmentation of clerical stipends. They pointed out that lay rectors (or impropriations) were directly responsible for the impoverishment of many livings. The situation was one of great difficulty and complexity, aggravated by steadily rising prices.

There were churches which were "appropriate" and others which were "impropriate". An "appropriate" church was one annexed to an ecclesiastical person or corporation, such as a bishop or a religious house. With the dissolution of the monasteries, a considerable number of appropriations fell to the Crown, and these, in turn, were often granted to laymen. When an "appropriate" church passed into lay hands it became "impropriate". It was the exploitation and extortion of many of the lay impropriators which moved Bancroft to indignant protest. Whitgift estimated that the annual loss to the Church through impropriations amounted to £100,000 per annum:[3] in these circumstances it is not surprising that many parishes were unable to provide "a competent maintenance". By impropriations, "above any other one means", W. Crawshawe said, "an ignorant and unteaching ministry is set over a great part of our people, which is the source and fountain of all other evils in our church".[4] Crawshawe saw impropriations as the root of all evil: "it is both unseasonable and

---

[1] T. Ball, *The Life of the renowned Dr Preston*, 1628.
[2] S. D'Ewes, op. cit., p. 339.   [3] J. Strype, op. cit., Vol. I, p. 535.
[4] W. Crawshawe, *The Sermon Preached at the Crosse*, Feb. xiiij. 1607.

unreasonable", he said, "to complain of the ignorant, or to crave a learned ministry",[1] without the redress of this inherited evil. The gentry, however, were no more willing to surrender their impropriated tithes under James than they were to restore secularized monastic lands under Mary. There were further complications. When a vicarage was endowed with *portio congrua* of the income of a benefice, the appropriator or rector (or, when in lay hands, the impropriator or lay rector) took the great tithes, and the vicar the small tithes. Tithes were divided in two ways: first into predial, mixed and personal; secondly into great and small. Predial tithes were due from "that which doth arise and grow by reason and virtue of the grounds as fruits and increase of beasts, fishes and fowls". Personal tithes were due from "lawful and honest commodity obtained and procured by art, science and the manual occupation of some person". They were to be paid at the rate of "one-tenth of clear gains, after expenses had been deducted". Mixed tithes came largely from the produce of livestock —milk, cheese, wool. Great tithes, those which went to the rector, normally comprehended tithes due from corn, hay, and wood; small tithes, due by endowment or prescription to the vicar where there was one, arose from all other predial tithes, plus mixed and personal tithes.[2]

The Puritans contended that clerical stipends should be increased from the appropriations held by bishops and deans and chapters. Bancroft, on the other hand, maintained that the problem was more complex: it was due, not only to appropriations and impropriations (on which latter subject the Puritans were strangely silent), but also to the commutation of tithes. Bancroft held that only the most unimpeachable proof of the existence of *modus decimandi* should be recognized, and that when it was not forthcoming, tithing in kind should be restored.

The real value of benefices had greatly declined. They were assessed, for the payment of first fruits and tenths, on the values recorded in the *Valor Ecclesiasticus* of 1535. Since that time the value of the tithe had risen with the price of corn, but the increase in tithes had not been commensurate with the general increase in

---

[1] W. Crawshawe, *Epistle to Sir John Savile.*

[2] (Anon.) *Tithes and oblations According to the Lawes established in the Church of England*, 1595.

prices.[1] Frequently a composition or *modus decimandi* had been adopted in place of the payment in kind of tithes, and especially of small tithes, but such customary payments had often become a mere fraction of their market value. The great tithe was derived from corn, and the laying down of arable land in grass had resulted in further impoverishment.

There is a wealth of evidence to illustrate the consequences of these economic and social changes. John Hockley, "a yeoman of the age of threescore ten yeares or thereabouts", gave evidence about the decline in the real value of the vicarage of Alton in the diocese of Winchester:

> Many olde inclosures in Alton and Halliborne by estimacion an hundred acres of grownde or there abowts are now imployed to the sowing of Oade [i.e., woad], whereof the parson hath the tythes uppon which inclosures were before tyme kept kyne all the sommer and sheepe all the winter, And the tythes and proffitts of the same so used then weare the Vicars which nowe he looseth, And further . . . the tythes oblacions Revencions and proffitts of Bensted and Kingsley Chappells beelonging to the said Vicarage are at much less yearlie value at this present tyme then it was certified into the Court of Exchequer in Anno xxvi Henrici regis octavi, by reason, first that verye many olde seuerall grownds in Bensted and Kingesley which before time allwayes had remayned in the nature of Cowe-pastures are now of late yeares converted into Tyllage, and some onelye for arable grownds, Whereof the parsonage impropriate hath the Tythes And so the vicarage Tythes of Bensted and Kingesley are diminished yearlie as much as the tythe Calfe and Whittage of twoe hundred kyne and upwards may ammount unto.[2]

Another witness testified:

> the Common Feildes . . . by measure one thowsand fowre hundred Acres of ground or there abowts are of late yeares inclosed and converted into Tyllage and sowing of Oade whereof the parsonage impropriate hathe the tythes, uppon which Downes and Commons Feildes he saythe heertofore haue usuallie bin kepte two thousand two hundred sheepe, and then the Tythe wooll yearlie gathered and

---

[1] For details of the actual increase in the diocese of Lincoln, cf. *Valuatio Beneficiorum* the actual net value (*communibus annis deductis deducendis*) 1604, and *Valor Ecclesiasticus*, 1535. On an average incomes had rather more than doubled between 1535 and 1603. This increase, however, was not proportionate to the far greater rise in prices.

[2] *Plea Roll*, E.337, 13, no. 59.

comming to the Vicar ... was ordinarilie twentie sixe todds which now he thincketh not in any one yeare to be aboue fowre or five todds. Also he saythe that the Vicar hath not nowe so many tithe lambs.[1]

The situation had been aggravated by other economic changes:

Alton hathe in tyme paste bin a Towne of great clothing, and very welthie and populous and the Easter-booke and privie Tythes of the same were known to bee of verie good Commoditie and proffitt, but nowe since the trade of clothing hath decayde, both the number of Communicants ... is much lessened, and the Inhabitants for the moste parte are become verye poore.[2]

But besides these economic factors, which tended to impoverish livings and diminish stipends, there was also much shameless exploitation, and simony was rife. Many patrons required payments in money, or pensions, or favourable leases, or surrenders of glebe, or easy compositions, or remission of tithes and dues, before appointing men to benefices.

During the previous reign the Queen had set an evil example, keeping the see of Oxford vacant for forty-one years, Ely for nineteen, and Bristol for fourteen. In 1596 the Bishop of Durham used the ugly word simony to describe the royal demands that he should grant certain leases as a condition of being promoted to the Archbishopric of York. The Bishop's protest was dismissed by Sir Robert Cecil and Sir John Wolley as "very absurd": "These niceties will hardly be admitted where such a prince vouchsafes to entreat."[3] It is not surprising that the nobility and other ranks of society were quick to follow the royal example. In 1595 an Oxford Fellow was moved to preach a sermon on the text: "My house shall be called the house of prayer, but ye have made it a den of thieves", with pointed reference to "the noblemen of this realm especially, and in sort also to the bishops."[4] Some years previously Whitgift referred to the fact that "patrons nowadays search not the universities for a most fit pastor, but they post up and down the country for a most gainful chapman. He that hath the biggest purse to pay largely, not he that hath the best gift to

---

[1] Ibid.   [2] Ibid.

[3] Ed. J. Raine, *The Correspondence of Dr Matthew Hutton* (Surtees Soc., 1834), pp. 93-4. Quoted, C. Hill, op. cit., p. 17.

[4] J. Strype, op. cit., Vol. II, p. 319.

preach learnedly, is presented."[1] Convocation complained that it was hard "to wring a full presentation from a lay patron".[2]

A Supplication of Some of the Students of the Universitie of Cambridge to the parliament, contained a bitter indictment of the existing system:

> if we ourselves use some means to have entrance into a charge, the covetousness of patrons is such, and so insatiable for the most part, that there is no waie by them but by simonie, perjurie, and afterwards almost plaine beggerie. So that, in this great want of labourers we stand idle in the market place all the day, for almost no man regardeth us to use our labours, so lamentable is the state of this our Church at this time.[3]

The bishops pointed out that five-sixths of all the benefices in the country were in the patronage of the laity. Not only were the laity in a position to exploit and impoverish the clergy, they were also in a position to appoint the minister of their choice.[4] The bishops complained that the Church had not the same control as formerly over those who were admitted to livings.[5] On 24 January 1604/5, Cranborne, speaking of the "Common knowne highe wayes for obtaining church livings and cures", said that the Puritans would never "fill up a long register, if the ministers Recusants were not backed, flattered, and encouraged by Gentlemen or Countries, that make a good reason for it, if private ends may justifie such formes, as keep oyle still in the Lampe".[6]

Complaints about pluralities and non-residence were rife during the reign of Elizabeth. As early as 1575 there was a Puritan plan to take the appropriations that were in the hands of

---

[1] Ibid., Vol. I, p. 368.   [2] Ibid., Vol. I, p. 500.

[3] Transcribed, A. Peel, *Seconde Parte of a Register*, Vol. II, p. 186.

[4] "The rights of patrons were defended both by those who wished to nominate Puritan ministers for the benefit of parishioners' souls, and by those who wished to exploit patronage for the benefit of their own pockets. God and Mammon were once again in alliance." C. Hill, op. cit., p. 71.

[5] *Additional MSS.*, 28,571, f. 191. The extent of lay patronage may be judged from an examination of a Puritan survey like "The Lamentable Estate of the Ministry in Staffordshire" (*Morrice MSS.*, published in the *English Historical Review*, Vol. xxvi, p. 341), and an episcopal survey like the *Liber Cleri* of the Lincoln diocese in 1603 (printed in C. W. Foster, *The State of the Church* p. 337): both indicate how extensive were lay impropriations.

[6] *S. P. Dom., Jas. I*, 14, Vol. XII. Viscount Cranborne to Sir Thomas Lake.

the bishops and to use them to supplement the stipends of the
poorer clergy. Whitgift informed the Bishop of Ely that

> considering how that every man sought to pull from the Church;
> how also the temporalty did envy any prosperity in the Clergy; and
> what enemies the most part of them were to the cathedral churches,
> bishoprics, colleges, and other places of learning; and that the most
> part of these consisted of impropriations; he feared, lest under the
> pretence of reforming the one, the dissolution and utter undoing of
> all the other would be sought for.[1]

The Puritan laymen were ready to relieve the ecclesiastical
hierarchy of their appropriations, but they were not prepared to
endanger their own impropriations in any way. There were fresh
Bills against non-residence and pluralities in the Parliament of
1584, to which the Archbishop replied that pluralities "could
not bee taken away, without discouraging the best sorte of
Ministers, and taking away the reward of learning".[2] There were
certain insuperable practical difficulties:

> of eight thousand eight hundred and odd benefices, with cure,
> there are not six hundred sufficient for learned men; neither (if they
> were all sufficient) could there be found the third part of learned men
> to supplie that number.

Concerning the Bill to take away appropriations Whitgift said:

> It is a most dangerous bill for the beste sorte of the Clergie, and for
> such as beste deserve to be rewarded; and will assuredlie discomfort
> and discourage them, and incourage the worste sorte, and such as
> are factious and contentious in the Churche; whose end is, to seek the
> spoyle and overthrowe of the same.[3]

Convocation urged weighty reasons against the Bill,

> shewing her Majesty the bad consequences thereof, even to the
> ruin of the good estate of the Church of England, and her poor
> Clergy, and the lessening of her own prerogative and revenues.[4]

Convocation declared the Bill

> depriveth men of the livings they do lawfully possess; beggareth
> the Clergy; bringeth in a base unlearned ministry; taketh away all

---

[1] J. Strype, op. cit., Vol. I, p. 145.   [2] J. Strype, ibid., Vol. I, p. 360.
[3] Ibid., Vol. I, pp. 380–1.   [4] Ibid., Vol. I, p. 383.

hope of a succession in learning; will breed great discontentment in the younger sort of students. . . .[1]

The Queen, ever jealous of her prerogative, forbade Parliament to legislate in matters concerning the Church, which matters must be left to the bishops and Convocation.

In 1558 Parliament again essayed to deal with ecclesiastical affairs and several Bills were introduced dealing with pluralities and non-residence. Convocation, in an address to the Queen, pointed out that "the pretence being made, the maintenance and increase of a learned ministry, when it is throughly weighed, decayeth learning, spoileth their livings . . . and is the means to bring in confusion and barbarism".[2]

In the *Advice tending to Reformation,* circulated preparatory to the Hampton Court Conference, the Puritans made diligent efforts to obtain independent statistics concerning the state of clerical learning.[3] It was in these circumstances that the Archbishop sent out letters to the bishops on 12 May 1603 desiring them to collect statistics of beneficed men and preachers.[4] In obedience to this direction, the Bishop of Lincoln wrote to the archdeacons of the diocese:

I haue lately receaued lettres . . . requiring mee to sende . . . with convenient speede the names of all the preachers within my dioces with their degrees and places of residence, and therefore I pray you presently to make diligent inquirie of all such ministers . . . as well in places exempt as not exempte . . . and so wishinge you not to fayle in the premisses, as you haue often done heretofore, for that

---

[1] Ibid., Vol. I, p. 384.
[2] Ibid., Vol. I, p. 534.
[3] *Additional MSS.*, 28,571, f. 199; 38,492, f. 62. For some of the Puritan statistics, see:

(*a*) "Certaine briefe observations truly gathered . . . comprehending the whole estate of Lancashire clergy, rightly divided into its six proper hundrethes, with the severall parishes contained in the same." 1604, *MSS. of Lord Kenyon,* no. 14. H.M.C., Fourteenth Report, Appendix, Part IV, p. 7.

(*b*) "Essex, A short Survey of the Mynisterie." *Additional MSS.*, 38,493, f. 83. Cf. "A View of the State of the Clergie in the County of Essex." 1604.

(*c*) "The Lamentable Estate of the Ministry in Staffordshire." Feb. 1603/4. *Morrice MSS.* (E.N.R., Vol. XXVI, p. 341.)

(*d*) "The State of the Severall Parishes within the Deanery of Doncaster in the Diocese of Yorke in this yeare 1603." 19 March 1603/4. *Morrice MSS.,* G., f. 546 b.

[4] See above, p. 61.

there dependeth some matter of consequence herevpon, with my heartye commendacions I committ you to god.[1]

On 29 June Whitgift sent a further communication on the same subject to the bishops, enclosing certain articles which he desired them to answer "secretely and particulerly". He directed the Bishop of Lincoln to admonish his archdeacons and commissaries:

yf they thought of it how much these things which I desire to bee informed in may concerne their seuerall jurisdiccions, they would both haue more care particulerly to informe themselues by all meanes of euery such matter required of theim and spedely to returne Certificate of theim.

There were certain matters about which the Archbishop desired "to bee aduertized of withall convenient spede":

The particuler name of euery double beneficed man in your dioces, who holdeth two benefices with cure, his degree of schoole and qualificacion, the names of the seuerall benefices with cure which hee so holdeth, how many miles distante ech of the benefices which hee holdeth is from the other, and as nere as you can the valuacion of theim in the Kings books. How many seuerall Impropriacions there bee within your dioces, whether they bee endowed with vicaredges, or served by curates, if with vicaredges, what euery of these seuerall vicaredges is valued at so nere as you can informe your self, in the Kings books. If by curates what the ordinarie stipend is that the proprietarie payeth for the maineteynance of the Curate. The name of euery parsonage within your dioces which is endowed with a vicaredge, what the said parsonage is valued at in the Kings books, and what the vicaredge is valued at. Who is patrone of eyery seuerall benefice within your dioces, so nere as your records of Institutions can geue direccion.[2]

On 10 July 1603 the King sent a letter to the vice-chancellors of the Universities, informing them that he had resolved to devote the royal impropriations to the betterment of ecclesiastical livings, "for no one thing is greater impediment, than want of competent living to maintain learned men in such places . . . where the ordinary benefit of the vicarages doth not suffice, and the parsonages are impropriate, and in laymens hands". He expressed the hope that the Universities would follow his royal example, as

[1] *Brown Book*, ff. 185, 185 d. Printed, C. W. Foster, op. cit., p. 246.
[2] *Brown Book*, f. 187. Lincoln Diocesan Registry.

divers of them had impropriations, which could be used "to prouide for ... such liuings, as shall fall within their power to dispose".[1] Whitgift, who knew how dependent the Universities were upon these royal impropriations, prayed the King to stay the order "untill opportunitie may serue mee to attend uppon you and to make knowen the Inconveniences that may ensue ... for sure I am, that it will bee in tyme the ouerthrowe of the Universities and of Learning".[2]

On 29 October 1603, the King wrote to both the Archbishops requiring a fresh census of all the clergy:

> We require you for our satisfaction to cause ye seuerall Bishopps of your province within some convenient time to make certificate to you in writing what nomber of churches with cure of soules be vnder each of them, what ye Incumbents are, of what degree in schoole, and how qualified to preache, and what ye seuerall liuings of each church is worth, which certificate you shall send vnto vs, or bringe them your selfe.

He was determined to assist in the increment of ecclesiastical incomes:

> yet shall we be content in all such vicarages, whereof ye tythes be impropriate and are in our hand, if they be not able to mainteyne a sufficient minister, to add some reliefe to them by some convenient meanes, and as we may and as vpon deliberation of our Councell shalbe thought fitt.[3]

In accordance with this communication, Whitgift wrote to the bishops, demanding the speedy return of certificates, and these were in due course forwarded to the King.[4]

At the final session of the Hampton Court Conference on 18 January 1603/4 it was resolved that the principle be adopted: "as few double beneficed men and pluralities as may be, where they have double benefices to maintaine preaching, and to have their livings neare one to the other."[5]

The Archbishop wrote to the bishops on 28 January 1603/4 informing them that there were some defects in the previous certificates which had been supplied and sent to him, and that a

---

[1] *Additional MSS.*, 1,856, f. 11.   [2] *S.P. Dom., Jas. I*, 14, Vol. XI, no. 39.
[3] *Egerton MSS.*, 2,877, f. 172 b; *Harleian MSS.*, 677, f. 107.
[4] *Harleian MSS.*, 280, ff. 157 ff.
[5] *S.P. Dom., Jas. I*, 14, Vol. VI, no. 25.

more accurate and precise survey of all ecclesiastical benefices and incomes was required:

> It is his maiesties pleasure to knowe the qualities and degrees of the present Incumbents in euerie seuerall parishe with in your dioces whether they be preachers, or able to cathecise or otherwise learned or vnlearned of good and euill conversacion and reporte, what is the value of theire seuerall livings and howe in your opinion they may be augmented where they are not competent, you shall doe well in this busines to vse the helpe of your learned Clergie, whom you can best trust and whoe knowe the state of their neighbour ministers, so shall it be better and sooner performed and with lesse troble to your self and to the rest of your Cleargie.

In connection with impropriations, the Archbishop particularly demanded the name of the proprietary, and in this business the bishops were to proceed

> effectuallie and speedely all excuses sett aparte. For I assure you that his maiestie doth looke for a speedie returne of these mattres and thinketh it to be a verie great negligence for anie Bishopp not to know the state and Condicion of his Cleargie within his dioces.[1]

The Bishop of Lincoln, writing from King's College, Cambridge, forwarded copies of this letter to his archdeacons and other officials on 10 February 1603/4, and informed them that

> there is with great speed anewe Survay in some points to be made of the Ministers and their livings with in my Dioces, And that my opinion is desired howe their wantes may be supplied if their maintenance be not competent.

He explained that

> the valuacion which is required is to be rated (as I take it) accordinge as the Benefice is worthe *communibus annis* to be letten, and not as it is valued in the Kings Books, for that hath bene done allreadie and Myght with more ease haue bene taken out of the office of the first fruitts, if that were intended, nether is that valuacion equall for that some Benefices are over valued and some farre vnder.[2]

In a postscript the Bishop added,

> it weare not amisse if anie glebe, or Tithes, bee with holden from anie Incumbent to inquire dilligentellie the estate thereof, and to examane those Ministers who want a competent maintenance, in the

---

[1] *Brown Book*, ff. 202 d, 203. Lincoln Diocesan Registry.   [2] Ibid., f. 199.

proportion of their worthiness, and charge, howe that may be
supplied, and to make certificate of both accordinglie.[1]

Fragmentary returns are extant only for the archdeaconry of
Stow and the deanery of Walshcroft in the diocese of Lincoln,[2]
but these returns give valuable particulars about clerical marriage,
the behaviour and hospitality of the clergy; about degrees, plurality, residence, and preaching; and about patrons, impropriations,
and the leasing of benefices. The most interesting returns concern
the method of augmenting ecclesiastical incomes: in the deanery
of Walshcroft the "leading clergymen" advised:

> Wee thinke the best means to encrease the liveings is that payement
> of all manner of tithes in proper kinde and all prescripcions and
> customs of paienge lesse then the tenth and all exempcions from
> payemente of tithes to be taken away and that the parishioners be
> compelled to answer vppon theire oathes for theire privie tithes and
> all ancient commons and glibe restored to the church, the frequent
> vse of prohibicions taken awaie or abridged and allowance owte of
> impropriacions to poore incumbents.

Again, the returns from the deaneries of Aslackhoe, Corringham,
Lawres, and Manlake, in the Archdeaconry of Stow, show that
the clergy were convinced that "the meanes to increase the
liveings which are not competent is by deducion from the impropriacions and payement of all tithes to be made in proper kinde".
In one deanery it was suggested that "twoe contiguous small
Rectories are not two seuerall competent livings but might be
helped by vnitinge them in one, they are but one towne and both
the churches stand in one churchyard", and at another, "2 contiguous small Rectories in the deanrie are not two seuerall
competent liveings, but mighte be helped by vnittinge them in
one as they are now possessed by one incumbent".

Prior to the meeting of Parliament on 19 March 1603/4 the
bishops met under the presidency of Bancroft (Whitgift having
died on 29 February), to consider how a competent maintenance
might be provided for a preaching minister in every parish. The
statistics which had been obtained from the previous survey were
made the basis for various constructive suggestions. As regards

[1] Ibid., f. 200 d.
[2] *Valuatio Beneficiorum*, 1603/4, Lincoln Diocesan Registry. Printed, C. W.
Foster, op. cit., p. 355.

"the nomber of ministers and the places where they remayne",
it was reported that

> there are as many ministers as there are parishes in England besides
> those which remayne in both Vniversityes: which serve cures vnder
> other Ministers: and which remayne in divers noble men and gentle
> mens houses: the nomber whereof is greate, but the certainty of it as
> yett is not knowne.

Concerning their qualifications and provision, it was reported that

> very many are Preachers, and many are no Preachers. Many beinge
> no Preachers have ecclesiastical livings, and many that are Preachers
> doe want, viz: such as remayne in the Vniversities serve cures vnder
> other ministers, and remayne in noble and gentle mens houses.

The following remedies were proposed:

> For those parishes where the Incumbents are no Preachers, these
> may be remedies:
>   1. that asmuche as may be allotted out of the livinge towards the
> mayntenance of a Preacher as the Incumbent may any wayes spare
> so as he may live, and the rest is to be supplyed by the parishe.
>   2. that after the said Incumbents deathe who is no preacher: it
> may not be lawfull for any Bishop to admitt any vnto it who is not a
> Preacher.
>   3. Whereas partly vppon necessitie and partly through oversight
> divers insufficient persons have heretofore ben made ministers: it
> woulde now be provided for, that when any insufficient minister
> either for his learninge or conversation shoulde be presented to a
> Benefice: it may be lawfull for the Bishop to reject him and vppon
> any Quare impedit brought the Bishops certificate thereof to the
> Judges may suffice without further triall by any course att the
> temporall lawe.

The really difficult problem, however, was the augmentation of
ecclesiastical incomes:

> how every parishe maye afforde a competent mayntenance for a
> Preacher, for that once effected, in short tyme there woulde be
> able ministers almost for every parishe in England.

The following suggestions were recorded:

>   1. There are many Personages and Vicaredges in England nowe
> scarce able to finde a Reader who woulde afforde a competent

livinge for a Preacher if it might be provided for by Acte of Parliament that all Vicars and persons havinge benefices with cure of soules might have the tithes payd vnto them in kinde accordinge to the auncient ecclesiasticall constitutions of the churche, notwithstandinge any custome privilege or composition to the contrary.

2. If some small vicaredges and personages notwithstandinge the said payments of tithes in kinde, shoulde not be able to mainteyne a Preacher: then one or two of the small benefices next adioyninge and lying fitt for that purpose might be conioyned into one.

3. In Cities and Towneshipps where there are no praediall tithes att all or litle, and where in auncient tymes the Priests livinge did rise vppon offeringes, oblations, and personall or privie tithes which nowe are vtterly decayed: it would be provided by acte of Parliament that tithes in suche places should be payed accordinge to the house rents of the inhabitants as it is in London. And that where in suche cities or Towneshipps there are diverse litle parishes which are not able euery one of them to maynteyne a Preacher notwithstandinge they had tithes payed vnto them accordinge to the manner of London: there two or three might likewise be ioyned together to make one parishe.

4. Where the Personages are impropriate, there the Cure is discharged either by a Vicar or by a Stipendary. The Vicars are mainteyend with such tithes only as were allotted vnto them by composition when the Personages were first impropriate which in many places notwithstandinge they should be payed in kinde, would not be able to mainteyne a Preacher. But where the Cure is served by a Stipendiary his mayntenance is commonly much worse. In which cases and where there can be no convenient vnyon of divers livinges in one as aforesaid, these wants would be supplied and remedied if the Bishop of the diocesse might have authoritie by acte of Parliament to allott to every such vicar or stipendiary congruam portionem out of the impropriations and all other personages that have vicaredges indowed.

The bishops were aware that one of the major problems was that of lay patronage:

If all the Benefices with cure in England were divided in 6 parts 5 of them and more are of laymens patronages whereby many of the saide Benefices are made vnable through the patrones greediness to mainteyne a Preacher in any honest sorte. for remedy whereof there would be a more severe statute made against symonye.[1]

---

[1] *Additional MSS.*, 28,571, f. 191. Printed, R. G. Usher, *The Reconstruction of the English Church*, Vol. II, p. 331.

The first Parliament of James I met on 19 March 1603/4, and the following month consideration was given to ecclesiastical affairs. The Commons drew up a series of Articles or Heads to be handled in Conference with the Lords, among which Articles some were devoted to the abuses of non-residency and pluralities. It was moved

> that from henceforth noe dispensation or tolleration shall bee allowed to any to haue or retaine twoe or more Benefices with Cure of Sowles or to bee non-resident; and that suche as nowe haue double benefices or bee non-resident shall giue sufficient allowance yearely to maintaine a Preacher in their absence. And that for this purpose the incombent shalbee allotted to make his residency in one of his Personages to th' intent that in the other Church a certen and constant minister maye bee maintained and kept.

Further, it was added,

> yt is thought meete where the lyuinge of the Vicar or Curat is vnder xxL. by the yeare that for the better maintenance of the Vicar or Curate (beinge a Preacher) there may be some increase made of his lyuinge as shalbe thought conuenient.[1]

At the Conference between the Lords and the Commons, the latter proposed "An Act for planting a learned Ministry", and also "A Bill against pluralities".[2] On 20 June the Commons prepared an Apology, in which they stressed the need for a "learned, religious, and godly ministry". For the maintenance of such a ministry the Commons declared that they would have been prepared to grant "no small contributions" if they had "found that correspondency from others which was expected".[3] They wisely refrained from specifying the sources from which it was proposed the "contributions" should be made. When the bishops sponsored a Bill "for a convenient portion to be assigned out of every Impropriation for the maintenance of a preaching minister", it was rejected by the Commons on its first reading.

James was perturbed by the temper of the Commons and by these further attacks on the evils of pluralism and non-residency. The King admonished the Archbishop to write to the bishops. Bancroft accordingly wrote to each one:

---

[1] *Journals of the H. of C.*, Vol. I, pp. 199–200.   [2] See above, pp. 250–1.
[3] Printed, G. W. Prothero, *Select Statutes*, p. 286.

I would your Lordship had been presente, and heard his Maiesty discourse thereof, and what griefe he conceiueth, that men whome he so much endeavoreth to mainteine and supporte, should so greatly forgett them selues, and neglect his Maiesties most Princelie and religious desire, there beinge no one thinge in the worlde which he more wisheth from his harte, then that his people should be instructed in the feare of God, and that they who are possessed of diuers livings accordinge to their former deserts, and for the countenancinge of their degrees (hauinge many enimies that repine and barke at such their preferments) should discharge their duties with all faythfulnesse, to the comforte of their owne consciences, and the preventinge of all iust exceptions.

The King was greatly exercised and concerned:

his remembrance of the late Session of Parliamente, and his desire to haue all calumniators prevented in the next, which ensueth, doe make his Maiestie exceedinge earnest in theis poyntes: And therefore his further commaundment is, that you shall not onely informe your selfe . . . but likewise write unto me in the meane tyme, to be imparted to his Maiestie, concerninge the trueth of the saide information, which hath begotten and brought forthe theis his most princely cogitations and directions.

The King required detailed statistics about the names and places of pluralists:

His Maiesty hath commaunded me to procure, with all conuenient speede, a true and exact information of the names of all such persons, as do holde at this presente two or more ecclesiasticall preferments, whether they be with Cure or without Cure . . . sende unto me, as soone as possibly you can, the seuerall names of euerie one within your diocesse, who is so preferred, togeither with the names of the benefices, prebends, dignities, and donatives whereof they are possessed: Your Lordship shall fynde some that haue but one liuinge in your diocesse, who hath notwithstandinge a seconde livinge in an other diocesse: and thereof I desire you also to certifie me, with the name of livinge where he is: I wishe this order to be obserued. First, set downe your Deane with the names of all his seuerall preferments, the diocesses where they lye, and the distance of myles betwixt such benefices, as he holdeth with cure: and so in order downewards, your Archdeacons, your Doctors of Divinitie; your bachelors of Divinitie, your Masters and bachelors of Arts . . . with their seuerall liuings, if they haue aboue one of anie nature whatsoeuer (beinge ecclesiasticall preferments) with their names and distances, as is before mentioned.

Information was also required concerninge the competence of curates and deputies:

> his Majestie is informed, that such as haue divers ecclesiastical liuings, are verie negligent, not onelie in forbearinge them selues to preache at anie of them, or at least in preachinge verie seldome, but likewise in supplyinge their owne absence with verie insufficient Curates, either no Preachers at all, or men very meanly qualified.

Bancroft earnestly hoped that the King would also proceed to curb the rapacity and greed of the impropriators:

> And thus hopeing that when we of the Clergie are refined, there will be some course taken for such as haue all the best ecclesiasticall lyueings in the Land, named impropriations, and yett make noe conscience in sufferinge them to be served with very simple Curats, god knoweth such as will be content in effecte to serve the same (as the disdainefull speeche of many runneth) for tenne groates a yeare, and a Canvas dublett: I committ your Lordship . . . to God.[1]

Bancroft was fully alive to the realities of the situation. He pleaded strenuously for a restoration of the full value of tithes, preferably by a renewal of payment in kind, or alternatively, by a new commutation based on prevailing prices. Between 1500 and 1640 the cost of living rose by some 650 per cent. Wherever tithes were commuted, the tithepayer gained substantially at the expense of the parson.[2] Bancroft proposed that a new and more realistic commutation should be negotiated. Bancroft insisted that, in the case of *modus decimandi*, its validity must be legally established: otherwise tithing in kind restored.[3] There was protracted discussion over what constituted a valid *modus decimandi* in law. The ecclesiastical judges insisted that something reasonably equivalent in value to the actual tenth commuted should be assured to the vicar, and quoted common law to show that if the commutation reduced the income, then the vicar had the right to reinstate by legal process the original tithes in kind. The common lawyers

---

[1] Bancroft's *Register*, f. 131 b. 30 April 1605. Printed, D. Wilkins, *Concilia*, Vol. IV, p. 413.

[2] C. Hill, summarizing the conclusions of Miss D. M. Barratt's D.Phil. Thesis: *The Condition of the Parochial Clergy from the Reformation to 1660 with special reference to the Dioceses of Oxford, Worcester and Gloucester*, says: "In most parishes there was *some* commutation. . . . Tithes on wheat were never commuted." Op. cit. p. 95.

[3] *Tanner MSS.*, 280, ff. 342–417.

challenged this contention. The question was "whether vpon a suite commenced in the spirituall Courte for tithes in specie, and a prescription or custome *de modo decimandi* pleaded, a prohibition maye be brought in the temporall Courtes? or Whether the spirituall Court may not trie that yssue and soe sentence the intire Cause."[1] The common lawyers declared that the legal *modus* was whatever had been substituted in the past by mutual consent for the actual tenth: "*Modus Decimandi* is either when land or a yearelie pension or some of money or other profitt belong to the Parson Vicar etc. by Composition or Custome in satisfaction of Tithes in kind." If any question touching *modus* arose, it was a matter of civil rather than spiritual cognizance: "Where there is a *Modus Decimandi* we are of opinion that the Parson Vicar etc suing for tithes in kinde: and thereby seeking to infringe the Custome of *Modus Decimandi* claymed by the parishioner, that is, Custome, ought to be tried by the Common Lawe, and not in the ecclesiastical Court."[2]

The Archbishop found himself confronted by formidable opponents. With the common lawyers there was a lengthy controversy about "whether if Tithes in kind, be not deuided and sett foorth, an action may be brought in any of the King's Courts at Westminster by the parties greeued for treble damages, grounded vpon the Statute of the 2. Ed. 6. cap. 13".[3] Bancroft claimed that if tithes in kind were not forthcoming, the clergy might sue for the "recouerye of the treble value in the spirituall courte",[4] but the common lawyers rejoined that the Statute only permitted the recovery of treble value in connection with predial tithes, and not in the case of personal tithes.[5]

The common lawyers claimed that even in the case of the

---

[1] *Rawlinson MSS.*, B.157, f. 1; B.202, f. 165 b; C.731, f. 63; *Tanner MSS.*, 120, f. 72.

[2] *Lansdowne MSS.*, 161, f. 253; 421, f. 183; *Cotton MSS., Cleopatra*, F.1, f. 191; *Harleian MSS.*, 1,299, f. 56; 7,161, f. 111 b; *Additional MSS.*, 25,270, f. 4; *Rawlinson MSS.*, c.731, f. 73; *Tanner MSS.*, 120, f. 90; 280, f. 432.

[3] The Statute declared that "noe person shall carry away any prediall Tithes ... before he hath iustly devided or sett forth for the Tithe thereof, the Tenth part of the same vnder the paine or forfeiture of treble value of the Tithes so taken or carried away ...". *Lansdowne MSS.*, 161, f. 258.

[4] *Rawlinson MSS.*, 157, f. 12.

[5] *Lansdowne MSS.*, 161, f. 258; *Cotton MSS., Cleopatra*, F.1, f. 173; *Harleian MSS.*, 1,299, f. 143.

"treble value of prediall Tithes not sett out or devided according to the said Statute, the partie greeved ought to sue in the Kings Courts, and cannot sue for it in any ecclesiastical court".

In the meantime, Parliament continued to initiate Bills concerned with the establishment of a godly and resident ministry, and the abuses of pluralities and non-residence. On 9 March 1606/7, Bills were read three times in the Commons, and then forwarded to the Lords with a note especially commending the Bills, because "the Abuse sought to be redressed by those Bills was a great Scandal to the Church, and the greatest Hindrance to the instruction of Gods people".[1] None of these Bills became law; the Bill about non-residency was stopped by order of the King.[2]

In the session which began on 9 February 1609/10, two separate Bills were brought into the House of Commons, and proceeded with, against pluralities and non-residence; and a committee of grievances was appointed, which collected materials and made reports to the House. A Bill on pluralities was sent to the Lords, to which Bancroft desired to add a rider dealing with the augmentation of ecclesiastical incomes. He wished the abolition of pluralities to be conditional on the provision of an adequate stipend for each single benefice. Bancroft sent a communication to James on the whole subject, informing him that the Bill against pluralities was the same which had been rejected in Parliament for forty years. The ostensible object of the Bill was in itself entirely commendable: there was "a fair overture of an earnest desire to make every parsonage and vicarage in England a competent living for a learned preacher", but Bancroft feared that there were other and less desirable objects latent in it. He suspected that the Commons were simply proposing a redistribution of ecclesiastical incomes: diminishing the funds of the cathedrals and of the bishops by as much as they increased those of the parish clergy. The result would be

> rather to deprive them all indeed of sufficient living, than to make the lesser benefices able to maintain men so qualified, as now it is with such earnestness desired. But God's will be done; we that are bishops will do our best (as heretofore we have to our powers

[1] *Journals of the H. of C.*, Vol. I, p. 350.
[2] Ibid., Vol. I, p. 384.

endeavoured) for the increasing of a learned ministry; but we may
never yield to any course that shall procure apparently their utter
overthrowe.

While the Bill forbade any clergyman to receive tithes from two
benefices, it nevertheless permitted laymen to retain the income
from any number of impropriations: "so as for mine own part,
I hold it a very unequal and scandalous project . . . considering
to whom, by God's ordinance, tithes ought to be paid." Bancroft
earnestly besought the King to stop the Bill, and all other measures

> against the clergy by the lower house of parliament, as hoping, now
> or never, to obtain that which divers of them for many years had
> aimed at, and that your Majesty, for the gaining of your own ends
> towards your supply and support, may be inclined to give more way
> unto them therein, than, I judge, may stand . . . all is one: reason or
> no reason, it forceth not; it is importunity and opportunity, that is
> relied upon; and we must again endure a new brunt to no purpose
> except your Majesty shall be pleased to prevent it: and I think it
> very necessary you should do so.[1]

Bancroft and his colleagues were themselves busily engaged in
submitting to the House of Lords some far-reaching "Projects for
the bettering of Ministers livings".[2] The proposal was "that all
prediall tithes of Benefices with Cure" should "be payd in kinde
hereafter", and "that personal tithes" should "be urged upon
oath being confessed to be due by law". The Archbishop aimed
at recovering those tithes which had been secularized at the
Reformation, and, where possible, at securing a renewal of
payment in kind.

> That as oblations are due by Law to parsons and vicars, that have
> Cure of soules; they may accordingly be paid unto them, as hereto-
> fore hath bin accustomed: viz, at marriage, Burialls, and upon
> solemn feast dayes; as Christmas day, Easter day, Whit Sonday,
> All hallow-day, and at times of receauing the holy Communion.
> That all Abbey lands now exempted may pay tithes in kinde to
> the parsons and vicars in whose parishes they lye.
> That all lands altered within these 60 years past from tillage, may
> pay tithes according to the value they formerly payd.

[1] Quoted, D. Dalrymple, *Memorials and Letters*, Vol. I, p. 18.
[2] *S.P. Dom., Jas. I*, 14, Vol. LVI, no. 57; *Harleian MSS.*, 828, f. 30. Quoted
J. Collier, *Ecclesiastical History*, Vol. VII, p. 352.

That all parkes and warrens made within these 60 years last past, may pay tythes, viz: according to their former value, when they were in tillage, or according to some reasonable rate by the Acre. That parke disparked within these 60 years may pay tythes in kind.

That the occupiers of lande of such parishes, that haue ben within these 60 years past utterly depopulated, and doe now pay no tithes at all, may hereafter pay all their tithes in kind, to your next poore parsons adioyning.

Where the population had decreased, Bancroft proposed "that smale Benefices nowe adioyning" should "be so united, as they may be holden by one man"; and where migration had taken place, he proposed "that Ministery in Cities and Townes incorporate, and other greate townes" should "have their tithes according to the Rente of howses after the rate of London", and "that the landlord of such houses in every Citie Incorporate and greate Townes" should "be chargeable with such paymente to their Ministers, and not their under tenants". Bancroft was anxious that the clergy should have their legal and ancient rights recognized:

that parsons and vicars may haue right and freedome of Commin with the rest of the parishioners; that the auncient Ecclesiastical Constitution in England for paying of tithe lambes, and wooll may be renued and established . . .; that parsons and vicars may have tithe wood duely payd unto them, according to the Constitution of John Stratford Archbishop of Canterbury; that all pensions may be hereafter discharged which are not payd to Ecclesiastical persons . . .; that an order may be taken for the setting of glebe lande, which are by strong hand deteyned from divers parsons and vicars . . . and that it may be prouided, that no patron or lord of any Mannor in any parish may hereafter haue the glebe land in farme.

He recognized the prevalence of simony, and desired

that all lay-patrons when they present any Minister to an Ecclesiastical Living, may take the like oath against Symonie that Ministers doe; or else that they may forfeit their patronage for ever to the king, when it shalbe prooued that they haue committed Symonie, upon any such presentation;

and "that it may be held Symonie to sell aduousons aswell as Presentations; or that all Aduousons to be made hereafter may be utterly voyd". Bancroft insisted that tithes were due on "oade,

Hopps, Rootes, Coales, and other Mineralls, and likewise of Lyme-Kins, and brick-kilns ", together with tithes from "lands that haue ben . . . wonne from the sea or otherwise dreyned and recovered".

The greatest evil of all, tending to the diminution of ecclesiastical incomes, was the existence of a vast number of impropriations. The impropriator or lay rector took the great tithes of a benefice, with the result that the incumbents of many vicarages were reduced to desperate and squalid poverty. Bancroft made a bold and revolutionary suggestion: "That a Subsidie may be graunted for the redeeming of Impropriations, and that the same redeemed may be of that Bishops patronage in whose diocese they lye." As an alternative interim solution, he proposed:

> that if the last motion may not now be enterteyned, then there may be free passage given to the Law yet in force (as it is supposed) : That all Impropriations may be declared voyd and become presentations, which have no endowments for vicars.

In this connection, he further recommended:

> That where there are Vicarages endowed which doe belong to Impropriations, but yet are no competent livinge for a sufficient Minister, Bishops may haue authoritie in their diocese, where such vicarages are, to allott some further portions for their better maintenance out of the sayd Impropriations.
>
> That some Order may be sett downe for the repayring of Chancells of Churches Impropriate, which are everywhere in wonderfull decay.

Twenty-eight "projects" were proposed, all of which were designed to effect some improvement in the matter of ecclesiastical stipends. A further series of alternative schemes was also proposed. The question is whether these proposals are the work of Bancroft or the work of Salisbury. There is a break in the manuscript at this point, and a marginal heading, "The L: S:". The proposals presumably had the general support of Bancroft and are, like the "projects", designed to redress abuses and to remove anomalies. Among the alternative proposals was the following:

> a second means of raising sufficient maintenance may be done, by severing unto divers Churches such Vicarages and parsonages as are united into one: As for example, at Bampton in the County of Oxford there are three perpetuall Vicars, Canonically instituted

and inducted to serve the Cure in that parochial Church: Every
one of the said vicars having maintenance sufficient, according to
one of the values aforesaid.

Other instances were also cited.

Now then it seemeth there being 8 or 9 ministers every of them
enioying competency of maintenance appointed to serve these
3 Cures, that 6 of these livings, as they shall happen to fall voyd,
might serve 6 other parochial churches being neere adioyning and
wanting maintenance.

In cases where tithes became payable on new goods or products,
the suggestion was made that these tithes should be paid direct
to the vicars:

That all Noualia arising within any parish wherein there is a perpetuall vicar endowed, whether the same Noualia be of hopps, oade,
yron, myne, coales, turfe, peate, etc. Shall from henceforth onely be
payable to the vicars of the same parochial church, and not to any
owner, farmor, or proprietary of the Impropriations.

In times past it had been customary for those who owned gardens
to pay a penny in lieu of tithes—a very inadequate commutation—
but it was now proposed

that from henceforth out of all gardens, and garden plotte be paid
unto the said parsons and vicars, not onely the said penny, but also
the tenth of all hoppes, beanes, wheate, rye, barly, roote, roses,
applies, cherries, strawberries, hartichokes and such like.

Again:

Where it is pretended in many places that by custome there is not
any tithe milke to be paid by him, who hath not had seaven Calfes
at the least: by which meanes, some that may keepe seaven or eight
kyne will never keepe aboue six, that from henceforth this custome
as an unreasonable custome be annulled; And that the tith milk of
all kine be paid in specie, as by the Ecclesiastical Law it is due, and
that alwayes either to the parson of the Church not appropriate, or
to the vicar of the same Church appropriate.

And again:

Whereas much fraud is dayly used among the meaner sort of people
about the payment of their tith wool, lambe, calfes, etc. by reason of
taking grounde and keeping cattell in divers parishes, and of remov-

ing them out of one parish into another, at, or immediately before the sale, and shering their sheepe, whereupon much trouble and wrangling for small matters often ensued: I leave it to be considered, whether it were not meete, that their tith of wooll, lambe, calfe, should entirely be paid to the minister of that parochial church wherein the same sheepe and cattell for the greatest part of the yeare be feeding. And if they happen to be feeding within two parishes alike, that then the said tithes be paid yearly to that minister only within whose parish the owner shall inhabite. Provided, that the minister to whom such entire tithes shalbe paid, or to whom the said ought to be paid, be aunswerable to the Minister of the other church for such part of these tithes as for the feeding of the same sheepe and cattell within his parish proportionately shalbe due.

Tithes should again be paid by the royal parks "out of which tithes and other Ecclesiastical Commodities are due, and out of which also tithes in times past have been paid". Some maintenance, out of the "Imperiall grounde" should be allowed "unto the Ministers within whose parishes where the same parkes are situate", so that

the same Ministers from henceforth might enioy a competent allowance of some patronage within the said parks for the keeping of a certain number of kyne or other Cattell towards the provision of their houses and keeping hospitality.

To prevent the alienation of Church property or the surrender of traditional rights, it was proposed

that it may not be lawful for any Minister instituted to any benefice with Cure, to demise the Mansion house, glebe land, or any part of the tithes thereof directly or indirectly, mediatly or immediately to the patron, or to his use.

The final proposal concerned the surrender of impropriations for their original and proper purpose:

That it may be lawful for any person holding any impropriations or tithes of the king in capite, or knights'-service, to give the same impropriations and tithes or any parte thereof to the use of a learned and able preaching Minister to be placed within the same parish.

The problem of augmenting ecclesiastical incomes was complicated by the existence of vested interests. At the Reformation much ecclesiastical property had been secularized. Even Queen

Mary had found herself unable to restore to the Church monastic lands and other alienated property. The beneficiaries of these changes were strongly entrenched in the House of Commons. They were implacably opposed to any solution based upon the abolition of lay impropriations, or the restoration of tithes in kind. Religious reasons were added to financial: it was this same class which was most sympathetic to the Puritan cause. Any acceptance of Bancroft's schemes would strengthen that ministry which accepted the ceremonies and persecuted the Puritans. The solutions proposed by Bancroft and his colleagues were therefore rejected.

Nevertheless the Commons continued to inveigh against the evils of pluralism and non-residence, while rejecting the only practical proposals for their redress. In an Apology presented to the King on 7 July 1610 the Commons renewed their complaints. They rejected the bishops' attempts at self-justification: they

> frame excuse of the smalenes of some livinges and pretend the maintenance of learninge: yet we finde by experience that they couplinge manie of greatest livinges doe for the most parte leaue the least meanlye furnished and the best as ill served, and supplyed with the preachers as the meanest . . . the non-residents (neglectinge theire pastorall charges) doe leaue the people in apparante daunger to be seduced.

Consequently, the Commons desired that

> yt might therefore please your most excellent Maiestie for remedie of those evills in the Church, to provide that dispensacions of pluralitie of benefices with cure of soule may be prohibited, and that tolleracion of non Residencie maye be restrayned, so that true Religion bee better vphelde and the people more instructed in devine and Civill duties.[1]

In a summary reply to the grievances on 10 July 1610 James declared that he had ever had a great detestation of the "Covetous and ymmoderate heaping of many Benefices togither especially when the neglecte of the Cures is ioyned therewith", but that reform was impossible

> vntill some further provision be made that the Benefices of this Realme might be made Competent Livinges for godlye Ministers

---

[1] *S.P. Dom., Jas. I*, 14, Vol. LIII, no. 123; *Cotton MSS., Titus*, F.LV, f. 134 ff.

and Learned Preachers, and that with some difference in proporcion answerable to the guiftes and meritts.

The King promised that he would

> lay a streight Charge vpon the Bishoppes vnder the paine of our displeasure that such Ministers as either now haue, or herafter shall haue, two Benefices with Cure, shall Carefully observe the 41 and 47 Constitutions Confirmed by vs Anno 1603—Wherby it is provided, that every such person, as hath two Benefices shall (when he doth not reside) mainteyne a Preacher lawfully allowed, that is able sufficientlye to teache and instructe the people in his absence.[1]

A final considered reply to the grievances of the Commons was made on 23 July at the prorogation of Parliament, and on 27 July Bancroft, in pursuance of the royal directions, sent out letters to all the bishops.[2] The Archbishop explained that his letter was due to "the grievances exhibited unto his Maiestie by the lower howse of Parliament", which had resulted in the King laying a great burden upon him, which he was "not otherwise able to beare, but by the assistance of . . . the Bisshopps".

> These are, therefore in dischardge of myne owne dutie, very hartely to praye and requier your Lordshipp, that you forthwith informe your selfe how many ministers haue twoe benefices within your diocesse, and whether every one of them hath a preacheinge minister to supply his absence where he doth not reside himself, accordinge to the xli and xlvii Constitutions: And if herein you finde any wante, sende presently for the parties, and Chardge them by vertue of the saide Cannons, and in his Maiesties name, as they will avoyde his displeasure, that without any delaye they supplye that defecte. Perhapps some may give your Lordship froward answeares, and either refuse or delaye to give you satisfaction therein: which if they doe, I requier you, in his Maiesties name, to suspende them for theire Contempte, and to certefie me thereof presently, that I may give order to staie all inhibitions in that Case. If any suche person keepe the benefice in his owne handes, whereuppon he doeth not reside, then I would haue you to sequester the fruits of it, and to allowe out of them a reasonable portion for a Curate that is a preacher. If a Pluralist, haueing one benefice in your Lordships

---

[1] *Journals of the H. of L.*, Vol. II, p. 658; *S.P. Dom.*, *Jas. I*, 14, Vol. LVI, no. 39.
[2] Bancroft's *Register*, f. 173a. 27 July 1610. *Wharton MSS.*, no. 595, p. 126. Lambeth Palace Library. *The Brown Book*, 1580–1618, ff. 221 b. Lincoln Diocesan Office. Printed, E. Cardwell, *Documentary Annals*, Vol. II, p. 120; D. Wilkins, *Concilia*, Vol. IV, p. 440.

dioces, be resident in another, then you are to call him by processe;
if he be a delinquent herein, I hartely desier your Lordship to use
your beste diligence in this matter: to the ende that notice thereof
may be had throughout your diocesse before the next Session of
Parliament; and faile not to write unto me before that tyme what
you haue done therein, and uppon any wilfulnes shewed to your
Lordship, or other impediment, whereby you canne nott prevaile
with some partie, lett me presently be informed of his name, and I
will sende for him my self.[1]

Bancroft asked for "the names and degrees of all those that haue
twoe benefices within your diocesse, or but one in your diocesse
and another in another diocesse". In accordance with the canons,
the Archbishop informed the bishops that it was

his Maiesties streighte chardge, that your requier all your Prebendaries to be resident uppon their benefices, and there to preache
every Sonday . . . and takeinge the Course before mentioned, write
unto me the names of such as shall refuse to obeye you herein.

In connection with pluralities Bancroft wrote:

It beinge more then notorious, that many parsons and vicars, and
especially such as haue twoe benefices, doe suffer theire howses to
runne into decaye, where they doe not reside them selves: it is his
Maiesties pleasure, that you do take present care in that behalfe, by
appoynting all your under officers to looke uppon presentments
already made of such defects, and otherwise, by all wayes and meanes
to informe your selfe, and thereuppon to call the parties offendinge

---

[1] The Archbishop's admonition was not without effect. The Bishop of
Lincoln immediately took action against a flagrant case of non-residence at
Eton. Writing to Sir Henry Savil, Provost of King's College, Eton, the Bishop
said: "In one thing I am not well satisfied, and the lesse, because the clamor
is re-echoed of your Schoole-master his Non-residence (I forbeare to add the
Epithites which other annex thereto). . . . Is it not a sinne against God and a
scandall to the world, that the charge of Christs sheepe, in two seuerall flocks,
should bee neglected, and only for a little accrument of profitt to one man?
Will it not prooue an occasion of check both to you and mee (his Maiesty
openly in Parliament, and now againe very lately and freshly by Cammaund-
ment from the Arch-Bishop, hauing inioyned vs to call men to their local and
personal Residence vpon their Benefices) that wee shall suffer such an example
in Eton Schoole? . . . I wish the man as well as you; his good quallities I
esteeme and loue; but . . . his Churches haue neede of him; send him to his
charge: his vertues for example, his sufficiency for learning, can not bee too
great nor too good for Gods People."
In a subsequent letter, the Bishop said that he thought the schoolmaster
"tooke the wisest course by his voluntary Resignation". *Tenison MSS.*, no. 663,
ff. 13, 17, 23.

herein before you, and to take such order as that either they them
selves shall presently repaire their howses or else doe you sequester
theire liuinges, allottinge a fitt portion for them to live uppon and
causing the reste to be soe imployed: for besides that such neglectinge
of theire howses doth argue too much greedines, and is a greate
scandall to the beste affected in the parrish, it is very iniurious unto
theire successors.

He also mentioned the scandal occasioned by the dress and
worldly ostentation of "Chauncellors, Commissaries, Archdeacons
and officialls", who seek nothing but "theire owne profitt",
and about whom "many true complaynts and mischiefs doe
indeede thereof ensue".

There haue been many Constitutions formerly made concerninge the
apparell of ministers, but never was theire pride in that respecte so
greate as now it is, from the deane to euery Curate, nothinge beinge
lefte that waye to distinguish a Bishop from any of them: you shall
find deanes usually either in their velvate damaske or sattin cassocks,
with their silk netherstocks; nay some Archdeacons and inferior
ministers, haueing twoe Benefices are likewise for the most parte soe
attired: to omitt that theire wives, in the Coste and vanitie of theire
apparell, doe exceede asmuch and more, which is one principall
motive why there is such exclamation againest double beneficed
men, and such as beside theire twoe benefices haue some other
preferrement sine cura.

Bancroft informed the bishops that if any so attired came before
them, they were to be sternly rebuked for

these so chardgeable vanities, many of them hauing more Care, to
theire owne scorne, so to garnish themselves and theire wives, then
to furnishe their studies with such bookes as might enable them the
better to dischardge their duties, aswell for the confirmation of the
truthe, as for the refutinge of all theire opposites and aduersaries.

The Archbishop emphasized his resolution in the matter: if, at
the next session, there was no improvement and reform, he would
personally petition the King so that "so chardgeable a vanitie
should not bee still continued; whilst manie other men endure
great want": for these "by such theire braverie in apparell . . . do
procure, no manner of credyt unto them selues, but rather . . .
great envy and hartburninge againste their callinge and estates".
Bancroft concluded:

I must tell your Lordship, that I am to sende to his Maiestie, by his Commandment, a Copie of this letter, and that I keepe likewise a Coppie of it my selfe, to the ende, that both his Maiestie may know what I haue donne, and I be able to justifie my selfe for the dischardge of myne owne dutie, and so leave the blame and burthen uppon them, whoe shall, through their negligence, deserve it.

This was virtually Bancroft's last labour on behalf of the Church which he had served faithfully and well. He had been ill throughout the session of Parliament, and he was not to live to see the next. He cannot be reproached for his failure to achieve any major financial reform. The forces arrayed against him were too firmly entrenched. He failed to abolish the inequitable *mode*. He believed —and he reiterated—that ecclesiastical incomes could not be augmented without either a partial resumption of some of the impropriations and other property secularized at the Reformation, or, alternatively, by a restoration of the full payment of tithes in kind. Both these proposals were unacceptable: the House of Commons was prepared neither to restore impropriations nor to tax itself. Was there another way? There were not wanting bold voices who said that there *was* another way: let the property of "proud prelates" be usefully employed in the service of poor preachers.[1]

[1] "Bancroft had grim forebodings. He cancelled the will in which he left his library to Canterbury, because he feared that all cathedrals might be despoiled." C. Hill, op. cit., p. 49.

11

ARTICLES OF VISITATION

IT IS TIME to consider other aspects of the administrative
life of the Church, and, in particular, to note the subjects
about which Bancroft was primarily concerned as Bishop of
London and Archbishop of Canterbury. The matters of pressing
concern are sufficiently indicated by the subject matter of the
articles he compiled for his various visitations as diocesan and
metropolitan. As Bishop of London he conducted three visitations. Unfortunately the visitation articles for the primary visitation are not extant, but it is possible to examine those used for the
visitation of St Paul's Cathedral in 1598. They occupy no less
than seventy pages in manuscript form.[1] The articles are detailed
and specific, with the reiterated question: "which of them are
most negligent in their duties therein; and when were they
negligent and what be their names?"

The first section, concerning the proper and due observance of
the services of the Cathedral, makes searching inquiry whether
there be any who do not come "orderly in their gowns and
surplices, according unto the decent and laudable orders and
ordinances of the Church"? Bancroft is rightly concerned about
"their reverent behaviour and conversation of life", both in the
services at the Cathedral and outside its precincts, and pertinent
questions are asked. Even the wives of the clergy are not exempt
from the scope of this vigorous inquisition. There are pointed
questions about the "wives of the peti-canons, vicars, and other
ministers".

The replies indicate a sad state of negligent disorder: many of

[1] "Articles to be inquired in the first visitation of the Reverend Father in
God, Richard, Lord Bishop of London holden in the Chapter House of the
Cathedral Church of St Paul's in London upon Monday the three and twentieth
day of October in the year of our Lord God 1598, for the peti-canons, vicars-
choral, choristers, vergers, and all other inferior officers and ministers of the
said church touching Divine Service in the said church and the hearing of
the word of God preached there." Printed, W. P. M. Kennedy, *Elizabethan
Episcopal Administration*, Vol. III, p. 305.

the Chapter come late to service and leave before the sermon; many sit instead of kneel for the Confession; when they should stand for the Psalms, many sit and talk to each other in audible tones; and "in the upper quier, wher the communion table doth stand, there is much unreverente people walking with hattes on their heads commonlye all the servyce tyme, no man approvinge [*sic*] them for yt".[1]

The articles for Bancroft's second and third diocesan visitations in 1601 and 1604 are extant.[2] The first twenty-five articles are concerned to discover whether there is an exact and conscientious observance of the Prayer Book:

> whether is Common Prayer read by your minister in your church or chapel distinctly and reverently upon all Sundays and Holy Days, and in such order as is set forth by the laws of this realm in the Book of Common Prayer, without any kind of alteration omitting or adding anything, and at due and convenient hours?[3]

More particularly,

> doth your parson, vicar, or curate, read public prayer and administer the Sacraments ordinarily himself, using such rites and ceremonies as are prescribed in the Book of Common Prayer; as namely whether doth he kneel at the receiving of the Holy Communion; make the sign of the Cross upon the child's forehead in the administration of Baptism; baptize any without godfathers and godmothers; use the ring in marriage; and generally whether doth he in discharging of all these duties and when he readeth Common Prayer either upon Sundays, Holydays, Wednesday and Fridays wear a surplice?[4]

Again,

---

[1] W. S. Simpson, *Registrum Statutorum et Consuetudinum Ecclesiae Cathedralis Sancti Pauli Londoniensis* (1873), pp. 272–80.

[2] "Articles to be inquired of within the Diocese of London, in the Visitation of the Reverend Father in God, Richard, Bishop of London, in his Second general Visitation holden in the three and fortieth year of the reign of our most gracious sovereign Lady, Elizabeth, by the grace of God, Queen of England, etc." London 1601.

"Articles, to be enquired to vvithin the Dioces of London, in the third generall Visitation of the reuerend Father in God, Richard, Bishop of London, Holden in the yere of our Lord God 1604. In the second yeere of the raigne of our most gratious Soueraigne Lord Iames etc." London 1604. Printed, W. P. M. Kennedy, op. cit., Vol. III, p. 335; *Second Ritual Report*, Appendix E, p. 436.

[3] Article 1.   [4] Article 4.

Doth any man, being neither minister nor deacon read Common Prayer openly in your church or chapel, or administer the Sacrament of Baptism . . . or take upon him to practise any other ministerial duty in the church, that is prescribed to be executed particularly by such as are either ministers or deacons; and what is his name that so doth?[1]

The Puritan controversy is never forgotten: this is the reason for a series of questions dealing with matters of doctrine and practice:

Doth your parson, vicar, or curate administer the Holy Communion unto any communicants which do not receive the same devoutly and humbly kneeling upon their knees; or some either sitting, or standing, or walking?[2]

Doth your parson, vicar, or curate, or any other minister or preacher baptize in your parish church or chapel any infants not in the font according to the ancient custom, but in a basin, and urge the parents of the said infant to be present, in place of godfathers for their children?[3]

Hath your parson, vicar, or curate, or any other minister preached, declared or spoken anything in your parish in derogation of the Book of Common Prayer, which is set forth by the laws of this realm, dispraising, or depraving the same, or anything therein contained, or against the present estate of the ecclesiastical government, established by the same authority, or against any office, function, or part thereof, affirming the same to be unlawful?[4]

Bancroft is eager to know the identity of all recusants, whether papist or Puritan:

Whether there be in your parish any popish or sectary recusant or recusants, which for any cause whatsoever forbear to come to church to Common Prayer or to hear God's word preached, pretending it unlawful to come to our assemblies, as the church of England now standeth established by her Majesty's authority.[5]

Whether your minister and you the churchwardens or any other in the parish have in your vestries made any orders, or do use to call any parties before you for any cause to be ordered by the ecclesiastical laws, and so do use a kind of presbytery or censuring over your neighbours under pretence of your vestry meetings?[6]

---

[1] Article 8.   [2] Article 16.   [3] Article 18.
[4] Article 20.   [5] Article 48.   [6] Article 56.

There is a like concern about the dissemination of subversive literature:

> whether there by any person or persons ecclesiastical or temporal within your parish or elsewhere within the diocese who have retained and kept in their custody, or that read, sell, utter, disperse, carry or deliver to others any English books or libels, set forth either on this side or beyond the seas, by papists or others against the Queen's supremacy in causes ecclesiastical, or against true religion or catholic doctrine, or the government or discipline of the church of England now within this realm received and established by common authority; and what their names and surnames are?[1]

Other articles relate to routine ecclesiastical matters of a multifarious character.

Early in 1605 Bancroft held his first metropolitan visitation in the diocese of Bath and Wells. He issued an inhibition to the Bishop, Dean and Chapter, and the Archdeacons of Bath and Wells, according to form, during the period of the visitation.[2] To the Bishop, whom he appointed one of his commissioners, he wrote:

> After my hartie commendations I have nowe thought fitt to send out the commission for the Visitation itself, wherein I have named your Lordship the first Commissioner, findinge that some of my predecessors have done the like, albeit others have used their owne Officers and Divines and Lawyers as they thought fittest, omittinge the Bishop in that service. But for my owne parte, as I hold not fitt, that your Lordship should be left out in that Commission (my selfe beinge well presuaded of your good government and carriage in your Diocesse) soe my purpose is not to troble or charge you with further travale or expenses, then onelie to be present at the visitinge of your Cathedral Church, and such other places as your Lordship and your Chauncellor shalbe thought fitt to be called thither; for the Sessions abroad, which cannot be performed without great troble and charges especiallie as your Lordship should be attended as is fitt for your place and callinge. I have taken order and given special directions to Mr Dr James your Chauncellor, whose service and indeavours I doe at this tyme especiallie relie upon, without your Lordships further travayle, but for the deprivinge of anie minister, or for the doeinge of anie other thinge (wherein your Lordships consent is required by the Canons) as I have charged

---

[1] Article 46.   [2] Bancroft's *Register*, f. 178 a.

him to take your direction, so I presume he will not attempt anie thing herein without your advice.[1]

On the same day, 28 May 1605, Bancroft wrote to the Chancellor, Dr James, concerning matters of special importance:

Salutem in Christo. Mr Doctor James, I haue made choyse of you to be a commissioner in this my Visitation within the Diocesse of Bath and Wells, therein there be diuers things of waight to be considered, the burthen whereof I must speciallie laye upon you. For albeith I doubt not, but the rest of my Commissioners wilbe readie to ioyne you as occasion shalbe offered, yet I must looke for an accompt of these thing at your hands alone, being speciallie appoynted for the orderinge and censuringe of such misdemeanours, as shalbe presented unto you, accordinge to the tenor of my commission: And therefore, as I doe desire, that you should have care to see all the Canons and Constitutions published by his Maiesties authoritie to be carefullie and diligentlie observed; Soe in perticuler, I doe require you to see that the 43, 44, 45, 46, 47, the 59 and 74 Canons be trulie and thorowlie put in execution, all of them concerninge the increase of the preachinge of the Worde of God; the catechisinge and instructinge of the yonger sort in the principles and grounds of christian religion; the sober and discreet carriage of the ministers and preachers; and the meanes to meete with and prevent that soe much spoken against non-residence, the defects whereof you knowe have bynn often and soe violentlie complayned of in parliament. And therefore I must desire that these things which are nowe soe well ordered and settled by authoritie, maye with all diligence be put in execution, and soe I doubt not but it will give full satisfaction to all men of moderate and reasonable affections; and if you and others, whom it concerneth, will doe that herein which is fitt, I shalbe the better able to answeare for us all in Parliament, when occasion shalbe offered. Further, you know, that there hath byn manie complaints against the taking of greater fees in ecclesiastical Courts, than weare fitt, against the number of apparitors, and the offensive proceedinge of office by inferior Officers and their Deputies; all which beinge nowe ordered by speciall Constitutions, I doe require you diligentlie to enquire of the offenders against anie of them, and especiallie to foresee that noe other, or greater fees be taken by anie, of what qualitie soever, in this my visitation, then the table of your owne Diocesse will warrant; wherein if anie shalbe found contemptuous or disobedient, those I would have you to make knowen unto my selfe, that their punishments may be made examples unto

1 Bancroft's *Register*, f. 181 b.

22

others. And above the rest, I would have you to looke into peculiers and exempt jurisdictions, where manie Recusants of both sorts (as I am crediblie informed) doe remayne where manie most ungodlie and unlawfull marriages are celebrated, and where manie notorious and most lewde offenders are harbored and protected. ... Soe nothing doubtinge of your best endevour in this service, I bid you heartily farewel. From Lambeth the 28. day of May, 1605.[1]

There are striking differences, not only in number but also in content, between Bancroft's articles and those of his predecessor. Whitgift used the same articles for each successive visitation for Salisbury,[2] Canterbury, and Rochester in 1589,[3] Ely and Landaff, in 1591,[4] Exeter in 1593,[5] Ely[6] and Salisbury in 1597,[7] and St Asaph in 1600.[8] The number was twenty-two, whereas Bancroft's articles numbered seventy-six—a total not previously approximated except on the occasion of Bancroft's own visitation of London in 1601 and 1604.[9]

Many of the other articles are based on the newly licensed canons, and the question is immediately raised, in the first article, whether a copy of the said canons is available and in use:

Whether haue you in your seuerall Churches and Chappels, the booke of Constitutions, or Canons Ecclesiasticall ready to be Read by your Minister, according to his Maiesties pleasure, Published by his Highnes aucthoritie, vnder the great Seale of Englande: And whether hath your minister read the same, or any part thereof, vppon Sundayes and Holydayes in the afternoone, before divine Seruice accordingly; yea or no?[10]

Again and again reference is made to the canons as setting forth the prescribed standard of order and practice:

---

[1] Bancroft's *Register*, f. 181 b. Printed, D. Wilkins, *Concilia*, Vol. IV, p. 414.
[2] Whitgift's *Register*, Vol. I, f. 400.   [3] Ibid., Vol. I, f. 254.
[4] Ibid., Vol. I, ff. 327, 422.   [5] Ibid., Vol. II, f. 236.
[6] Ibid., Vol. III, f. 164.   [7] Ibid., Vol. III, f. 194.
[8] Ibid., Vol. III, f. 217.
[9] Bancroft's articles for London totalled seventy items.
[10] "Articles to be inquired of, in the first Metropoliticall Visitation of the most Reuerend Father: Richarde by Gods Prouidence, Archbushop of Canterbury and Primat of all Englande: in, and for, all theise Diocesses following, (viz.) Exeter, Norwich, Chichester, St Davids, Landaffe, Heriford, Worcester, Bristol, Bath and Welles, and Coventrie and Litchfielde, in the yeare of our Lorde God, 1605, and in the first yeare of his Graces Translation." London 1605. Printed, *The Second Report on Ritual*, 1868, Appendix E, p. 450.

Whether is that due Reuerence, and humble submission vsed within your Church or Chappel, in the time of diuine Seruice, as by the Eighteenth Constitution is prescribed? Whether each one in the Church or Chappell, do apply, and order himself there, in time of diuine Seruice, as by the latter part of the same Constitution is most commendably enioyned?[1]

Whether doth your Minister administer the Holy Communion so often, and at such times as that euery parishioner may receiue the same, at the least thrice in euery yeare, whereof, once at Easter as by the Booke of common prayer is appointed? And whether doth your Minister receiue the same himselfe, on euery Day that he administreth it to others, and vse the wordes of the Institution, according to the Booke, at euery time that the Bread or Wine is receiued, in such manner and forme, as by the Proviso of the one and twentieth Cannon is directed, or wherein is the facultie? And whether is warning giuen by him beforehand for the Communion, as the 22 Canon requireth?[2]

Whether hath your minister admitted any notorious Offenders, or Shimatickes, to the Communion: contrary to the Six and Twentieth, and Seauen and Twentieth Constitutions?

Whether your Minister preach vusally according to the constitutions: either in his owne cure with you, or else in some other church or chappell neere adioyning, where no preacher is? or how often hath he bin negligent in this behalfe?[3]

Is there any in your parish, that doe refuse to haue their children baptised: or themselves to receiue the Communion at the hands of your minister because he is no preacher.[4] You shall present their names. And if your Minister sithence the publishing of the said booke of Canons, hath receiued any such Persons (being not of his owne Cure) to the communion or baptised any of their children: you shall likewise present him.[5]

[1] Article 14.
[2] This article practically reproduces the whole of Canon 22. There was some precedent in Bishop Cotton's *Articles for Exeter*, 1599: "Whether all persons of convenient age do not repair unto the Church upon Sundays and Holy-days, and receive the Communion thrice yearly humbly kneeling, and not standing, nor sitting?"
[3] Article 23. Cf. Article 3 of Whitgift's *Articles for Salisbury diocese*, 1589: "whether you have had monthly sermons in your parish church at the least, or no; and whether are the Homilies read when there is no sermon?" Cf. Canons 45, 46 and 47.
[4] Cf. Canon 57. The Sacraments not to be refused at the Hands of unpreaching Ministers.
[5] Article 31. Cf. Article 49 in Bancroft's *Articles for the London diocese*, 1601:

Whether hath your Minister without license from the Archbushop, Bushop of the Diocesse or his Chancellor, solemnized mariage betwixt any parties, the banes not being three seuerall sundaies or hollidaies first publisht in time of diuine seruice, in the seuerall Churches or Chappels of their seueral abode according to the booke of Common prayer, and that also betwixt the houres of eight and twelue in the forenoone. And furthermore, whether hath your minister since the last Cannons published, solemnized any marriage betwixte anye persons beeing vnder the age of one and twenty yeares, although the banes be thrice asked, before such time as the parents haue made knowne vnto him their consent thereunto, and whether hath he married any of an other Diocesse, who are they? And by what authority, and when?[1]

Whether is there in your church or chappell one parchment Register Booke, prouided for the Christnings, Mariages and Burials, and whether is the same duely and exactly kept according to the constitutions in that behalfe prouided;[2]

Whether doth your minister vse such decencye and Comliness in his apparell, as by the 77 Constitution is inioyned?[3]

Bancroft was anxious to discover the names of those who declined to recognize the validity of the canons on one pretext or another:

Do any, of, or within your parish, affirme, or haue they affirmed that the sacred sinode of the Nation assembled by the Kings aucthority, is not the true Church of Englande by representation: or hath, or doth any of your parish affirme, that noe persons eyther of the Clergie or Layty that were not personally present in the said late sinod are subject to the Decrees thereof in causes Ecclesiastical, made and ratified by the Kings supreame aucthoritie: because they gaue not vp their Voyces vnto them, yee shall present their names.[4]

Is there any among you, that haue or do depraue the fore-said late sinod, saying or affirming that the same was a Company of such

---

"whether any do refuse to receive the Holy Communion at their own minister's hands either because he is not a preacher or because he duly observeth the order of ministration appointed by the book; and who they be that go from their own parish to receive at any other minister's hands?" Cf. Canon 28.

[1] Article 34. Cf. Articles 16–22 of Bishop Bickley's *Articles for the Chichester diocese*, 1586.

[2] Article 40. There were many precedents for this article, e.g., Whitgift's *Articles for the deanery of Shoreham in the diocese of Rochester*, no. 13.

[3] Article 44.   [4] Article 73. Cf. Canons 139 and 140.

persons as did conspire together against godly and religious professors of the Gospel, and that therefore, both they and their proceedings in that behalfe, are and ought to be dispised and contemned, or wordes to the like effect, you shall not fayle to present their names?[1]

Bancroft's chief concern, of course, was the maintenance of the Royal supremacy, and the doctrines, rites, and ceremonies of the Church of England. The articles relating to these matters are basically the same as the subject matter of the first twelve canons. There are articles directed against those who deny that the Church "established vnder the Kinges most Excellent Maiestie, [is] a true Apostolicall church, Teaching and mainteyning the doctrine of the Apostles";[2] and against those who reject the ceremonies and repudiate the episcopal government of the Church:

Is there any in your Parish, that doe impugne or speak against the Rites and Ceremonies, established in the Church of Englande, or the lawfull vse of them? . . . Are there any in your Parish, that doe impugne the gouerment of the Churche of Englande, vnder the Kings most excellent Maiestie, by Arch-bushops, Bushops, Deanes, Archdeacons, and the Rest that beare Office in the same: Affirming that the same is Ante-christian, or repugnant to the Worde of God.[3]

Is there any in your Parish, that doth impugne any of the Articles of Religion, agreed vpon in Anno 1562, and established in the Church of England?[4]

Is there any in your Parish that doth hold or frequent any Conventicles, or priuat congreagations: or any that do eyther make or mainteine any Constitutions agreed vpon, in any such priuat conventicles or assemblies?[5]

[1] Cf. Canon 141.
[2] Articles 3 and 4. Cf. Archdeacon King's *Articles for the Archdeaconry of Nottingham*, no. 7, 1599.
[3] Cf. Bishop Bancroft's *Articles for the diocese of London*, no. 20, 1601: "Whether hath your parson, vicar or curate, or any other minister preached, declared or spoken anything in your parish in derogation of the Book of Common Prayer, which is set forth by the laws of this realm, dispraising or depraving the same, or anything therein contained, or against the present estate of the ecclesiastical government, established by the same authority, or against any office, function, or part thereof, affirming the same to be unlawful?" Cf. Canons 6 and 7.
[4] Article 4. Cf. Canon 5.
[5] Cf. Archbishop Whitgift's *Articles for the deanery of Shoreham*, no. 23, 1597: "And whether there be . . . any that wilfully or obstinately doth defend or

Is the prescript form of diuine Seruice vsed by your Minister, vpon Sundayes and holydayes, according to the Booke of Common Prayer? And whether doth your Minister duely obserue all the Orders, Rites and Ceremonies, prescribed in the Booke of Common Prayer: as well in Reading publicque Prayers, the Letany: as also in administring the Sacraments, in such manner and forme as in the Booke of Common Prayer is inioyned?[1]

A number of the articles can only be understood in the context of the struggle with Puritanism. A question about godparents demands some knowledge of Puritan objections at this point:

Haue any in your owne parish bin Godfathers or Godmothers to their owne children: or whether your Minister, or any Godfathers or Godmothers haue vsed, or doe vse any other forme, answere or speach in Baptisme: then is in the Booke of common praier appointed? Or any which haue not communicated, been admitted to be Godfathers or Godmothers?[2]

A like knowledge is essential to appreciate the ecclesiastical preoccupation with the sign of the cross, the wearing of the surplice, and the practice of spiritual exercises:

Whether doth your minister vse to sign the Children with the signe of the crosse, when they haue baptised: according to the booke of Common praier? and whether he hath referred or wilfully refused, to baptise any Infant in his Parish being in danger, hauing bin duly informed of the weakenes thereof: and whether the child hath dyed in his defaulte without baptisme?[3]

Whether doth your Minister wear the Surplice, while he is saying the publike prayers, and ministering the seacraments? And if he

maintain heresies, errors, false or schismatical opinions or doctrines against the Book of Common Prayer and the Holy Scriptures and true religion now publicly established and professed; or do use any conventicles or meetings, handling or expounding of Scriptures in any private house or place: when and where they do and have so done?"

[1] Article 12. Cf. Canon 14.

[2] Article 20. Cf. Whitgift's *Articles for Shoreham*, no. 11, 1597: "Whether any person or persons be admitted to answer as godfathers or godmothers at the christening of any child except he or they have before received the Holy Communion and can say by heart the Articles of the Christian faith ...?" Cf. Canon 29.

[3] Article 21. Cf. Archdeacon King's *Articles for the archdeaconry of Nottingham*, no. 14, 1599: "whether doth your parson ... use ... the Book of Common Prayer; if not, then what other form or manner doth he or they use in the premisses, or any of them; and do not they use the ring in marriage, and crossing the child's head in Baptism?" Cf. Canon 30.

be a Graduat, Whether then doth he also were vpon his Surplyce, during the times aforesaid, such a whood as by the orders of the Uniuersity is agreeable to his degree?[1]

Whether hath your Minister taken vpon him to appoint any publique or priuate Fastes, prophecies, or exercises not approued and established by Law or publique authoritie, or hath hee attempted vppon any pretence eyther of possession or obsession, by fasting and prayer to cast out deuils yea or no?[2]

Hath your minister or any other person or persons within your parish vsed to meet in any priuat house or other place, there to consult togither, how to impeach or depraue the booke of Common prayer, or the Doctrine or Discipline of the Churche of Englande, if yea, then you shall present them all.[3]

There are articles relating to such contentious matters as residence and preaching. These matters, Bancroft said, have been "soe well ordered and settled by authoritie" in the canons[4] that they should now, "with all diligence . . . [be] put in execution".[5] The language of the articles reflects the language of the canons.

Bancroft's interrogation is nothing if not searching. Is the minister

continually resident . . . vpon his benefice: or how long time hath he been absent? And where is he Resident for the most part, and what other benefice hath he? . . . is your Minister a Preacher allowed, if yea: then by whom? if not, Whether doth he procure sermons to be preached among you once in euery month at the least, by such as are lawfully licensed?[6]

There are probing questions about curates and visiting preachers;[7] about the proper and strict observation of the services of the Church, about the catechizing of the youth,[8] and the bidding of

---

[1] Article 32. Cf. Bancroft's *Articles for the diocese of London*, no. 4, 1601. Cf. Canon 58.

[2] Article 42. Cf. Canon 72.

[3] Article 43. Cf. Whitgift's *Articles for the Salisbury diocese*, no. 19, 1589: "whether you know any that use conventicles or meetings for expounding scriptures or saying of prayers in private houses or places?" Cf. Canon 73.

[4] Canons 41–50.   [5] Bancroft's *Register*, f. 181 b.

[6] Article 24. Cf. 45 and 47.

[7] Articles 25–27. Canons 48–50, and Bishop Cotton's *Articles for the diocese of Exeter*, no. 15, 1599.

[8] Article 33. Cf. Canon 59.

"hollidaies and fasting daies, as by the booke of common praier is appointed".[1] The inquiry is relentless:

> Hath your minister or any other preacher baptised children, solemnized Marriage, churched any woman or ministred the holy communion in any priuate house or houses, otherwise then is by law allowed, yea or no? if yea, then where? whom? when and how often hath he offended in anye of the Premisses?[2]

Again

> Doth your Minister being a Preacher, endeuor and dilligently, to reclaime the popish recusants in his parish from their errors: if there be any such abidinge? and whether is he painefull in visiting the sick according to the book of Common Prayer?[3]

Another section deals with material things: books and furniture and the position of the Holy Table:

> Whether you haue prouided the booke of common prayer lately set forth by his Maiesties aucthoritie, and the booke of Homylies, and whether haue you in your church or chappell a Fonte of stone set vp in the ancient vsual place, a conuenient Table with a carpet of silk or some other decent stuffe, and a faire linnen cloth to laye thereon at the Communion time, and whether is the same table then placed in such conuenient sort within the chauncell or church, as that the minister may be best hearde in his prayer and administration, and that the greater number may communicate: And whether are the ten commaundements set vpon the east end of your church or chappell, where the people may best see and reade them and other sentences of Holy Scriptures written on walls likewise for that purpose?[4]

> Whether haue you a conuenient seate for your minister to read seruice in, together with a comely pulpit set vp in a conuenient place with a decent cloth or cushion for the same; a comely large surplice, a faire communion cup of gold, siluer, or other pure mettle, and a couer agreeable for the same with all other things and ornaments necessarie for the celebration of diuine seruice and administration of the sacraments?[5]

---

[1] Article 35. Cf. Bancroft's *Articles for the London diocese*, no. 6, 1601. Also Cf. Canon 64.
[2] Article 41. Cf. Archdeacon King's *Articles for the archdeaconry of Nottingham* no. 21. 1599. Also Cf. Canon 71.
[3] Article 37. Cf. Canons 46 and 47.
[4] Article 48. Cf. Canons 81 and 82.   [5] Article 49. Cf. Canon 83.

There are additional questions about church seats, the churchyard, the chancel, the vicarage house, and other ecclesiastical property,[1] and the usual dreary questions about incontinence and drunkenness.[2]

"Churchwardens and Swornemen" were required to answer these articles faithfully:

> You shall sweare, that all Affection, Fauour, Hatred, hope of Reward and Gaine, or feare of displeasure or malice set aside; You shall vpon due Consideration of the Articles giuen you in chardge: present all and euery such person, of, or within your parish: as hath committed any offence or fault: or made any default mentioned in theise, or any of theise Articles: or which are vehemently suspected and defamed of any such Offence: fault or default: wherein you shall deliuer vprightly, and according to truth: neither of malice, presenting any contrary to truth: nor of corrupt affection sparing to present any, and so conceale the truth: Hauing in this action God before your eyes: with an earnest Zeale to maintaine truth and to suppresse vice: so help you God, and the contents of this booke.[3]

A separate series of questions was prepared for the visitation of the cathedral church of the diocese. As metropolitan, Bancroft only used thirteen articles,[4] in contrast to the thirty-one articles he compiled for the visitation of St Paul's Cathedral in 1598.[5] There is the same appeal to the canons as the standard to which obedience must be given. Bancroft asks, for example,

> howe the xlij and xliiij Chapters of the Constitutions made the last Convocation anno M.DC.IV. and confirmed by his Majestie under the Great Seale of England, for the residencies of your Deane and other prebendaries, as well upon their Prebends, as upon their other benefices, are observed?[6]

There is a series of similar questions:

> Whether all the members of your Church, especiallie the Prebendaries and ecclesiastical persons, doe use seemlie garments and attires, as namelie all graduates there Surplice and hood for their degree of Schoole, and other inferiors there Surplice and Capp accordinge to the Cannons. . . . M.DC.IV.?[7]

---

[1] Article 50. Cf. Canon 85.
[2] Articles 51, 54, 55, 57, 58, 61, 62, 63, 65, 66, 67, 68, 70, and 76.
[3] Preface to the articles.
[4] Bancroft's *Register*, ff. 181 a, 217 b, 230 b, 251 b. Printed D. Wilkins, op. cit., Vol. IV, p. 415.
[5] Bancroft's *Visitation MSS.*, f.7.   [6] Article 3.   [7] Article 6.

Whether the Prebendaries and Preachers of your Church doe preach yearlie the full number of Sermons appointed by the Statutes and Ordinances of the said Church, and the late Constitutions ecclesiastical, in their owne persons, or by others; and who doth most usually preach them; and how often have you sermons or lectures in the weeke in the Cathedral Church, and by whom, and what be the Statutes of this church in that behalfe?[1]

Whether the prebendaries and other the preachers, of this Church, in their Sermons, doe use to praye for the Kings Maiestie, the Queens, Prince, and all his highnes issue; and doe give unto his highnes in their prayer, accordinge to the late Constitutions, his whole stile, and so doe pursue the perticulers in the said Constitution appointed for that end to be observed?[2]

Other articles relate to the reverent observance of services of the cathedral:

Whether the number of those that serve the Quire, and all other ministers of this Church, be kept full, and the Quire sufficiently furnished with able singers, and daylie service there songe according to the foundation of this church?[3]

Whether the Choristers be well ordered, and the number of them furnished, and who hath the Charge of Catechisinge and instructinge of them in the principles of Religion; and whether are they soe brought upp?[4]

There are questions about the dean and other ministers as well as about the choir: whether they are pluralists,[5] and whether they are conformable:

Whether your divine service be used, and the Sacraments administered in due tyme, and accordinge to the book of common prayer, and by singinge and note according to the Statutes of this Church?[6]

There is also a question about the fabric:

Whether the Cathedral Church be sufficientlie repayred both in the bodie Chauncell, and in all other iles, and places belonginge to the Church; by whose default it is unrepayred, and who ought to repayre it?[7]

[1] Article 7.   [2] Article 12.   [3] Article 4.
[4] Article 9.   [5] Article 2.   [6] Article 5.
[7] Article 11.

Shortly after the visitation of the Cathedral Church of Wells, the Dean and Chapter demurred at the Archbishop's appointment of Dr Barker as Canon residentiary. Bancroft replied with some asperity:

I understand you refuse or delaie to performe the order which, in the cause of residentiarishippe lately voide, committed unto me by speciall reference from his Majesty, I sett downe uppon the hearinge thereof, as most agreeable in my judgement to your statutes and to equitie and right. I wishe you yet once againe frendlie to be better advised. And least any of your companie should pretend ignorance of the saide order, I have sent a coppie thereof here inclosed, requiringe you in his Majesties name (whoe hath referred this matter to me to be determined and ordered) that you see the saide order, sett downe by mee therein, to be presentlie put in execucion and performed, or in default thereof, that everie one of you refusinge to obaie and fulfill the saide order, doe make your personall appearance before me at Lambeth, the eight daie after the receipte hereof, to answeare your contempts in that behalf. Whereof I require you not to faile, as you will answeare the contrarie at your further perill.[1]

Bancroft was elected Chancellor of the University of Oxford in 1608. He was appreciative of the high honour:

Consideringe what great Care I have to give you especiall Thankes, in that of your owne accord with one consent, and without any suite of mine, you made choise of me to be your Chancellor, I will ever acknowledge the same as an undoubted Argument of your true love and affection towards me, fully assuringe you, that as I am thereby bounden, soe I will ever to my abilitie, endeavour not only to advance the common good of the whole Universitie, but likewise the preferment and benefit of everie one of you, as fit occasion shalbe offered.

Concerning the appointment of a Vice-Chancellor, he added:

Findinge not any thinge hitherto wherein I may more pleasure you, then to use a carefull and diligent circumspection in makinge choise of him, that shalbe Vice Chancellor (upon whose government the prosperous estate of your Universitie will much depend) neither knowinge any man at this present, more meete, for many his singular virtues, learninge, judgement, gravitie, discretion and synceritie, in all his actions, to supply that place, than my very

---

[1] *The MSS. of the Dean and Chapter of Wells*, Ledger F, f. 203. 19 July 1606. H.M.C., Vol. II, p. 350.

lovinge freind Mr Dr King, Deane of Christ Church. I doe therfor appoynt him. . . .

He sought their loyal co-operation in certain important matters:

Firste and aboue all thinges I require that your ancient Statutes for the frequentinge of divine Service and Sermons and the Cate-chizing and traininge up of your youth in true Religion, be diligently observed, because the foundation and groundwork of Gods true worship and pietie being once well layd, all other your doinges and Studies will undoubtedly prosper and have happier successe. And for that (as I am crediblie informed) there is an old Statute or Decree made by yourselves in your Convocation, and confirmed by my Predecessor your former Chancellor, which to this purpose may greatlie avayle, viz. That noe private Tutor or Reader shalbe allowed for the instructinge of youth, but such as shalbe first ap-proved by the Vice Chancellor and some other Divines mentioned herein, forasmuch as that Course being held, it will easily prevent or Supplant all popish and schismaticall corruptions in Religion, which otherwise might perhaps rise up amongst you. I doe likewise seriously expect you to see the sayd Statute duly kept and observed, resolvinge within my selfe, if hereafter any neglect hereof shall happen to be found, to exact with all due severitie an account at the hands to whom it doth appertaine to have redressed it. And so beseeching Allmighty God to blesse you in all your meetinges and consultations, I commit you all by my heartie prayers to his most merciful goodnesse and protection.
    From Lambeth July 6⁰ 1608
        R. Cant.[1]

Bancroft was prepared to sanction the appointment, to collegiate posts, only of men who were loyal and conformable. Writing to Salisbury on 12 March 1609 he stated frankly that he would not deliver a letter in favour of Mr Murray for appointment as Warden, "till Mr Murray has made his mynd fully knowen . . . touching his conformitie".[2]

In 1608 Bancroft undertook a metropolitan visitation of his own Cathedral Church of Canterbury. The result was a series of Orders for observance by the Dean and Chapter.[3] First, in accordance with Canon 24, order is given

---

[1] *S.P. Dom., Jas. I*, 14, Vol. XXV, no. 8. 6 July 1608.
[2] *S.P. Dom., Jas. I*, 14, Vol. XLIV, no. 22. 12 March 1609.
[3] Bancroft's *Register*, f. 226 b.

that the Epistle and Gospel be everie Sundaye and holie daye read, accordinge to the booke of common prayer, in some convenient place neere to the Communion Table, and in coapes.

Regular preaching is enjoined:

that upon solempne feast dayes, the Sermon be made before the Communion: The moveable pulpitt beinge placed either in the presbyterye or Quire: and everie afternoone of such dayes, there be a Sermon for the Citie in the ordinarie place.[1]

The stipends of the choristers are to be augmented:

that the poore singinge men, especially such as are cunninge, diligent, and inoffensive, havinge but meane stipendes, maye have (for their better encouragment and sustinance) some more sufficient allowance appointed them at the discretion of the Deane and Chapter, and that they certifie, what they will allowe them.[2]

Choristers are to be tested by an independent judge of proved musical competence:

That Choristers be not admitted upon their maisters allowance, but that the Deane doe appoint them to be examined and approved by some others of the Quire, And that their said Master, doe not take of them a yeares wages at their first enterance.

There are matters of internal order and discipline: the Master is not

under pretence of goeinge to the Grammar or writinge schoole [to] suffer anie of his schollers to be absent in the afternoones, without the privitie and speciall licence of the Dean.[3]

The accounts of the Cathedral are to be accurately kept, and the "particuler bills of Expences" are to be written in a book, and at "the Audite, every Prebendary present, and at home, [is to] be called to the viewe of the Accompt, and the examination of the particuler bills of expences".[4] Great care is to be taken "for the preservation of all the churchwoods", and none are to be sold but by the consent of the Dean and Chapter,[5] and similarly no timber is to be felled in the said church woods, except by the consent of the Dean and Chapter.[6]

[1] Order 2.
[4] Order 9.
[2] Order 4.
[5] Order 13.
[3] Order 6.
[6] Order 15.

These varied articles and orders are sufficiently indicative of the range of subjects about which Bancroft was particularly concerned. It is, of course, a comparatively easy matter to issue injunctions; it is a more difficult task to enforce them. In this connection, Bancroft was determined to use all available means to secure their execution. It is the canons, he contends, which define the law of the Church. And it is to the canons that obedience is to be given. Bancroft was not prepared to tolerate scandals in conduct or lawlessness in practice: on the contrary, he was resolved to punish with severity those who offended and transgressed.

The *detectiones* and *comperta* provide us with a vivid insight into the effectiveness of the Church's machinery through visitation to bring hidden evils to light, and to achieve reformation and correction, and it is to an examination of this evidence that we now turn.

12

DETECTIONES AND COMPERTA

THE PURPOSE of a visitation was to discover those matters in the life of each parish which needed correction and reform so that appropriate action might be taken, either by the threat of punishment or peremptory injunction. To facilitate this task, articles were submitted to the churchwardens which they were bound on oath to answer faithfully. The resultant information was listed under the two heads of *detectiones* and *comperta*: *detectiones* being matters made known to the visitors; *comperta* being matters discovered by the visitors.

Dr Usher rejects this material. He summarily dismisses it as unworthy of serious consideration. "The great obstacle to its use", he says, "is its untrustworthiness. The figures are usually so palpably inaccurate and incorrect that they cannot be accepted as even a basis for guesswork." In these circumstances, it is not surprising to find that Dr Usher rejects "the whole of this material as worthless and misleading. From its statements", he avers, "anything at all can be proved about the condition of the Church and the clergy."[1] This judgement is over hasty. The records are, in fact, a rich mine of information. Those parishes in which Puritanism is known to have been strong are just the parishes in which we find a wide variety of presentments for nonconformity. The Visitation Books and Act Books provide precisely the kind of detailed information which we need to understand the strength of Puritanism at grassroots. But not only Puritanism: they provide us with a wealth of material illustrative of every aspect of ministerial and parochial life—a window through which we can see the sorry state of the Church. At least a visitation provided some machinery through which to discover wants and to reveal abuses, and evidence is not lacking concerning resultant remedies and reforms.

A visitation was held in the diocese of Lincoln during the latter

---

[1] *Reconstruction*, Vol. II, pp. 384–6.

part of 1604. More breaches of church order were revealed than on the occasion of any previous visitation. In the archdeaconries of Lincoln and Stow, the churchwardens of no less than one hundred and ninety-four parishes had not obtained the new Prayer Book. They were admonished to provide it.[1]

The *detectiones* indicate that the churchwardens of twenty-eight parishes in the same archdeaconries presented their minister for not wearing the surplice:[2] the *comperta* that in thirteen other parishes the churchwardens failed to present their minister for not wearing the surplice.[3] In each case the churchwardens were admonished to provide one within a fortnight, to tender it to their minister on Sunday, and to certify the Bishop's Court at Lincoln whether he had worn it or no. The churchwardens of South Witham were "to provide a decent surplis against sonday next . . . and to tender yt that day vnto their minister and to certifie";[4] at Quarrington the churchwardens were examined "weather he weare the surplis yea or noe". His reply was unsatisfactory: a note adds: "the vicar Robert Hitchcocke" presented "for not wearinge the surplis".[5] His nonconformity was short-lived: on 20 November 1604 the churchwardens forwarded a certificate "wherin appeareth that their said vicar Mr Worshipp hath worne the surplis and signeth with the crosse in baptisme".[6] At Hareby the churchwardens were "to tender it to their minister and to certifie the court at Lincoln". A marginal note records: "he weareth yt".[7] At Sibsey the churchwardens were presented "for omitting to presente their minister for not wearing the surples", but from a later entry we learn "that nowe their vicar dothe weare the surplis and observe the book of common praier".[8] At Withcall, where the churchwardens had also been presented "for omitting to present Mr Walter Allen their parson for not wearing his surplis", a certificate was forwarded that "they have nowe provided a decent surplis and that their minister weareth it".[8] At Martin by Horncastle they certified "that whereas there was a presentment mayd of the want of a decent surplisse of a bible of

---

[1] E.g., Episcopal Visitation Book. Lincoln, 1608, Vj 18, f. 3.
[2] E.g., "Horblinge gard. for omitting to presente their minister for not wearing the surplice." Episcopal Visitation Book, Lincoln, Vj 18, f. 3.
[3] Ibid., Vj 18, f. 26.   [4] Ibid., Vj 18, f. 1.   [5] Ibid., Vj 18, f. 74.
[6] Ibid., Vj 18, f. 87.   [7] Ibid., Vj 18, f. 89.   [8] Ibid., Vj 18, f. 103.

the largest volume and of the booke of Cannons ... thes things before named ar already provided".[1] The churchwardens of Dunstable forwarded a certificate to the Chancellor:

These are to certifie vnto you that Mr Richardson our minister doeth vpon saboath daies and other daies reade the booke of common prayer last published by authority in our church and conformeth himselfe vnto the reverend or visitors of the reverende father in god the Lorde bishop of Lincolne in whose presence he did weare the surplice at the visitation.[2]

The churchwardens at All Saints, Hertford, proudly reported: "we saye that all things are well and that we haue a surplece and that our menyster doth weare it dyvers tymes";[3] and a similar report was sent from Chilton: "wee ... do certify that wee haue prouided suche a Surplice as by the L: B: his order was inioyned and that our minister doth orderly weare it and that we haue satisfyed him for his charges".[4] The churchwardens at North Somercotes reported that their Vicar was now more amenable: "he weareth not the surplis anie sondaie but is willing nowe to performe that dutie in wearing yt."[5]

The churchwardens at Welton in the diocese of Lincoln were charged "for not presenting that they want a newe booke of common praier", but on 4 September 1604 they were able to certify "that they have nowe provided a newe booke of common praier".[6] At Hamby in the same diocese a like certificate was sent: "they have a booke of common praier and cannons."[7] The churchwardens at Dunston reported: "Thomas Lovering our parson of Dunston in the Countie of Bucks hath conformed himself by wearing of the surplice and obseruing the booke of Common Prayer nowe by lawe established."[8] The churchwardens of Shalstone, with pleased self-righteousness, congratulated themselves on the punctilious performance of their tedious office:

---

[1] Churchwardens' Presentments and Certificates, Lincoln. Ch.P., 1606/7, no. 9, f. 35.
[2] Ibid., f. 15. [3] Ibid., Ch.P., 1604, no. 3, f. 1117.
[4] Ibid., Ch.P., 1605, no. 8, f. 14.
[5] Episcopal Visitation Book, Lincoln, 1604, Vj 18, f. 92.
[6] Ibid., Vj 18, f. 102. [7] Ibid., Vj 18, f. 111.
[8] Churchwardens' Presentments and Certificates, Lincoln, Ch.P., 1605, no. 8, f. 13.

23

These are once againe to certify your Lordshippe that this bearer, Mr Bursey, our godly paynefull minister doeth strictly obserue the booke of Common prayer and other Ceremonies of the church according to orders sett downe by the authoritie of our gracious Kynge. Which (if at anytime) he shall omitt, your L: shall vndoubtedly heare of it, though we, or others (hereafter to succedde vs, in our troblesome office) should be silent. ffor Mr Bursey hath watchfull overseers.[1]

The Vicar of Childerditch, in the archdeaconry of Essex, had conscientious scruples about the use of the new Prayer Book: he was presented "for refusinge to read the booke of common prayer established the last parliament".[2] His obduracy was short lived: a later entry in the Act Book states that after admonition "he hathe read the booke of common prayer nowe by authoritie established".[3] Ralph Firnies, Vicar of Morston in the diocese of Norwich, was also presented because he "doeth not reade service according to the booke of common prayer".[4] John Baldwyn, Vicar of Yaxham in the same diocese, was presented because he "doethe not reade the prescribed forme of Common prayer according to the booke of common prayer but omitteth most comonly the x commandments the Epistle and gospell ... he dothe not byd holy dayes and fastinge dayes ... he dothe not church women in such sort as is prescribed but vseth a prayer of his owne devisinge";[5] William Worship, Vicar of Croft in the Lincoln diocese, was presented because "there be noe holie dayes either bidden or kepte within the said parishe neither doe anie absteine from worke vpon the said dayes neither is there anie prayers on Wednesdaies or frydaies".[6] At Radwell, in the diocese of Lincoln, it was reported that "the minister doth not say service on frydaies and saterdayes", but the explanation was simple: "noe body comes to heare him."[7] From the *detectiones* and *comperta* we learn that Thomas Cotton, Vicar of Little Laughton in the same diocese, "dothe not read the holy service neither morninge

---

[1] Ibid., f. 7.
[2] Set Book Archdeaconry, London, D/AEA, no. 23, f. 209.
[3] Ibid., f. 224.
[4] Episcopal Visitation Book, Norwich, 1606.
[5] Ibid. Unfortunately there are no folio numbers to enable more precise references to be given.
[6] Visitation Book of the Archdeaconry of Lincoln, 1608, no. 12, f. 158.
[7] Episcopal Visitation Book, Lincoln, 1607, Vj 19, f. 20 b.

nor eveninge prayer noe further then the second lesson".[1] The churchwardens of Ludborough refused to answer the articles of the Bishop of Lincoln, "beinge so many and so harde". Being threatened with excommunication, they applied themselves to the task and testified:

Art. 14. Our minister sometime omitteth some parts of the common prayer sometimes readeth prayer accordinge to the booke. . . .

Art. 15. We have prayers on the Wednesdayes and frydayes very seldome. . . .

[Art. 22. We know] not what theise articles of the convocation are and theirfore . . . we knowe our minister nor any other haue not preached against them nor Against the booke of common prayer and gouerment of the church: albeith we thinke he desireth many things therein weare reformed.

Art. 23 . . . our minister alway at the ministration of the sacrament doth vnfould the meaninge of the sacrament and declareth the vse of some of the cerimonies observing the forme and order of the booke: but alway he vseth not the signe of the crosse.[2]

Mr Hulkes, Vicar of Kempston in the same diocese, was presented because he "doth not vse the prescribed forme of common prayer neyther doth obserue the orders rights and Ceremonies Commaunded".[3] Similarly, John Lowes, Vicar of Brandiston in the diocese of Norwich, was presented because he "hath not allwayes vsed the prescribed forme of Common prayer prescribed in the boke but for the most parte since the publishing of the Cannons he hath obserued the same";[4] while John Baker, Vicar of Chattisham in the same diocese, was presented because he "doth impugne and speake against the rights and ceremonies established in the Church of England . . . doth not vse the prescribed forme of Common prayer but readeth psalmes of his owne chosinge neyther doth obserue all the rights and ceremonies prescribed in the said booke".[5]

There are numerous presentments for offences against Church discipline and breaches of Church order. In many cases the offences are simply the consequence of clerical negligence or sloth; more rarely, they testify to Puritan convictions and beliefs. At Appleby in the diocese of Lincoln "Hollie daies and

[1] Ibid., ff. 29 b, 70 b. [2] Ibid., 1604, Vj 18, ff. 106–7.
[3] Ibid. [4] Ibid. [5] Ibid.

fastinge dayes"[1] were not observed. William Wood, Vicar of Somerby in the same diocese, was presented "for ommittinge to reade the Epistle and ghospell but when he ministers the sacrament, neither dothe hee read the x commandements but when there is a communion".[2] John Cheveley, Curate of St Michael's in the city of Lincoln, did not say "prayers on sundayes and holidayes in suche due sort as the articles and Cannons doe require".[3] Frequently the Litany was not read on the appointed days.

Benjamin Alexander, Curate of Torksey in the diocese of Lincoln, was presented because "hee omitteth to read the letanie on Wednesdaies and fridaies";[4] and Henry Peacham, Rector of Leverton in the same diocese, "for not reading the letanie on Wednesdayes and fridaies nor eny service and likewise for not saieinge the praiers and Service on diuers Wednesdaies for the tyme of the visitation of Sicknkes sett downe according to his Majesties auchoritie", but shortly afterwards it was certified that "he doe hereafter reade the letany and doe service accordinge to the booke of common praier".[5] The same offence was found at Tendring in the diocese of London, where the churchwardens reported "that we haue no letanye nor prayers vpon ffrydayes or Wednesdayes and ffor that in November last we had no service nor sermon two sondayes togither nor no service vpon Michelmas daye last nor the Sonday following".[6]

There was widespread resistance to the canons enjoining the use of the surplice (as previous quotations have indicated), and it is not surprising that there were a host of presentments for failure to obey this order. On 3 October 1604 the Bishop of Lincoln cited ninety-three men to appear in the church of St Benedict to answer to articles charging them with not wearing the surplice.[7] Excuses, both cogent and specious, were offered in extenuation: Christopher Dynys, Vicar of Calceby, had aesthetic scruples: "I will not refuse to weare a Surplusse so that it be a comely or

---

1 Ibid., Vj 20, f. 110.
2 Visitation Book of the Archdeaconry of Lincoln, 1608, Vij. no. 11, f. 8.
3 Ibid., f. 55.   4 Ibid., 1607, Vj 19, f. 56 b.
5 Ibid., 1604, Vj 18, f. 53.
6 Act Book, Archdeaconry of Colchester, London D/ACA, no. 29, f. 43 b. December 1604.
7 C. W. Foster, *The State of the Church*, p. lxix.

decent one . . . yet will I not wear this yow haue bycause there is
no comlines in yt."[1] The churchwardens certified that Robert
Campbell, Curate of Owston and Newbold "weareth the surplisse
and neuer refused yt but there was not a sufficient surplesse and
therefore he did not weare yt but nowe there is a sufficient surplisse
he weareth yt".[2] John Fisher, Rector of Ingoldsby, appeared
before the Bishop of Lincoln on 3 and 13 October, 22 November,
and 12 December 1604, and was admonished. On each occasion
he declined to conform. Evidence was subsequently submitted
that "he hath not yet conformed himself nor hath anie certificate
neither will now conforme himself".[3] On 8 April 1605, however,
it was certified that he "did weare the surplesse vppon soondaye
last both at morning and euening praier, and sayth he would
haue done soe one easter daye and the holidais . . . if it had not
bene a meane one and sayth he will weare it hereafter".[4] The
question of "seemliness" caused much anxious debate. Richard
Sherwood, Rector of Thurlaston, refused to wear a surplice
until he had examined it. "Two surplisses haue beene tendered
him," the exasperated churchwardens said, "which he reteyneth
at his howse, sayeing he tooke them thither to see what condicion
they were of."[5] Thomas Cade, Vicar of Ilston, could not shelter
behind the convenient question of seemliness: the churchwardens
certified that they had "a good and sufficient surples". The plain
truth was that the Vicar had "neuer worne the surples in their
parishe churche since hee came thither".[6] William Cade of
Lillingstone Dayrell invoked the principle of desuetude: the
churchwardens said he "hath made some doubt of wearinge the
surplice bie reason of the discontinuance thereof amongst vs these
fiue and twenty yeares".[7] Thomas Wooll, Vicar of Boston, con-
temptuously spurned the popish rag: he was presented "for not
wearinge the surplice . . . and sithence the visitacion notice hath
bene given to the courte that the surplis hath bene tendred him
and he in scorne thereof (as yt seemeth) maketh it his cushion to

---

[1] Episcopal Visitation Book, Lincoln, 1604, Vj 18, f. 115.
[2] Ibid. Cf. Episcopal Court Book, 1602–9, Cj 14, f. 67 d.
[3] Episcopal Visitation Book, Lincoln, 1604, Cj 14, f. 76 d.
[4] Miscellaneous Correspondence, Lincoln, 1605, Ch.P., no. 8, f. 38.
[5] Episcopal Court Book, Lincoln, 1604, Cj 14, f. 167.
[6] Episcopal Visitation Book, Lincoln, 1607, Vj 19, f. 74 b.
[7] Miscellaneous Correspondence, Lincoln, Ch.P., 1605, no. 6, f. 70.

sitt on".[1] John Browne, Rector of Loughborough, in a letter to
the Chancellor of the Lincoln diocese, Dr Belley, explained:

> we have obserued the forme prescribed by lawe in prayer and
> administration of sacraments except kneeling at the communion,
> the vse of the crosse in baptisme and wearing of the surplice, which
> we take libertye in . . . for that they were disused by my predecessor
> all her majestye raigne and the people had conceaved some dislike
> of them.[2]

Other parishes claimed a like freedom from the letter of the law:
at St Martin's, Colchester, in the diocese of London, "the
minister doeth not weare the surplice for that there ys not anye
nor hath bene these xx years".[3] At Earls Colne in the same
diocese, the churchwardens also admitted that they did not
possess "a surplesse".[4] The churchwardens of Little Leighs in the
same diocese presented their Vicar, William Buckley who was
later deprived, "for not wearinge the surplice at anie tyme".[5]
The churchwardens of Farlish in the Chichester diocese confessed
that they lacked "a fayer surplice with sleeves".[6] At Catfield in
the diocese of Norwich the churchwardens reported that their
Vicar, Gabriel Gloude, "neuer weareth the surples neither in
reding devine service nor administeringe the sacraments".[7]
William Wood, Vicar of Somerby in the Lincoln diocese, was
presented on two counts: "for wearing a wrought nightcap"
contrary to Canon 74 (surely a sad case of nocturnal frivolity),
and for "not wearinge his surplice according to the Canons".[8]
The churchwardens were frequently enjoined "to prouide a
decent surplis against sondaie next . . . and to tender yt that day
to their minister and to certifie".[9] The churchwardens of Padwell

---

[1] Episcopal Visitation Book, Lincoln, 1605, Cj 14, f. 46.
[2] Miscellaneous Correspondence, Lincoln, Ch.P., 1605, no. 6, f. 77.
[3] Act Book, Archdeaconry of Colchester, London D/ACA, no. 31, f. 191,
Jan. 1607/8.
[4] Ibid., London D/ACA, no. 27, f. 166, March 1604/5.
[5] Ibid., D/ACA, no. 24, f. 142. March 1607/8.
[6] Act Book, Chichester, C.18, f. 42 b. September 1605.
[7] Episcopal Visitation Book, Norwich. Cf. Witton, Morston, Stiffkey,
Yaxham, Kempston and Brandiston in the Norwich diocese.
[8] Archdeacon's Visitation Book, Lincoln, 1608, Vij 11, f. 8.
[9] Scrafield, Holbeach, South Witham, in the Lincoln diocese. Episcopal
Visitation Book, Lincoln, 1604, Vj 18, ff. 26, 41, 63, etc.

in the Lincoln diocese dissociated themselves from the sin of their minister: "they had a surplice, but what the minister hath done with it they knowe not."[1] Some churchwardens connived at the offence of their minister and were found out: the churchwardens of Bolingbroke, Hagworthingham, Fulletby, Dunstry, Edlington and South Ormsby in the diocese of Lincoln all failed (according to the evidence of the *comperta*)[2] to present their parsons for not wearing the surplice.

Again and again explicit reference is made to the canons as the standard to which practice must conform. Richard Forman, Vicar of West Halton in the diocese of Lincoln, was culpable "for not wearing the surplice according to the Canon".[3] Sir Nicholas Larke of Waddingworth in the same diocese was likewise guilty: "he doth not weare the surples euery sabaoth daie according to the Canons."[4] The churchwardens of Burlingham in the Norwich diocese presented their minister: "he doeth not conforme himself in such ornaments as is mentioned in the Constitution 74"[5]—the canon which prescribes "comely and scholar like apparel" for clergymen, "provided that it be not cut or pinkt", and forbids their going about in public in "doublet and hose, without coats and cassocks", and particularly the enormity of "light coloured stockings". The canon expresses the hope "that in time newfangleness in apparel in some factious persons will die of itself". Tantalizingly enough, evidence is lacking concerning the particular indiscretions of which Sir Nicholas Larke was guilty. The Vicar of Witton also offended in this respect: "he hath not conformed himselfe in his apparel as by the 74 Constitution he is inioyned."[6] The same canon states that "all ecclesiastical persons ... shall usually wear in their journeys cloaks with sleeves, commonly called priests' cloaks". Israell Tailour, Vicar of Thornton in the diocese of Lincoln, was without this serviceable and useful garment: "hee hath not a cloke according to the Canon."[7] The churchwardens of Gainsborough certified: "The minister is in all thinges conformable,

---

[1] Ibid., 1607, Vj 19, f. 20 b.   [2] Ibid., 1604, Vj 18, ff. 68, 69, 70, 85, etc.
[3] Ibid., 1608, Vj 20, f. 51 d.
[4] Ibid., 1607, Vj 19, ff. 41 b. 128 b. *Comperta.*
[5] Episcopal Visitation Book, Norwich, 1606.
[6] Ibid., Cf. also the Vicars of Lyng, Bastwick, and Yaxham for the same.
[7] Episcopal Visitation Book, Lincoln, 1607, Vj 19, ff. 48 b, 167.

savinge they never saw him weare a cornerd cap or ride in a cloke with sleeues."[1] Mr Sankey, Vicar of Brandiston in the diocese of Norwich, was apparently a dissolute gambler: he was presented "for not conformeinge himself as in the 75 Constitution he is inioyned".[2] Clergymen are forbidden by this canon from resorting to "taverns or alehouses", and are warned against spending their time "idly by day or by night, playing at dice, cards, or tables, or any other unlawful games". The churchwardens had other grounds for complaint: Mr Sankey "is not resident vppon his parsonage howse but dwelleth on his temporall howse", and "doeth not Catachise the yeouth euery sondaye". John Baldwyn, Vicar of Yaxham in the same diocese, was presented because "he hath not redd all the cannons published";[3] and John Love of Martham in the diocese of Norwich because "he haue not vsed that due reuerence and humble submission in time of divine service as he is inioyned by the xviij Constitution".[4] Mr Hilton, Vicar of Lingwood in the same diocese, was another of whom the churchwardens reported: "he hath not conformed himself accordinge to the late constitutions."[5] The churchwardens of Holy Trinity, Colchester, in the diocese of London, in January 1607/8, admitted that they did not possess "the book of Cannons",[6] and six months later they confessed the same again.[7] Benjamin Alexander, Curate of Torksey in the Lincoln diocese, was presented "for not reading the Cannons the 12 months last past".[8] The churchwardens of Ludborough in the same diocese confessed that they did not know "what theise articles of the convocation are".[9] Hugh Blythe, Vicar of Appleby in the diocese of Lincoln, was censured "for not wearing his hoode and Tippett according to the Cannon".[10] Richard Kent and his wife, parishioners of St Benedict's, city of Lincoln, were presented "for not receaueing the sacrament of Easter last and for not comeing to church according to the Canon".[11] The Curate of St Paul's, Lincoln, was accused of not saying "prayers on Sundayes and

---

[1] *Liber Cleri*, Lincoln, 1607, f. 52.
[2] Episcopal Visitation Book, Norwich, 1606.
[3] Ibid.   [4] Ibid.   [5] Ibid.
[6] Act Book, Archdeaconry of Colchester, London D/ACA 31, f. 18 b.
[7] Ibid., f. 96 b. June, 1608.
[8] Episcopal Visitation Book, Lincoln, 1607, Vj 19, f. 56 b.
[9] Ibid., 1604, Vj 18, ff. 106–7.   [10] Ibid., 1608, Vj 20, f. 110.
[11] Archdeacon's Visitation Book, Lincoln, 1608, Vij 11, f. 54 d.

holidayes in suche due sort as the articles and Canons doe require".[1] Simon Bradstreet of Horbling in the diocese of Lincoln, was charged "for yt he [doth not] wholly conforme himselfe vnto the orders and ceremonies set downe and appointed in the booke of common praier . . . the Canons latelie established and in crosse and surplice".[2]

The traditional subjects of Puritan protest, from the earliest days of the Elizabethan settlement of religion, concerned the wearing of the surplice and the use of the sign of the cross in baptism. There are numerous presentments for the omission of the sign of the cross, many of those who were presented for failing to wear the surplice also being presented for a like omission of the sign of the cross. Hugh Tuke, Rector of Silk Willoughby in the diocese of Lincoln, for example, was presented at the episcopal visitation in 1604[3] and 1607[4] for "not wearing the surples and not signinge with the crosse". The churchwardens of Stubton in the Lincoln diocese were charged with "omitting to present their minister who signeth not with the signe of the crosse in baptisme".[5] Robert Hargrave, Curate of Stanton under Bardon in the diocese of Lincoln, achieved a local reputation for his militant nonconformity. Certain people who had brought their children from neighbouring parishes "to be christened . . . without the signe of the Crosse by Robert Hargraue Curate" were presented for this offence.[6] Others repeated the offence: in 1607 James Ware alias Farmer was in trouble "for carryenge his child to bee christened in a boate to Stanton without the signe of the Crosse by Roberte Hargraue curate there".[7] Nicholas Chauntler, Vicar of Udimer in the Chichester diocese, believed that an important theological principle was involved: he was presented "for not signing the children with the signe of the Crosse according to the book of Common Prayer, but vseth these words to signe with, the outward signe of inward baptism without Crossing them".[8]

Robert Hargrave was accused of other Puritan offences. The

[1] Ibid., 1608, Vij 11, f. 55.
[2] Episcopal Visitation Book, Lincoln, 1607, Vj 19, f. 36.
[3] Ibid., 1604, Vj 18, f. 1. Cf. Saltfleetby, Humberston (Lincoln); Great Stambridge, Little Leighs (London); Salehurst, Litlington (Chichester); etc.
[4] Ibid., Vj 19, f. 35 b.   [5] Ibid., Vj 18, f. 18.
[6] Ibid., 1604, Vj 19, f. 27.   [7] Liber Cleri, Lincoln, 1607, f. 27.
[8] Act Book, Chichester, C20.

irate churchwardens of the neighbouring parish of Peckleton complained that "Robert Hargrave, minister of Staynton" had presumed "to administer the Communion to one ffrauncys Brokelbie beinge of Pekilton" who refused "to take the Communion at his owne minister bycause he would not give yt him standinge".[1] During the episcopal visitation of Lincoln in 1607 it was discovered that Thomas Buckley of Little Marlow was guilty of similar irregularities: "he doth administer the Communion to those that sitt givinge the cup at one end of the seat with the words of benediction and soe it is delivered from the hands of one of them to the other. And doth vsually christen without the signe of the crosse."[2] Buckley had been instituted to the living of Little Marlow after the deprivation of Thomas Heape in 1605, who refused to conform himself after many admonitions.[3] It is clear that Buckley continued the Puritan tradition of the parish. His namesake, William Buckley, Vicar of Little Leighs in the diocese of London, adopted the same practice: he was presented "for administeringe the sacrament to those that doe not receyue the same kneelinge".[4] William Whatley in the diocese of Oxford was another: he was presented "for administring the Communion to such as wold not kneele".[5] What was more serious was the failure of some ministers to provide the sacrament at all.

Mr Fermeley in the diocese of Norwich was presented because "he doeth not administer the sacrament thrice in the yere"[6] as required by Canon 21; John Law because "he ded not administer the Communion at Whitsontyde last nor since Easter";[7] Thomas Jackeler because "he did not reade divine prayers in his parish Church vppon Easter daye last neyther did he procure any other minister in his place to saye service or minister the holly Communion that daye nor Easter was twelve moneth to the greefe of the parishioners";[8] Mr Pencewall because "he hath administered the Communion by [sic] twise this yere".[9]

The besetting sin of clerical indolence took its characteristic

---

[1] Episcopal Visitation Book, Lincoln, 1608, Vj 20, f. 110 d.
[2] Ibid., 1607, Vj 19, f. 19 b.   [3] See above, p. 191.
[4] Act Book, Archdeaconry of Essex. D/AEA, No. 23, f. 337. 25 June 1606.
[5] Oxford Archdeaconry Papers, Oxon., b. 52, f. 11. 6 April 1607.
[6] Episcopal Visitation Book, Norwich, 1606.   [7] Ibid.
[8] Ibid.   [9] Ibid.

toll: it manifested itself in a failure to read prayers, to celebrate the sacraments, to preach sermons.[1] Thomas Taylor, Rector of Martin by Horncastle in the diocese of Lincoln, was presented "for not preaching in his Cure monethlie sermons iuxta Canon".[2] Mr Jeffrys in the Norwich diocese was presented because "he doeth not preach aboue once in the yere and for other sermons they haue none"; and Mr Stebben of the same diocese because "they haue scarse a sermon in the yere".[3] The complaint about William Whatley in the diocese of Oxford was not that he failed to preach but the subject matter of his sermons: he was presented, first of all, "for not praying for the Bishops in his prayer before the sermon" (contrary to Canon 55), and secondly, "for preaching agaynst the Ceremonyes".[4]

The difficulty was that there were those who ought to have preached, and did not do so, and that there were those who ought not to have preached, and did so. Henry Lord, Rector of Great Steeping in the diocese of Lincoln, was presented "for preaching without license";[5] Mr Sankey of Brandiston in the diocese of Norwich was known to preach but the churchwardens confessed, whether "Licensed they know not".[6] Nicholas Banester, Vicar of Little Cotes in the diocese of Lincoln was in the curious position of being presented "for preaching without a licence and not shewing any beinge demaunded and saying noe prayers at all oftentimes on the sabaoth daye and for not preachinge his quarter sermons".[7]

There were negligent clergymen who failed to catechize, in defiance of Canon 59. "Mr Stebben readeth service disorderly and omitteth parte thereof ... doeth not Catechise the yeouth"; "Mr Jeffers ... doeth Catachise sometymes but not euery sondaye";[8] John Hickling "doeth seldome Catachise"; Mr

---

[1] E.g., Crostwick, Felthorpe, Horsham, Spixworth, Sallowes, Catton, Burlingham, Braydeston, Freethorpe, Halvergate, Moulton, Hempton, Longham, Toftrees, West Lexham, Dersingham, etc.

[2] Episcopal Court Book, Lincoln, Cj 16, f. 133.

[3] Episcopal Visitation Book, Norwich, 1606. Cf. Crostwick, etc.

[4] Churchwardens' Presentments, Archdeaconry of Oxford, Oxon., b. 52, f. 15. 6 April 1607.

[5] Episcopal Court Book, Lincoln, Cj 16, f. 135.

[6] Episcopal Court Book, Norwich, 1606.

[7] Episcopal Visitation Book, Lincoln, 1608, Vj 20, f. 19.

[8] Cf. Mr Sankey, Vicar of Brandiston in the same diocese.

Slyne "doth not Catechise the yeouth"; John Baldwyn "hath not Catechised the youth but on the 14 day of July he did request them to come vp to be catechised"; "Mr Hilton [doth] not Catachise the yeouth as he ought to doe".[1]

There were presentments about clergymen who absented themselves from their parishes, and failed to make adequate provision for the pastoral needs of the flock.

At Skirbeck in the Lincoln diocese the churchwardens complained: "Mr Johannes Prat Rect. for that [he] hath not byn resident there these x yeares neither doth he giue any thinge to the poore, and also his parsonage there goeth greatly to decaye by his meanes."[2] At Mablethorpe in the same diocese the churchwardens declared that the Rector was not resident "vpon his parsonage", and that there was no "curate in his roome".[3] At Moulton in the Norwich diocese the situation was scandalous. Concerning the Vicar, Mr Bredhurst, the churchwardens charged: "he is not resident vppon his vicaredge. eundem. he is noe preacher neyther haue there ben any sermons these xij monethes, eundem. he beinge a vicar they present him for a Common Drunckard."[4] The vicars of Catton and Shadingfield in the same diocese were also presented for non-residency.[5]

Inquiries were made concerning the condition of the fabric and the state of the furnishings. The churchwardens of Earls Colne in the London diocese reported a catalogue of needs: "they want . . . a covering for the communion table A handsome Communion Cupp of sylver or pewter to sethe wine in to serve the lords table a surplesse the first tome of homilyes and a decent patent of sylver to minister the lords bread vpon."[6] Four years later the churchwardens again presented "the Communion table Clothe ys torne and worne and not sufficient for the table";[7] at another parish in the same diocese there were "no potts to bring the wine to the Communion table".[8] At Hellingly in the diocese of Chichester

---

[1] Episcopal Visitation Book, Norwich, 1606.
[2] Episcopal Visitation Book, Lincoln, 1604, Vj 18, f. 44.
[3] Ibid., Vj 18, f. 110. Cf. Great Cotes: "Mr Tho: fforman R. ibidem resideth not vpon his parsonage his curate preacheth not." F. 120.
[4] Episcopal Visitation Book, Norwich, 1606.   [5] Ibid.
[6] Act Book, Archdeaconry of Colchester, London, D/ACA, no. 27, f. 183. March 1604/5.
[7] Ibid., D/ACA, no. 32, f. 58. July 1609.
[8] Ibid., D/ACA, no. 29, f. 297 b. Jan. 1606/7.

they wanted "a fflagon pott for wyne to furnishe the communicants", and they were enjoined to get "a standing pott" before Michaelmas;[1] at another parish in the same diocese they needed "a Carpett for the Communion table".[2] Elsewhere they lacked the ten commandments painted on the wall, the churchwardens excusing their want on the plea of ignorance: "we only present the want of the tenne commandements because we haue had noe commandment to provyde them before this tyme, and therefore crave some respit iff it please you to be certified at the next visitation."[3]

The impropriator of a benefice was responsible for the maintenance of the chancel in good repair, but the duty was often neglected. Originally the responsibility rested on the rector or vicar, but in the case of an impropriated rectory, the responsibility was that of the impropriatory or the person to whom he farmed or leased the parsonage. Conditions varied greatly from diocese to diocese and from parish to parish: in the diocese of Lincoln the situation was fairly satisfactory; in the diocese of Chichester many chancels and churches were in a state of woeful disrepair. In the Lincoln diocese there were some exceptions: the churchwardens of Ludborough admitted: "our church and chancell are neyther of them in sufficient repayre . . .[4] churchyarde is vtterly vnfenced the parson is in falt for the [chancel?] but the church and churchyarde our whole towne are in [fault?]."[5] The dilapidation was of recent date, for in 1602 it was reported that "the churcheis and Chauncells of theis seuerall parishes are well repayred and kept decently".[6] The rectory of Ludborough was neither appropriate nor impropriate,[7] so that the responsibility for repairing the chancel belonged to the Rector.

The practice of "farming" encouraged the evils of exploitation. The churchwardens of the parish of Legbourne in the diocese of

---

[1] Act Book, Chichester, C. 18.
[2] Ibid., C. 18, f. 42 b. 10 September, 1605.
[3] Churchwardens' Presentments, Oxford Archdeaconry, b. 14, f. 45. 4 April 1605.
[4] The MS. is damaged in places.
[5] Episcopal Visitation Book, Lincoln, 1604, Vj 18, ff. 106–7.
[6] *Libri Cleri*, 1570–1603, f. 18 d. The State of the Churches in the archdeaconries of Lincoln and Stow, August, 1602.
[7] *Libri Cleri*, 1603, f. 62.

Lincoln presented that the chancel "is in decay and so it hath beene presented these .20. yeares and as yet neuer amended".[1] In 1602 it was reported that the church "ys in reasonable good repaire and kept decently"; but the same could not be said of the chancel: "the chauncell ys ruinated and yt ys sayd to be her majesties and that Wylliam henneage esq. ys farmer to her majestie of this parsonage."[2] At Boxted in Essex the churchwardens reported that the impropriator "hath stripped the vicarage stark naked, without glebe, word, hay or corn".[3] At Ugley in the same year (1610) the churchwardens reported that the vicar "has been dispossessed of his dwelling place, some forty-five acres of Glebe, and all the corn", the consequence of the purchase of the rectory by Sir William Maynard.[4]

The rising middle class was seldom inhibited by scruples of conscience from pursuing a policy of cynical opportunism. The fact is that the rapid revolutionary changes of the previous century had bred a spirit of religious scepticism which found expression in worldly self-aggrandisement. Only among the Puritan gentry and popish recusants a different spirit prevailed. In the meantime, the ecclesiastical authorities, despite frustrations and discouragements, sought to repair the waste places and to build up the desolations of many generations. Bancroft, for his part, was determined to lay the burden of repairs upon the impropriators who were legally responsible. One difficulty was that there was no effective machinery to coerce those who, with selfish indifference, allowed churches to fall into decay. The injunction of an ecclesiastical court could often be frustrated by the issue of a prohibition in the Court of Common Pleas. It was easy to admonish; it was difficult to compel.

As a final resort the parishioners might be exhorted to undertake the work of repair themselves.[5] This sometimes had the desired result. A number of examples may be cited. The churchwardens of Little Staughton certified "that whatsoever was decayed concerning eyther the doores or floore of our Chauncell

---

1 Episcopal Visitation Book, Lincoln, 1604, Vj 18, f. 114.
2 *Libri Cleri*, 1570–1603, f. 5.
3 R. Newcourt, *Repertorium Ecclesiasticum Parochiale Londinenne*, Vol. II, p. 79.
4 Ibid., Vol. II, p. 614.
5 D. Wilkins, *Concilia*, Vol. IV, p. 460–1.

in Staughton parua is sufficiently amended and repayred";[1] the churchwardens of Houghton Regis informed the Chancellor that "where as Mr Wyngate was presented for not repayring the chancell of Houghton Regis in the countie of Bedford at Dunstable in my Lords Last visitation. Theise ar to certify that nowe the chancell is new tilled and in very good repayre and the glasse windowes very well glassed";[2] of Broughton the churchwardens testified:

> whereas there hathe bynne Complainte made vnto your Worshipp in your Chauncellors Courte of the Reuynge and decaye of the Leades and walls aboughte our parishe Churche of Broughton ... wee ... do certifie ... That the Churche Leades, walls, Tenne Comaundements, Kynges Armes, and Sentences are all in good plighte and in due manner and fforme as they oughte to be;[3]

the churchwardens of Martin by Horncastle were able to report

> that whereas there was a presentment mayd of the ... bell frames and bell roapes and churchyard fences and divers other things presented that all these things named ar already prouided and repayred. In witnesse wherof we the Minister and churchwardens ther have to this certificate set our hands the ix th. of November anno 1607.[4]

At Ewerby the churchwardens certified that "the churche of Ewarbye beinge in decaye in the northe Ile thereof in the tyme of Stephen Wyelles and William Mosseys churchwardens is Repayred and covered". The following letter was sent to the Chancellor from Surfleet:

> Theis shalbe to certifie your worsshipp that Wheras the great Bell at Surfflett in the Countie of Lincoln was presented defectyve into your court and day geuen for the Amending the same, that the said Bell was newe made and is hanged vpp in the steple ffullye fynished in all good order as yt ought to be before the said day appoynted. Thus we leve you to the tuition of the allmightie who haue you in his kepeing ffrom Surfflett. this xv th. of November 1607.
>
> Yours to their powers
> Thinhabitants of Surfflett.[5]

---

[1] Churchwardens' Presentments and Certificates, Lincoln, Ch.P., 1608, no. 10, f. 8.
[2] Ibid., Ch.P., 1605, no. 8, f. 4.　　　　[3] Ibid., f. 22.
[4] Ibid., Ch.P., 1606/7, no. 9, f. 35.　　　[5] Ibid., f. 37.

John Gartsyde, Vicar of Witham on the Hill, certified "that the bodie of church of Witham is borded and ther is some part of Mr Hanles Ile and some other odde places is yet to doe and youre wurshippe hath given vs time to doe yt and our churche is both whitelined and paved".[1] John Hutchin, the Rector of Wyfordby, forwarded a certificate, also signed by the church-wardens, John Hall and William Warde, stating:

> whereas the Churche of Wiverby standeth presented in this Courte for not beinge paved The truthe is, it is nowe tyled thorowghe owte, with very good workemanshippe, to the great Charge of our small parishe. Thus hopinge of your favourable acceptance hearof wee leave you to the protection of Thallmightie. . . .[2]

Henry Tuke, the nonconformist Rector of Silk Willoughby,[3] was proudly conscious of a job well done. He wrote:

> Mr Clarke, may it please yow to vnderstand that wheras our churchwardens were appointed to repaire our church porche against midsomer that it was don sufficiently aforr Whitsunday and the windowes that needed now glassed, so that now I thinck we haue the comelyest churche in all our countrye.[4]

The Vicar was responsible for the repair of the chancel at Potter Hanworth, and the churchwardens certified "that Mr Bedford our minister hath verie sufficientlie and substantiallye repayred his chauncell".[5] A certificate was sent from Milton Ernest "that the seats in our Church and our Chest for the safe kepeinge of the Regester are sufficientlie repared and doone as our churchwardens were enioyned. Also they haue provided a Stoop of Puter for wyne for the holye Communion as they likewyse weere enioyned."[6]

The evidence from other dioceses indicates a less satisfactory state of affairs. At Earls Colne the churchwardens confessed "that the pulpett ys decayed and not sufficient for our preacher";[7]

---

1 Ibid., f. 23.   2 Ibid., f. 18.

3 He was presented for his nonconformity on 3 and 31 Oct., 30 Nov., and 1 Dec. 1604. He received four admonitions, but on 23 Oct. 1605 he was, in hope of his conformity, dismissed until he should be cited again. Cf. C. W. Foster, *The State of the Church*, pp. 363 ff.

4 Churchwardens' Presentments and Certificates, Lincoln, Ch.P. 1606/7, no. 9, f. 42.

5 Ibid., Ch.P., 1606/7, no. 9, f. 42.

6 Ibid., Ch.P., 1608, no. 10, f. 1.

7 Act Book, Archdeaconry of Colchester, London, D/ACA, no. 32, f. 58.

and at St Martin's Colchester, the churchwardens presented that the "Churche ys in great decaye", adding that they were "not able to repayre yt".[1] Three years later the situation had further deteriorated: the report stated: "there is no decent table, no stoope for the wine, no Chest for the poore, the Church is not in reparations in the windowes and the Chauncell also no stooles nor seats no seat to read prayers no Cushen".[2] The church at Great Wigborough was ruinous: the "Chauncell ys defective in reparations lik to fall downe and wanteth glasse windowes yf not shortly amended yt will fall downe".[3] At Great Bentley the "chauncell ys out of repayer beinge vnpaued"; there is "not a decent pulpett neither doth it stand in a convenient place so that the prayer cannot be harde of them in the lower end of the churche". There were difficulties of one kind and another: "our ministers seat ys not convenient it wanteth a convenient Waye into it and he Cannot knele in yt. we want the table of the tenne comaundments the people sitt confusedly without order the youth prevent the maried people of ther seats."[4]

The situation in the diocese of Chichester was not dissimilar. A typical presentment, by Richard Wickins and Edward Payne, churchwardens of West Hoathley, dated 16 February 1607/8, may be cited:

> The walles of the Church in some places faulty, betweene the Roof and steeple, the Rayne may fall into the Church, the glasse windowes in some places broken, the paving in some places of the Church and Ile faulty, some seats in the Church and Ile not planked, stone-cealing of the Church porch in some Decay The fences of the church-yard in some places are downe and wanting, or otherwise faulty.[5]

The judge admonished them to repair these things before the feast of St John the Baptist. At Farlish, "the Church wants repairinge the seats of the Church want amendment the Church-yeard is not fenced". The judge admonished John Baker, the churchwarden, to repair the decay of the church and cemetery before the feast of All Saints.[6] Likewise in the diocese of Norwich: at St Augustine's the "parsonage howse is in greate decaye and

---

[1] Ibid., D/ACA, no. 29, f. 16 b.   [2] Ibid., D/ACA, no. 31, f. 19.
[3] Ibid., D/ACA, no. 31, f. 1999.   [4] Ibid., D/ACA, no. 29, f. 47.
[5] Act Book, Chichester, C. 20.   [6] Ibid., C. 18, f. 42 b.

ready to fall downe"; at Spixworth, "the parsonage howse is in greate decaye throughe his [i.e., John Hickling's] defaulte"; at Shadingfield "the chauncell is decayed in thachinge the parsonage howses be decayed in thachinge";[1] at Beetley "the chauncell greatly wanteth glasseinge so that the vermine Come into the Church and defile the same".[2] There were other scandals at Beetley:

The reporte and fame hath gone publiquely in Beetley yt Mr Thomas Jackler Came to his benefice of Beeteley by Simony viz[t] that he should give xx*l* to one Mr Lingford for the benefice of Beetley aforesaid. allso he hath omitted to reade service in his parish Church vppon diuerse holly dayes this last yere, vz[t] vppon maye daye St Peters day and St Marks daye last . . . he neuer as yet wore his whood he beinge a graduit.[3]

There are a variety of depressing presentments for offences against the moral law. The incumbents of Moulton, Lyng, and Shadingfield, in the diocese of Norwich, were presented for common drunkards. At Shadingfield the Vicar "was druncke vppon the 14 of July 1605 and was indited for a common drunckard".[4] The Rector, Edmund Stanhope, was also accused of a variety of offences: "he is not resident .2. he preacheth and expoundeth without Licence .3. he weareth no whoode being a master of art .4. he omitteth to catechise the youth .5. he doth not byd holy dayes nor fasting dayes .6. he weareth not a corner Cap." "The parishe clarke" was also presented because he could "neyther wright nor read."[5] The Vicar of Lyng in the same diocese was, to common knowledge, "a common gamster and Alehowse Keeper"; it was also reported that "he hath sould aways xxij acres of glebb Lande from his parsonage to one Salomon Leech for the some of vij*l*x*s* or there abouts".[6]

The initial purpose of a visitation was to bring to light the hidden things of darkness. The articles were framed accordingly: their subject matter ranged from Puritanism to profanity, and their inquiry related to the laity no less than the clergy. The evidence for the existence of lay Puritanism is abundant: at Fenny Drayton in the diocese of Lincoln, George Heard and

---

[1] Episcopal Visitation Book, Norwich, 1606.   [2] Ibid.
[3] Ibid.   [4] Ibid.   [5] Ibid.
                            [6] Ibid.

George Pegge, together with eleven other parishioners, were presented because they refused to receive the Holy Communion kneeling.[1] At Holy Trinity, Colchester, the wife of Robert Barnard was presented "for that she affirmeth that she never will receive the Communion except at the hands of suche a minister as will suffer her to receive yt sitting".[2] At Brandiston in Norwich diocese, Abraham Hubberd was presented "for receauinge the communion settinge and not knelinge", and John Lowes, the Vicar, was also presented "for minstringe the Communion to the said hubberd settinge and not knelinge".[3] Robert Hargrave "minister of Staunton" in the diocese of Lincoln, was presented "for presuminge to administer the Communion to one ffrauncys Brokelbie being of Pekilton and Refusinge to take the Communion at his owne minister bycause he would not give yt him standinge".[4] James Ware of Thornton and Bagworth was presented "for carryeinge his child to be christened in a boate to Stanton without the signe of the Crosse by Roberte Hargraue Curate there". A note in the *Visitation Book* gives the explanation: "Hargraue dwells in a peculiar."[5]

There is a wealth of illuminating detail in a letter from William Osborne to the Chancellor of the diocese of Oxford:

> I heare Mr Holton hath moved the churchwardens to present mee for not Catachising on the Sabaoths . . . all this ariseth on ill will because they dislike mee for not administring the Sacrament to such as will not kneele. I beseech your Worship let them not presse mee downe, nor impose farther burdens upon mee then belonges to my place. for their drift is to expell mee, thinking that if I bee tyed to such things, my other place will Call mee away.[6]

John Brown, Vicar of Loughborough in the diocese of Lincoln, described the efforts which he had made to achieve conformity among his people:

> Ever since my Coming first to Loughborough we haue obserued the forme prescribed by Lawe in prayer and administration of Sacra-

---

[1] Episcopal Visitation Book, Lincoln, 1607, Vj 19, f. 27.
[2] Act Book, Archdeaconry of Colchester, London. D/ACA, no. 29, f. 108 b.
[3] Episcopal Visitation Book, Norwich, 1606.
[4] Ibid., Lincoln, 1608, Vj 20, f. 110 d.
[5] Ibid., 1607, Vj 19, f. 27.
[6] Churchwardens' Presentments, Oxford, b. 52, f. 11. 26 Feb. 1606/7.

ments except kneeling at the Communion, the vse of the Crosse in Baptisme, and wearing of the Surplice: which we take Libertye in, not for that we hold them vnlawfull but for that they were disused by my predecessors all her maiestys raigne and the people had conceaued some dislike of them whom I would not striue with vntill I were vrged thervnto by authority. Now that it hath pleased his maiesty to require an exact obseruation of these thinges I haue Laboured privately and publikly to perswad the people of the Lawfull vse of them: And haue brought them for the most parte to kneele at the communion, to approue the vse of the surplice, hoping I shall prevaile likewise with them to do the like concerning the vse of the crosse. Theis courses of drawing them one by degrees I haue presumed that my Lord would allowe me in my chardges and thinke well of it, especially in one who hath laboured by work and writting to drawe other ministers vnto conformity. . . .[1]

Margaret Aris of Chesham in the diocese of Lincoln was another lady of outspoken religions views: she was presented for

taking away the childe of Rich. Springhall before the minister had signed yt with the crosse and read the prayers and performed the ceremonies incident to the same according to the booke of common praier and in vsinge speeches againste the said booke of common praier and the ceremonies of the churche, as well at the baptisinge of the said childe as at the time of her appearance before doctor Hill his Courte.[2]

After suitable apology, Richard Chaloner was ordered by the Chancellor, Dr Belley, to absolve her. Chaloner reported:

Sir, I haue receiued from your Court an order to absolue one mrs Aris of Chessham vpon hir priuate acknowledgment of hir fame before me, our churchewardens and six more with hir oathe to obey the lawes of the Churche heareafter. The oathe she dothe sticke at, but dothe promise to lyue quietly in word and dede to hir power: and to obey the lawes so farr as she can. And she saith, she is very sory that she did offend in withdrawing the child from the crosse in baptisme heare, or speaking any vndewtifull wordes in that court, and will behaue hir selfe now dewtifully heareafter . . . Howbeith because this answereth not the strictnes of your forme sett downe, I haue thought good to signify vnto you what I finde, and to desire you to lett this be accepted; and the charges forgiuen because of

---

[1] Miscellaneous Correspondence, 1601–43, Lincoln. Cor/m/2, f. 11. 22 July 1605.

[2] Episcopal Court Book, Lincoln, 1605–10, Cj 16, f. 16.

theire pouerty./And that ye wilbe pleased vpon this acknowledgment to giue power to Mr Saunders or me at Chressham or Amersam
to publisshe hir absolution ... it weare pity the woman should
stand out any longer, being nowe almost one yeare. for my part, I
rest satisfied with this, if it please you to accept it.[1]

Thomas Aris, her husband, in a letter to Dr Belley, said:

my wife hath bene with Mr doctor Challoner and hath so acknowledged her desire to be sorrowfull that any should be offended by
her withdrawing the child from the crosse and ... also for the time
to come hathe promised through the grace of god to walke so
peaceably in her place, not meddling willingly where she hath
nothing to doe and in other mens matters not concerning her. . . .[2]

At Thurlaston in the diocese of Lincoln, Agnes Wallen was
presented "for goinge out of the parishe to bee deliuered of child
because it should not bee baptized with the signe of the crosse
and bee churched after the booke of common prayer";[3] and at
Great Bentley in the diocese of London, John Ellis was presented,
"for pulling of the Child awaye at the tyme of the Baptizinge
thereof when the minister cam to signe yt with the signe of the
Crosse".[4] Six months later, the wife of John Ellis was presented
because "she irreligiously Covered hir face with hir hands to
thentente she might not see the Crosse vsed in Baptisme".[5] At
Hinckley in the diocese of Lincoln, five men were presented on
28 September 1608, "for denyenge and refusing . . .[6] stand kneele
or put (?) of [f] th[eir] hatts in the time of d[ivine service] accordinge to the booke of com[mon] prayer";[7] and at Edlington in the
same diocese "mr: Roger Carter was Cited vnto Stamford for
haveing his hat on in the tyme of the devine service". He was
ordered to make public apology: "the said Mr: Carter before
diuerse of the neighbours of horncastle vpon the xviij th. daie of
October being the Sabaoth daie did acknowledge his over sight
in haveing his hat on at that tyme and doth promise not to doe

[1] Churchwardens' Presentments and Certificates, Lincoln, Ch.P., 1605,
no. 8, f. 9.
[2] Ibid., Ch.P., 1605, no. 8, f. 11.
[3] Episcopal Visitation Book, Lincoln, 1607, Vj 19, f. 24.
[4] Act Book, Archdeaconry of Colchester, London, D/ACA, no. 26.
[5] Ibid., D/ACA, no. 29, f. 27 b.
[6] The MS. is badly eaten in places.
[7] Episcopal Visitation Book, Lincoln, 1608, Vj 20, f. 111.

the like againe."[1] At Martham in the diocese of Norwich, John Love was presented because he had "not vsed that due reuerence and humble submission in time of divine service as he is inioyned by the xviij Constitution".[2] Sometimes lay Puritanism took a more militant form, as when Robert Burbedge of the parish of Harborough, in the diocese of Lincoln, called

> tho: Gower minister of great Bowden, Lowsy Rogue, cogginge companion, and scurvy Rascall and did challendge him to the feild and did laye waite for him for vsinge the rites and ceremonies of the churche as by proof it may appeare and further hee said hee would incense the parishioners of great Bowdon against their minister which hee did indeede and they expostulated of him therefore And alsoe did call his minister puppye.[3]

At Barholm, in the same diocese, Francis Bunyge was presented "for layeng violent hands vpon John Ball minister without anie cause and callinge him paltrie priest".[4] Richard Bury, Vicar of Utterby in the diocese of Lincoln, showed a spirit of commendable forbearance and petitioned the Registrar on behalf of Robert Taylor:

> Mr Stirrop my kinde salutations vnto you and good Mrs Stirrop first Remembered. Theise ar to Lett you vnderstand that this bearer Roberte Taylor seems to be sorie for his Lewde speeches and at the request of somme of my best ffrends in Regarde of impoverishinge of his pore wife and Children I am Contented to haue no further proceedinge in the matter. therefore good Mr Stirrop Lett all things bee quite dispatched and Lett him haue a note what the Charge is and at your Comminge over at Lammas I will see you Answered. I praye you Lett theire be as mutche mittigation of Charge as you Can both for your Brothers fee and your owne, and what you doe herin I will take yt as done vnto my self.[5]

It is clear that some of the Puritans had already embraced independency or congregationalism. Clementine, wife of George Tallmage, of the parish of Hyntlesham in the diocese of Norwich,

---

[1] Churchwardens' Presentments and Certificates, Lincoln, Ch.P., 1606/7, no. 9, f. 34.
[2] Episcopal Visitation Book, Norwich, 1606.
[3] Ibid., Lincoln, 1607, Vj 19, ff. 30, 72.
[4] Ibid., 1608, Vj 20, f. 74.
[5] Churchwardens' Presentments and Certificates, Lincoln, Ch.P., 1608, no. 10, f. 70.

was presented "for denyinge the church of England to be the trew church of Christe [and] for speakinge against the rites and ceremonies in the church of England saying they be not Lawfull". A note explains: "she refuseth to come to church being taken to be a browniste."[1] Another Brownist was presented at Cressingham in the same diocese: "Elizabeth Barker: there be often meetinges at her howse to conferre about religion and that the said Elizabeth is a brownest."[2] There were a number of presentments at Coggeshall in the diocese of London, and it appears that these Puritans were in fact Brownists: "Edward Taylor wold not acknowledge the Churche of England to be the Churche of Christ", or acknowledge the "minister to be a Lawfull minister",[3] and John Taylor "did saye that he wold not putt of [f] his hatt when the book of Comon prayer was in reading and that the Bishopes ought not to be prayed for at service and sermon, and that the book of Comon prayer was nothing but mingell mangell".[4] Mr Jagger was presented because he "will not abid in the Churche when the minister putteth on the surplice but goeth [out] of the Churche".[5] William Paternoster was presented "for refusing a long tyme to communicate with vs and tending hertofore his insufficiency as the only Cause of his absence from the holy Communion but now yt appeareth that he Cannot fanncey our churche government and iudge yt vnlawfull to receiue of our minister". Two others were also presented for "this peevish opinion".[6] William Belvis of Tolleshunt Major objected to the Prayer Book:

Speaking vpon the xj th. daye of November last in the Churche yeard before divers of the parishioners that he verye well knewe that the booke of Comon prayer which ys now sett forthe was not caused to be published and sett forthe by the Kings Maiestye but by the Bishopes and that he hoped verye shortly ther shoulde be reformation had by reason yt Came not out by due authoritye neither was yt Agreeable to the word of god, and that divers other parishes had not bought yt neither wolde bye yt.[7]

William Lambe of Salcott in the diocese of London, in similar

[1] Episcopal Visitation Book, Norwich, 1606. [2] Ibid
[3] Act Book, Archdeaconry of Colchester, London, D/ACA, no. 27, f. 127.
[4] Ibid., D/ACA, no. 30, f. 113 b. [5] Ibid., D/ACA, no. 30, f. 199.
[6] Ibid., D/ACA, no. 27, f. 187 b. [7] Ibid., D/ACA, no. 27, f. 161 b.

strain, "sayd that the booke of Comon prayer was but trumperye and Came from the divell and was mad by the divell".[1] William Dowseing was contemptuous of his minister's lack of preaching ability: he was presented because he "doeth refuse to receaue the Communion at the hands of ther Minister bycause he cannot preach".[2]

There are a host of presentments for moral offences as distinct from ecclesiastical: a depressing catalogue of diverse sins of the flesh. A single example will suffice: William Phillipe, of the parish and deanery of Risborough in the diocese of Oxford, was presented "for keeping in his house a woman great with child, and for suffering her to depart vnexamined and without punishment". His sentence was:

the said William Phillipe shalbe present in the parish church of Risborough aforesaid on sundaie being the seaventh daie of July next at morninge praier, and haue a white sheete wound about him from ye shoulders to ye anckles, and a white rod in his hand, bare legged and bare footed, and open faced, shall kneele in the sight of the congregation vntill the gospell bee read, and then standinge vppe in some open place where hee maie well bee seene of the congregation shall saie after the minister as followeth viz

Good people Whereas I not haueinge the feare of god before my eies nor regarding my soules health, gods holy commandements, nor the wholesome lawes established in this Realme, haue kept in my howse one Katherin Adams great with child, whome I suffered to depart vnexamined and without punishment, to the evill example of others: I am nowe come hither to acknowledge such my fault, and am right hartely sorie for the same, beseeching god and you all whome I haue offended not onely to forgiue mee but also to take example by this my punishment, that neyther you or I offend in the like sort againe, saieing as our sauior christ hath taught vs Our father which art in heauen &c.

And the performance of this order is to bee certified vnder the hands of the Minister and churchwardens the next court daie following together with these presents.[3]

The question, of course, is to what extent a visitation achieved

---

[1] Ibid., D/ACA, no. 30, f. 102.
[2] Episcopal Visitation Book, Norwich, 1606.
[3] Churchwardens' Presentments, Oxford Archdeaconry Papers, Berks, b. 14, f. 98. 28 May 1606.

its intended object. How effective was it in discovering sins of omission and of commission? The evidence is clear: a visitation was an invaluable means of gaining accurate information, thereby making possible disciplinary action of one kind and another. After a visitation a court went on circuit and those who had been presented were summoned before it. Such courts were of summary jurisdiction: the accused had to answer directly to the judge who charged him with the presentment made against him. The impressive thing is the speed with which so many things were remedied and reformed. The churchwardens of the church of Dunsby in the Lincoln diocese certified:

> pleaseth yt your worshipp to be aduertized That wheras the Churchwardens of Dunsby within the dioces of Lincoln were convented before you at Stamford in Lent last because that the seats or desks in the Church there were not so sufficient and decent as by the Canons and Constitutions thei should haue been, though then in as good manner as to the remembrance of any man they haue heretofore bene Wherefore the Mynyster ... doe hereby Certifye your Worshipp that all the said seats or stooles in the said our Church are now sufficiently and decently made, and framed in such sorte (though to our great coste) as there is not many like them in our Country.[1]

The certificates necessarily concern a great variety of subjects. The churchwardens of Lillingstone forwarded a certificate touching the conformity of their Vicar, William Cade:

> Right reuerende father in God and our verie good Lorde Whereas wee the churchwardens of Lillingston haue beene required bie our minister Mr Cade to certifie your Lordship of his conformitye, may it please your Lordship to vnderstande that as for these twentie yeres hee hath liued peaceablie and orderlie amongst vs, Labouringe painfullie in his callinge both by preaching and catechisinge and hath alwaies vsed the booke of common prayer sett forth by auctoritie, and none but that, soe hee contynueth still the same course, and doeth strictly obserue the saide booke of common praier lately corrected and sett forth by auctoritie, reading the same throughout. And whereas heretofore hee hath made some doubt of wearinge the surplice bie reason of the discontinuance thereof amongst vs for thes fiue and twentie yeeres now notwithstandinge hee weareth the

---

[1] Churchwardens' Presentments and Certificates, Lincoln, Ch.P., 1608, no. 10, f. 26.

same and doeth obserue the other ceremonies prescribed in the booke.[1]

The churchwardens of Thurcaston, in like manner, certified to the conformity of their Curate:

These are to signifie vnto you that our minister Mr William Arme [*sic*: Orme] curate of Thurcaston in the countie of Bedford is conformable to the booke of common prayer and other his Majesties lawes concerning the church of England.[2]

The churchwardens of Thurleigh wrote to the Bishop:

Whereas (right reverend father) diverse articles haue bene exhibited to your Lordship against Mr William fforde vicar of Thurleigh in Bedfordshire wherein is shewed to your Lordship that he is not conformable to the rytes and ceremonyes of the church (we therefore whos names are subscrybed) doe hereby signify to your Lordship that the sayd Mr fforde hath behaued himself (according to his vocation) orderly in his ministry, and hath bene and is very conformable to the lawes of this realm established, and doth paynfully and profitably instruct his parishioners . . . furthermore, we certify your Lordship that we can not possibly remember that Mr fford at any tyme dyd preach against any the lawes of this realme established, or against the boocke of Canons lately sett forth: or condemned (in any of sermons) the surplice whood with other ceremonyes and orders of the church, as vnlawfull to be vsed of him or others. . . .[3]

A certificate from Leasingham was forwarded about the provision of monthly sermons:

Whereas ovr minister being called vpon for his certyficate to be brovght into the covrt of Stavingfort for his monthly Sermons how they be discharged and by whom we that are the churchwardens at his request in this matter and knowing it for a certayntie to be trve that they be preached and that monthly as it is commanded every month a sermon: We . . . do write thes feaw Lynes vnto yovr worshipp to certifie yov of the trveth in this matter his own son doth com monthly from his own place Lendnam where my Lord Byshop appoynted him to preach: and doth preach with vs at Lessingham his fathers Sermons and that monthly: being appoynted to preach with vs for his father by my Lord byshop.[4]

[1] Ibid., Ch.P., 1605, no. 8, f. 6.   [2] Ibid., Ch.P., 1606/7, no. 9, f. 16.
[3] Ibid., f. 2.   [4] Ibid., f. 40.

The churchwardens of Leverton, who had presented the Rector, Henry Peacham, "for not reading the letanie on wednesdayes and fridaies nor eny service and likewise for not saieinge the praiers and Service on diuers wednesdaies for the tyme of the visitation of sicknes sett downe according to his Majesties aucthoritie", certified on 15 January 1604/5 "that he doe herafter reade the letany and doe service according to the booke of common praier".[1]

It is clear that a visitation, as a method of inquiry, was an invaluable aid to administrative efficiency. The *detectiones* and *comperta* indicate the comprehensive range of subject matter included and investigated, and the detailed and exact nature of the inquiry itself. The answers, so painstakingly obtained, provided the evidence required for the issue of admonitions and injunctions. The subsequent certificates show that many offences were indeed remedied and wants supplied. The method of inquiry by means of a visitation was not an empty formality; on the contrary, it was a flexible and efficient instrument of undoubted usefulness.

[1] Episcopal Visitation Book, Lincoln, 1604, Vj. 18, f. 53.

13

CONCLUSION

WHETHER PURITANISM would finally have triumphed apart from the bloody arbitrament of war is a matter for speculation: the fact is that the victorious Commons, in accomplishing the destruction of the Crown, also overthrew the Church. It is not surprising that the downfall of the one involved the ruin of the other. The fortunes of the Crown and the Church had become inseparably allied, and it was widely believed that the Church had supported and encouraged those doctrines of divine right which had found expression in royal absolutism. On one occasion Bancroft had been moved to indignant protest: "some . . . [give] it out very seditiouslie . . . that I labour by all waies I can devise to make the Kinge believe that he is one absolut monarch and maie *iure Regio*, doe what he list . . . all these imputations are cast vpon mee, as god knoweth very uniustlie."[1]

James himself had stressed the close identification of interest between the Church and the Crown, and, in the first year after his accession to the English throne, had coined the slogan: "No bishop, no king." With the development of royal autocracy in conjunction with Laudian authoritarianism, there were not wanting voices to say that prelacy no less than monarchy must be curbed.

An attempt must be made to assess the notable achievements of Bancroft: he cannot be held responsible for the holocaust of destruction which engulfed the Church three decades later. By the codification of the canons and other disciplinary measures, he gave to the Church a new sense of unity and order; and by his emphasis on the need for proper qualifications and adequate rewards he raised the status of the ministry. He was jealous for the rights of the Church; at the same time, he was concerned

---

[1] *Cotton MSS., Cleopatra*, F.11, f. 121.

about the conscientious and diligent performance of clerical duties and the proper fulfilment of responsibilities. Above all, he successfully resisted the resolute attempt to rivet upon the Church the presbyterian form of government. He knew that the innocuous phrase in the Millenary Petition about "the discipline . . . according to Christ his owne institution" masked nothing less than the Genevan system. He was also responsible for expelling persistent nonconformists from the ranks of the Church, on the ground that no self-respecting institution can tolerate the open flaunting of its laws.

The consequences of these policies were not immediately apparent. They rendered negative the Reformation concept of a Church identical in membership with the body politic. A Church, comprehensive of all citizens, must necessarily make provision for a wide latitude in belief and practice. The difficulties of achieving such a settlement had already become apparent, in the early days of Queen Elizabeth's reign;[1] they were to be multiplied tenfold with the vigorous enforcement of a more exacting conformity.

At first sight the points at issue appear trivial. Nevertheless these matters of contemptible triviality masked great issues. Mandell Creighton remarks that the vestiarian controversy bequeathed to the English Church "the unfortunate legacy of fighting great principles over outward trifles".[2] He points out that, to the Puritans, these outward trifles signified great issues. "The Puritan clergy would have neither surplice, hood, nor square cap. Clothes worn by Papists were like meat offered to idols: they were bound to abstain from all appearance of evil."

[1] Ronald Marchant, in his illuminating study of *The Puritans and the Church Courts in the Diocese of York 1560-1642*, writes: "Elizabeth's ministers and bishops produced the basic paradox of Church government in England: doctrinal latitude was allowed within wide limits, but ceremonial and liturgical detail was fixed and unchanging. The result was not a lessening of party strife, but the diverting of it to disputes over inessentials—the wearing of the surplice, the use of the cross in Baptism, bowing at the name of Jesus, and the like." His conclusion is that "these matters, secondary in themselves, were magnified into spiritual issues of profound significance", and that "the church found itself trying to administer a canon law which not only regulated necessary legal requirements—church courts, ordination, the solemnization of matrimony and similar affairs—but also practices about which many clergy and laity had deep conscientious convictions". Pp. 205–6.

[2] *Queen Elizabeth*, London, 1908, p. 129.

These Puritans were not concerned about some abstract principles of liberty; they were concerned about the achievement of a "pure" reformation (hence the name "puritan") in liturgy as in doctrine. They argued, with passionate conviction, that the principle *sola scriptura* must control liturgical worship in precisely the same way as doctrinal belief. Despite Hooker, they argued that this principle applied both to the vesture of the minister and to the polity of the Church.

During this period under review Puritanism was steadily expanding its influence, despite the fact that outwardly its professors were subject to regimentation and coercion. Nevertheless there is a limit to what can be achieved through threats of punishment and deprivation.

> A man convinced against his will
> Is of the same opinion still.

Castellio's celebrated declaration that persecution, if it does not make martyrs, turns heretics into hypocrites, was little understood: the principle of toleration was not yet accepted. According to the accepted practice of the time there were only two alternatives: either outward conformity or the pains of punishment. The separatists, aware of the realities of the situation, sought freedom and sanctuary in exile overseas. The main body of Puritans, however, continued, until forcibly restrained, their quiet work of ministry.

Certain centres were notorious for their Puritan activity. Such a centre was Cambridge. It was in Cambridge that Cartwright first enunciated the doctrines of classic presbyterianism, suffering the consequences of deprivation, and it was in Cambridge that Sir Walter Mildmay established Emmanuel College in 1584. Lawrence Chaderton continued as master for nearly forty years, only to be succeeded by John Preston. Emmanuel became the chief breeding ground for Puritan preachers. William Bradshaw, a graduate of Emmanuel, became one of the first fellows of Sidney Sussex, and, as the author of *English Puritanisme*, published in 1605, one of the intellectual fathers of independency.

Certain men made an inestimable contribution to the growth of Puritanism during these formative years. Chief among these were Arthur Hildersham and John Dod, who were appointed to take charge of Cartwright's papers after his death: Hildersham survived until 1632 and Dod until 1645. They were patriarchal figures revered for their learning as for their sufferings. Their influence did not cease with their "silencing". "I am sure", says Fuller, in his inimitable fashion, "Master Dod, when his mouth was shut, instructed almost as much as before by his holy demeanour and pious discourse."[1]

The Puritans magnified the office of preaching and it was through preaching that they exercised their greatest influence. They cultivated a style which, to use their own descriptive terms, was plain, perspicuous, pithy, and powerful. A faithful preacher, according to the testimony of William Perkins in his *Treatise of the Duties and Dignities of the Ministrie*, must "observe an admirable plainnesse and an admirable powerfullnesse".[2] John Downame, in the *Christian Warfare*, stresses the paramount importance of "simple and plaine speech" in the service of God: a sermon, "though never so adorned with the flowers of eloquence, and sharpe conceits of wit and learning, cannot so deeply pearce the heart of man, nor so forcibly worke upon his affections . . . as the word of God".[3] These Puritan preachers scornfully rejected the pretentious style of preaching adopted by the new school of court preachers: they abhorred the employment of rhetorical devices and pretty conceits. The Puritan Samuel Crook was not one of those "who for want of wares in their shops, set up painted boxes to fill up empty shelves", nor did he feed his flock "with airy dews of effiminate Rhetorick . . . nor yet with the jerks, and quibbles of a light spirit, which he ever abhorred as the excrementitious superfluities of frothy brains, and unhallowed hearts".[4] The Puritan preacher, whose abhorrence of "excrementitious superfluities" did not extend to the repudiation of pungent and highly picturesque language, did not find it difficult to attract an appreciative auditory (often from neighbouring parishes), and the result was the steady increase in the number of laymen who were instructed and informed. Fuller justly observes: "What won them most repute was their ministers' painful preaching in populous places; it being observed in England that those who

---

[1] *Workes*, p. 181.　　　　[2] *Workes*, Vol. III, p. 430.
[3] P. 340.　　　　[4] Quoted, W. Haller, op. cit., p. 132.

hold the helm of the pulpit always steer people's hearts as they please."[1]

Evidence may be cited to prove the truth of this contention. The evidence is slight but it is sufficient. It was only occasionally, for example, that a layman publicly indicated his conscientious opposition to the rubrical requirements of the Prayer Book, and thereby his Puritanism, by stubbornly refusing to kneel. German and Jane Ireton—the parents of Cromwell's famous general— were of this number. German was presented for not receiving the Communion kneeling; Jane, for not being churched.[2] They were dismissed with an admonition. They may have exercised a greater circumspection for the future: the fact remains that they did not fail to train up their son in the zealous profession of a like Puritanism. No doubt there were many others of a like persuasion who consoled themselves with the hope and expectation of more propitious days.

Puritanism was not, as Usher erroneously opined, exclusively a clerical movement. The evidence provided by presentments has already been examined. But the actual presentments do not tell the whole story (although they vividly illustrate part of the story). It is now clear that there were others who were never presented despite their Puritan practices. A single example will suffice. A document,[3] prepared for Arthur Hildersham in connection with the Millenary Petition, contains some revealing particulars about the parishes in the deanery of Doncaster in York: the primary purpose was to provide comparative statistics about the number of "idle drones" in relation to the number who were "diligent, learned and zealous" preachers. Of more immediate concern, however, is the information provided by this document about the conformity of those listed. In the sixty parishes of the deanery there were three men who were nonconformists in all things, one who was nonconformist in some things, and thirteen who were "seeming weary of ceremonies". Of this third group there are additional items of information: "sometimes useth the ceremonies and is indifferent for them"; "useth the ceremonies sometimes, would be rid of them"; "wishes the ceremonies removed". The arresting and surprising thing is that of those

---

[1] *Church History*, Vol. III, p. 101.
[2] Quoted, R. Marchant, op. cit., p. 178.   [3] *Birch MSS.*, 4293.

thirteen only one ever came before the Church courts for non-conformity. The others conformed sufficiently to escape official censure, and yet, their sympathies were plainly on the side of those who desired further reform. It is clear that we cannot make accurate generalizations about the extent of Puritanism by simply relying on the number of recorded presentments: Puritanism was, in fact, more extensive and widespread than the evidence sometimes suggests.

The official promulgation of the canons, and the systematic enforcement of conformity, confronted the Puritans with a critical situation. A clearly thought out strategy was necessary to meet this new situation. A conference was convened at the home of Lady Bowes of Coventry, in the presence of certain of the recently deprived ministers, and such hardy veterans as Arthur Hildersham and John Dod. The object of this conference was to formulate a common policy. The conference was also attended by the separatists John Smyth and John Robinson who argued that the Church of England was no longer a true Church, and that all Christians must separate from it. The majority of those present rejected this view. Nevertheless John Smyth and John Robinson proceeded to establish a "covenanted" church outside the established Church—the former at Gainsborough, the latter at Scrooby. Richard Bernard, recently deprived from Worksop, followed their example and organised another in his late parish. These men quickly gathered together fervent disciples. The presentments tell their own story. On 1 June 1605 John Denman and his wife of East Retford[1] were cited before the archdeacon's court and confessed that "they were absent from theire owne parishe church uppon the laste Saboath daye and there (at Sturton) did here Mr Robinson a strainger preache who whether he was licensed sufficientlie or not theie knowe not". Five other persons from East Retford, a man and his wife from Clareborough, three men and their wives from Ordsall and John Broome (the ex-churchwarden of Babworth) and his wife all admitted that they also were at the sermon. They were fined twelve pence (except two

[1] Ellen Denman was a Puritan lady of fiery zeal. On Easter Day 1606 she went to Babworth (Richard Clifton's parish prior to deprivation) "and did disturbe the minister for the time beinge from exequucion of divine services and did also impugne the rite and ceremonies of the crosse in the sacrament of Baptisme by force and violence contrarie to the booke of common prayer".

25

men who were fined sixpence each), the legal fine for absence from church on one Sunday.[1]

It is abundantly evident that the word spoken in these separatist congregations often fell on to receptive soil. Thomas Jessop, a layman, was presented because "he doth refuse the taking the communion at Easter untill he be resolved whether he may take it kneeling sitting or standing lawfully". Jessop was cited before the Commissary:

... he saith that the iudge dothe all things for his private gayne he saithe that it is to dishonour Christe to saye that a man must receave the communion kneeling he further said to the iudge you are like a painted wall et per dominum examinatus sponte fassus est that he hath not received the communion.[2]

Later in the year three men and a woman of Burton Joyce were fined the usual shilling for absence from church for a month; they alleged that their absence was "because the word was not there preached", and did not pay the fine. Two men and their wives and another man, all of Bothamsall, were reported to the court at Retford for saying in public that they would not go to church where the minister was not a preacher.[3]

The greater number of those laymen or ministers who had Puritan sympathies, did not elect to adopt the hazardous course of deliberate separation from the established Church. Some, making a virtue of necessity, gave a grudging conformity; others patiently awaited the dawning of a better day.

It is not easy to evaluate Bancroft's achievements, particularly in relation to Puritanism. He was a political prelate—the Church was his career—but he brought to his high office an intense dedication of mind and will. He was incontrovertibly a doughty defender of episcopacy, an efficient administrator, a zealous disciplinarian. With purposeful determination he sought to mitigate the prevalent evils of pluralism by the sedulous augmentation of ecclesiastical incomes; he resisted, with pertinacious energy, the encroachment of the common-law judges, contending for the rights and privileges of the ecclesiastical judges; he was diligent in the conduct of visitations and the execution of reforms.

[1] Quoted, R. Marchant, op. cit., p. 152.
[2] Archdeacon's Act Book, 24. 2 July 1607.　　[3] Ibid., 24. 12 Dec. 1607.

He saw the Church threatened by the machinations of her enemies, and he gave himself ceaselessly to the task of defence and consolidation. The Church was finally overwhelmed by the very forces against which he had long contended, and the explanation is to be found in the fact that he never fully understood the nature of those forces. He failed to realize that differences of biblical interpretation and the intractable problems of ecclesiastical polity cannot be resolved and settled by legislative enactment, and that those who professed Puritanism were not simply swayed by considerations of political expediency. To say this is to confess that he shared the prejudices and limitations of his own age.

His primacy was contemporaneous with that of the first years of the new King's reign. Bancroft had the heavy disadvantage of being called upon to serve under a vain and inexperienced monarch. James was not without intellectual attainments, but he was politically inept and inordinately conceited. He understood little (and wished to understand less) of the complexities of the English scene: it is not too severe a judgement to say that his major preoccupation was the delights of hunting, and his second, the lavish reward of his chosen favourites. Henry IV of France gave him the contemptuous sobriquet of "the wisest fool in Christendom".

The events associated with the reception of the Millenary Petition indicate the kind of difficulties with which Bancroft had to contend. James, having received the petition, forthwith agreed to the summoning of a conference at Hampton Court. The consequence was to confer on the Puritans a *de facto* recognition. It was a tactical blunder: it placed the bishops of the established Church in the position of accused men. The situation was only partly retrieved by the issue of a royal proclamation stating: "we have reason to think the estate of the Church here established, and the degrees and order of ministers governing the same, to be agreeable to the word of God."[1] Another characteristic example concerns the royal impropriations. The King, without prior consultation, informed the Vice-Chancellors of the Universities that he proposed to devote all the royal impropriations to the betterment of ecclesiastical livings. On the surface it was an

---

[1] *Patent Roll*, 1 Jas. I, Part 3.

entirely laudable intention. But the problem of bettering ecclesiastical livings was one of vast complexity and not so easily resolved. The Archbishop communicated in haste with Cecil expressing his general concern and anxiety: His Majesty, he wrote, "is altogether ignorant of this our state".[1] Nevertheless, Bancroft was compelled to rely on the King to defend the Church against the Commons. When a Bill for the abolition of pluralities was introduced in 1610, Bancroft pleaded with the King to stop it: "We must again endure a new brunt to no purpose except Your Majesty shall be pleased to prevent it: and I think it very necessary you should do so."[2] This unhappy dependence was to bear a bitter harvest.

Professor A. L. Rowse, in his eminently readable history of the Elizabethan age, excludes the bishops from his general encomium. "When one looks at their portraits, high shouldered with their furred tippets, their puffy, lined faces with their atribilious, constipated expressions, always grave, often sour, one cannot find them congenial."[3] This highly subjective judgement is less than generous. Bancroft, on any score, was a gifted administrator (according to Professor Hugh Trevor-Roper "one of the greatest of ecclesiastical administrators")[4] and Usher was entirely justified in describing his work as nothing less than "the reconstruction of the English Church".[5] His achievements were solid and substantial; however, it is not unfair to say that, in relation to the challenge of Puritanism, the peace which reigned was more apparent than real; the conflict was only postponed and not concluded.

---

[1] *Cecil MSS.*, 101, f. 20.   [2] *S.P. Dom., Jas. I*, 14, Vol. LVI, no. 57.
[3] *The England of Elizabeth*, London, 1950, p. 415.
[4] *Historical Essays*, London, 1957, p. 135.   [5] Op. cit., Vol. I, p. 30.

APPENDIX 1

PRELIMINARY DRAFT OF THE CANONS

"Artickells agreed one by ye Convocatione House, 1604." (*Additional MSS.*, 29,546, f. 77.)

1. That the service shalbe redd intirely withowt omitting any parte.

2. That euery househoulder dwelling within a mile of his parishe churche shall either com him selfe to churche or at the least send one of his famelie euerie whensdaie and ffrydaie.

3. That euery man shall sitt in the Church with his head vncouered and duringe the tyme of devine Service vnlesse he haue some necessary infirmity to the contrary.

4. That parents shall not be vrged to be present or if they be present not to answeare to any questions at the baptizinge of the children nor yt Godfathers or Godmothers shalbe admitted to make any other answeare then suche as the booke requirethe.

5. That no bread and wyne be vsed at the Communion but such as by the minister hathe bene blessed by reding the word of institution and therefore if the want of either any newe which waste not one the table at the beginninge of the administration be brought in by the Churchwardens the minister shall not delivere it before he haue agayne red ouer the words of institution.

6. That the bread shalbe brought to the table in a fayer lynen clothe.

7. That the minister shall deliver the bread and wyne to every severall person.

8. That he shall delivere it to none that shall deprave the booke of commone prayer nor to any standinge or sitting but only kneeling.

9. That all ministers shall weare the Serplise at the tyme of service and administration of the Sacrament and it shalbe Lawfull for him also to weare a whodde vpon the Serplisse if he be a graduatt if no graduatt then a Teppett of any Stuffe vnder silcke.

10. That it shalbe lawefull for any man in casse of necessitie and whear his Child shalbe weake and in danger of Death to

send for the minister to baptize it in his howse which if the minister Refuse to doe if he convenianly may and the child die vnbaptized and he is to be Suspended for three moneths. . . .

11. That the ministers that haue curatts vnder them shall read ye service Administer the Sacraments of the lords supper and ye order of baptisme if occasion serve at the least twice euery yeare vpon a sundaie or speciall holidaie according to the order and forme appoynted in the Communion booke.

12. That every one to be admitted in to the ministery or reders of divenitie lectures or instituted in to any place of the Chardge or dignitie in the Churche shall subscribe to the Kings supremacie the articles of Religion sett forthe anno 1562 the Communion booke of ordayninge Archbishop Bishop preists and deacons bookes of homelies and in the whole discipline and gouernment of the Church of Englande nowe established ther is nothinge contrary to the Worde of god.

13. That everie minister that ether refuseth to vse the said communione book in all or in parte or sheweth or willethe any thing agaynst it after twise admonition geven by the Bishop shalbe suspended and if he persist deprived and at the lengthe degraded.

14. That no minister shall suffer any man to preach in his parishe without his licence first shewede.

15. That no man shall preach or expounde any part of the Scripture without ye licence of the ordinary.

16. Every minister in his prayer before the sermone besids such things as concerne the church King and Queene prince and roiall issue shall also pray for Archbishop Bishops and curatts and at the end shall praise god for all suche as are departed in the trewe faithe of Christ and so Conclude with the lords prayer.

17. Every minister halfe ane hower before Eveninge prayer shall Instruct the youthe of his parishe in the Catechessme sett forth in the Communione booke and no other vpon payne of Admonishion ye first offence and for the second suspenssion and for the third deprivation.

18. A cannone to be made which yet is not redd that none shalbe mariede but suche as are conferminde of the Bishops.

19. No minister may Administere the Communione in privett hovvses vnlesse ther be in the same howse some impotente sicke persone that doth Requier the same.

20. No minister shal apoynt any sollemn taste or shalbe willingly presently at them nor at any lectures in marckett Townes Commonly called exercizes nor at any privatt fastinge and prayer vnder pretence of Castinge out Devilles vnder payne of suspension and deprivation from the ministre.

21. That observation of the Sabothe daie and holidaies commandede be equally [kept] except the fayers and marketts may be kept one holidaies.

APPENDIX 2

STATEMENTS OF JOHN BURGESS CONCERNING SUBSCRIPTION

(a) John Burges to the King. The Reasons which induced him to resign his benefice rather than subscribe.[1]

Most dread and gracious Soveraigne, when Josephs Cup was found in Beniamins sacke, Judah assured of the fact, ignorant of the meanes, falleth to Confession of a fault vnexcuseable, And yet there was noe fault. To subscribe and to deny to subscribe to the same Articles, Appeareth so manifest a fault of vnconstancie or vnhonestie, as were I not privie to a iust reason of both, I should say with Judah what shall I say vnto my Lord? What can I speake? How can I iustifie my selfe? God hath found out the wickednes of thie Servant. But if it may appeare that the Compas of our Churches Intention (to which my former Subscription made reference) be either varied by some degrees toward the Antartique, or be newly discovered to be other than I conceaved yt, I may be Censured of former blindnes in not seeing, but not of falshood then or now.

My most humble suite vnto your gracious Majestie, is (even in the bowells of Jesus Christ) That you would vouchsafe to reade a rude and long but plaine and vpright narration of my proceedings past and present and motives to both, which haveing too suddenlie prepared to give vp with my ministerie and liveing into the hands of my Ordenarie, and not haveing tyme to cast

[1] *Rawlinson MSS.*, D.353, f. 46.

into an other mould, or fairer hand, I make bould vpon my knees
to present as my accomt vnto your sacred Majestie. If suspicion
growe that I have studied better defences of the booke of Common
prayer to iustifie my former subscription, then I sawe before hand,
I can cleare that by many witnesses. If on the contrarie, that now
I seeke quarrells against it causelessly I take God to witnes that
I meane it not, my reasons following that I doe yt not will shewe.
And to say truth, vpon what reason could I doe yt. Is it a pleasure
to be in disgrace with the tymes? especiallie of your Majestie
whose favour I doe esteeme as your person next vnto Gods? Is yt
nothing to loose all my living and to behold the daylie miseries of
a wife and ten deare Children besides the feeling of myne owne?
If this weare nothing, yt wilbe something to loose (the life of my
selfe) the vse of my poore Ministerie and to see the flockes (at least
for a tyme) without Sheapheards or vnder such, as cannot
sodenly knowe how to handle them.

Would God your Majestie would beleeve of vs That the onely
feare of Gods displeasure hazerdeth vs vpon your Maiesties,
whom if we did not feare lesse then God, neither should wee long
feare so much as wee ought. If may be wee are misled in opinion,
thanked be God, it is not here. But he that once will goe against
the vnknowen error of his Conscience, will at last have no Conscience to goe against knowne error. The conscience foyled is
like a distempered locke, that no key will open. If the matters be
looked on which be imposed (I now speake of the Ceremonies)
they seem slight, but if there derivation be from Antichrist
they are hatefull. If the simple vse of them be considered, they
are shaddowes, byt yf the late abuse (which is hardly servered
from the things) they are gyants, but if there vse not so, while the
Papists insult, the zealous mourne, and both stumble at them.
And both they that like and they that like them not cast vs, that
have not vsed them out of their Consciences, as men ready to say
Masse rather then to loose our livings, And the very boyes and
girls laugh at our most grave and reverend Ministers, whom
before they looked vpon with feare. Let the Kings Majestie
please to remember how pardonable good men differ in lighter,
and that our opinion is neither newe, nor vncountenanced from
as learned as this age hath knowen, nor soe concluded in the
Ministers breasts, as that the quenching of them and of the cause

will prove one worke. And if your Majestie measure our desires and spirites by ... some in Scotland, God and tyme will surely cleare vs, and it will appeare that wee affect not any popularity or parietie in the Churche of God. And a little of Abrahams Indulgence to his Inferiour would have drawne a peace farr more speedy and safe, then can be inforced. Your excellent Majestie is perswaded first to draw all into conformitie and then to sett vpon Poperie with a compleate army, It is a probable Course, but if yt be suggested vnto your Majestie out of any mans heart but your owne, let me beseech you to consider if it may not be (at least in sequell) like that of Hushay and Absolom, which first overthroweing the good counsell of Achitophell did after over-throwe the very intention which it seemed to support.

Give me leave once to sweare vnto your Majestie by the God of Gods that never any thing in my memorie more greeved the subiects than the present Course against the Ministers, nothing in my Opinion would more gratifie them then the contrarie, which (if God pleased) I could wish derived imediatly from your noble breast that your highnes might receive the sole honour and thanks for such favour, and refresh the affections of your most loyall subiects.

John Burges

(*b*) "A Particular of those Interpretations of some things Questioned in the matter of subscription, with which I had satisfied my selfe in former times, and with which I offered to subscribe the same day wherein I was deprived for not subscribing, which were presented to his Maiesty by the Bishop of Winchester, and after to his Lo: Grace of Canterbury, vpon which I was restored to my ministry."[1]

To the first Article concerning his Majesties supremacy, and to the third concerning the Article of Religion agreed vpon in the Convocation house &c I doe willingly and absolutely subscribe. To the second Article (viz) that there is nothing contayned in the booke of Common prayer, the booke of ordination of Bishopps, priests and Deacons, and in the two bookes of Homilies contrary to the word of God I doe willingly subscribe if I may haue leaue to satisfie my selfe in such interpretation of some things questioned,

---

[1] *Rawlinson MSS.*, A.419, f. 48.

as I may stand with the words of subscription and things subscribed to in the maner following:

1. Concerning the translations of some scriptures printed in the
booke of Comon prayer.

I vnderstand that our subscription to the booke of Common
prayer is to approue the forme of Common prayer Contained in
that booke and consequently the reading of such scriptures as
are therein appointed to be read. And not to iustify the printer
or translators errors which may be noted in any part of the
Scriptures contayned in the closure of that booke. for I see that
men are allowed to read the same scripture after his Majesties
translation.

2. Concerning Apocryphal Scripture appointed to be read.

I vnderstand by subscription to acknowledge that the reading
of these (which is all the booke requireth) not as Canonicall but
as Apocryphall for instructions sake so farr as they accord with
the Canon as lawfull.

3. Concerning the rites and Ceremonies required as the vse of
the surplice, Crosse in Baptisme, kneeling in receaving the
Communion in generall.

I vndertake not by subscription to determine how well these
be imposed, but only to acknowledge that the vse of them, vpon
his Maiesties command, and that in the best construction of them,
is lawfull.

4. Of the vse of the Surplice in particular.

I vnderstand it not to be imposed as an holy vestment as were
the priestly garments vnder Moses by reason of Gods institution,
nor as a thing necessary to the worship of God, or any part
therof, neither take I it to be enioyned as any sacramentall
significant signe, but onely for order and vniformityes sake.

5. Of the vse of the Cross in Baptism.

I know it is not made any part of the sacrament of Baptisme
which is acknowledged by the Canon to be compleat without it,
and not perfected or bettered by it. I vnderstand it not as any
sacramentall, operative or efficient signe bringing any vertue to
Baptisme or to the baptised, where the booke sayth, and *Doe
signe him with the Signe of the Crosse in token* &c I vnderstand the
booke not to meane that the signe of the Cross hath any vertue

in it to effect or further this duty, but onely intimate or express
by that Ceremony, by which the ancients did avow their profession of Christ crucified. What the Congregation hopeth and
expecteth from that Infant, viz: that he shall not be ashamed to
profess the faith of Christ crucified into which he was even now
baptized.

And therefore when the thirtieth Article, that the Infant is of
that signe dedicated, vnto the servise of Christ, I vnderstand that
dedication to import not a reall consecration of the Child, which
is done in Baptisme itselfe, but onley a Ceremoniall declaration
of that dedication like the preist is sayd to make cleane the Leper,
whose being cleane he onely declareth.

6. Of the Interrogatories in Baptisme.

I conceaue that these Interrogatories made to the Infant and
answered as in his name by the suerties intend onely *an advmbra-
tion of that stipulation* and covenant made which is really entred
into by receaving the Sacrament of baptisme and not to import
that the child actually had such a distinct faith, repentance or
desires as are there professed, or that he is indeed supplyed therof
from his suerties, who cannot make over their owne faith and
repentance to others as good and Chattells vse to be converted.

7. Of Kneeling in the Act of Receaving the Lords Supper.

I confesse I never sawe cause to think this vnlawfull to be done
and therefore I doe it. first. because I knowe that the Church of
England abhorreth all adoration and the papists knowe it
.secondly. because it holdeth sitting or standing as lawfull and
holy as kneeling putting noe necessity or worship of God in any
of these arbitrary gestures, yea because in this church a prayer
is vsed for each Communicant, this gesture may seeme more
agreeable to the externall arbitrary forme here vsed, then to the
fashion of other Churches whose liberty is not abridged by ours,
nor ours by theirs.

8. As for phrases of doubtfull Construction I take them in the
best sence, and soe subscribe to the Booke of Comon Prayer.

9. Of the Bookes of ordination of Bishops Preists and Deacons.

I conceaue that subscription to this booke doth not intend an
approbation of every phrase or application of every place of
scripture therein alleadged as fitly applyed, but onely that the

calling of Bishopps to government in the Church and the order of inferiour ministers by them to the vses there assigned, are not contrary to the word of God, and so I subscribe to that booke.

10. Of the two bookes of Homilies.

I vndertake not to approue of every phrase or allegation of scripture as fittly applied to the word of the Holy Ghost, but that dogmatically there is nothing delivered in those Homilies that I knowe to be contrary to the word of God, but that they may lawfully and profitably be read to the people for their edification when better meanes are wanting; and in this I subscribe to those bookes also. These Interpretations K. James accepted and my L^{ds.} Grace of Canterbury affirmed them to be the true sense and meaning of the Church of England.

APPENDIX 3

THE LAST WILL AND TESTAMENT OF RICHARD BANCROFT, ARCHBISHOP OF CANTERBURY

In the name of God, Amen. I Richard Bancrofte by the providence of God Archbishop of Canterbury being in my body diseased, but of good and sound memory, doe make this my last Will and Testament, in manner and forme following. First I bequeath my soule into the hands of Almightie God through Jesus Christ my onely Saviour and Redeemer in whome I stedfastly beleeve point by point as it is conteyned in the Apostles Creed being a briefe compendiom of the Holy Euangelists, assuring myself consequently that by his death and bitter passion my sinnes are for giuen me, that I shall rise againe in the later day, and enioy that eternall and blessed life which my said Saviour hath purchased for me, and for all other faithfull beleevers. And for my body I bequeath the same to the earth from whence it came, and to be buryed in Lambeth Chauncell: for bidding any other monument then a plaine stone to be layd uppon my graue. Item, my will is, that my body be not opened, but layd into my graue as it came into the world with all the parts and members of it compacted and knitt together as my soule left it. Item, my will is, that my body be buryed within fourty or fiuety howers after my death: and likewise that all needelesse expences may be avoyded in the manner of my buryall. For my body being interred within the time limited and the following of an empty coffin being both idle and absurd: my will is, that all these chargable Ceremonies may be omitted. Onely upon some Sonday within a moneth after my death I desire the now Lord Bishop of London, or the Bishop of Chichester, or some of my Chaplaines to preach in Lambeth Church, and to make such mention of me, as may tend to God's glory. At that sermon I would wish all my servants to be present: for whome partly for that end, my will is, that my Executors should make prouision of Commons for them for one moneth after my death. And now as touching my worldly estate, I doe giue and bequeath to my Successor whosoever he shalbe my fower Dutch coach geldings, and my best coach. Item, I doe giue to my Nephew doctor Newman my fower english coach geldings and my second coach. Item, I doe giue to my Sister Elizabeth Wenland one hundred pounds. Item I giue to her youngest daughter one hundreth pounds to be paid unto her by my Executors when she is marryed, or commeth to the age of eighteene yeares. Item, I forgiue my Nephew John Gough one hundreth pounds which I lent him. I giue to my Nephew doctor Tigh, and to my Neece his wife my second siluer bason and yeuer. Item, I giue to my Nephew Thomas Hunt all my Instruments of musick and my two liuery potts of siluer not guilt. Item, I giue unto him all my siluer candlesticks, and silver Chasingdish: likewise my siluer sugar box. Likewise I giue to him my said nephew Thomas Hunt, two dozen of my best siluer spoones, desiring him herewith to be content. Item, I giue to the poore in Lambeth fourty pounds, and to the poore in Croydon twenty pounds. I giue to my Brethren the now Bishops of Lincolne of Bath and Wells, of Rochester and of Chichester, euery one of them a round hoope ring of gold of a marke in weight with this inscription Sic Sanctorum Communio, two hands being ioyned together within the round at the beginning of the said Inscription. Item I giue to my lovinge frends Sir Christoper Hatton, Sir Christopher Parkins, Sir George Paule, doctor Pasfield, Mr Nicholas Kemp, Mr Barckham, Mr Rob: Hatton, Mr Wilson and Mr Alsop, and to such other of my frends as my Executors shall think I haue forgotten, to euery one of them a round hoope ring of gold in weight ten shillings with the inscription in manner aforesaid. Item I giue all the Bookes in my Study ouer to the Cloisters unto my Successor, and to the Archbishops of Canterbury successively for euer if he my next Successor will yeeld to such assurances as shalbe deuised by such learned Councell as my superuisor and Executors shall make choice of for the continuance of all the said Books unto the said Archbishops successively according to my true meaning: otherwise, I bequeath them all unto his Majestys Colledge to be erected at Chelfry, if it be erected within these six yeares, or otherwise I giue and bequeath them all to the publick library of the Universitie of Cambridge. Touching this my bequest and Legacie, there may be some defect in the same, which I desire may be supplyed as that all my said Bookes may remaine to my Successors, for that is my chiefest desire. And if it might please his most Excellent Majesty, and his most Royal Successors, when they receaue the homage of any Archbishop of Canterbury, first to procure him to enter Bonde to leaue all the said Books to his Successors, my desire herein would be greatly strengthened. Item I giue to my next Successor all the maps and pictures in my gallery at Lambeth, and all my writings and papers concerning Church Causes, which are in my paper Study and in my greate Study. And I doe most hartely intreate my next Successor, that he wilbe good and gratious to my seruants, and namely to these six: Alsop, Scot, Langley, Lyne, Dobson, and Sleinehead, more seruiceable and faithfull men in their places I suppose he shall not readily find; and more particularly I hartely desire him to be good unto Langley, that he may enjoy my graunt unto him for the keeping of Lambeth House. Item, I giue unto Walter Dobson fourtie pounds, and to Wilton Sleinhead thirty pounds. Item, I doe reserue to my self power and authoritie to make and add hereunto such Codicells as I shall think convenient. And as touching all the rest of my goods and Chatells of what nature soeuer which I haue not here giuen and bequeathed, or shall not hereafter giue or bequeath by any Codicell by me to be made, I giue and bequeath them all unto my nephew Richard Bancrofte of Wilsden, whom I doe by these presents make my sole and onley Executor. Lastly, of this my last Will and Testament, I doe nominate and appoint by their

good fauor and relying uppon their friendship the now Bishops
of London and Chichester the ouerseers, and doe giue to the
Bishop of Chichester for his paines herein my best basin and yewer
of siluer guilt: And touching my Lord of London, if it should
not please God and his Majesty, that he may succede me in the
Archbishoprike, then I giue and bequeath unto him for his said
paines the summe of one hundreth markes to bestow in plate at
his pleasure in remembrance of me his faithful frend. In witnesse
of all which the promises conteyning my last Will and Testament
I haue with my owne hand subscribed my name to euery page of
the same: and also haue hereunto affixed my seale the eight and
twenty day of October Aᵒ Domini 1610.

                    Richard Bancrofte
                    Archb: of Canterbury
              28 Oct: Aᵒ 1610
I declare this to be my last Will and Testament in the presence of
        Saᶜ: Licestren
                Jo: Bowyer   Goo: Paule
                Jo: Wilson   Walter Dobson[1]

[1] *S.P. Dom., Jas. I*, 14, Vol. LVII, no. 115. *Wharton MSS.*, Lambeth, no. 577,
f. 58; no. 578, f. 42.

BIBLIOGRAPHY

PRIMARY

I. MANUSCRIPTS

Bodleian Library, Oxford
Oxford Archdeaconry Papers:
Libri Actorium, Berks, 1603–11
Allegations, Attestations, Depositions, Berks, 1601–11
Churchwardens' Presentments:
Banbury, Oxon, 1605–23
Newington, Oxon, 1605–24
Thame, Oxon, 1603–19
Rawlinson MSS.
Tanner MSS.
British Museum
Additional MSS.
Baker MSS., Vols. I–XXIII
Birch MSS.
Burney MSS.
Cotton MSS., Vespasian, Titus, Cleopatra
Harleian MSS.
Lansdowne MSS.
Sloane MSS.
Stowe MSS.
Cambridge University Library
Baker MSS., Vols. XXIV–XLII
Diocesan Registry, East Pallant, Chichester
Bishop Andrewes' Register
Parish Register Extracts
Liber Exhibitorum
The Book of Reparations, 1602
Act Book, 1605
Essex Record Office, County Hall, Chelmsford
Archdeaconry of Essex:
Act Books, D/AEA, 1603–11
Cause Books, D/AEC, 1601–13
Visitation Books, D/AEV, 1591–1613
Depositions, 1600–13
Archdeaconry of Colchester:
Act Books, D/ACA, 1601–11

Visitation Books, 1604/24
Cause Books, 1604–24
Lambeth Palace Library
Bancroft's Register
Codices Manuscripti Lambethani
Codices Manuscripti Whartoniani
Codices Manuscripti Tenisoniani
Codices Manuscripti Gibsoniani
Codices Manuscripti Miscellanei
Lincoln Diocesan Record Office, Exchequer Gate, Lincoln
Liber Cleri, 1603
The Brown Book: Episcopal Register, 1580–1618
Correspondence of William Stirrop, Registrar of the diocese of
Lincoln, Cor/R
Correspondence of William Chaderton, Bishop of the diocese of
Lincoln, Cor/B
Miscellaneous Correspondence, 1601–43, Cor/M
The Bishops' Act Book, 1589–1622
Citations to Ecclesiastical Courts, 1604/6, 1607, 1608, 1609. Cit/
10–14
Episcopal Court Books, Cj 14–17
Archidiaconal Court Books, Cij 12–74
Responsa Personalia, x 1604–1704
Churchwardens' Presentments and Certificates, Ch.P. 1604–9
Visitation Books, Vj 18–19
Archdeacons' Visitation Books, Vij 11–13
Presentation Deeds
Somerset House, London
Liber Vicarii Generalis, Stanhope, 1601–5, no. 9
Liber Vicarii Generalis, Crompton, 1607–11, no. 10
The Diocesan Registry, The Cathedral, Norwich
Visitation Book, 1606
Institution Books, Bishops' Registers, Vols. XXI–II
Court Books, 1605–10
The Muniment Room, Norwich Castle
Archdeacons' Visitation Books, 1604–9
The Public Record Office
Dispensation Rolls, C.58
Patent Rolls, C.66
Exchequer of First Fruits and Tenths:
Bishops' Certificates, E.331
Commission Book, E.336
Plea Rolls, E.337
Miscellaneous, E.347

26

Exchequer, K.R.:
  Ecclesiastical Documents, E.135
  Decrees and Orders, E.123–4
  Depositions by Commissioners, E.134
  State Papers Domestic, James I, S.P. 14, Vols. VI–LVI

2. PRINTED MANUSCRIPTS

Calendar of State Papers, Venetian, Vols. V–XI
Historical Manuscripts' Commission:
  Calendar of the MSS. of the Most Honourable the Marquess of Salisbury, preserved at Hatfield House, Herts, Parts XV–XVII.
  Appendix to the Fourth Report, Part 1. MSS. of Trinity College, Dublin; MSS. of the House of Lords, Supplementary Calendar, 1873.
  Appendix to the Sixth Report, Part 1, MSS. of the Rt. Hon. Lord Leconfield, Petworth House, Sussex, 1877. Report on Various Collections, Vol. IV, MSS. of E. H. T. Jervoise, Esq., 1907.
  Tenth Report of the Historical MSS. Commission, Part 2, 1509 to the death in 1606 of Sir B. Gawdy, 1885. Report of the MSS. of Lord Montagu of Beaulieu, 1900.
  Fourteenth Report, Appendix, Part 4, MSS. of Lord Kenyon at Gredington Hall, Shropshire, 1894.
  Report on the Laing MSS. preserved in the University of Edinburgh, Vol. I, 1914.
Journals of the House of Commons, Vol. I, 1547–1628
Journals of the House of Lords, Vol. II, 1578–1614

3. CONTEMPORARY PUBLICATIONS

R. Abbott, *The Old Waye: A Sermon Preached at Oxford, The eighth day of Iuly, being the Act Sunday 1610.*
H. Ainsworth, *An Epistle sent vnto tvvo daughters of VVarwick from H.N. The oldest Father of the Familie of Love. VVith a refutation of the errors that are therein,* 1608.
H. Ainsworth, *Covnterpoyson: Considerations touching the poynts in difference between the godly ministers and people of the Church of England, and the seduced Brethren of the Separation; Arguments That the best Assemblies of the present Church of England are true visible Churches; That the Preachers in the best assemblies of England are true ministers of Christ . . .,* 1608.
H. Ainsworth, *A Defence of the Holy Scriptures, Worship and Ministerie, used in the Christian churches separated from Antichrist: against the challenges, cavils, and contradiction of Mr Smyth: in his book intituled The Differences of the Churches of the Separation,* 1609.

An Abridgment of that Booke which the Ministers of Lincoln Diocess delivered to his Maiestie upon the first of December last. 1605. Being the First Part of an Apologye for Themselves and their Brethren that refuse subscription and conformitie which is required.

Wherevnto is Annexed, a Table of Sondry Poynts not handled in this Abridgment which are other exceptions they take to the subscription requyred, and shalbe the Argument of the second part of their Apology, 1605.

The Answere of the Vice Chancelovr, the Doctors, both the Proctors, and other Heads of Houses in the Vniversity of Oxford. (Agreeable, undoubtedly, to the ioint and Vniforme opinion, of all the Deanes and Chapters, and all other the learned and obedient Clergy in the Church of England.) To the humble Petition of the Ministers of the Church of England, desiring Reformation of certain Ceremonies and Abuses of the Church, 1603.

Articles to be inquired of, in the first Metropoliticall Visitation of the most Reuerend Father: Richarde by the grace of Gods Prouidence, Archbushop of Canterbury and Primat of all England: in, and for, all thiese Diocesses (Viz.) Exeter, Norwich, Chichester, St Davids, Landaffe, Heriford, Worcester, Bristol, Bath and Welles, and Coventrie and Lichfielde in the yeare of our Lorde God, 1605 and in the first yeare of his Graces Translation 1605.

Articles, To be enquired of vvithin the Dioces of London, in the third generall Visitation of the reuerend Father in God, Richard Bishop of London, 1604.

E. Askew, *Of Brotherly Reconcilement, preached in Oxford for the vnion of somme, and now published with longer meditations for the vnitie of all, in this Church and common welth,* 1605.

Sir F. Bacon, *Certaine Considerations touching the better pacification, and Edification of the Church of England; Dedicated to his most Excellent Maiestie,* 1604.

R. Bancroft, *A Sermon Preached at Paules Crosse the 9. of Februarie, being the first Sunday in the Parleament, Anno 1588,* 1588.

R. Bancroft, *Dangerous Positions and Proceedings, Published and Practiced within this lland of Brytaine, under Pretence of Reformation, and for the Presbiterial Discipline,* 1593.

R. Bancroft, *A Survey of the Pretended Holy Discipline, Contayning the beginnings, successe, parts, proceedings, authority, and doctrine of it: with some of the manifold and materiall repugnances, varieties and uncertainties, in that behalf. Faithfully gathered, by way of historicall narration, out of the bookes and writinges, of principall fauorers of that platforme,* 1593.

H. Barrowe and J. Greenwood, *A Plaine Refvtion of M. Giffards Booke, intituled, A Short treatise against the Donatistes of England. Wherein is discouered*

1. *The forgery of the vvhole Ministerie.*
2. *The confusion.*
3. *False VVorship.*
4. *And Antichristian disorder of these Parish Assemblies, called the Church of England . . ., 1605.*

W. Barlow, *The Svmme and Svbstance of the Conference, which it pleased his Excellent Maiestie to haue with the Lords Bishops, and other of his Clergie, (at which the most of the Lordes of the Councell were present) in his Maiesties Priuy-Chamber, at Hampton Court, Ianuary 14, 1603, 1604.*

W. Barlow, *The First of the foure Sermons Preached before the Kings Maiestie, at Hampton Court in September last. This concerning the Antiquity and Superioritie of Bishops. Sept. 21. 1606, 1607.*

H. Barrowe, *Henry Barrowes Platform. Which may serve as a Preparative to purge away Prelatisme: with some other parts of Poperie. Made ready to be sent from Miles Mickle bound to Much beloved England. Togither with some other memorable things. And, A familiar Dialogue in and with the which, all the severall matters conteyned in this booke, are set forth and interlace. After the untimely death of the penman of the aforesaid Platform &c. and his fellow prisoner; who being constant witnesses in points apperteyning to the true worship of God, and right government of his Church, sealed up their testimony with their bloud, 1593.*

T. Bell, *The Regiments of the Church as it is agreable with Scriptures, all Antiquities of the Fathers, and moderne writers from the Apostles themselves unto this present age.*

R. Bernard, *Christian Advertisements and Counsels of Peace. Also disswasions from the Separatists schisme, commonly called Brownisme, which is set apart from such truths as they take from vs, and other Reformed churches . . ., 1608.*

R. Bernard, *Plaine Euidences: The Chvrch of England is Apostolicall; the Seperation schismaticall. Directed against Mr Ainsworth the Separatist, and Mr Smith the Se-baptist: Both of them seuerally opposing the Booke called the Separatists Schisme, 1610.*

W. Bradshaw, *A Short Treatise of the Crosse in Baptism, 1604.*

W. Bradshaw, *A Consideration of Certaine Positions Archiepiscopall, 1604.*

W. Bradshaw, *A Treatise of Divine Worship. Tending to prove that the Ceremonies imposed upon the Ministers of the Gospell in England, in present Controversie, are in their use unlawfull, 1604.*

W. Bradshaw, *A Proposition on Concerning Kneeling in the very act of receiuing. Howsoeuer Published to satisfie professours, yet humblie Submitted to the iudgment of Prophets, 1605.*

W. Bradshaw, *A Treatise of the Nature and Use of Things Indifferent. Tendinge to proue, That the Ceremonies in present Controuersie amongst the Ministers of the Gospell in the Realme of England, are neither in Nature or Use Indifferent, 1605.*

W. Bradshawe, *Twelve General Arguments, prouing that the Ceremonies imposed upon the Ministers of the Gospel in England, by our Prelates, are unlawfull; and therefore, That the Ministers of the Gospel, for the bare and sole omission of them in Church-Service, for conscience sake, are most unjustly charged of disloyalty of his Maiestie,* 1605.

W. Bradshaw, *A Protestation of the Kings Supremacie. Made in the Name of the afflicted Ministers and Opposed to the shamefull Calumniations of the Prelates,* 1605.

W. Bradshaw, *English Puritanisme Containening the maine opinions of the rigidest sort of those that are called Puritanes in the Realme of England,* 1605.

W. Bradshaw, *Informations, or a Protestation, and a Treatise for Scotland. Seconded with D. Reignoldes his letter to Sir Francis Knollis and Sir Francis Knollis his speach in Parliament. All suggesting the usurpation of Papal Bishops,* 1608.

W. Bradshaw, *The Vnreasonablenesse of the separation, Made apparent, by an examination of Mr Iohnsons pretended reasons, published an. 1608. Wherby he laboureth to iustifie his schisme from the Assemblies of England,* 1614.

H. Broughton, *An Advertisement of Corrvption in ovr Handling of Religion,* 1605.

The Brownists Petition to King James. With a Dispute upon the Question of kneeling in the act of receiving the Sacramental Bread and Wine, 1608.

R. Buckland, *An Embassage from heauen; wherein Christ giueth to understand his iust indignation against al such as being catholikely minded, dare yeelde their presence to rites and praier of the malignant church,* 1609.

J. Burges, *A Sermon Preached before the late King James his Majesty at Greenwich, the 19. of July, 1604. Together with two letters in way of Apology for his Sermon: The one to the late King James his Majesty; the other to the Lords of his Majesties then Privie Councell,* 1642.

Constitvtions and Canons Ecclesiasticall, Treated vpon by the Bishop of London, President of the Conuocation for the Prouince of Canterbury, and the rest of the Bishops and Clergie of the said Prouince: and agreed vpon with the kings Maiesties Licence in their Synode begun at London. Anno. 1603.

Certaine Arguments to Perswade and Provoke the most Honorable and High Court of Parliament now assembled, and also all other in any high authority, or in any grace and credite with them that are in high authority, to promote and advance the sincere Ministery of the Gospell; as also zealously to speake for the Ministers thereof now degraded, deprived, silenced, or admonished, or afterward like to be called in question, for Subscription, Ceremonyes, strict observation of the booke of Common prayer, or for other Conformitie, 1606.

Certain Considerations drawne from the Canons of the last Sinod, and other the Kings Ecclesiasticall and statute law, ad informandum animum Domini

Episcopi Wigornensis, seu alterius cuiusuis iudicis ecclesiastici, ne temere et inconsulto prosiliant ad depriuationem ministrorum Ecclesiae: for nor subscription, for the not exact use of the order and forme of the booke of common prayer, heeretofore provided by the Parishioners of any parish Church, within the Diocesse of Worcester, or for the not precise practise of the rites, ceremonies, and ornaments of the Church, 1605.

Certaine Demands with their grounds drawne out of holy Writ, and propounded in foro conscientiae by some religious Gentlemen vnto the reverend Fathers, Richard Archbishop of Canterbury, Richard Bishop of London, William Bishop of Lincolne, Garvase Bishop of Worcester, William Bishop of Exeter, and Thomas Bishop of Peterborough, whereunto the said Gentlemen require that it would please their Lordships to make a—true, plaine, direct, honest and resolute aunswere, 1605.

Certayne Reasons and Arguments proving that it is not lawfull to heare or have any spirituall communion with the present Ministerie of the Church of England, 1608.

H. Clapham, *Doctor Andros his Prosopopeia answered, and necessarily directed to his Majestie, for removing of Catholike scandale:* (2) *Sacred policie, directed of dutie to our sweet yong prince Henry:* (3) *An Epistle directed to such as are troubled in minde about the stirres in our Church*, 1605.

H. Clapham, *Errour on the Right Hand, through a preposterous zeale, acted by way of dialogue*, 1608.

H. Clapham, *Errour on the left hand through a frozen securitie*, 1608.

H. Clapham, *A Chronologicall Discourse, touching the Church, Christ, Antichrist, Gog and Magog . . .*, 1609.

Sir E. Coke, *The First part of the Institvtes of the Lawes of England, or a Commentarie vpon Littleton, not the name of the Lawyer onely, but of the Law it selfe*, 1628.

Sir E. Coke, *The Second Part of the Institutes of the Laws of England: Containing The Exposition of many ancient, and other Statutes; whereof you may see the particulars in a Table following*, 1642.

S. Collins, *A Sermon preached at Paules-Cross, upon the 1. of November, being all Saints day, anno 1607*, 1608.

The Confession of faith of certayne English people, living in exile, in the Low Countreyes. Together with a brief note of the special heads of those things wherein we differ from the Church of England . . ., 1607.

W. Couell, *A Ivst and Temperate Defence of the Five bookes of Ecclesiastical Policie written by M. Richard Hooker: against an vncharitable Letter of certain English Protestants (as they tearme themselues) crauing resolution; in some matters of doctrine, which seeme to ouerthrow the foundation of religion, and the Church amongst vs*, 1603.

W. Couell, *A Modest and Reasonable Examination of some things in vse in the Church of England, sundrie times heretofore misliked, and now lately, in a Booke called the (Plea of the Innocent:) and an Assertion for true and Christian Church policy . . .*, 1604.

W. Couell, *A Briefe Answer vnto Certaine Reasons by way of an Apologie deliuered to the Right Reuerend Father in God, the L. Bishop of Lincolne, by Mr Iohn Bvrges: wherein he laboureth to prooue, that hauing heretofore subscribed foure times, and now refusing (as a thing vnlawfull) that he hath notwithstanding done lawfully in both*, 1606.

R. Crakanthorpe, *A Sermon at the Solemnizing of the Happie Inauguration of our most gracious and religious soueraigne King James I Wherein is manifestly proued, that the soueraignty of Kings is immediatly from God and second to no authority on Earth whatsoeuer*, 1609.

W. Crasshawe, *The Sermon Preached at the Crosse, Feb. xiiij. 1607. Iustified by the Author, both against Papist, and Brownist, to be the truth . . .*, 1608.

A Dialogue wherein is Plainly laid open, the tyrannicall dealing of the L. Bishopps against Gods children: with certaine points of doctrine, wherein they approue themselues (according to D. Bridges his judgment) to be truly the Bishops of the Diuell, n.d.

J. Dove, *A Defence of Church Government; wherin the chh. government established in England is directly proued to be consonant with the word of God; together with a defence of the cross in baptisme . . .*, 1606.

G. Downame, *Two Sermons, The One commending the Ministerie in Generall: The other defending the Office of Bishops in particular . . .*, 1608.

G. Downame, *A Treatise vpon Iohn 8.36. Concerning Christian Libertie. The chiefe Points whereof were delivered in a Sermon preached at Pauls Cross, Nov. 6.1608 . . .*, 1609.

R. Eburne, *The Maintenance of the Ministerie Wherein is plainly declared how the Ministers of the Gospell ought to be maintained: And the true and Auncient practize of our Church in this case, shewed to be agreeable to the word of God, and all antiquitie*, 1609.

P. Fairlambe, *The Recantation of a Brownist, Or, a Reformed Puritan. Written by one that hath altogether, bin led in the same erroneous oppinions for many yeares together: and thereupon banished this Realme. And now since his conuersion, hath and doth approue, the holy Discipline, by the auncient Pastors, Doctors and Elders (which Disciplinarian malecontents would obtrude vpon our Church) and hath found it far shorter, then the Discipline vsed either in the Primitive Church, or in this our Church of England*, 1606.

R. Field, *Of the Chvrch. Five Bookes*, 1606.

N. Fuller, *The Arguments of Nicholas Fuller of Grayes Inne Esquire, in the case Tho. Lad, and Rich. Mansell his Clients. Wherein it is plainly proved, that the Ecclesiastical Commissioners have no power by their Commission, to imprison, or to fine any of his Majesties subjects, or to put them to the Oath Ex Officio*, 1607.

S. Gardiner, *A. Dialogue or Conference between Irenaeus and Antimachus, about the rites and Ceremonies of the Church of England,* 1605.

J. Hall, *Pharisaisme and Christianity: Compared and set forth in a Sermon at Paules Crosse, May. 1 1608,* 1608.

J. H[all], *A Common Apologie of the Chvrch of England: Against the vniust Challenges of the ouer-iust Sect, commonly called Brownists. Wherein the grounds and Defences of the Separation are largely discussed . . .,* 1610.

[J. Hall], *A Description of the Chvrch of Christ, with her peculiar Priuiledges, and also of her Common and Entercommers with some Oppositions and Answers of Defence, For the maintenance of the Truth which shee professeth: Against certaine Anabaptisticall and Erroniovs Opinions, Verie hurtfull and dangerous to weake Christians . . .,* 1610.

Sir I. Hayward, *A Reporte of a Discovrse concerning svpreme power in affaires of Religion. Manifesting that this power is a right of Regalitie, inseparably annexed to the soueraigntie of euery State . . .,* 1606.

S. Hieron, *A Short Dialogue proving that the Ceremonyes, and some other Corrvptions now in question, are defended, by none other Arguments then such as the Papists have heretofore used; And our Protestant writers haue long since answered. Whereunto are annexed, Certayne Considerations why the Ministers shovld not be removed for the Subscription and Ceremonies,* 1605.

[S. Hieron], *A defence of the Ministers Reasons, for Refusall of Subscription to the Booke of Common Prayer, and of Conformitie . . .,* 1607.

[S. Hieron], *The Second Parte of the Defence of the Ministers Reasons for refusal of Subscription and Conformitie to the book of Common Prayer . . .,* 1608.

[S. Hieron], *A Dispute upon the Question of Kneeling, in the Acte of Receiving the Sacramentall bread and wine, proving it to be unlawful. Or a Third Parte of the Defence of the Ministers Reasons, for refusall of the Subscription and Conformitie requyred . . .,* 1608.

S. Hieron, *Three Sermons: A remedie for Securitie. The ruine of Gods Enemies. The Worldlings Downfall,* 1609.

F. Holyoke, *A Sermon of Obedience, especially unto Authority Ecclesiasticall . . .,* 1601.

R. Hooker, *Of the Lawes of Ecclesiastical Politie,* 1592.

L. H[utten], *An Answere to a Certaine Treatise of the Crosse in Baptisme . . .,* 1605.

T. Hutton, *Reasons for Refvsal of Svbscription to the booke of Common praier, vnder the hands of certaine Ministers of Devon, and Cornwall word for word as they were exhibited by them to the Right Reverend Father in God William Coton Doctor of Divinitie L. Bishop of Exceter. . . . With an Answere at Severall times returned them in publike conference and in diverse sermons . . .,* 1605.

T. Hutton, *The Second and Last Part of Reasons for Refusall of Subscrip-*

tion to the Booke of Common Prayer, vnder the hands of certaine Ministers of Deuon and Cornwall, as they were exhibited by them to the right reuerend Father in God William Cotton . . ., 1606.

[H. Jacobs], *Reasons taken out of Gods Word and the best humane Testimonies proving a Necessitie of Reforming Our Churches in England . . .*, 1604.

[H. Jacobs], *A Christian and Modest Offer of a most Indifferent Conference, or Dispvtation, abovt the maine and principall Controversies betwixt the Prelats, and the late silenced and deprived Ministers in England: Tendered by some of the said Ministers to the Archbishops and Bishops, and all their Adherents*, 1606.

[H. Jacobs], *To the right High and Mightie Prince, Iames by the grace of God, King of great Britannie, France, and Irelande, Defender of the faith, &c. An Humble Supplication for Toleration and libertie to enioy and observe the ordinances of Christ Iesue in th'administration of his Churches in lieu of humane constitutions*, 1609.

H. Jacobs, *A plaine and cleere Exposition of the Second Commandement*, 1610.

H. Jacobs, *The Divine Beginning and Institution of Christs True Visible or Ministeriall Church, Also the unchangeableness of the same by men; viz. in the forme and essentiall constitution thereof*, 1601.

[H. Jacobs], *An Attestation of many Learned, Godly, and famous Divines, Lightes of Religion, and pillars of the Gospell, iustifying this doctrine, viz. That the Church governement ought to bee always with the peoples free consent. Also this, that a true Church under the Gospell contayneth no more ordinary Congregations but one . . .*, 1613.

E. James, *A Retraite sounded to certen Brethren latelye seduced by the schismaticall Brownistes to forsake the Church*, 1607.

[F. Johnson and H. Ainsworth], *An Apologie or Defence of svch Trve Christians as are commonly (but vniustly) called Brovvnists: against such imputations as are layd upon them by the Heads and Doctors of the Vniversity of Oxford, in their Ansvver to the humble Petition of the Ministers of the Church of England, desiring reformation of certayne Ceremonies and abuses of the Church*, 1604.

F. Johnson, *Certayne Reasons and Arguments proving that it is not lawfull to heare or have any Spirituall communion with the present Ministerie of the Church of England*, 1608.

F. Johnson, *A Brief Treatise containing some grounds and reasons against two Errors of the Anabaptists . . .*, 1610.

F. Mason, *The Avthoritie of the Chvrch is making Canons and Constitutions concerning things indifferent, And the obedience thereto required: With particular application to the present estate of the Church of England . . .*, 1607.

F. Mason, *Of the Consecration of the Bishops in the Church of England: With their Succession, Jurisdiction, and other things incident to their calling: As also of the Ordination of Priests and Deacons . . .*, 1613.

*A Myld and Ivst Defence of Certeyne Argvments, at the Last Session of Parlia-
ment directed to that most Honorable High Court, in behalfe of the
Ministers suspended and deprived &c.: for not Subscribing and Conforming
themselues &c. Against an Inteinperat and Vnivst Consideration of them*
by M. Gabriel Powell . . ., 1606.

O. Ormerod, *The Pictvre of a Puritane: or, a Relation of the opinions,
qualities and practises of the Anabaptists in Germanie, and of the Puritanes in England. Wherein is firmely prooued that the Puritanes doe
resemble the Anabaptists, in aboue forescore seuerall thinges* . . ., 1605.

[R. Parker], *A Scholasticall Discovrse Against Symbolizing with Antichrist
in Ceremonies: especially in the Signe of the Crosse,* 1607.

J. Penry. *Historie of Corah, Dathan, and Abiram &c. Applied to the Prelacy
Ministrie and Church assemblies of England* . . ., 1609.

W. Perkins, *Of the Calling of the Ministerie. Two treatises describing the
Duties and Dignities of that calling,* 1605.

G. Powell, *A Refutation of an Epistle Apologeticall written by a Puritan-
Papist to perswade the permission of the promiscuous use and profession
of all sects and heresies,* 1605.

G. Powell, *The unlawfulness and danger of Toleration of diuers Religions,
and conniuance to contrary worship in one monarchy or Kingdom,* 1605.

G. Powell, *A Reioynder unto the Mild Defence, iustifying the Consideration of
the silenced Ministers Supplication unto the high Court of Parliament.
Wherein is plainly Discouered the vanitie of the Ministers Arguments for
their Restitution; and they irrefutably euinced to be properly Schismatiques,
Unworthie to be restored againe to the use and liberties of their Ministerie,* n.d.

G. Powell, *De Adiaphoris. Theological and Scholastical Positions Concerning
the Nature and Use of Things Indifferent. Where also is methodically
and briefly handled, of Ciuill and Ecclesiasticall Magistrates, of Humane
Lawes, of Christian Libertie, of Scandall, and of the worship of God* . . .,
1607.

*The Reformation of Religion by Iosiah. A commendable example for all Princes
professinge the Gospell to followe. With a warninge to all faithfull and
true-hearted Subiects, to encourage theire Princes in so happie a course,* n.d.

*The Remoouall of Certaine Imputations laid upon the Ministers of Deuon: and
Cornwall by one M.T.H.[utton] and in them, upon all Ministers els
where, refusing to subscribe,* 1606.

T. Ridley, *A View of the Civile and Ecclesiastical Law, and wherein the
practice of them is streetened and may be relieved within this Land,* 1607.

T. Rogers, *Two Dialogues, or Conferences . . . concerning kneeling in the
very act of receiving the Sacramentall bread and wine, in the Supper of the
Lord* . . ., 1608.

J. Smyth, *The Differences of the Churches of the separation. Contayning A
description of the Leitovrgie and Ministerie of the Visible Church annexed,*
1608.

J. Smyth, *The Character of the Beast, or the false constitution of the Church discovered in certain passages betwixt Mr R. Clyfton and John Smyth, concerning the Christian baptism of new creatures, or newborn babes in Christ* . . ., 1609.

T. Sparke, *A Brotherly Perswasion to Unite and Uniformitie in iudgement, and Practise touching the Received and present Ecclesiasticall gouernment, and the authorised rites and ceremonies of the Church of England* . . ., 1607.

J. Sprint, *Argvments: That the best Assemblies of the present Church of England, are true visible Churches; That the Preachers in the best assemblies of England, are true ministers of Christ* . . ., 1607.

J. Sprint, *Considerations touching the poynts in difference, between the godly ministers and people of the Church of England, and the seduced brethren of the Separation* . . ., 1607.

[W. Stoughton?], *An Assertion for True and Christian Church-Policie. Wherein certaine politike obiections made against the planting of Pastours and Elders in every Congregation, are sufficientlie answered* . . ., 1604.

A Supplication to the Kings most excellent Majestie, wherein several reasons of state and religion are briefly touched: not unworthy to be read, and pondered by the lords, knights, and burgesses of the present parliament, and other of all estates . . ., 1604.

A Suruey of the Booke of Common Prayer, By way of 197. Quaeres grounded upon 58. places, ministring iust matter of question, with a view of London Ministers exceptions. All humbly propounded, That They may be syncerely answered or els Offences Religiously remoued, 1610.

J. Tichborne, *A Triple Antidote, against certaine very common Scandalls of this time* . . ., 1609.

W. Tooker, *Of the Fabriqve of the Church and Church-mens liuings*, 1604.

A Triall of Subscription, by way of a Preface unto Certaine Subscribers; And, Reasons for lesse rigour against non-subscribers, 1599.

T. Whitenhall, *A Discourse of the Abuses now in Question in Churches of Christ. Of their Creeping in, Growing up, and flourishing in the Babilonish Church of Rome* . . ., 1607.

T. White, *A Discoverie of Brownisme: or, A briefe declaration of some of the Errors and Abhominations daily practised and increased among the English Company of the Separation remayning for the present at Amsterdam in Holland*, 1605.

W. Wilkes, *Obedience or Ecclesiasticall Vnion*, 1605.

INDEX

285.9
B11

Date Due
